KT-474-552

THE ROUGH GUIDE TO

Devon & Cornwall

There are more than two hundred Rough Guide titles
covering destinations from Alaska to Zimbabwe
and subjects from Acoustic Guitar to Travel Health

Forthcoming travel guides include

Chicago • Corfu • First-Time Round the World
Grand Canyon • Philippines • Skiing & Snowboarding in North America
South America • The Gambia • Walks Around London

Forthcoming reference guides include

Chronicles series: China, England,
France, India • The Universe

Rough Guides Online

www.roughguides.com

Rough Guide Credits

Text Editors:	Polly Thomas and Sam Thorne
Series Editor:	Mark Ellingham
Editorial:	Martin Dunford, Jonathan Buckley, Jo Mead, Kate Berens, Ann-Marie Shaw, Paul Gray, Helena Smith, Judith Bamber, Orla Duane, Olivia Eccleshall, Ruth Blackmore, Geoff Howard, Claire Saunders, Gavin Thomas, Alexander Mark Rogers, Joe Staines, Richard Lim, Duncan Clark, Peter Buckley, Lucy Ratcliffe, Clifton Wilkinson, David Glen, Alison Murchie, Matthew Teller (UK); Andrew Rosenberg, Stephen Timblin, Yuki Takagaki, Richard Koss (US)
Online:	Kelly Cross, Anja Mutić-Blessing, Jennifer Gold, Audra Epstein, Suzanne Welles (US)
Production:	Susanne Hillen, Andy Hilliard, Link Hall, Helen Prior, Julia Bovis, Michelle Draycott, Katie Pringle, Mike Hancock, Zoë Nobes, Rachel Holmes, Andy Turner
Cartography:	Melissa Baker, Maxine Repath, Ed Wright, Katie Lloyd-Jones
Picture Research:	Louise Boulton, Sharon Martins
Finance:	John Fisher, Gary Singh, Edward Downey, Mark Hall, Tim Bill
Marketing & Publicity:	Richard Trillo, Niki Smith, David Wearn, Chloë Roberts, Birgit Hartmann, Claire Southern (UK); Simon Carloss, David Wechsler, Kathleen Rushforth (US)
Administration:	Tania Hummel, Demelza Dallow, Julie Sanderson

Acknowledgements

This book is dedicated to Jo Morgan, with love. Robert Andrews wishes to thank Kate Hughes, Peter Hughes, Peter Hack and Jo Morgan for sundry research and generous assistance; George Burke of the Ramblers Association; Juliana Uhart for artistic consultation; the staff at Devon and Cornwall's various tourist offices, national park offices and museums for their time and information; and Polly Thomas for her patient editing. Thanks are also due to Paul Gray for guidance and support, Ed Wright for his hard work on the maps, Rob Evers and Rachel Holmes for typesetting and Russell Walton for proofreading.

This first edition published June 2001 by Rough Guides Ltd, 62–70 Shorts Gardens, London WC2H 9AH.
Reprinted January and August 2002

Distributed by the Penguin Group:
Penguin Books Ltd, 80 Strand, London WC2R ORL.
Penguin Putnam, Inc. 375 Hudson Street, New York, NY 10014, USA.
Penguin Books Australia Ltd, 487 Maroondah Highway, PO Box 257, Ringwood, Victoria 3134, Australia.
Penguin Books Canada Ltd, 10 Alcorn Avenue, Toronto, Ontario M4V 1E4, Canada.
Penguin Books (NZ) Ltd, 182–190 Wairau Road, Auckland 10, New Zealand.
Printed in England by Clays Ltd, St Ives PLC.
Typography and original design by Jonathan Dear and The Crowd Roars.
Illustrations throughout by Edward Briant.

ISBN 1-85828-678-6

THE ROUGH GUIDE TO

Devon & Cornwall

Written and researched by
Robert Andrews

With additional contributions by
Peter Hack

ROUGH GUIDES

Help us update

We've gone to a lot of trouble to ensure that this first edition of *The Rough Guide to Devon & Cornwall* is accurate and up-to-date. However, things inevitably change, and if you feel we've got it wrong or left something out, we'd like to know: any suggestions, comments or corrections would be much appreciated. We'll credit all contributions and send a copy of the next edition – or any other Rough Guide if you prefer – for the best correspondence.

Please mark letters "Rough Guide to Devon & Cornwall" and send to:
Rough Guides, 62–70 Shorts Gardens, London WC2H 9AH or
Rough Guides, 4th Floor, 345 Hudson St, New York, NY 10014.

Emails should be sent to:
mail@roughguides.co.uk

Online updates about Rough Guide titles can be found on our Web site at **www.roughguides.com**

The Author

From his lair in Bristol, **Robert Andrews** makes frequent expeditions down west, either in the company of his family or on solo research missions. He has previously written and researched Rough Guides on England, Italy, Sicily and Sardinia. When not travel-writing, he compiles dictionaries of quotations.

Rough Guides

Travel Guides • Phrasebooks • Music and Reference Guides

We set out to do something different when the first Rough Guide was published in 1982. Mark Ellingham, just out of university, was travelling in Greece. He brought along the popular guides of the day, but found they were all lacking in some way. They were either strong on ruins and museums but went on for pages without mentioning a beach or taverna. Or they were so conscious of the need to save money that they lost sight of Greece's cultural and historical significance. Also, none of the books told him anything about Greece's contemporary life – its politics, its culture, its people and how they lived.

So with no job in prospect, Mark decided to write his own guidebook, one which aimed to provide practical information that was second to none, detailing the best beaches and the hottest clubs and restaurants, while also giving hard-hitting accounts of every sight, both famous and obscure, and providing up-to-the-minute information on contemporary culture. It was a guide that encouraged independent travellers to find the best of Greece, and was a great success, getting shortlisted for the Thomas Cook travel guide award, and encouraging Mark, along with three friends, to expand the series.

The Rough Guide list grew rapidly and the letters flooded in, indicating a much broader readership than had been anticipated, but one which uniformly appreciated the Rough Guides' mix of practical detail and humour, irreverence and enthusiasm. Things haven't changed. The same four friends who began the series are still the caretakers of the Rough Guide mission today: to provide the most reliable, up-to-date and entertaining information to independent-minded travellers of all ages, on all budgets.

We now publish over 200 titles and have offices in London and New York. The travel guides are written and researched by a dedicated team of more than 100 authors, based in Britain, Europe, the USA and Australia. We have also created a unique series of phrasebooks to accompany the travel series, along with the acclaimed series of music guides, and a best-selling pocket guide to the Internet and World Wide Web. We also publish comprehensive travel information on our Web site: *www.roughguides.com*

Contents

Chapter 11:   The North Cornwall Coast   263–295

Chapter 12:   Bodmin and Bodmin Moor   296–311

Part Three: Contexts   313

Index   332

List of maps

MAP SYMBOLS

– – –	Chapter division boundary	▲	Mountain peak
	Motorway (regional maps)	⌂	Hills/mountains
===	Major road	ⵢ	Lighthouse
—	Minor road		Rocks
	Pedestrianized street (town maps)	⌇	Waterfall
- - - -	Path	ⵣ	Gardens
	Railway	♦	Museum
— —	Ferry route	P	Parking
	Waterway	◉	Accommodation
⌣	Bridge/tunnel	Δ	Campsite
◆	General point of interest	ⓘ	Tourist office
♜	Castle	▬▬	Wall
ⵝ	Fortress	⊠	Post office
⊞	Stately home		Building
ⵞ	Church (regional maps)	→	Church
⌂	Abbey	+	Cemetery
∴	Ruin/archeological site		National Park
⌒	Caves		

Introduction

Pointing away from England into the Atlantic, the dangling limb of land holding the country's westernmost counties of **Devon and Cornwall** has long wielded a powerful attraction for holiday-makers – not to mention second-homers, retirees, artists and writers, and anyone keen on rugged landscape and ever-changing coastal scenery. The two counties have a markedly different feel and look: Devon's rolling swards of pasture, narrow lanes and picturesque thatched cottages are a striking contrast to the craggy charms of Cornwall, imbued with its strong sense of Celtic culture. The essential elements, however, are shared, first among which is the **sea** – the constant theme and the strongest lure, whether experienced as a restless force raging against rocks and reefs, or as a serene presence bathed in the kind of rich colours more readily associated with some sultry southern Mediterranean shore. You're never very far from the coast in Devon and Cornwall, where the panoramic sequence of miniature ports, placid estuaries, embattled cliffs and sequestered bays are linked by one of the region's greatest assets, the **South West Coast Path**, stretching from the seaboard of Exmoor to the Dorset border. Most visitors, however, are primarily drawn to the magnificent **beaches** strewn along the deeply indented coast, ranging from grand sweeps of sand confronting ranks of surfer-friendly rollers to intimate creeks and coves away from the crowds and holiday paraphernalia. The **resorts** catering to the armies of beach fans which inundate the southwest every summer also come in all shapes and sizes, from former fishing villages to full-blown tourist towns offering every facility, from sedate Victorian watering-holes to spartan beaches backed by caravan parks and hot-dog stalls. It is this sheer diversity which accounts for the region's enduring popularity, and which has made it the destination of travellers since the Napoleonic wars forced the English to look closer to home for their annual break.

Inland, the peninsula offers a complete contrast in the form of three of the country's most dramatic wildernesses, Exmoor,

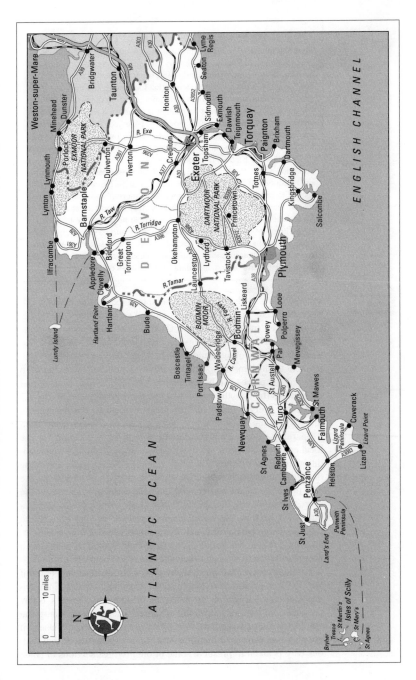

Dartmoor and Bodmin Moor, whose appeal extends to cyclists, riding enthusiasts and nature lovers as well as to walkers. Alongside these barren tracts, Devon and Cornwall can also boast supreme specimens of English rural life – unsung hamlets off the beaten track, where clustered cottages and brilliant flower displays perfectly complement the lush meadows and tidy dells surrounding them. But even these idyllic places can be invaded and spoiled in high season, and therein lies the rub: the millions of tourists who descend on the M5 motorway every summer are the biggest threat to the beauty and integrity of the West Country, some corners of which have been irreparably ruined. Though tourism represents a godsend for the local economy at a time when both farming and fishing – which traditionally provided the main employment in these parts – are in the doldrums, it can only favour the small proportion of locals who are well-placed to adapt and benefit from the passing trade, while the seasonal nature and fluctuating trends of the work leave many without much backup. Moreover, the demand for second homes and inflated prices have meant that many locals are literally priced out, and you'll find hotels and B&Bs managed and staffed by people with every kind of accent except the local one. The pressures of the holiday industry have also given many places an artificial veneer, as if they've been preserved to match some ideal vision of a pre-industrial, "authentic" England, as apparent in some of Devon's cosily gentrified villages or Cornwall's quainter fishing ports, where the cloying nostalgia is underpinned by a sharp commercial sense. On the plus side, though, the southwest's popularity has meant that zealous care is taken to preserve some of the prettiest sections of coast and countryside in a more or less "natural" condition, limiting development and unconsidered exploitation. Though this has not proved sufficient in the case of, say, Land's End, whose spectacular glory has been desecrated by an amusement complex, other equally dramatic headlands remain relatively unscathed.

Where to go

Where you go in Devon and Cornwall will depend on your primary interest. If beaches are the priority, you can pick just about any stretch of coast with the guarantee of finding a patch of sand or rocks to swim from. As a rule, the cliffier northern littoral has fewer beaches, though some of these are first choice for surfers, notably at **Woolacombe** and **Croyde** in Devon, and in Cornwall, those around **Bude**, **Padstow** and **Newquay**. Devon's most popular **seaside towns** are on the more sheltered southeast-facing coast, where there is superb swimming to north and south of **Torquay**, self-styled capital of the **"English Riviera"**. Elsewhere in Devon, you'll find less coming and going around the classic resorts of the **east Devon** coast, where the predominantly shingle shores are backed by eroded sandstone-red cliffs and interspersed with such classic old resorts as **Sidmouth**. In Cornwall, crowds home in on **St Austell Bay** and the **Falmouth** locality, but the beaches are far more inviting at the western end of the region, where the twin prongs of the **Lizard and Penwith peninsulas** are liberally studded with small sheltered bays such as **Porthcurno** and **Kynance Cove**, as well as more extensive surfing beaches such as **Sennen Cove** and **Poldhu**. All, however, pale into insignificance when compared with the dazzling white-sand strands found in abundance on the **Isles of Scilly**, where the sea can take on a tropical brilliance, though the water temperatures are decidedly chilly.

Likewise, hikers need only head for the nearest coast to find some of the choicest walking in Britain. Circling the entire peninsula, the coast path allows endless opportunities for long-distance or shorter jaunts, and links up with other routes such as the **Tarka Way**, around **Barnstaple** and **Bideford** in north Devon, and the **Camel Trail**, which goes inland from the coast at **Padstow** to **Bodmin Moor**. Unsurprisingly, it is the moors which hold the greatest range of paths and bridleways, and of these **Dartmoor** holds the densest concentration, though the walks and rides on the smaller, more cultivated **Exmoor** should not be discounted.

The pleasures of Devon and Cornwall are not confined to the great outdoors, however. History and culture can be soaked up at the region's main centres, not least at **Exeter**, the most satisfying ensemble of medieval architecture, with a first-rate museum. Devon's leading part in England's maritime history is well evident here and at **Plymouth**, which has preserved its medieval core around the old harbour despite severe bomb damage during World War II.

On a smaller scale, the nautical tradition is perpetuated in such estuary ports as **Dartmouth** and **Fowey** on the south coast, and **Bideford** on the north, all favourite anchorages of yachting folk. More tangibly, the West Country's past can be encountered in the numerous ruins scattered throughout the peninsula. These range from the primitive hut circles and Iron Age remains on the moors and even on the remote **Isles of Scilly**, to the various castles of diverse eras – fragmentary but dramatic, as at **Tintagel**, King Arthur's fabled home on the north Cornish coast, or immaculately preserved, such as the Tudor **St Mawes**, in south Cornwall, and **Castle Drogo**, on Dartmoor. The region's former wealth, derived above all from mining and wool, is reflected in a rich assortment of stately homes, usually tucked out of sight in the midst of splendid countryside, as at **Hartland Abbey**, in north Devon, and **Lanhydrock**, on the edge of Bodmin Moor. The endowments of landowners and merchants helped to fund some of Devon's most striking examples of ecclesiastical architecture, as at **Crediton**, in mid-Devon, while Cornwall's myriad **Methodist chapels** are testament to the markedly different style of popular religion proselytized by John Wesley in the eighteenth century. On a very different note, **Truro's** twentieth-century cathedral – a bold neo-Gothic statement which has divided local opinion – has, literally, raised the profile of Cornwall's county town.

The region's more modern face is well evident a few miles west at **St Ives**, whose branch of the Tate celebrates the various schools of art which colonized the area in the nineteenth and twentieth centuries. Most recent of all, the ambitious **Eden Project** near St Austell, a clay pit converted into an immense complex of conservatories, has married technology with ecology on an eye-popping scale, and is already drawing record crowds.

For many people, however, the magic of Devon and Cornwall lies in the multitude of remote villages dotted along the coast, often sandwiched between rocky headlands, where a few fishing vessels still operate and a timeless tranquillity sets the tone. There are any number of well-known examples – **Boscastle** or **Port Isaac**, say, on Cornwall's northern coast, or **Beer** and **Brixham** in south Devon – but the best ones are usually serendipitous discoveries. At the same time, many places have succumbed to their own myth and turned into synthesized versions of the ideal coastal hamlet, as is the case at **Clovelly** in north Devon and **Polperro** in south Cornwall. Drop in on these places outside the tourist season and you'll find authentic charm still managing to shine through.

When to go

With the highest average year-round temperatures in Britain, Devon and Cornwall make a viable destination in all seasons. This makes an even more compelling case for avoiding the peak **summer** months, if at all possible, when your visit will coincide with that of crowds of other holiday-makers. Admittedly, the sea is at its warmest and the possibility of rain at its lowest in July and August, but given the unpredictability of the English climate at any season, it's worth missing the hassle of this period, which includes congested roads and paths, packed beaches and reduced availability for all forms of accommodation. Other busy periods include the Easter holiday and, to a lesser extent, around Christmas and New Year. Individual places can get very busy when a local **festival** is being staged (see the Festivals and Events Calendar box on pp.18–19). At other times, weekends see most movement, and Saturday in particular is traditionally the worst day for traffic.

On the other hand, don't expect to enjoy all that the peninsula has to offer in the middle of **winter**. Wet weather can ruin any outdoor pursuits, and in the case of walking can be downright risky. This is particularly true on the coast and on the moors, where mists and blinding rain can descend with amazing suddenness – and note that the moors attract more rainfall than other areas: Dartmoor, for example, gets nearly twice as much annually as Torbay, just 15 miles away. Moreover, attractions, including most stately homes, often close during the winter months, and many B&Bs and hotels are also shut between October and Easter, as well as most campsites. Public transport services, too, are severely curtailed. On the other hand, you can get splendid weather in winter, when you'll have many places pretty much to yourself, and if you're in the Isles of Scilly, you'll be well-placed for the flower harvest – the best time to appreciate the scale of this local industry.

Spring sees the famous plants and shrubs of the peninsula's south coast at their most spectacular, and the countryside everywhere at its most exuberant, while the turning of the colours in **autumn** is a sight to behold, especially on the moors. All the same, you'll have to guard against the strong winds which can still blow fairly cold, and only the hardiest will risk swimming in the sea. On balance, the ideal would be to plan your visit between May and late July, before the schools' summer break, or between September and October, when everything is open, but you won't find yourself spending too much of your holiday in a queue.

Average daily temperatures in Plymouth

	Jan	Feb	March	April	May	June	July	Aug	Sept	Oct	Nov	Dec
max°F	47	47	50	54	59	64	66	67	64	58	52	49
max°C	8.3	8.3	10	12.2	15	17.8	18.8	19.4	17.8	14.4	11.1	9.4
min°F	39	38	40	43	47	52	55	55	53	49	44	41
min°C	3.8	3.3	4.4	6.1	8.3	11.1	12.8	12.8	11.6	9.4	6.7	5

Average monthly rainfall in Plymouth

	Jan	Feb	March	April	May	June	July	Aug	Sept	Oct	Nov	Dec
inches	3.9	2.9	2.7	2.1	2.5	2.1	2.8	3.0	3.1	3.6	4.5	4.3
mm	98	73	68	53	63	53	70	75	78	90	113	108

Basics

Getting there

Getting to Devon and Cornwall is easily accomplished along one of the main westward-bound road and rail routes. By road, most use the M5 motorway, which swoops south from Birmingham and connects with the M4 from London at Bristol. The M5 terminates at Exeter, from where roads radiate out to different parts of Devon and further west. The A30 offers a slower route from London and Salisbury, extending via Exeter all the way to Land's End. Exeter is also the junction of the two main rail lines – from Salisbury, and from London, the Midlands and Bristol – and is the hub of a network of bus routes throughout Devon.

By bus

National Express (☎ 0870/580 8080) buses connect **Exeter** with London, Bristol, Birmingham, Bradford, Leeds, Sheffield and Derby. Standard ticket prices for all National Express services are slightly reduced if you buy at least seven days in advance, and are subject to a minor increase if you travel on Fridays or, in July and August, on Saturdays. From **London's Victoria Coach Station**, there are nine daily departures to **Exeter** (4hr–4hr 30min; £28 return); the same service carries on to Torquay and Paignton. A separate service leaves seven times daily from Victoria Coach Station to **Plymouth** (5hr; £32 return). If you want to go straight to Cornwall, there are four daily departures from London to **Truro** (7–8hr; £40 return) and six to **Penzance** (8–9hr;

£40 return). Bodmin, Falmouth and Newquay are connected by less-frequent daily services.

From **Birmingham**, there are two to three buses daily to **Exeter** (3hr 35min–5hr; £29 return); three to five daily to **Plymouth** (4hr 45min–5hr 25min; £36.50 return); three daily to **Penzance** (8–9hr; £43.50 return), and two daily to **Truro** (7hr–7hr 30min; £43.50 return). **From Bristol**, there are four daily buses to **Exeter** (2hr; £12.50 return); four daily to **Plymouth** (2hr 30min–3hr; £22.25 return); one daily to **Truro** (5hr; £31.50 return) and two daily to **Penzance** (6hr; £33 return).

Between May and September, Stray Travel's **backpacker bus** makes a round trip between London and the West Country two or three times a week, making selected stops. It operates as a cross between a jump on/jump off service, with a travel pass (£99) good for transport over each section of the route once only, and a tour with commentary included. Currently, there are overnight halts at Ilfracombe and Newquay, and other stops include Torquay and Land's End. The pass is valid over four months, but does not include accommodation for overnight stops, which can be booked through the company. Call ☎ 020/7373 7737, or book online at the Web site, www.straytravel.com.

By train

From London Paddington, First Great Western, and Wales and West run all trains to Exeter, Plymouth and Penzance, with roughly one departure hourly. Journey time **to Exeter St David's** is two to three hours, and the cost of the ticket varies according to how far ahead you book and the restrictions imposed – from £98 for a completely unrestricted open return to £53.80 for a Saver return (allowing travel on all days but not before 9.25am or between 4pm and 7.05pm, which are peak times), £40 for a Supersaver (not Fridays or before 9.25am and between 4.32pm and 6.20pm any day), £34 for a Super-advance ticket (limited availability; book before 6pm the previous day) and £24 for an Apex (limited availability, to be booked at least a week ahead with specified date and time of return travel). Services from London **to Plymouth**, taking around three and a half hours, cost £126 for an open return, £56.90 for a Saver return, £45 for a Supersaver return, £39 for a Super-advance ticket and £28 for an Apex. You can reach **Penzance** from London Paddington in five or six hours, with return fares at £140 for an open return, £61.30 for a Saver, £55 for a Supersaver, £46 for a Super-advance and £31 for an Apex.

From London Waterloo, South West Trains take slightly longer – around three and a quarter hours – to reach **Exeter**, running via Salisbury (where you may need to change) and Honiton in east Devon, but are cheaper: £78 for an open return, £52.60 for a Saver return, £40 for a Supersaver, £27.50 for a Super-advance ticket and £20 for an Apex. On this line, you can also purchase a Network Stayaway ticket to Exeter (for more than five days away, travelling outside peak times) for £49.20.

Virgin Trains run **from Birmingham New Street Station to Exeter** in under three hours, and offer a Saver (an open return) for £52.60, or a Virgin Value ticket, for which the outgoing and return journeys must be booked before you travel; these cost £30 if booked three days in advance, £20 if booked seven days in advance and £15 if booked fourteen days in advance. From Birmingham, Virgin trains also run **to Plymouth** in three and a half to four and a half hours, with Saver tickets costing £68.30, and Virgin Value tickets at £55 (three days in advance), £30 (seven days in advance) and £20 (fourteen days in advance). **To Penzance**, trains take about five and a half hours. Saver tickets cost £84, and Virgin Value tickets are £55 (three days in advance), £30 (seven days in advance) and £25 (fourteen days in advance).

From Paddington, **bikes** are carried free on Wales and West, and for £1 (with advance reservation) or £3 (without reserving) on First Great Western trains. Availability is limited, and reservations are advised. From Waterloo, South West Trains carry up to five bikes per train free on non-peak services; bikes are prohibited on trains that depart on weekdays from 4.30pm to 6.30pm, and those that arrive in Devon and Cornwall between 7.45am and 9.45am. On services from Birmingham, Virgin Trains charge a similarly small fee but insist on advance reservations (call ☎0845/722 2333, 8am–10pm); again, space is limited. For information on taking bikes on trains run by companies within Devon and Cornwall, see p.6-7.

Train and bus information

For all information on **train** services run by all companies, call National Rail Enquiries on ☎0845/748 4950, or access the Web site *www.railtrack.co.uk*. You can also get information by visiting the Web sites of the individual operators: *www.virgintrains.co.uk* (Virgin Trains); *www.walesandwest.co.uk* (Wales and West); *www.great-western-trains.co.uk* (First Great Western); *www.swtrains.co.uk* (South West Trains). For National Express **buses**, call ☎0870/580 8080 or visit *www.gobycoach.com*.

By car

Although drivers from Salisbury may be on the **A30** or the faster **A303** (which branches off the London–Southampton M3), the most direct route into Devon and Cornwall by car is along the **M5** motorway, which runs to Exeter from Birmingham, and links with the M4 from London outside Bristol. You can calculate less than two-hours' driving between Bristol and Exeter, depending on the volume of traffic. Bank holiday weekends and high summer see intense traffic, particularly on the M5 around Bristol, which is frequently exacerbated by roadworks over the Avon bridge where tailbacks can be expected. Saturday is "changeover day", when holiday-makers on weekly rentals clog up the roads in and around the region, and should be avoided if possible. You can get up-to-date **information** on bottlenecks and other possible delays from the AA (☎0870/550 0600; *www.theaa.co.uk*) and RAC (☎0906/470 1740; *www.rac.co.uk*); both also provide a route-planning service; it's also worth tuning in to local radio stations for traffic news – frequencies are posted up at the side of major roads.

If you want to reduce your fuel costs, you might consider joining one of the two **liftshare** schemes operating in the UK, which put members in touch with others travelling the same way. Contact National CarShare (☎01344/861600; *www.nationalcarshare.co.uk*) or visit the Liftshare Web site (*www.liftshare.com*).

Ferries and flights

Travellers from France and Spain can cross over to Plymouth **by ferry** with Brittany Ferries (☎0870/901 2400; *www.brittanyferries.co.uk*)

from Roscoff in Brittany (Feb–Dec from 1 weekly to several times daily) and Santander in Spain (mid-March to mid-Nov 2 weekly).

Exeter, Plymouth and Newquay have the region's main airports for anyone intending to **fly to the southwest**. There are frequent flights **to Exeter** from Birmingham; Jersey and Guernsey in the Channel Islands; and Cork and Dublin in Ireland, all run by British European Airways (☎0870/ 567 6676). Brymon Airways (☎0845/779 9977) operate regular flights **to Plymouth** from Bristol, Aberdeen, Edinburgh, Glasgow, London Gatwick, Newcastle, Cork and Paris. **Newquay's airport** has four flights per day from London Gatwick; for flight information contact British Airways on ☎0870/551 1155.

Getting around

While your own vehicle can seem like a cumbersome burden in **Devon and Cornwall's** towns and villages, which are prone to traffic snarl-ups, a car does provide the freedom to explore more remote parts of the region and avoids being at the mercy of sporadic public-transport timetables, which can be woefully limited in some of the most attractive areas of the region. There are viable alternatives to cars both for longer and shorter journeys, however, not least the various walking and cycling routes which traverse the peninsula. Additionally, you may need to make use of a sketchy network of ferries, and there's also the option of flying to the **Isles of Scilly or Lundy**.

Although general points are covered below, you'll find detailed listings of transport schedules and frequencies at the end of each chapter in the *Guide*. Comprehensive transport **timetables** for the region are listed in booklets available free from tourist offices and travel shops. Regional transport Web sites and information lines are detailed in the box overleaf.

By train

The **train network** in Devon and Cornwall is a mere shadow of the system which covered the region in Victorian times – later dismantled – notably by Lord Beeching in the 1960s. The main spine survives today, running from Exeter through Plymouth, Bodmin and Truro to Penzance, and this provides a quick and efficient way to travel through the peninsula. With the exception of Bodmin Parkway, stations are generally centrally located. A few **branch lines** remain, too, providing unique opportunities to see some of the region's most scenic parts. From Exeter, South West trains run the brief distance south alongside the Exe estuary to Exmouth, and **Tarka Line** trains run northwest to Barnstaple, making a handy link to mid- and north Devon. From Plymouth, the **Tamar Valley Line** runs north to Gunnislake, close to a cluster of sights as well as to Dartmoor. In Cornwall, the **Looe Valley Line** links Liskeard, on the main line from London, with Looe, on the south coast, while from Par in St Austell's Bay, a branch line goes northwest to Newquay. From Truro, there is a line to Falmouth, while from St Erth (the last stop on the London line before Penzance), one of the most beautiful West Country tracks runs along the Hayle estuary to St Ives.

There are also a few restored private lines running in summer and school holidays, chiefly the

PUBLIC TRANSPORT INFORMATION LINES AND WEB SITES

TRAINS

Call National Rail Enquiries on ☎0845/748 4950 for details of all train services.
The Devon and Cornwall Rail Partnership (☎01752/233094)
provides information on all branch lines as well as walks from stations.
For **pocket timetables** for the Tarka, Tamar and Looe Valley Lines, call ☎0870/900 0772.

BUS INFORMATION IN DEVON

All Devon	☎01392/382800.	Plymouth and around	☎01752/402060.
	or ☎01271/382800.	Plymouth Citybus	☎01752/222221.
Exeter and around	☎01392/427711.	South Devon	☎01752/402060.
North Devon	☎01271/345444.	Torbay area	☎01803/613226.

BUS INFORMATION IN CORNWALL

For First Western National and First Red Bus call
☎01752/402060 in east Cornwall,
☎01208/79898 in mid- and north Cornwall
☎01209/719988 in west Cornwall.
For Truronian services, call ☎01872/273453.

WEB SITES

www.devon-cc.gov.uk/devonbus
Bus information for the whole of Devon.

www.firstwesternnational.co.uk
Information on First Western National and First Red Bus services in Cornwall.

www.truronian.co.uk
Truronian bus routes and schedules.

www.carfreedaysout.com
Excellent site comprehensively covering timetables, tickets, maps,
attractions, walks and cycle routes in Cornwall, Devon and Exmoor.

Paignton and Dartmouth Steam Railway (see p.80), tracing the Dart estuary from Torbay to Kingswear, which is connected by ferry to Dartmouth; and the **South Devon Railway** (see p.84) between Totnes and Buckfastleigh on the edge of Dartmoor. They're both touristy but fun, and provide useful links in the transport network.

Although they're not valid on the private steam lines, **rail passes** are a worthwhile investment if you're going to make regular use of the trains. Covering Devon, Cornwall and places east as far as Weston-super-Mare and Salisbury, a **Freedom of the South West Rover** allows eight-days' travel in fifteen at a cost of £71.50 in high season (end May to end Sept) or £61 in low season (end Sept to end May). A **Cornwall Rover** pass valid for three-days' travel in seven costs £25.50 in high season and £18 in low season; for eight-days' travel in fifteen, you'll pay £40.50 in high

season and £33 in low season. Similarly, a **Devon Rover** costs £30 for three-days' travel in seven during the high season, or £24 in low season; for eight-days' travel in fifteen, you'll pay £46.50 in high season and £39.50 in low season. A further third discount on all these passes is given for holders of a Young Person's or Senior Railcard. Passes can be obtained from any staffed train station or booked in advance by credit card on ☎0870/900 0773 or ☎0845/700 0125, allowing five days for delivery.

Bikes can be carried on most trains operated by Devon and Cornwall-based companies, and on all of those of the Tarka Line. Note that if you want to load your bike onto a train, reservations and usually a small fee are required on services between Plymouth and Penzance. Bikes travel free on the Plymouth–Gunnislake, Liskeard–Looe, Par–Newquay, Truro–Falmouth and St Ives–St

NATIONAL CAR RENTAL COMPANIES

Avis Main office ☎ 0870/606 0100; Exeter office ☎ 01392/259713; *www.avis.com*.

Budget Main office ☎ 0800/181181; Exeter office ☎ 01392/496555; *www.budgetrentacar.com*.

Europcar Main office ☎ 0870/607 5000; Exeter office ☎ 01392/498630; *www.europcar.co.uk*.

Hertz Main office ☎ 0870/844 8844; Exeter office ☎ 01392/207207; *www.hertz.com*.

National Car Rental (formerly Eurodollar) Main office ☎ 01895/233300; Exeter office ☎ 01392/250858; *www.nationalcar-europe.com*.

Thrifty Main office ☎ 01494/751600; Exeter office ☎ 01392/204460; *www.thrifty.co.uk*.

Erth branch lines on a first-come, first-served basis (availability is limited). For further details and reservations, ask at train stations or contact the company operating the service, either Wales and West (☎ 0870/900 0773), South West Trains (☎ 023/8021 3600), Virgin Trains (☎ 0845/722 2333), or First Great Western (☎ 0845/700 0125).

By bus

While National Express provide a long-distance service linking the main centres of Devon and Cornwall, the main companies running **bus services** between small villages in the region are Stagecoach Devon and First Red Bus, covering mainly south and north Devon respectively, and First Western National and Truronian in Cornwall – the latter confined to a few routes in the Lizard, around Falmouth and in north Cornwall. Most villages in Devon and Cornwall are covered at least once daily, though others, for example on the moors or on remote sections of coast, may be visited just once or twice weekly, or on school days only. Day-return **tickets** are cheaper than two singles, but are only available at weekends and after 8.45am from Monday to Friday. If you're going to be using buses extensively, you might want to consider buying a **pass**. The **Explorer** ticket covers travel on the complete Stagecoach Devon network and costs £5.95 for one day, £15 for three days and £24.40 for seven days. The equivalent for Cornwall costs £6 for one day, £15 for three days and £27 for seven days. The **Red Rider** is valid only on First Red buses, which mainly operate in north Devon, and costs £4.60 for a day and £14.40 for a week. You can buy all the passes listed here at travel shops, some tourist offices and on board the bus – though the Red Day Rider is not sold on the #300 Minehead–Ilfracombe route. Note, too, that students can use their NUS cards to travel at the children's price on single and return journeys.

By car

Though a **car** is often the fastest way to get around Devon and Cornwall, the nature of the region's roads and the level of summer traffic mean that you may often get embroiled in irritating hold-ups. The peninsula's three main roads – the A39, running along the north coast, the A30, which strikes through the middle as far as Land's End, and the A38, which takes the southern route through Plymouth, joining the A30 near Bodmin – can get seriously clogged in holiday season, with caravans and farm vehicles adding to the congestion. As soon as you leave the main roads, you'll often find yourself in narrow, bendy country lanes, flanked by high hedges and with minimal visibility, where a low speed is unavoidable. Other rural hazards include horses and riders, straying sheep and ponies and hunt followers on the moors.

If you're driving, you'll find that the best policy is to deposit your vehicle at the first available car park whenever you reach a destination – negotiating convoluted one-way systems while trying to map-read can be a nightmare and parking spaces on streets are few and far between. **Car parks**, though, are relatively cheap; most are pay-and-display, so a small cache of change is a useful item to have to hand.

Car rental companies are distributed throughout the region, and a selection of them are detailed in the *Guide* (see box, above, for the national companies). Prices start at around £100 per week.

By bike

A significant stretch of the National Cycle Network has recently opened in the South West, linking Bristol and Bath with Padstow in Cornwall and making biking through the region a particularly attractive possibility. Known as the **West Country Way**, the stretch connects and overlaps with the **Cornish Way**, which runs between Bude and Land's End. Parts of the West Country Way run along the **Tarka Trail** in north Devon, and the **Camel Trail**, which runs between Bodmin Moor and the Camel Estuary at Padstow, two first-class walking and cycling routes. Other cycleways have been developed along the old tramways in Cornwall's mining country (see p.267). For more information on the South West and Cornish Ways, and on the entire National Cycle Network, contact Sustrans, 35 King St, Bristol BS1 4DZ (☎0117/929 0888; www.sustrans.co.uk). **Bike rental** outlets are found throughout the region, especially around the main trails. A selection are included in the *Guide*; expect to pay around £8.50 per day including helmet; a hefty deposit and proof of identity is usually required as well.

See p.6-7 for information on taking bikes onto trains in Devon and Cornwall.

On foot

The longest footpath in Britain, the **South West Coast Path** tracks the peninsula's coast all the way round from Minehead in Somerset to Poole in Dorset, and offers an unrivalled way to experience coast and sea. The path was con-

ceived in the 1940s, but it is only in the last thirty years that – barring a few significant gaps – the full **six-hundred-mile route** has been open, much of it on land owned by the National Trust, and all of it well signposted with the acorn symbol of the Countryside Agency. Local shops stock maps of the route (the 1:25,000 Explorer and Outdoor Leisure series are most useful) and there are several books giving detailed directions, including a series of four describing different stretches of the path which include Ordnance Survey maps; they're published by Aurum Press (25 Bedford Ave, London WC1B 3AT ☎020/7637 3225; www.aurumpress.co.uk).

The **South West Coast Path Association** (Windlestraw, Penquit, Ermington, Devon PL21 0LU ☎01752/896237; www.swcp.org.uk) also publishes an annual guide to the route, costing £7 including postage. Though lacking much detail and without maps, it does include **tide tables**, which can also be bought from tourist offices, newsagents, souvenir shops and bookstores for less than £1. The south Devon stretch in particular needs careful timing, as there are six ferries to negotiate and one ford to cross between Plymouth and Exmouth. Accommodation, which is relatively plentiful along the way, should also be booked ahead.

TOUR COMPANIES

Coast and Country Tours, 2 Basset Place, Falmouth TR11 2SS ☎01326/211889; www.coast-country-tours.co.uk. Full-day minibus tours from Falmouth (£29–34), or evening excursions to the Minack Theatre (about £17.50 including transport and theatre ticket). Trips run from Easter to mid-September, and can also be booked through Falmouth's tourist office.

First Western National, 38 Lemon St, Truro, Cornwall TR1 2NS ☎01209/719988. Full- and half-day coach excursions from Penzance and St Ives around the north Cornwall coast (£4.50), the Lizard (£6) and King Arthur country (£7.50). Other excursions are also available.

Road Trip, 501 International House, 223 Regent St, London W1R 8QD ☎0800/056 0505; www.roadtrip.co.uk. Five-day and weekend trips to Devon and Cornwall aimed at backpack-

ers, with stops at Tintagel, Totnes, Land's End, Exeter and Newquay, and rides and barbecues thrown in. Prices start at around £89 for two nights away including accommodation and food.

Stray Travel, 171 Earls Court Rd, London SW5 9RF ☎020/7373 7737; www.straytravel.com. Three-day tours on a backpacker bus operating between May and September from London, with commentary, barbecues and other entertainments. There are overnight stops in Ilfracombe and Newquay, and short stops at Tintagel, Land's End and Torquay. Your ticket, or pass, is valid for two months, so you can rejoin a tour later if you want to jump off for a sojourn somewhere. Tickets currently cost £99, and hostel accommodation is paid for separately (but can be arranged through the company). Bookings can also be made on line.

Even campsites can fill up, though campers have the flexibility of asking farmers for permission to pitch in a corner of a field.

The South West Coast Path also touches on other long-distance paths in the region, including the **Saint's Way**, crossing between Cornwall's coasts between Padstow and Fowey, and the **Two Moors Way**, which links Exmoor and Dartmoor between Lynmouth and Ivybridge. Local tourist offices have route maps of both, and you can write to the Two Moors Way Association (Coppins, The Poplars, Pinhoe, Exeter EX4 9HH) for leaflets (50p plus an SAE) or the official guide (£3).

Tours

Taking a **tour** allows you to see and learn a lot quickly with minimum effort. Most are conducted in minibuses by guides who possess an expert knowledge of the area and mix personal experience with history and context. Some of the best focus on individual **themes**, such as the archeology of Penwith, Arthurian links in Cornwall and wildlife on the moors, giving you a deeper insight into one particular area, and a new angle on the region as a whole. Specialist tours tend to change frequently, but local tourist offices can update you on what's currently on offer. The box opposite, suggests a selection of the best general tours.

Information, maps and the media

Unless you want to plan your trip in minute detail, it's not necessary to stock up on maps and brochures before you leave – all can readily be picked up in the region. Local bookstores and outdoor shops have the relevant walking and touring maps, while much information can be gleaned from Web sites relating to places and attractions in the region; these are listed throughout the *Guide*, and there's a selection of the most useful general sites in the box overleaf.

Visitor information

While regional tourist boards (see box overleaf) can supply maps and general information, local **tourist offices** have their ears closer to the ground and are better placed for practical information. Fairly ubiquitous, they are always well supplied with reams of information on transport, local attractions and accommodation, though it's worth noting that much of the material relates only to places which have paid for their entries and listings in the official brochures – there are many other attractions and places to eat or sleep on which tourist offices have nothing at all. All the same, it's worth grabbing whatever accommodation and dining listings they have for the area you're interested in – in summer especially, places fill up quickly and places listed in this *Guide* may not always be available. Though mostly overworked, staff are knowledgeable and extremely helpful as a rule. **Opening hours** for most tourist offices are Monday to Saturday from 9am to 5pm, with some variations at weekends and in winter. In high summer, many are open daily, while in winter some close altogether. Larger offices will also change money, and all will book accommodation.

REGIONAL TOURIST BOARDS

South West Tourism, Woodwater Park, Exeter, Devon EX2 5WT ☎0870/442 0830; *www.westcountrynow.com*.

Cornwall Tourist Board, Pydar House, Pydar St, Truro, Cornwall TR1 1EA ☎01872/274057; *www.cornwalltouristboard.co.uk*.

Devon Tourist Information Service, PO Box 55, Barnstaple, Devon EX32 8YR ☎0870/608 5531.

Local publications

Local publications are often an excellent source of up-to-date information and entertainment listings. One of the southwest's most widely read local **newspapers** is the daily *Western Morning News*, covering the whole of Devon and eastern Cornwall, a sort of middle-England paper with national as well as local news. Weekly publications include, in Devon, the *North Devon Journal* and *Mid-Devon Gazette*, and in Cornwall the *Cornishman*, *Cornish Guardian* and *West Briton*, part of the same publishing stable and covering, respectively, Penwith, mid-Cornwall and The Lizard, and east Cornwall; all are strong on local news and events and general tittle-tattle. **Magazines** geared toward the region, usually available from tourist offices or newsagents in the area, include the monthly *Inside Cornwall*, *Cornwall Today*, *Devon Life* and *Devon Today*, and the quarterly *Devon County Magazine* – all of them with articles on food, culture, local issues and other aspects of living in the West Country. The quarterly *Dartmoor: The Country Magazine* and the bimonthly *Dartmoor News* cover books and local history.

You'll pick up more practical information from **free newspapers**, which relate to specific regions and are published annually. Look out particularly for the *Exmoor Visitor*, the *Dartmoor Visitor* and *Coastlines and Countryside News* (the latter covering the north Cornwall coast); both have information on walks, wildlife, accommodation and services. For music, theatre and other events, seek out the monthly free **listings magazines** *tdb*, *twenty4-seven* and *What's On Southwest* for the latest places and dates. Newquay's *Woz On* publishes two issues every summer, in May and July. All these publications can be found in tourist offices and in pubs, clubs and hotels.

Local radio

Providing the usual mix of chat and chart music, **local radio stations** can be useful sources of information on traffic and sea conditions, weather and local events. The BBC's **Radio Cornwall** (95.2, 96 or 103.9FM) and **Radio Devon** (94.8, 95.8 or 103.4FM) are staid but authoritative, with the accent on local issues; phone-ins tend to feature complaints about the state of the roads and problems with gulls. The

WEB SITES

www.chycor.co.uk General information on Cornwall, including dining and accommodation.

www.chycor.co.uk/buzz Excellent for music, festivals, pubs, clubs and general nightlife.

www.cornwall-online.co.uk Information on e vents, weekend breaks, attractions and local products, with the accent on Falmouth and southwest Cornwall.

www.devon-connect.co.uk Attractions, accommodation and general info site for Devon, but limited in scope.

www.english-heritage.org.uk General information about historic attractions run by English Heritage.

www.gaycornwall.org.uk Gay-friendly restaurants, hotels, beaches and clubs in Cornwall.

www.nationaltrust.org.uk Background and practical details on National Trust properties.

www.resort-guide.co.uk Basic information on, and links to, hundreds of hotels, restaurants and other facilities throughout the southwest.

www.thisiscornwall.co.uk The Web site for the *West Briton* newspaper, with surf reports and local news from Cornwall.

www.west-cornwall-tourism.co.uk Official site of west Cornwall's tourist offices.

www.2000cc.co.uk Great site for clubbing and nightlife in Cornwall.

main independent stations are **Gemini FM** (96.4, 97 or 103FM) and **Plymouth Sound** (97FM) in Devon, and **Pirate FM** (102.8FM), broadcast throughout Cornwall as well as Plymouth; all have national and local news, but mainly transmit a fairly bland musical output.

Maps

The best general **map** of the southwest is the **A–Z Devon Cornwall Visitors' Atlas and Guide**, showing the region at a scale of 2.5 miles to the inch. Produced by Geographers' A–Z Map Company, and available from most newsagents in the region, it has visitor information and large-scale town plans at the back. Drivers will find this more compact than the countrywide **road atlases**, usually three-miles-to-one-inch, pro-duced by the AA, RAC, Ordnance Survey, Collins and others. Walkers, however, should get hold of the 1:50,000 maps of the **Landranger Series**, or, better still, the more detailed 1:25,000 maps of the **Explorer Series** and of the **Outdoor Leisure Series**, which concentrates on Exmoor, Dartmoor and other specific areas of outstanding beauty. All three series are published by Ordnance Survey and are for sale at outdoors shops and book-shops in the region, or from dedicated **map outlets** such as Stanfords, whose nearest branch is in Bristol (29 Corn St, Bristol BS1 1HT; ☎0117/929 9966; *www.stanfords.co.uk*) and who also do mail order. It's also worth checking the Web site *www.multimap.com*, which has town plans and maps of the whole area with scales of up to 1:10,000.

Mail and money

The most important shop – and usually the only one – in many small rural communities is the post office, which will often offer a variety of services in addition to its traditional role. Banks are less common, though most larger villages have a branch, while Internet cafés are only to be found in bigger towns and cities. As for costs, what you spend on holiday will depend chiefly on where you stay and what you eat – the two biggest expenses on a daily basis.

Post offices, the Internet and mobile phones

Most **post offices** open from Monday to Friday between 9am and 5.30pm, and on Saturdays from 9am to 12.30pm. As well as the usual services, main post offices have facilities for changing travellers' cheques and foreign currency. **Internet cafés** are still surprisingly scarce in the southwest, but we've listed those that do exist – in Exeter, Plymouth, Barnstaple, Newquay, Truro and Penzance – in the *Guide*. Many hostels also offer Internet access. **Mobile phone** users should note that at time of writing, parts of the southwest peninsula are out of range or have only a weak signal – patches of the north coast of Devon and Cornwall, for example, and the moors.

Money and banks

If you're watching your budget – camping and buying some of your own food in shops and markets – you could get by on as little as £20–30 a day, but a more realistic **average daily budget** is around £45–55 a day, including B&B accommodation and some travel costs, while on

£60–80 a day you could be living pretty comfortably: staying in a decent hotel and eating out every night. **Cash** is easy to come by, with the main banks represented in all the towns and some larger villages; some smaller villages also have branches with cash dispensers (ATMs) that accept most cards. If you're stuck, ask around for **cashback** facilities in supermarkets; some stores even have cashpoint machines. You can rely on **credit cards** for most daily expenditure including petrol and train tickets, though pubs and cafés prefer cash, and the majority of B&Bs will not accept them (they will generally accept cheques, however). We've highlighted which accommodation establishments and restaurants don't take plastic in the *Guide* (pubs and cafés are assumed not to). Where credit cards are accepted, MasterCard and Visa are the most popular, with relatively few places taking American Express or Diner's Club.

Accommodation

Though Devon and Cornwall are awash with accommodation options, rooms can be scarce in high season. At peak periods – New Year, Easter, public holidays and school holidays (particularly the six-week summer break from late July to early Sept) – you should always book ahead.

There's a whole range of places in all price categories, and if you're economizing, hostels, private rooms, campsites and camping barns are all possibilities. Local tourist offices can usually make **bookings** in hotels and B&Bs over the phone, for which a deposit (normally ten percent) is charged (this is then deducted from your bill). Tourist offices are usually abreast of vacancies, and when offices are closed, staff often pin up a list of nearby possibilities on the door.

Hotels and B&Bs

Tariffs in hotels, guesthouses or B&Bs reflect the level of comfort, their location and the season. Within the same establishment, rooms with panoramic views or four-poster beds generally cost more, while most hotels and some B&Bs and guesthouses increase their rates in summer. Most places offer discounts for stays of two or more nights, or "special breaks" – usually referring to packages including meals. Single rooms can be hard to come by at any time of year.

Most ubiquitous are **B&Bs**, often quite modest places with a couple of rooms attached to a private home. On the whole these offer more personal service than more expensive places; owners usually are friendly and informative, and will often give you a fairer picture of a place than

---

ACCOMMODATION PRICE CODES

Throughout this *Guide*, hotel and B&B accommodation is coded on a scale of ① to ⑨, the code indicating the lowest price you can expect to pay per night for a double room in high season. The prices indicated by the codes are as follows:

① under £40	④ £60–70	⑦ £110–150
② £40–50	⑤ £70–90	⑧ £150–200
③ £50–60	⑥ £90–110	⑨ over £200

the tourist office can. As a rule, **B&Bs** (also known as guesthouses) are cheapest where they're remotely located; some of the best deals are on rural farms, where prices can be as little as £12 per person; more commonly, prices start at around £17 per person in double or twin rooms, with singles paying a few pounds more. You'll sometimes get en-suite facilities at this price – little more than a cupboard with a toilet and shower in many cases – though you can usually expect to pay a little extra for your own bathroom. Most rooms have a sink nowadays, along with tea- and coffee-making facilities, and, increasingly, a television. In many places, smoking is banned, either throughout the building or just in bedrooms (mentioned in the *Guide* where this is the case). There's a great uniformity of style in B&Bs; most are decked out in either functional or chintzy furnishings (according to the price) and offer identical breakfasts of juice, toast, cereals, fry-up and tea or coffee. Facilities are generally minimal, though some have guest lounges and some provide evening meals. Though it's rarely spelled out, B&Bs often discourage much coming and going during the day, and if you're not staying a second night you're expected to vacate your room by 10 or 11am.

Hotels in Devon and Cornwall come in all shapes and sizes. Many are little more than B&Bs with fire doors, while others are the acme of comfort, character and class. On the whole, though, you can expect at least a bar, restaurant and parking space; some places offer a pool, gym or games room at correspondingly higher prices. Guests can always come and go as they please, and all hotels should accept **credit cards** – we've noted hotels and B&Bs which don't in the *Guide*.

Hotels, and some B&Bs, offer a combined dinner, bed and breakfast rate, which can work out to be an excellent deal. In some places, particularly in rural areas or on the Isles of Scilly, half- or full-board is obligatory, especially in summer.

Hostels

There are twenty-three official **YHA youth hostels** in the area covered by this *Guide*, and we've listed them all at the relevant places in the text. Outside the cities, most close during the winter months, and many are also closed for one or more days in the week (usually Sun) in spring and autumn. You'll find the majority of the

hostels clean and well-equipped with laundrettes and self-catering **facilities**; Internet access and bike rental are also frequently available. On the minus side, most places still operate a curfew and are closed during the day. They can also get full, particularly in summer and at weekends, with group bookings often taking over an entire hostel; it's always worth booking ahead. **Sleeping arrangements** are pretty similar in all hostels: dormitories rarely have more than eight or ten bunk-beds, most are en suite and there are usually twin and family rooms available. Expect to pay around £10 for a dorm bed, or a little more per person for a double; bed linen is free, but towels are not provided. Membership of the Youth Hostel Association is required to stay in their hostels; this costs £12.50 per year; contact the YHA, Trevelyan House, 8 St Stephen's Hill, St Alban's, Herts AL1 2DY (☎01727/855215; *www.yha.org.uk*), or join online or at one of the hostels. Most members of hostelling associations in other countries have automatic membership of the YHA.

Accessibility is the biggest problem with YHA hostels: they're often hidden away in remote rural settings which are difficult, if not impossible, to reach by public transport. Most of the **independent hostels**, on the other hand, are conveniently located in the centre of towns. They generally have a less institutional atmosphere, but offer as good a range of facilities – kitchen, laundry, Internet access and bike rental – as you'll find in the YHA hostels. On the downside, they can sometimes be scruffy, and you might not be comfortable with the fact that dorms are occasionally mixed-sex. **Prices** are around the same as YHA hostels, with discounts negotiable for longer stays, and linen is usually supplied for an extra £1 or so per stay. The *Independent Hostel Guide*, available for £4.95 (plus £1 post and packing) from Backpackers Press, 2 Rockview Cottages, Matlock Bath, Derbyshire DE4 3PG (☎01629/580427), contains comprehensive listings of independent hostels. Alternatively, the free twice-yearly backpacker's magazine *Backpax*, usually available from the hostels themselves (or from Backpax Publications, 14a Arlington Villas, Bristol BS8 2EG *www.backpaxmag.com*), lists recently opened hostels, and *www.far2go.co.uk* has information on hostels, as well as tours, surf and other activities. A US-based site, *www.hostels.com*, also has information on hostels worldwide, including Devon and Cornwall, and allows you to book online.

Holiday rentals

Self-catering holiday properties can be a cheaper alternative to hotels and B&Bs. There are literally thousands of properties on offer, ranging from flats by the sea to rustic barn conversions, though many of the best are booked a year in advance. Prices range from £100 to £800 a week, according to size and season, and usually include bed linen and towels. Most are rented by the week only – Sunday to Saturday – though three-night short breaks are sometimes available in low season.

The agencies listed in the box, below, will send out brochures with photos and full details of individual properties; the info is generally repeated on the Web site as well. Local tourist offices, newspapers and notice boards are also worth consulting.

Campsites and camping barns

Camping is popular throughout Devon and Cornwall, and you'll find sites in all coastal areas and a smaller number inland. Many are mega-parks dominated by caravans and motor homes, but the ones we've recommended in the *Guide* are mainly tent-friendly. Most are closed in the winter months (usually October to May) though smaller sites attached to farms or pubs stay open – always ring first, however. **Prices** vary from three or four pounds for pitches in farmers' fields to £10 per pitch for the best equipped places, which often have a pool, nightclub and on-site store.

Another popular option, especially on the moors, are **camping barns**: rudimentary but weathertight dormitories fitted with showers, toilets and usually kitchens. Costing around £4 per night, most are run by, or associated with, the YHA (see p.13), which can supply a full list; you don't need to be a YHA member to stay in a camping barn. Bed linen and blankets are usually available, but most people just roll out their sleeping bag and bed-mat. Camping barns are often rented out to groups, so always call first. Places in the YHA-affiliated barns can be booked by phoning ☎01200/420102; for others, call the numbers printed in the *Guide*.

By and large, **camping rough** is not so easy. Most land is privately owned and on most of the rest – for instance on parkland or National Trust property – it's illegal, though it's always worth asking around, as some easygoing farmers will provide a pitch. Expect a hostile reception if you camp without asking. On Dartmoor, you are allowed to camp out for a maximum of two nights as long as you're out of sight of houses and roads, away from reservoirs and not on certain commons, as specified in the *Camping and Backpacking Code* – Princetown's tourist office (☎01822/890414) will send you a free copy, and it's also posted on the Web site: *www.dartmoor-npa.gov.uk*. Open fires are forbidden, but you can use stoves, taking due care especially after a spell of dry weather. Free camping is not allowed on the other moors unless permission by landowners is granted first, and overnight camping in any of the region's car parks is also prohibited.

Food and drink

Eating out in Devon and Cornwall has improved immeasurably in recent years, and it's now possible to find a wide range of quality restaurants as well as more modest places serving traditional local fare or more adventurous modern dishes. Staples such as the Cornish pasty are a permanent feature of the culinary landscape, while the appetite for seafood, prepared in a myriad of ways, has seen a huge renaissance. The fish restaurants at Dartmouth and Padstow are among the best in the country, though don't expect invariably decent fish and chips to munch along the region's quaysides, and there is as much junk food about as you would expect to find in any English holiday region.

Eating out

Even the region's smallest villages often have surprisingly sophisticated eating houses along-

---

Meal prices

Each restaurant listed in this guide has been graded according to the following scale: inexpensive (under £10); moderate (£10–20), expensive (£20–30) and very expensive (over £30). The grades relate to the price per person for a two- or three-course meal, excluding drinks and service.

---

side cheaper **restaurants** and **cafés**, and in the larger towns, you'll find the gamut of Indian, Thai, Chinese and Italian eateries; there's also **pub food** a-plenty in every direction. What really marks out the menus of Devon and Cornwall, however, is the **fish**, ranging from the salmon caught in the rivers of Exmoor and Dartmoor to the fresh seafood from the local ports. Despite drastic reductions in the catches and restrictive quotas, the fishing industry is still going relatively strong. Most of the haul is landed at the ports of Brixham in Devon and Newlyn in Cornwall, from where it's transported across the country, but enough remains to supply the local restaurants, some of which have their own boat. Seafood restaurants abound throughout the region, and places such as Padstow, where TV chef Rick Stein has carved an empire, have become meccas for foodies. Other good places for fish restaurants are Dartmouth, Falmouth, St Ives and Port Isaac. Restaurants aren't the only places to sample the freshest seafood, though – crab sandwiches are sold in most pubs and make an excellent light lunch.

In the *Guide*, **telephone numbers** are only given for restaurants where it's advisable or necessary to reserve a table in advance.

The speciality **meat** found in most of Devon and Cornwall's restaurants is lamb, cooked all ways, while Exmoor and Dartmoor are renowned for grouse and other game. Though they may not rise above a nut roast, **vegetarian** dishes are almost always available, and there are wholefood and vegetarian restaurants in remote villages as well as the cities.

Devon and Cornwall specialities

Though some have claimed Cornwall's greatest export has been the **Cornish pasty**, the form has been so adulterated and debased that much of what is sold under the name fails to live up to the genuine article. Pasties were originally made as a full meal-in-one for miners to take underground, with vegetables at one end and jam at the other. The crimped edge ensured that they didn't need to wash their hands, and was not eaten. At home, each member of the family would have their own tastes catered for and marked with initials in the corner of their pasty.

If you're in search of a good pasty, forget about the cellophane-wrapped lumps stuffed with gristle and mince that you'll see in chill cabinets, and head for the local baker's. Ideally, the pasty should have a rich, short or flaky pastry, neatly crimped on the rounded edge and filled with steak, turnip and potato – and dripping with gravy. You can also find a wide range of **non-traditional fillings** in some delicatessens, but the best (and probably the biggest) pasties in Cornwall are to be found at Trevaskis Farm near Hayle (see p.243).

Other local specialities include **star gazy pie** (also known as starry gazy pie), a fish pie with the heads and tails of the fish, traditionally pilchards or mackerel, sticking out of the pastry. Tradition has it that this originated after a local fisherman returned from a fierce storm with seven types of fish, which were then cooked in a pie with their heads sticking out for easy identification. In Devon, you may come across **cobbler**, a baked meat dish with a scone topping, and you'll also find casseroles of pork or rabbit cooked in cider. Sweet dishes include fruity **Cornish heavy cake** and **saffron cake**, a sort of loaf baked with currants and locally produced saffron; these days, though, genuine saffron is rarely used, and even when it is, it's probably been imported. Everywhere in the West Country, from quaint tearooms to farmhouses and cafés, you'll be tempted by **cream teas**: fluffy scones thickly spread with strawberry jam and clotted cream. The best advice is to surrender to the temptation, at least once. Lastly, it's also worth

looking out for Cornish **Yarg cheese** – mild, creamy and covered in nettles.

Drinking

Devon and Cornwall boast some of the snuggest **pubs** in the land, often of the thatched and inglenook variety, and equipped with old slate floors, beamed ceilings and maritime paraphernalia. Most pubs are open all day from 11am until 11pm (10.30pm on Sun), and many offer food – Sunday lunches can be exceptionally good deals at £5–8. The region is dominated by the St Austell brewery, responsible for superlative **beers** like Hicks Special and Wreckers Bitter. Skinner's is the leading local independent though there are shining examples of smaller operations, notably the *Blue Anchor* pub at Helston, where renowned Spingo bitter is brewed on the premises.

You'll occasionally come across **meaderies** in the southwest – usually faux-bawdy banquet halls that serve meals alongside the various types of mead on offer, which can be surprisingly strong with a corresponding effect on the customers. They're pretty tacky places, but are relatively cheap and can be a good laugh.

In Cornwall, where it's common to see cider advertised in farm shops, you might also look out for home-made **scrumpy** which, while not as well known as the Somerset variety, holds its own nonetheless. It's available on draught in some pubs, with names like "Cripplecock", "Legless but Smiling" and "Dead Man's", and weighs in at around 8 percent alcohol by volume.

Look out, too, for local **wines** such as Sharpham, from around Totnes, or Camel Valley, a light red, white or sparkling concoction from Cornwall. If you're interested in the wine-making process, you can tour the Camel Valley vineyard near Nanstallon (☎01208/77959; *www.camelvalley.com*) where you can also sample and buy.

Festivals and annual events

The demands of the tourist industry have combined with authentic local traditions to ensure a full programme of annual festivals and events, especially over the summer. Some have been held continuously for centuries, others have been lately revived, while others are arts festivals of recent date.

As nearly every village stages an annual event of some sort, and carnivals surface year-round, it would be impossible to detail them all. The main events listed in the box overleaf are arranged according to the week in which they occur, as most are fixed to weekends or specific days; contact the local tourist office for precise dates.

Public and bank holidays

January 1

Good Friday (late March or early April)

Easter Monday (as above)

First Monday in May

Last Monday in May

Last Monday in August

December 25

December 26

Note that if January 1 or December 25 or 26 falls on a Saturday or Sunday, the next weekday becomes a public holiday.

Traditional festivals, food fairs and sporting events

Unsurprisingly, given the region's long seaboard, a large proportion of events in Devon and Cornwall hinge around the sea. The smartest of these are the various **regattas** which take place throughout the summer; larger ones, such as at Dartmouth and Fowey, get jam packed, so if you're contemplating visiting in those weeks, book accommodation well ahead. A peculiarity of Cornwall is **gig races** – rowing-boat races held in the summer between teams from different west Cornwall villages or from different islands in the Isles of Scilly. You need to get pretty close to appreciate the passion (tickets are usually on hand for seats on passenger boats), but the races generate a thrilling atmosphere. Foodies might take more interest in the **Newlyn Fish Fair** on August Bank Holiday, when the port's harbour is crammed with boats, and the quaysides have all sorts of fish on display, cookery demonstrations and Celtic entertainment.

Other festivals are resolutely tied to the land, especially those with an element of fertility ritual such as Padstow's May Day **Obby Oss** celebration (see p.279), when a weird and wonderful hobby horse in circular hooped skirt prances its way through the town, and Helston's **Flora Day** (see p.208), which has smartly turned out couples dancing to the tune of the *Floral Dance*, taking place on May 8th. Dance features strongly in both events, as it does in many other Cornish festivities such as the midsummer **Golowan Festival** in Penzance, a week-long community celebration with pagan elements, featuring fireworks and roots music and culminating in Mazey Day, with street processions and a free programme of music and dance events at the festival marquee in St Anthony's Gardens. You're most likely to come into contact with Cornish – or at least Celtic – heritage at the **Lowender Peran** festival, held at Perranporth over four days in the middle of October: there's Celtic dance and a parade through the village.

For a winter festival, you'd be hard pressed to beat the **Flaming Tar Barrels** ceremony at Ottery

FESTIVALS AND EVENTS CALENDAR

MARCH

Third week
Cornwall's Festival of Spring Gardens, various venues.

EASTER

Classical Music Festival, St Endellion.

MAY

First week
Obby Oss, Padstow.
Boscastle Beer Festival, Boscastle.
Isles of Scilly World Pilot Gig Championships.
English National Surfing Championships, Newquay.
Flora Day, Helston.

Second week
Jazz Festival, Looe.
Daphne du Maurier Festival of Arts and Literature, Fowey.
Re-enactment of the Battle of Stamford Hill, Bude.

Third week
Tiverton Spring Festival, Tiverton. Maypole dancing, workshops and concerts.

Fourth week
Newquay Surf Festival, Newquay.

JUNE

First week
Gala Week, Budleigh Salterton. Mainly family-oriented events over a week, including dog

shows, a madhatters tea party and an open-air barbecue.
Maritime Weekend, Topsham.
Tavistock Steam Fair, Tavistock.
Salcombe Festival, Salcombe. Sailing displays, races, jazz bands, processions, workshops and barbecues.

Second week
Royal Cornwall Show, Wadebridge.

Third week
St Ives Regatta, St Ives.

Fourth week
Golowan Festival, Penzance.
Music and Art Festival, Exmouth.
Cornwall Theatre and Heritage Festival, Bodmin. Eight days of storytelling, music, dance and theatre events (sometimes taking place during the first week of July).

JULY

First week
Truro Jazz Festival, Truro.

Second week
Launceston Agricultural Show, Launceston.
Dartington Literary Festival, Dartington.

Third week
Cutty Sark Tall Ships Race, Falmouth.
Plymouth Regatta, Plymouth.
Stithians Show. One of the biggest agricultural shows in the west, held in this village between Redruth and Falmouth.
Exeter Arts Festival, Exeter.

St Mary in early November (see p.64), when people rush through the narrow streets with flaming barrels on their shoulders.

Arts festivals

Probably the most famous of the West Country's arts festivals is the **Dartington International Festival of Music** (see p.84), spread over five

weeks from July to late August, where you might take in three concerts a night ranging from classical to contemporary jazz and world in the refined setting of Dartington Hall. Fowey's **Daphne du Maurier Festival of Arts and Literature** in May (see p.183) includes plenty of walks, concerts, workshops and exhibitions as well as talks by literati and others, while the **St**

Fourth week
Ale Tasting and Bread Weighing, Ashburton.
Exmouth Carnival, Exmouth.
Honiton Hot Penny Ceremony and Fair,
Honiton. Highlight of the town's annual fair is,
as its name suggests, catching heated pennies.
Newquay International Surf Festival, Newquay.

AUGUST
First week
Padstow Carnival, Padstow.
St Endellion Summer Music Festival, St
Endellion.
Re-enactment of The Battle of Camlann,
Tintagel.
Falmouth Carnival, Falmouth.
St Mawgan Air Day, St Mawgan.
Sidmouth International Festival, Sidmouth.

Second week
Falmouth Regatta Week, Falmouth.
Paignton Regatta Week, Paignton.

Third week
Beer Regatta Week, Beer.
Bude Carnival Week, Bude.
Fowey Royal Regatta, Fowey.
St Mary's Arts Festival, Penzance.
Contemporary, classical and choir music in St
Mary's Church, spread over a week.
Torquay Royal Regatta, Torquay.

Fourth week
Wadebridge Folk Festival, Wadebridge. Three-
day event with mainly British performers plus a
few from America and Europe.

Bude Jazz Festival, Bude.
Newlyn Fish Festival, Newlyn.
British National Surfing Championships,
Newquay.
Dartmouth Royal Regatta, Dartmouth.
Tavistock Hot Air Balloon Fiesta, Tavistock.
Newquay Beach Festival, Newquay.

SEPTEMBER
First week
County Gig Championships, Newquay.

Second week
County Gig Championships, Newquay.
St Ives Festival of Music and the Arts, St Ives.
Widecombe Fair, Widecombe.

OCTOBER
Second week
Goose Fair, Tavistock.
Beer Rhythm and Blues Festival, Beer.

Third week
Lowender Peran Celtic Festival, Perranporth.

Fourth week
Surf's Up Foamie Festival, Polzeath.

NOVEMBER
First week
Tar Barrel Rolling, Ottery St Mary.

DECEMBER
Fourth week
Tom Bawcock's Eve, Mousehole. Celebrated the
day before Christmas Eve, featuring choirs and
the consumption of star gazy pie.

Ives Festival of Music and the Arts in September has an eclectic brief, featuring music and theatre.

For **music**, the biggest and best known of the region's folk-music festivals is the **Sidmouth International Festival** (see p.59), which attracts a diverse audience for one week at the beginning of August. The **Cornwall Folk Festival** at Wadebridge (see p.283) towards the end of August concentrates more on British performers, though it does have a few guest players from abroad. **St Endellion** (see p.286) hosts two classical-music festivals, for a week at Easter and for ten days or so at the beginning of August.

Outdoor activities

There's plenty of scope for experiencing the outdoor life in Devon and Cornwall, as the region is replete with excellent opportunities for hiking and biking. But the biggest draw for visitors is probably the coastline, chiefly for its beaches, which number among Britain's finest. If the water is too cold for total immersion, you can still get to grips with the sea on a boat trip.

Hiking

In addition to the long-distance footpaths crossing the region, detailed on p.8–9, the southwest also boasts a multiplicity of shorter-distance **hiking** routes, most notably the network of tracks over Exmoor, Dartmoor and Bodmin Moor, and around the region's river estuaries. The excursions outlined in the *Guide* present a cross-section of the kinds of walks you can find, with terrains ranging from bare moorland to wooded valley. These are more general descriptions than specific route guides, however, and the walks should not be undertaken without a proper 1:25,000 or 1:50,000 map (see p.11) and a compass that you know how to use. Ask at local tourist offices for leaflets – either free or costing around 50p each – detailing circular routes which take in places of interest. If you're not on a circular route, you'll probably have to rely on public transport to get you home at the end, so you should acquaint yourself with local timetables

before setting out. On the moors, bus routes often link up with walking routes and the local timetables even suggest walks with good directions. Coastal transport routes lend themselves to spurts of hiking on the South West Coast Path, too, with frequent intersections of path and bus route.

All walks should be approached with forward planning and suitable **equipment**. Supportive, waterproof hiking boots are ideal – moorland is particularly uneven terrain – and you should carry a waterproof jacket and hood, a warm, dry change of clothing on wet days and around two litres of water per person on a hot day. For longer hikes something to eat is also essential. Take advice on the **weather** (the info lines on p.22 are useful, as are local tourist offices, local press, radio and TV – see p.10–11): bad conditions can set in fast, and fogs are a particular hazard on the coast and moors. If you're inexperienced, consider joining one of the regular **organized walks** on Exmoor and Dartmoor of varying length and difficulty: contact the visitor centres at Princetown (☎01822/ 890414; *www.dartmoor-npa.gov.uk*) or Dulverton (☎01398/323841) for details.

Riding

Ponies have been synonymous with Dartmoor and Exmoor for centuries, and these areas are particularly ideal for **riding**. Stables can be found in some of the best parts of the moor, as well as in coastal areas, and are detailed in the *Guide*. Expect to pay £10–15 per hour for riding or tuition.

On the beach

The West Country's biggest asset for visitors is probably its hundreds of miles of **coastline**, most of it more or less unspoilt and studded with many of Britain's cleanest **beaches** and bathing waters. The prestigious **Blue Flag**, denoting top-quality water, has been awarded to the beaches at Blackpool Sands, Dawlish Warren, Torbay's Meadfoot and Oddicombe beaches (all in south Devon), and Woolacombe (north Devon), but (in 2000) none in Cornwall. The Marine Conservation

Society recommends many more than these – a third of the total number of beaches in the region – which have achieved 98 percent compliance with the EU Mandatory Standard: the full list can be consulted in their free annual booklet (available for £3 by calling ☎01989/566017 or writing to 9 Gloucester Rd, Ross-on-Wye HR9 5BU) or free on their Web site (*www.goodbeachguide.co.uk*). The area is certainly not free of problems, however, with various forms of **pollution** affecting a number of beaches; untreated sewage is still discharged close to the shore in some places and is washed back on to the sands. Both the local water companies have put considerable investment programmes in place to deal with the continuing scandalous condition of some coastal stretches, but they're still regularly criticized by groups such as Surfers Against Sewage (The Old Counthouse, Wheal Kitty, St Agnes, Cornwall TR5 0RE; ☎01872/ 553001; *www.sas.org.uk*).

Remember that the **currents** around the peninsula are powerful and can quickly pull you out to sea; it's best not to swim alone, or to swim too far out. Between June and September, the most popular beaches are under lifeguard surveillance, and a system of **flags** is in operation: a red flag indicates danger and means that the beach is closed for swimming and surfing; the zone between two red-and-yellow flags designates an area safe for swimming, belly-, boogie- and body-boarding, while the area between black-and-white chequered flags is reserved for surfing, wave skis, canoes and windsurfing.

Note that the beaches all around the Devon and Cornwall coasts – including the Isles of Scilly – are subject to **tides**, which dramatically transform the appearance of the seashore. Low tide can leave you feeling like you're sitting in a bath after the water has run out, while sudden high tides can pose a significant risk by cutting off your return from a rock or strip of sand. Take local advice, or buy tide times booklets (usually less than £1) from tourist offices or newsagents.

Surfing

The north coast of Devon and Cornwall has some of the country's most outstanding **surfing** beaches, which, thanks to wet suits, are used year-round by surf enthusiasts. The most popular areas are Woolacombe Bay and Croyde Bay

---

ACTIVITY HOLIDAYS

Adventure Sports Multi-activity Centre, Carnkie Farmhouse, Carnkie, Redruth TR16 6RZ ☎01209/218962; *www.adventure-sports. co.uk*. Paragliding, surfing and waterskiing.

Alternative Cornish Holidays, Karensa Cottage, St Issey, nr Wadebridge PL27 7QT ☎01841/ 540383. One-way coastal walking holidays.

Classic Sailing, Mermaids, St Mawes TR2 5AA ☎01326/270027; *www.axos.co.uk/classic-sailing*. Sailing and walking holidays.

Footpath Holidays, 16 Norton Bavant, Warminster, Wiltshire BA12 7BB ☎01985/840049; *footpath.holidays@ dmc. co.uk*. Five- or seven-day residential or day-pack walking tours available between May and October as well as around Christmas and New Year.

Gooseham Barton Riding Stables, Gooseham, Morwenstow, nr Bude EX23 9PG ☎01288/331204. Riding holidays with self-catering accommodation.

Haven Banks Adventure Centre, 61 Haven Rd, Exeter EX2 8BP ☎01392/434668. White-water kayaking, rock climbing and more.

Heart of Devon Ltd, Crediton Tourist Information Centre, The Old Town Hall, High St, Crediton, Devon EX17 3LS ☎01363/772006. Short special-interest and activity holidays in Exmoor and Devon, with hotel or farmhouse accommodation.

Hidden Cornwall, 5 Perhaver Park, Gorran Haven, St Austell PL26 6NZ ☎01726/842259. Guided walking holidays.

Shoreline Outdoor Pursuits, Crooklets Beach, Bude, Cornwall EX23 8NE ☎01288/354039; *www.bude.co.uk/shoreline*. Year-round outdoor activities including sea kayaking and rock climbing, plus a programme of half-day activities during summer.

Square Sail Shipyard, Charlestown Harbour, St Austell PL25 3NJ ☎01726/70241; *www.square-sail.com*. Two- to seven-day cruises along the coasts and rivers of Cornwall and Isles of Scilly.

in Devon, and the areas around Bude and Newquay, and the beaches at Polzeath, Constantine Bay, Porthtowan, Perranporth, Portreath and Sennen Cove in Cornwall. In summer, you'll find plenty of kiosks on the beaches renting out **surf equipment** – boards and wet suits, each about £5 per full day, plus a deposit of around £10; details of dedicated water-sports equipment:-rental outlets are given in the *Guide*. **Surfing courses** are also readily available, with two-to-three-hour lessons costing about £20, including all equipment. The British Surfing Association (☎01736/360250; *colin@britsurf .demon.co.uk*) has a list of approved surfing schools in the southwest which are open all year. Updated reports on **surf conditions** are available at Big G's five-day surf forecast for north Devon and Cornwall ☎0900/340 6864; *www.getaforecast.com*. Other useful lines for sea

and weather conditions are Marinecall (☎0891/ 505358) and Weathercall (☎0891/505304).

Diving and windsurfing

Apart from swimming and surfing, the most popular activities on the coasts of Devon and Cornwall are diving and windsurfing. With some of the clearest waters around the UK, the Isles of Scilly are particularly noted for their **scuba diving** possibilities, though you'll also find numerous places throughout the region offering tuition and equipment hire, charging around £15 for a couple of hours' taster. While **windsurfing** has ebbed in popularity in recent years, it's still practised all over the southwest, especially in sheltered spots such as Plymouth Sound and the Carrick Roads estuary. Basic tuition in a group starts from £10 per hour; and you'll pay around the same to rent equipment by the hour.

Directory

Emergencies Dial ☎999 for all emergencies, including police, fire, ambulance and coast guard.

English Heritage PO Box 569, Swindon SN2 2YR ☎01793/414910; *www.english-heritage.org.uk*. For enquiries specifically regarding the southwest, call ☎0845/301 0007. Properties managed by

English Heritage (denoted by EH in the *Guide*) include numerous castles and archeological sites, and are normally open daily during daylight hours, though many are closed in winter. Admission is free to members.

Hospitals Accident and Emergency departments are mentioned in the *Guide* where they exist. These are: the Royal Devon and Exeter Hospital, Barrack Rd, Exeter (☎01392/411611); Derriford Hospital, Derriford, outside Plymouth (☎01752/792511); Bodmin's East Cornwall Hospital (☎01208/251555); Treliske Hospital, Truro (☎01872/250000); West Cornwall Hospital, Penzance (☎01736/362382); Edward Hain Hospital, St Ives (☎01736/795044) and Newquay and District Hospital (☎01637 /893600).

Laundry Coin-operated laundrettes exist in all the cities and bigger towns, but are extremely sparse elsewhere. Most hostels have washing and drying facilities, and some B&B owners may be persuaded to help out.

National Trust PO Box 39, Bromley, Kent BR1 3XL
☎020/8315 1111; *www.nationaltrust.org.uk.*
Properties managed by the National Trust (denoted in the *Guide* by NT) include numerous stately homes and other historic buildings. They are normally open daily during daylight hours, but many are closed in winter. Admission is free to members.

Opening hours Opening hours to attractions are given in the *Guide*, though as these change regularly you might want to check in advance if you're making a long journey to a sight. Many paying attractions stop admitting visitors 45 minutes or an hour before closing. Larger and more important churches are almost always open during daylight hours, but you'll often find country churches locked up unless they're particular tourist attractions – most in any case close at 4 or 5pm. Shops generally open from 9am to 5pm Monday to Saturday, with an increasing tendency for bigger stores and supermarkets to open on Sunday as well. When all else is closed, you can normally find a garage selling basic items. In summer, food shops in tourist areas often stay open until 10 or 11pm.

Police For all enquiries or to report a crime, call ☎0990/777444 day or night.

Shopping and souvenirs You won't be short of ideas for gifts in Devon and Cornwall, which have always attracted artisans and craftspeople keen to merchandise their wares, which range from candles in Totnes to sword-and-sorcery trinkets in Tintagel. Fishermen's smocks are well in evidence throughout Cornwall, and you'll also find a bewildering range of objects fashioned from serpentine from the Lizard. It's worth checking out Devon's pannier markets – covered bazaars where a motley range of items are sold alongside the foodstuffs, and you'll find other markets in most towns.

The Guide

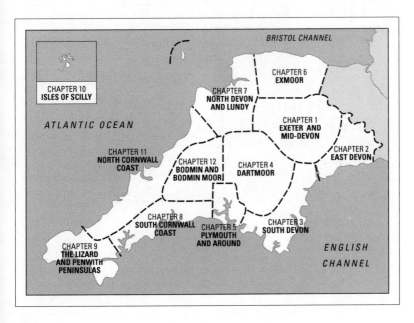

Chapter 1

Exeter and mid-Devon

One of Britain's oldest settlements, **Exeter** is also the most vibrant of Devon and Cornwall's cities, and the only one where you may be tempted to spend more than a day or two. A former centre of Devon's flourishing wool industry, Exeter has maintained its status as a chief commercial city and is today the terminus of the M5 motorway. You're likely to pass through at least once on your West Country travels, and it merits an extended exploration for its cultural life as well as its historical interest. The city's premier sight is also its most visible: rising above the concrete of the modern centre, Exeter's **cathedral** represents the apotheosis of one of the most brilliant periods of English architecture, its intricate web of roof-vaulting unique for its prodigious length. The other unmissable attraction is the dense collection of art and artefacts in the **Royal Albert Museum** – an excellent overview of the city and county, with everything from a menagerie of stuffed animals to the silverware and clocks at which the city excelled on display. Even without the city's traditional sights, Exeter's range of accommodation, pubs, clubs and restaurants makes it a fun place to soak up the more contemporary cultural scene, and an ideal base for visiting other places in Devon.

North of Exeter, sandwiched between the rugged moorland to north and south, **mid-Devon** has preserved its profoundly rural nature, its valleys and meadows still intensely farmed or dotted with sheep. North of Exeter, the A396 brings you to **Tiverton**, inland Devon's biggest town, brimming with interest itself and within easy distance of a cluster of the county's grandest country houses: **Knightshayes Court**, a showcase for the work of Victorian architect and designer William Burges; **Bickleigh Castle**, with a Norman chapel and fifteenth-century gatehouse, just across the river from the much-photographed village of **Bickleigh**, and, to the south, **Killerton House**, famous for its extensive collection of costumes. Elsewhere in the region, there's little to hold you for long in any one place, but there are some specific destinations which are worth visiting in passing. Northwest of Exeter, **Crediton** holds one of Devon's

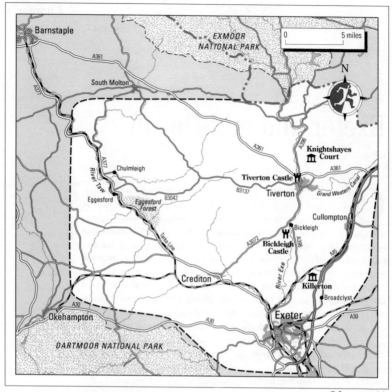

© Crown copyright

grandest churches, while further along the A377 Barnstaple road, you'll pass through good walking country around **Eggesford Forest**.

Served by frequent **trains** on the main line to Penzance, Exeter is the transport hub for the whole region, and is the departure point for trains following the **Tarka Line** to North Devon. A good network of **buses** extends out from the city, though your own vehicle would be most useful for reaching the various places around Tiverton. Bus

travellers can make savings by purchasing an Explorer ticket (see
Basics, p.7).

Exeter

Exeter

Devon's county town, **EXETER** is the first stop on many a tour of the
West Country, both as a transport hub and for its rich concentration
of sights. Despite having much of its ancient centre gutted by World
War II bombs, the city retains plenty of its medieval heritage, not
least its sturdy **cathedral**, whose two flanking Norman towers are
Exeter's most recognizable landmark. Other remnants of the old city
include a clutch of medieval churches, fashioned – like the cathedral
and the sparse remains of the castle and city walls – in the local pink-
ish-red sandstone, and a fascinating network of subterranean passages. The history and geography of the whole region is covered in
the town's fine **museum**, which also boasts a respected ethnographic
section. Away from the centre, sightseers often make the mistake of
missing out the **Quayside**, the starting-point of canalside walks and
bike rides during the day and a lively place by night for its pubs and
clubs.

Some history

Having been a settlement of the Celtic Dumnonii tribe, **Exeter** was
fortified by the Romans in around 50–55 AD, and re-named Isca
Dumnoniorum – the most westerly outpost of Rome in the British
Isles. Little of note has been excavated from this period, however,
suggesting that it was primarily a military occupation. The city was
refounded by Alfred the Great at the end of the ninth century, and
grew to become one of the largest towns in Anglo-Saxon England,
profiting from its position on the banks of the River Exe as the major
outlet for the inland wool industry. The Normans strengthened the
old Roman walls, rebuilt the cathedral and expanded the wool trade,
which sustained the city until the eighteenth century. Woven in rural
Devon, the serge cloth was dyed and finished in Exeter and exported
from the quays on the Exe to France, Spain and the Netherlands. By
the first quarter of the sixteenth century, Exeter was one of the
largest and richest towns in England – only York, Norwich, Bristol
and Newcastle were more important outside London. Although the
Countess of Devon diverted most of the shipping trade to Topsham
by building a weir across the Exe in around 1285, Exeter's role as a
major port was restored by the construction of the Quay and the
Exeter Ship Canal between 1564 and 1566 – the latter represented
the first canal to be built in England since Roman times.

  During the Civil War, Exeter – unusually for the West Country –
had predominantly Parliamentarian sympathies, but was besieged
and taken by the Royalists in 1643, becoming their headquarters in
the West and sheltering Charles I's queen. The city fell to a

Roundhead army in 1646, which stayed in occupation until the Restoration. Exeter subsequently entered its most prosperous age, its mainstay still the cloth trade; its scale moved the traveller and diarist Celia Fiennes, who visited in 1698, to marvel at the "incredible quantity of [serges] made and sold in the town . . . The whole town and country is employed for at least twenty miles around in spinning, weaving, dressing and scouring, fulling and drying of the serges. It turns the most money in a week of anything in England." Trade ceased during the Napoleonic wars, and by the time peace was restored, the centre of textile manufacturing had shifted to England's northern industrial towns, and Devon's wool industry never regained its former importance.

Useful Web sites for Exeter include www.thisisexeter.co.uk, www.exeter.gov.uk *and* www.exeterinfo.com

The severe bombing sustained during World War II miraculously spared the cathedral, but the bland reconstruction that followed, conforming to the postwar urban style, could not make up for the loss of much of the historic centre. In recent times however, an infusion of energy provided by the university and the tourist trade has prevented Exeter from sliding into provincial decline, and the daily bustle of the modern centre testifies to its economic well-being today.

Arrival and information

Of Exeter's two **train stations**, Exeter Central is smack in the middle of town on Queen Street, while St David's lies further north on Bonhay Road, though closer to some of the cheaper B&Bs. Trains on the London Waterloo–Salisbury line stop at both, as do Tarka Line services to Barnstaple (see p.157) and trains to Exmouth, but train travellers from London Paddington, Bristol or Birmingham will have to get off at Exeter St David's. Buses stop at the **bus station** on Paris Street, right across from the **tourist office** (April–Sept Mon–Sat 9am–5pm, plus Sun 10am–4pm in July & Aug; Oct–March Mon–Fri 9am–5pm, Sat 9am–1pm & 2–5pm; ☎01392/265700). There's a second, much smaller visitor centre in Quay House on Exeter's Quayside (Easter–Oct daily 10am–5pm; ☎01392/265213). The city is best negotiated on foot, but if you envisage using the buses during an intensive one-day visit, pick up a bus map from the tourist office and buy a £2.90 all-day bus ticket from the bus station. Useful routes include the #G, which goes down to the Quay from the High Street and Fore Street, and #H, which runs to the university campus and the Northcott Theatre from the High Street (both Mon–Sat only).

Accommodation

Most of Exeter's best B&B **accommodation** lies north of the centre, near the two train stations, though you'll find a row on Alphington Road, going out of town in the Plymouth direction. The nearest **campsites** are *Langford Bridge*, about four miles north of the centre off

Hotels and B&Bs

Bendene Hotel, 15 Richmond Rd ☎01392/213526. The central location and heated outdoor swimming pool are the main lures in this terraced house near Central Station; the en-suite rooms are quiet and reasonably sized. ③.

Cyrnea, 73 Howell Rd ☎01392/438386. Cheerful management, clean and spacious rooms and good rates. No credit cards. ①.

Glendale Hotel, St David's Hill ☎01392/274350. A little frayed, but comfortable enough for a short stay, with sinks and shower-units in the rooms and shared toilets. Several cats are also in residence. ②.

Maurice, 5 Bystock Terrace ☎01392/213079. Close to Exeter Central station, this is the best budget choice in the centre, and consequently often fully booked. Most of the quiet, inoffensively furnished rooms have views over the square. Non-smoking. ①.

Park View Hotel, 8 Howell Rd ☎01392/271772; *www.parkviewhotel .freeserve.co.uk*. Equidistant between the two train stations, this listed Georgian building has some chintzy furnishings but the rooms are spacious and quiet with shared bathrooms; en-suite rooms are also available. ①.

Raffles, 11 Blackall Rd ☎01392/270200; *www.raffles-exeter.co.uk*. Elegant Victorian house where the rooms are individually furnished with Pre-Raphaelite etchings and other items from the owner's antique business. Good fixed-price evening meals prepared with garden produce are available. ②.

Royal Clarence Hotel, Cathedral Yard ☎01392/319955. Dating from 1769 and enjoying a prize position opposite the Cathedral, this place claims to be the first inn in England to be described as a "hotel". The rates match the superb location, though rooms which don't face the front have no view at all. There's a chic restaurant on the ground floor. ⑦.

The White Hart, 65 South St ☎01392/279897. Centrally located old coaching inn with period trappings. The courtyard and bar are swimming with atmosphere but guestrooms are disappointingly ordinary. ⑥.

Hostels and university accommodation

Exeter YHA, 47 Countess Wear Rd ☎01392/873329; *www.yha.org.uk*. Country house two miles outside the city centre, where dorm beds cost £10.85. To get there, take minibus #K or #T from High St or South St, or #57 from the bus station, to the Countess Wear post office on Topsham Rd, from where it's a 10min signposted walk. Alternatively, you could do the whole journey on foot along the canal path from the Quayside.

Globe Backpackers, 71 Holloway St ☎01392/215521; *www.globeback-packers.freeserve.co.uk*. Clean and central, with good showers and an upbeat atmosphere. Bunk-beds in dorms of 6–10 go for £10 each, plus £1 for sheets. Cheap bike rental is also available. No credit cards.

University Halls of Residence ☎01392/211500; *Conferences@exeter .ac.uk*. Accommodation on the campus – east on Heavitree Rd (more useful for the bus station) or north off New North Rd (better for the trains) – in mostly single rooms for £12.50–16 per person, or £22 with your own bath. Available Easter & July–Sept. Book in advance.

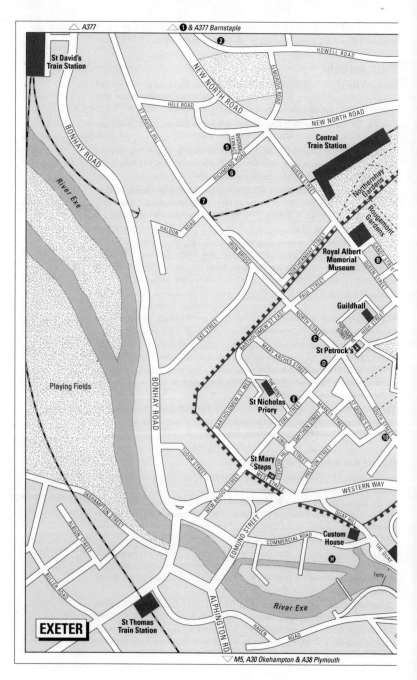

EXETER

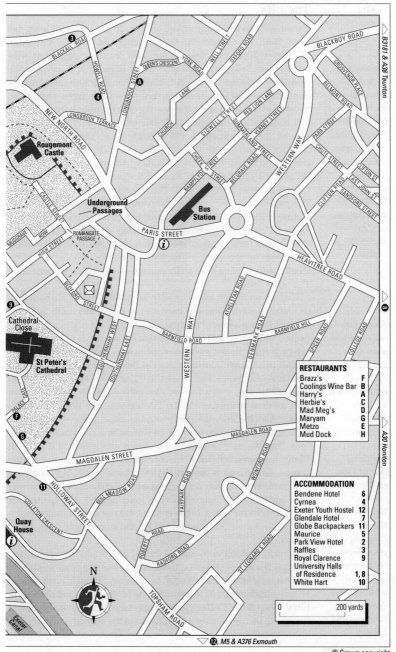

RESTAURANTS

Brazz's	F
Coolings Wine Bar	B
Harry's	A
Herbie's	C
Mad Meg's	D
Maryam	G
Metzo	E
Mud Dock	H

ACCOMMODATION

Bendene Hotel	6
Cyrnea	4
Exeter Youth Hostel	12
Glendale Hotel	7
Globe Backpackers	11
Maurice	5
Park View Hotel	2
Raffles	3
Royal Clarence	9
University Halls of Residence	1, 8
White Hart	10

0   200 yards

N

▽ **12**, M5 & A376 Exmouth

The City

Exeter's sights are easily visited on foot. In the centre of town, but aloof from its commercial bustle, stately **St Peter's Cathedral** (7.30am–6.30pm, Sat closes 5pm; £2.50 donation suggested) is the logical place to kick off your exploration of the city, its two massive Norman towers built – unusually and distinctively – on the transepts. Begun around 1114, the structure was thoroughly remodelled between about 1275 and 1369, leaving only the towers from the original construction but resulting in one of the country's finest examples of the Decorated Gothic building style. Close up, it is the facade's ornate Gothic **screen** that commands attention: its three tiers of sculpted figures – including Alfred, Athelstan, Canute, William the Conqueror and Richard II – were begun around 1360, though are now badly eroded. The **interior** however, has the chief interest: on entering, you're confronted by the longest unbroken **Gothic ceiling** in the world, an arresting vista of rib-vaulting which has been compared to an avenue of stately trees, the effect heightened by the multiplicity of shafts on each of the stout piers and of mouldings on the arches. The bulbous **bosses** running along the length of the ceiling are vividly painted – one shows the murder of Thomas à Becket.

High up on the left side, a **minstrels' gallery** is sculpted with fourteen angels playing musical instruments, below which are figures of Edward III and Queen Philippa. The walls of the aisles are densely packed with tombs and memorials that show a range of styles – most eye-catchingly in the right transept, where the fourteenth-century sepulchre of Hugh Courtenay, earl of Devon, and his wife is carved with graceful swans and a lion. A door from here leads to the **Chapter House**, with a fine wooden ceiling and an array of discordant modern sculptures. In the left transept, the fifteenth-century **Exeter Clock** shows the earth with the moon revolving around it, turning on its own axis to show its phases, and the sun represented by a fleur-de-lys. The minute dial above was added in 1760. The **Choir** is dominated by a spectacularly ugly sixty-foot **bishop's throne**, built in oak in around 1316 and boasting the largest canopy in Britain. You can also see some good **misericords** here, decorated with mythological figures: dating from around 1260, they are thought to be the oldest in the country. On the way out of the cathedral, note the simple plaque to R.D. Blackmore, author of *Lorna Doone*.

Outside, a studious-looking statue of the locally-born theologian Richard Hooker surveys the **Cathedral Close**, a motley mixture of architectural styles from Tudor to Regency, though most display Exeter's trademark red brickwork. One of the finest buildings is the Elizabethan **Mol's Coffee House**, impressively timbered and gabled. It's said to be named after a local Italian in the sixteenth-century, and is now a mapshop.

Starting from Cathedral Close, outside the Royal Clarence Hotel, free 90-minute walking tours of Exeter take place most days at 11am and 2pm; for more information, call ☎01392/ 265203.

Tours of the cathedral take place twice a day between April and October (11am & 2.30pm; £2.50 donation), and there's an additional tour at 11am on Thursdays between November and March. Evensong takes place throughout the year at 5.30pm on weekdays, and 3pm on Saturday and Sunday.

After the Cathedral, Exeter's most compelling attraction is the excellent **Royal Albert Memorial Museum** (Mon–Sat 10am–5pm; free), located north of the High Street on Queen Street. Housed in a neo-Gothic building whose boldly coloured interior sports an impressive central staircase, this rich assortment exudes a Victorian spirit of wide-ranging curiosity. The museum has an appropriately labyrinthine layout, with wildly contrasting eras and spheres of interest cheek by jowl, and unless you're here to see specific sights – for which consult the floor-plan at the entrance – you might as well let yourself get lost. Broadly speaking, however, archeology and local history are on the left as you enter, natural history on the right, while upstairs, the Rowley Gallery is devoted to art, next to rooms full of clocks, ceramics, glass and silverware, and the ethnography rooms.

The **archeological section**, displaying a mere fraction of the more than half-million artefacts stored in the museum, shows finds from the numerous Bronze Age barrows excavated in Devon, including a substantial haul from Hembury, near Honiton – arrowheads, axe-heads and such rudimentary tools as "chippers" and "bashers". **Local history** begins with the Romans, whose coins and other items from the legionary fortress at Exeter are displayed along with coins from the time of the Saxon, Danish and Norman rulers. The collection is enlivened by imaginative reconstructions of period rooms to illustrate typical building styles from various eras, notably a typical Devon wagon roof from the medieval period, with displays of bench ends carved with Gothic and Renaissance motifs. Other mock-ups include a heavily panelled room from the period 1550–1660, with a superb wooden overmantle above the fireplace showing the judgement of Paris, and a room from around 1700 complete with an original plaster ceiling and cornice.

Once you've had your fill of the stuffed kangaroos, polar bears, moose and bison in the **natural history** section, head upstairs to the **art gallery** which, when not devoted to temporary exhibitions, has some good specimens of West Country art – mainly landscapes by local painters alongside work by other artists associated with Devon such as Turner, Reynolds and Opie. The adjoining **clocks and watches** room is filled with the clicking and whirring of an eclectic display of timepieces from grandfather clocks to stopwatches. Showpieces include a "Turret clock" from 1741 – one of the earliest mechanical timepieces to have survived in Britain – and, from the same period, the Exeter Clock, an unbelievably complex mechanism of which only the painted dial – showing days of the week and month, phases of the moon, relative solar time and feast days – and a section of the intricate musical and automaton workings survive from bomb damage in 1941. Next door, the **glass** collection shows elegant examples of flasks and jars going back to the Roman era, as well as silver spoons, for which the West Country was famous, among other examples of

Exeter

The relaxed Albert's café on the ground floor makes the perfect pit-stop during or after your museum visit.

the **silverware** that has been crafted in Exeter from at least the twelfth century. Look out, too, for the case of Martin-ware – **pottery** by the Martin brothers, who were among the most successful of the so-called "art potters" of the late nineteenth and early twentieth centuries. Their slightly weird works include a two-faced jug and various grotesque jars incorporating birds and other animals.

Backtrack through the art gallery to get to the **World Cultures** room, particularly strong on items from the Pacific, West Africa and the Congo River area; an elaborate priest's garb from the latter is the most eye-catching, with a painted wooden mask and a flamboyant robe made from vegetable fibre and hornbill feathers.

The High Street

East of the Royal Albert Museum, Exeter's pedestrianized **High Street** holds a scattering of older buildings among the usual roster of retail outlets. The city's finest civic building is the fourteenth-century **Guildhall** (Mon–Fri 10.30am–1pm & 2–4pm, Sat 10am–noon; free), marked out by its elegant Renaissance portico (built in the 1590s from Beer stone), and said to be England's oldest municipal building still in regular use. The main attraction is the panelled main chamber, where the city's councillors meet; entered through an impressive oak door, the room has giant portraits of such worthies as George II and General Monck, the Devon-born Civil War veteran, and a fine example of a collar-and-brace timber roof from 1460–70. The brackets supporting the main roof trusses are in the form of bears holding a ragged staff, symbol of the earls of Warwick and possibly carved in honour of "Warwick the Kingmaker", a major player in the Wars of the Roses who visited the city while the roof was being constructed.

The Guildhall is closed when required for an official function (call ☎01392/ 265500 to check), but when things are quiet the doorman may give you a brief tour.

Just down from the Guildhall, the impossibly narrow Parliament Street, just 25 inches wide at this end, stands almost opposite **St Petrock's** – one of Exeter's six surviving medieval churches in the central area.

The Underground Passages and Rougemont Castle

Back at the north end of the High Street, Romangate Passage (an alley next to Boots) holds the entrance to a network of **underground passages**, first excavated in the fourteenth century. In the 1340s, masons at work on the cathedral were enlisted to improve the water supply intended for the cathedral precincts, laying down new lead pipes and creating conduits for which the vaulted passages visitable today formed a kind of maintenance tunnel. The townspeople were entitled to a third of this precious piped water supply, but in the 1420s the city went to the trouble of building its own network, which was later upgraded. The interlinking passages, unusual for their length and good state of preservation, can be explored on a diverting 35-minute **guided tour** (July–Sept & school holidays Mon–Sat

10am–5.30pm; Oct–June Tues–Fri 2–5pm, Sat 10am–5.30pm; £2.75, or £3.75 in July & Aug) – the narrow stone corridors, requiring much stooping, are not recommended for the claustrophobic. In summer the tours are often fully booked, while in winter they sometimes don't leave at all if not enough people show up: call ☎01392/665887 to check.

Just up Castle Street from the Underground Passages, you can see the red-coloured gatehouse from William the Conqueror's original fortress of **Rougemont Castle**, erected soon after his invasion of England. It was later rebuilt and augmented but little else remains today beyond the perimeter of red-stone walls extending from here through Rougemont and Northernhay Gardens.

Fore Street to the Quay

Southwest of the castle, High Street continues into Fore Street; on the latter's west side, around halfway down, The Mint leads to **St Nicholas Priory** (Easter–Oct Mon, Wed & Sat 2.30–4.30pm; 50p), originally part of a small Benedictine foundation that became a merchant's home after the Dissolution. The interior has been restored to how it might have looked in Tudor times, with some ecclesiastical items displayed alongside medieval pottery excavated hereabouts and, incongruously, a couple of rooms with guns, flags and other articles relating to the Devon and Dorset regiment. On the other side of Fore Street, King Street leads to cobbled **Stepcote Hill**, sloping down towards the river. It's difficult to imagine today that this steep and narrow lane was once the main road into Exeter from the west. At the bottom, surrounded by some wobbly timber-framed houses, **St Mary Steps** is another of Exeter's ancient churches, with a fine seventeenth-century clock showing a knight and two red-coated retainers on its tower, and a late-Gothic nave. The church is only open for Mass on Sunday mornings and evenings, and some Wednesday and Thursday evenings.

At the top of Fore Street, St George's Hall has an indoor market with fresh food as well as practical odds and ends, and there's a street market with similar merchandise on Sidwell Street, at the top of High Street (both Mon–Sat).

At the bottom of Fore Street, the red ruins of the **medieval bridge** lie below Western Way, tucked away from the traffic swirling over the more modern bridges across the River Exe, which marks the southwestern boundary of Exeter's centre. Walk along the river banks (or follow Commercial Rd) to reach the old port area, the **Quay**; now mostly devoted to leisure activities, the area comes into its own at night, but it's worth a wander at any time. Pubs, shops and cafés share the space with the smart **Custom House**, built in 1681, its opulence reflecting the former importance of the cloth trade; the fine plaster ceilings can only be seen by appointment, however. Ask at the main tourist office, or at nearby **Quay House**, which has an information desk; you can also view a video on Exeter's history upstairs (Easter–Oct). Further along, a handsomely restored pair of five-storey warehouses, with hatches and winches from their windows, date from 1835 and are prize examples of the industrial architecture of the period.

You can also rent out bikes and canoes (see p.40) from the Quay, with which to explore the **Exeter Canal** to Topsham and beyond, with good pubs along the route providing refreshment. The canal, which runs parallel to the river, to the southwest of it, was first built in the sixteenth century, and was the first to use pound locks (vertical guillotine sluice gates).

Eating and drinking

Exeter has a range of **eating places** which combine lively sophistication with a laid-back ambience. Most **pubs** also serve food, and the pubs and pizzerias around the Quay are especially popular in summer, and close to some of the city's clubs.

Restaurants

Brazz's, 10 Palace Gate ☎01392/252525. Trendy "style bar" and brasserie below the cathedral with a convivial atmosphere, a tall tubular fish tank and a "grazing" menu. Full meals are eaten upstairs; book a table in advance. Inexpensive–Moderate.

Coolings Wine Bar, Gandy St. Popular for lunch-time salads and pastas, and also open until late evening for drinking. On Fridays and Saturdays, when the place gets packed out, drinks are also available in the cellar. Inexpensive.

Harry's, 86 Longbrook St ☎01392/202234. Good-value Mexican and Italian staples are on the menu in this converted church. Moderate.

Herbie's, 15 North St ☎01392/258473. The city's only wholefood restaurant, with fast and friendly service and organic ice cream on the menu. Closed all day Sun & Mon eve. Inexpensive.

Mad Meg's, Fore St ☎01392/221225. There's an olde worlde atmosphere in this cellar, supposed to be an ex-nunnery (now buried below a bike shop) and the good-value menu has everything from "ploughpersons" and gammon-steak rolls to fish dishes in the evenings, and a gigantic plate of ribs for £13. Book for dinner at weekends. Closed lunch Mon & Tues. Inexpensive–Moderate.

Maryam, 28 South St ☎01392/496776. Alluring garlic smells waft out of this unpretentious trattoria, which is very popular locally, and offers the usual Italian staples. Closed Sun. Inexpensive–Moderate.

Metzo, 153 Fore St ☎01392/499666. Mellow café-bar and restaurant decked out in primary-school colours. The food is more subtle, including pasta, pizza, Mexican snacks and seafood salad. Inexpensive–Moderate.

Mud Dock, Kennaway Warehouse, the Quay ☎01392/27000; *www.muddock.com*. With sofas, newspapers and views over the river, this is a great place to come at any time from breakfast till late – DJs provide the sounds in the evenings; Sunday night is comedy. There's also an entrance on Commercial Rd. Inexpensive–Moderate.

Pubs

Prospect Inn, the Quay. You can eat and drink sitting outside at this seventeenth-century waterside pub, where TV drama *The Onedin Line* was filmed.

Ship Inn, St Martin's Lane. Claiming to have once been Francis Drake's local, this pub also serves food in the low-ceilinged bar adorned with knots and clay pipes (jacket potatoes, baps and French sticks), and main meals in the bistro upstairs. Inexpensive–Moderate.

Walkabout Inn, 99 Fore St. Australasian pub filled with screens showing live sport that serves big breakfasts and other meals. Live bands play on Tuesdays and Sundays.

Nightlife and entertainment

The pubs and clubs on the Quay make this a lively area to while away an evening, and other good nightspots are sprinkled around the centre. For something more challenging, the **Phoenix Exeter Arts Centre** (☎01392/667080), behind the museum off Gandy Street, is the focus of diverse cultural pursuits, including regular non-mainstream films, plays, concerts and various workshops; there are usually free exhibitions on and there's an excellent restaurant, bar and café. Of the town's **theatres**, the Northcott, on the university campus on Stocker Road (☎01392/493493) is the main venue, also staging ballet and opera performances, while the Barnfield, on Barnfield Road (☎01392/271808), is the home of Exeter's Little Theatre Company and stages chiefly amateur productions.

Available free from the tourist office and local pubs and venues, monthly listings and culture magazines tdb, twenty4-seven, The List *and* What's On Southwest *give Exeter plenty of coverage.*

Clubs and venues

Bar Bomba, 44 Queen St ☎01392/412233. Below *Fruta Bomba*, a Latin American restaurant, this cool pre-club bar has DJs on Friday playing funky house and garage until late.

Cavern Club, 83 Queen St ☎01392/495370; *www.cavernclub.co.uk*. With an entrance also in Gandy St, this venue for dance and live music is favoured by students and a mellower crowd. Open Mon–Sat until 1am, or 2am at weekends, also open 10.30am–4pm for snacks. £3–5.

Fizgig, Lower North St ☎01392/253284. A pub below the iron bridge at the bottom of St David's Hill, this has a good atmosphere and live acts – often big names – on Fridays and Saturdays. Tickets cost up to £10.

Lemon Grove, Cornwall House, university campus ☎01392/263528. Open term-time only, the university's club has live acts.

Porter Black's, 7 North St ☎01392/410680. Irish pub with live bands on Wednesdays and Thursdays.

St George's Hall, Fore St/Market St ☎01392/265866. Venue for regular dances, gigs and comedy evenings.

Timepiece, Little Castle Street ☎01392/493096; *www.timepiecenight-club.co.uk*. Formerly a prison and now offering indie, pop, jazz and cheese throughout the week, and a comedy club on Sunday nights. There's a good daytime bar here with a garden. Entry fees are £3–5.

Volts and **Hothouse**, The Quay ☎01392/211347; *www.volts-hothouse.co.uk*. Sharing the same premises, these twin clubs appeal to a young up-for-it crowd, who come for the mainstream dance sounds, Ibiza anthems (foam parties on Fridays) and pop tunes; Sundays have "radical karaoke", and there are occasional live acts. Closes 1am, 2am at weekends, Entry £3–5.

Warehouse, Boxes and Boogies, Commercial Rd ☎01392/295292; *www.wbb.org.uk*. By the Quay, these are three clubs in one, and open in

Mid-Devon

different combinations Monday–Saturday (not Mon in winter); all play a mix of dance music and retro, and stay open until 2am Thursday–Saturday.

Listings

The Exeter Festival takes place at various venues around town during the first three weeks of July, and features jazz and blues concerts as well as classical performances and cabaret. Contact the tourist office for details, or call the festival office on ☎01392/ 213161.

Bike and canoe rental Mud Docks Cycleworks (☎01392/279999) rents out hybrids and mountain bikes. Saddles & Paddles (☎01392/424241) has bikes and three- or four-person Canadian canoes. Both places are located on the Quay.

Car rental Most agencies have offices in the Marsh Barton Industrial Estate, off Alphington Rd (bus #D), including Abbey Ford, 30 Edwin Road (☎01392/254037); Avis, 29 Marsh Green Rd ☎01392/259713; and Budget, Unit 2, Grace Rd ☎01392/496555;

Hospital Royal Devon and Exeter Hospital on Barrack Rd (☎01392/411611) has an emergency department.

Internet access Try Hyperactive at 1b Central Station Crescent, right next to Exeter Central station (Mon–Fri 10am–7.30pm, Sat 10am–6pm, Sun noon–6pm; £2.50 for 30min; ☎01392/201544).

Laundrette St David's Laundrette is on the corner of Richmond Rd and St David's Hill (daily 9am–10pm).

Left luggage The bus station has a few lockers, and Capital Taxis, on the forecourt of St David's station, will also stash your bags (£1 per item per 24hr).

Post office Bedford St (Mon–Sat 9am–5.30pm).

Taxis A1 Cars (24hr), Richmond Rd ☎01392/218888; Capital Taxis, St David's station ☎01392/433433; Dartline Z Cars, 15 South St ☎01392/ 422888.

Mid-Devon

Covering the area between Exeter and Exmoor, **mid-Devon** is an intensely rural region of deep lanes and high hedgerows, its undulating landscape cut through by a number of rivers. Largely free of the cloying, tidily thatched appearance of much of the county, the few specific sights are scattered. Upstream of Exeter on the River Exe, **Tiverton** is the only town of any significance, often overlooked by tourists but holding some absorbing old buildings. Like many of the inland settlements around here, Tiverton thrived on the local wool industry, whose beneficiaries not only poured their largesse on the town but built some splendid mansions in the locality. Nearest of these is **Knightshayes Court**, which features rich decorative work by the exuberant Victorian Gothic designer, William Burges. Just downriver of the stereotypical Devon village of **Bickleigh**, you'll find plenty of genuine charm at **Bickleigh Castle**, while **Killerton** has a unique collection of costumes and an unusual bear's hut and ice house in the grounds.

If you're heading to Barnstaple from Exeter, you have the choice of taking the A377 or the Tarka Line (see p.157), the one surviving train service connecting north and south Devon. Either way, you'll

pass through **Crediton**, eight miles northwest of Exeter and site of
one of Devon's most splendid churches – the only reason for stopping here. Twelve miles further northwest, **Eggesford Forest** is one
of the few remaining areas of woodland in these parts, and well-sup-
plied with walking routes, while nearby **Chumleigh**, off the B3096, is
a picturesque village that provides some good places to sleep and
eat.

Tiverton and around

Thirteen miles due north of Exeter, **TIVERTON** lies at the heart of a
rich agricultural region of red soil and lush meadows. The town owes
its fortune to textiles, its mills powered by the Exe and Lowman
rivers that meet here. The main pedestrianized Fore Street leads
westwards down Angel Hill to the Exe Bridge, from where you can
see the last remaining textile factory, a prominent landmark that was
opened as a cotton mill in 1792 by a lace and textile entrepreneur,
John Heathcoat. Having been driven out of the Midlands by Luddite
machine-wreckers, Heathcoat rescued Tiverton from the decline
then overtaking other cloth centres in the west by building a lace factory which soon came to employ a significant portion of the local
workforce. Most of the remaining mills are now out of sight, however, and Tiverton today has the feeling of a prosperous market town.

*You'll find
some useful
information on
mid-Devon on
the district-
council Web
site:* www
.middevon
.gov.uk

The town's one-time wealth is reflected in its number of churches
– no less than eleven, including what is reckoned to be Devon's finest
Georgian church, **St George**, south of Fore Street on St Andrew
Street. Constructed partly of Purbeck stone in 1733, it lends a dignified air to the town's centre, and the harmonious interior has galleries equipped with Ionic columns. Further along St Andrew Street,
Tiverton Museum (Mon–Sat 10am–4.30pm; £3; *www.tiverton
museum.org.uk*) provides the background of the town's cloth industry, and also displays a variety of local items illustrating domestic
and social life, from agricultural implements, man traps and farm
wagons to cooking utensils and lace-making machinery from the
Heathcoat factory.

*At the time of
writing,
Tiverton
Museum was
closed for
refurbishment,
so to check
opening hours
and entry fees
before you
visit, look on
the Web site or
call* ☎*01884/
256295.*

Retracing your steps and crossing Fore Street brings you to St
Peter Street and **Slee's Almshouses**, a good example of one of the
many Tiverton buildings constructed using endowments from
wealthy wool merchants. Fronted by two storeys of wooden galleries,
it was built in 1613 with funds donated by one George Slee. He plied
his business next door in the **Great House of St George**, a substantial Jacobean edifice with mullioned windows and a wide stone
facade; you can visit the lovely walled garden at the back during
office hours (free). Another local benefactor, London Merchant
Venturer John Greenway, provided the south porch of **St Peter's
church**, whose tall pinnacled tower overlooks the River Exe at the
top of St Peter Street. Above the porch's door, the Gothic tracery
depicts an Assumption of the Virgin Mary flanked by images of

Greenway and his wife, while the church's south chapel, built in 1517 and also paid for by Greenway, is richly ornamented with a frieze of well-armed ships and accoutrements of his trade – bales of wool, ropes and anchors. The rest of the church is largely Victorian, but has a good set of modern hassocks depicting birds, butterflies and flowers.

Now surrounded by car parks and a modern shopping precinct, Tiverton's Pannier Market, between Fore Street and Newport Street, is a great place for picking up food or bargains, and there's a flea market every Monday.

Tiverton Castle

A few yards north of St Peter's on Park Hill stands the pinkish sand-stone **Tiverton Castle** (Easter to late June & Sept Sun & Thurs 2.30–5.30pm; July & Aug Sun–Thurs 2.30–5.30pm; £3.50), a rather unmenacing-looking fortification which traces its origins to 1106. It last saw action when Oliver Cromwell's general Thomas Fairfax attacked and took it in 1645, and has since slumbered as a family house. A wander through the renovated rooms brings you face to face with seventeenth-century armoury, and knowledgeable atten-dants point out such items as the "brass monkey" (a cannonball hold-er) and "morning star" (a spiked holy-water sprinkler) and encour-age you to try on some reproduction armour.

The Grand Western Canal

A mile southeast of the town centre, just off Canal Hill on the Cullompton road, you could spend a serene hour or two strolling along the **Grand Western Canal**. The waterway was originally con-ceived as a means of linking the English and Bristol channels, but only the stretch from Taunton to Tiverton was completed (in the early 1800s) – it was used by barges carrying coal and limestone. The canal fell into decline following the growth of the railway in the 1840s, but has recently been restored and now forms the focus of a country park; a leaflet describing **walks** along the canal banks can be bought at the Tiverton tourist office. From the wharf (signposted off Canal Hill), you also see the canal in the time-honoured manner by taking a trip on a **horse-drawn barge** (late April to Oct; ☎01884/253345; *www.horseboat.co.uk*) for one hour (£3.60 return) or three (£7.65 return). The same company also rents out **rowing boats** between April and September (£3.75 per half-hour; £5.95 per hour).

Practicalities

Tiverton's **tourist office** (April–Sept Mon–Fri 9.15am–5.30pm, Sat 9.15am–4pm; Oct–March Mon–Fri 9.15am–5pm, Sat 9.15am–3pm; ☎01884/255827; *www.devonshireheartland.co.uk*) is situated next to the **bus station** in Phoenix Lane, just south of Fore Street. The train station, **Tiverton Parkway**, lies six miles west of the town centre, connected by hourly buses #373 and #397.

If you're looking for somewhere to **stay** in the centre, the best bet is *Bridge House*, 23 Angel Hill (☎01884/252804; ①), a modernized red-brick Victorian house with a peaceful riverbank garden, where all the rooms overlook the river. A mile north of Tiverton on the A396, the Georgian *Hartnoll Country House Hotel* at Bolham (☎01884/252777; ③) provides a tranquil alternative: rooms are spacious and beautifully decorated, and the conservatory overlooks extensive gardens.

Daytime **eating** needs are taken care of by the small and busy *Up Stairs, Down Stairs*, 1 Angel Terrace, off Angel Hill (closed Wed & Sun), where the inexpensive menu changes daily and features home-grown vegetables; there's always curry available, and food to take away. The *White Ball Inn* on Angel Hill serves pub food all day.

Knightshayes Court

House April–Sept Sat–Thurs 11am–5.30pm; Oct Sat–Wed 11am–4pm; £5.40; garden April–Oct daily 11am–5.30pm; £3.80; NT.

A couple of miles north of Tiverton, off the A396 at Bolham, **Knightshayes Court** is a Victorian Gothic pile partly designed by the flamboyant and idiosyncratic architect William Burges for John Heathcoat Amory (1829–1914), MP for Tiverton and grandson of John Heathcoat (see p.41). Burges' dilatoriness in executing his designs, however, caused him to be replaced in 1874 by J.D. Crace, whose contributions were considerably blander than his predecessor's. Characteristic of Burges' work are the corbel figures in the hall stairwell, and the room itself, an imitation of a medieval vaulted hall which holds a bookcase designed by Burges and painted by the Pre-Raphaelites Burne-Jones and Rossetti. The library demonstrates one of Burges' favourite motifs in the jelly-mould-like miniature vaults of the ceiling; combined with cedar panelling and stencilling, heavily encrusted antique gold wallpaper and the leather and gold spines of the books, these give the library a truly sumptuous feel. It's a suitable complement to the magnificent arched red drawing room with its Burges-designed marble chimneypiece, originally from Worcester College, Oxford.

From Tiverton, you can get to Knightshayes Court via bus #398 to Bolham, from where it's a half-mile walk; the taxi fare from Tiverton is around £3.50.

Bickleigh

Four miles south of Tiverton on the A396, and connected by buses #55, #55a, #55b and #347, the picturesque village of **Bickleigh** suffers from coach-party fatigue but nevertheless makes an attractive stop, with a well-preserved castle and a five-arched bridge from 1630 that spans the tumbling waters of the River Exe. Idyllically sited by the river half a mile west of the village, the sandstone **Bickleigh Castle** (Easter to late; May Wed & Sun 2–5pm; late May to early Oct daily 2–5pm; £4) – more of a fortified manor house than a

Knightshayes Court and Bickleigh

You can rent bikes from Maynards Cycle Shop, 25 Gold St (☎01884/ 253979), and go horse riding at Mount Pleasant Riding Centre, Templeton, four miles west of Tiverton (signposted off the B3137 Witheridge road), for £8 per hour.

As there's no information on display, you'll need one of the guidebooks on sale (£2.95) to make the most of the house.

castle – has parts dating back to the Norman era, though many of the older sections were destroyed during the Civil War, when the building was a Royalist stronghold. The original **gatehouse** survives, however, now displaying weapons from the armoury and a vigorously carved stone overmantle showing a windmill, a walled city and figures in seventeenth-century dress. The courtyard holds the restored **Stuart farmhouse**, which incorporates ship's timbers and has an iron fireback celebrating the victory over the Spanish Armada.

Across the road from the gatehouse, you pass through seventeenth-century Italian wrought-iron gates to reach the thatched Norman **chapel**, one of Devon's oldest churches. Restored and whitewashed, the diminutive interior contains a wooden gallery and an hour-glass sermon-timer. Note the "sanctuary ring" on the church's door, where refugees were expected to cling for 48 hours to obtain protection.

Bickleigh makes a pricey place to **stay**, but if you're stuck you could do worse than the timbered and thatched *Fisherman's Cot* (☎01884/855237; *www.lionheartinns.co.uk*; ④), offering stylish rooms right on the river and a large restaurant and bar. For a slap-up **meal**, though, head for *The Exe-cargot* (reservations only; ☎01884/855680; closed daytime Mon–Sat in winter), right by Bickleigh Castle. The £20 set menu gets you a three-course feast of French and local specialities. Alternatively, seek out the small, sixteenth-century *Butterleigh Inn* at Butterleigh, three miles east of Bickleigh, which serves excellent-value meals such as veggie skins, home-made burgers and bacon chops with damson sauce. The wonderful puddings include saffron meringues.

Killerton House

House mid-March to end March & Oct Wed–Sun 11am–5.30pm; April–July & Sept Tues–Sun 11am–5.30pm; Aug daily 11am–5.30pm; garden daily 10.30am–dusk; house and garden £5.20, garden only £3.70; NT.

Five miles south of Bickleigh and twelve miles south of Tiverton off the B3185, **Killerton House** is attractively set on a hillside amid a landscaped garden of lawns and herbaceous borders. The elegant eighteenth-century house is most famous for its collection of **costumes**, one of the largest in the southwest. Displays on the first floor, drawn from the vast nine thousand-item store, are changed each year; recent ones include hats and underwear. On the ground floor, the **music room** has a rare nineteenth-century quartet table to the right of the organ and fake marble (scagliola) columns. The **laundry**, too, is worth looking at, accessible from the grounds; pride of place here goes to the Victorian pull-out floor-to-ceiling drier, its racks covered with paper to protect the whites, closely followed by a rare box mangle.

At the back of the house a path brings you to the **bear's hut**, a rustic summer house named on account of a pet bear formerly housed here. The three rooms are variously decorated with fir cones, cobbles, log sections, mullioned windows, stained glass and a floor made from the tiny knuckle–bones of deer. Close to the large and steep rockery nearby, the **ice house**, constructed in 1808, could store up to three years' worth of ice in its twenty-foot-deep brick-lined pit.

Killerton House has a café, but for evening and bar **meals**, the *Red Lion*, five miles south in the village of **Broadclyst**, offers good-value pies, steaks and home-made puddings.

Crediton and around

At the precise geographical centre of Devon, **CREDITON** has been an important settlement and market town since Saxon times, serving as the meeting point of trade routes from Okehampton, Exeter, Tiverton and Barnstaple. The great missionary **Saint Boniface**, originally called Wynfrith, was born here around 680; he went on to convert the German tribes east of the Rhine which even the Romans had steered clear of, for which he was later declared patron saint of both Germany and the Netherlands. At his request, a monastery was founded in his home town, and this helped to establish Crediton as an important ecclesiastical centre. The monastery's church became Devon's first cathedral in 909, but even after the diocese was transferred to Exeter in 1050, Crediton retained a central role, and by the fifteenth century it was one of Devon's most prosperous wool towns. However, fires in the eighteenth century destroyed most of its ancient buildings, and the only item of note today is its splendid red collegiate **Church of the Holy Cross**, whose cathedral dimensions and pinnacled central tower dominate what is now a mere village. It was started at or near the site of the monastery church in the mid-twelfth century, though only the base of the present tower remains from this period; most of what you see today dates from a reconstruction in the early Perpendicular style between 1410 and 1478. What might have been a gloomy interior is now flooded with the light coming in through two rows of generous windows (including those of the clerestory), the plain glass having replaced the stained glass blown out by a landmine in 1942.

The nave arch of the tower is dominated by a monument to local hero General Sir Redvers Buller, mainly remembered now for putting the British army into khaki; erected in 1911, this ornate neo-Gothic concoction of heraldry and Pre-Raphaelite imagery makes a gaudy contrast to the restraint of the rest of the church. At the eastern end of the nave, the dignified Lady Chapel may well have provided the model for the eponymous chapel in Exeter Cathedral. The south choir aisle gives access to the **Chapter House**, dating from around 1300; the lovely old room now displays a collection of local knick-knacks – pieces of seventeenth-century armour, a few musket barrels and the like.

Once you've taken in the church, there's little reason to hang around in Crediton, unless you're looking for refreshments or you're

Bike Shed on
Union Road in
Crediton
(☎01363/
774773) rent
out bikes.

stuck for a bed (see below). A fairly continual flow of traffic mars the flavour of the broad main street, and the rest of the town has little of interest.

Practicalities

Crediton's High Street has everything you might need: banks, pubs and the local **tourist office** (Mon–Tues & Thurs–Fri 9.30am–1pm & 1.30–5.30pm, Wed 2–5.30pm, Sat 1.30–4pm; ☎01363/772006; *www.devonshireheartland.co.uk*). The post office is just off the main drag on Market Street.

Taw Vale (☎01363/777879; no credit cards; ①) is the most central place to **stay**, a detached house at the southern end of town near the 24-hour garage, offering a pleasant double or twin, with en-suite shower or (for a bit less) with a private bathroom downstairs. Otherwise, try *Colt Chase* on Westwood Road (☎01363/774269; no credit cards; ①), with views of green fields from its windows.

The town offers a good choice of places to **eat**. Just down the road from the tourist office, *The Exchange* is a popular restaurant with a small patio and has cheap lunches, or you can dine on bangers and mash or nut roast in comfortable chairs across the road at the *General Sir Redvers Buller*, a free house with an open fire in winter. At 38 High St, *Treloar's Delicatessen* provides jam and hams, cheeses, patés and fruit juices as well as ready-made meals to take away, from cottage pies to vegetarian dishes.

Eggesford Forest and Chumleigh

Northwest of Crediton, the A377 and the Tarka Line follow the same route, passing through the village of Eggesford (where there's a rail stop) and the surrounding **Eggesford Forest**. This ancient wooded zone of high fir trees and birches on steep hillsides, where the Forestry Commission planted its first saplings in 1919, makes good **walking** country, and there are waymarked trails through some of the most scenic parts; look out for wild deer along the way. The prettiest village in the area is **CHUMLEIGH**, a couple of miles north of Eggesford as the crow flies but nearly four miles by road, turning right off the A377 onto the B3096 or heading east from Eggesford on the B3042 and left at the B3096. Once on the main Exeter–Barnstaple route, this was another centre of the cloth trade in the seventeenth and eighteenth centuries, but is now quiet and sedate. Turn right at the blue village pump at the end of the main street to reach its church, **St Mary Magdalene**, whose tall, grey pinnacled tower is surrounded by thatched cottages and offers clear views across the valley of the Little Dart river to the forest beyond. The interior of the church is worth glancing into as well, its wide, wagon-roofed interior crossed by a fine-traceried screen surmounted by four learned-looking figures. Below the roof, angels with painted golden wings add another decorative element.

Chumleigh makes the most congenial place to stay hereabouts, with several good **accommodation** choices. Of these, the best are the *Old Bakehouse* on South Molton Street (☎01769/580074; *the_old_bakehouse@talk21.com*; no smoking; ③), offering compact en-suite bedrooms, a tiny sitting-room for guests and evening meals. Right in front of the church, the flower-bedecked *Globe Inn* has neat, unfussy rooms (☎01769/580252; ②), and also provides a welcoming atmosphere for a meal or a pint of Butcombe ale. You can eat better, however, at the *Old Bakehouse*, which offers home-cooked pies and casseroles. If you don't want to hang around, pick up a fresh-cut baguette or other nibbles from the Dairy Delicatessen on East Street.

Travel details

Trains

Crediton to: Barnstaple (Mon–Sat 9–11 daily, Sun 5 daily; 55min); Eggesford (Mon–Sat 9–11 daily, Sun 5 daily; 30min); Exeter (9–11 daily; 12min).

Eggesford to: Barnstaple (Mon–Sat 9–11 daily, Sun 5 daily; 30min); Crediton (Mon–Sat 9–11 daily, Sun 5 daily; 30min); Exeter (Mon–Sat 9–11 daily, Sun 5 daily; 40min).

Exeter to: Barnstaple (Mon–Sat 9–11 daily, Sun 5 daily; 1hr 10min); Crediton (9–11 daily; 12min); Eggesford (Mon–Sat 9–11 daily, Sun 5 daily; 40min); London (hourly; 2–3hr); Penzance (hourly; 2hr 50min–3hr 25min); Plymouth (hourly; 1hr); Tiverton Parkway (6 daily; 20min).

Tiverton Parkway to: Bristol (5 daily; 55min); Exeter (6 daily; 20min); Plymouth (6 daily; 1hr 30min).

Buses

Crediton to: Chumleigh (Mon–Sat 2–3 daily; 50min); Exeter (1–3 hourly; 25min); Tiverton (Mon–Sat 5 daily; 55min).

Exeter to: Barnstaple (Mon–Sat 5 daily, Sun 2 daily; 2hr 20min); Bickleigh (Mon–Sat 1–2 hourly, Sun 9 daily; 25min); Bude (Mon–Sat 8 daily, Sun 2 daily; 1hr 45min); Chumleigh (Mon–Sat 2–3 daily; 1hr 10min); Crediton (1–3 hourly; 25min); Exmouth (every 20min; 40min); London (9 daily; 4hr 30min); Okehampton (hourly; 1hr); Plymouth (1–2 hourly; 1hr 10min); Sidmouth (hourly; 1hr 30min); Tiverton (Mon–Sat 1–2 hourly, Sun 9 daily; 40min); Torquay (every 30min; 1hr–1hr 30min); Uffculme (Mon–Sat 2 daily; 1hr).

Tiverton to: Bickleigh (Mon–Sat 1–2 hourly, Sun 8 daily; 10min); Crediton (Mon–Sat 5 daily; 55min); Exeter (Mon–Sat 1–2 hourly, Sun 8 daily; 40min); Uffculme (Mon–Sat hourly; 35min).

Chapter 2

East Devon

For comprehensive information on history, events, pubs and attractions in east Devon, visit http:// eastdevon.net. You'll also find some useful pages amongst the official council policies at www .devon-cc .gov.uk

Bordered by Dorset to the east and the Exe estuary to the west, east Devon is often bypassed by travellers speeding westward, and though the resorts and beaches can still get fairly busy in summer, the region is relatively free of the congestion which afflicts other parts of Devon. Popular with retirees and older holiday-makers, the area is renowned for the strength of its "grey pound", and remains a genteel, tranquil oasis of old-fashioned Regency-style seaside towns, majestic red-cliff coasts and, inland, a smattering of drowsy villages.

Immediately south of Exeter, the **Exe estuary** assumes a broad, marshy appearance along its five-mile length. At its head, the small port of **Topsham** is closely linked to the county capital, but with a very separate identity that's redolent of its seafaring past. Four miles south, off the A376, the Gothic fantasy of **A La Ronde** sits above the estuary, one of the most delightful architectural curiosities in the West Country, whose fascinating contents recall the travels of the two eighteenth-century women who designed it. At the head of the estuary, **Exmouth** is as busy as things get, a family resort embellished by some elegant Georgian terraces. It's the first of a succession of eighteenth- and nineteenth-century beach resorts strung along this coast, none of them over-commercialized, saved from mass tourism by the predominantly stony beaches, even if the water quality consistently rates highly. Though it can boast a sandy beach, Exmouth is not the most attractive of the coastal towns, but its range of accommodation makes it a possible base for exploring the pretty group of villages east of town, around the River Otter, which enjoy a quieter, more Elizabethan atmosphere. On the coast, **Budleigh Salterton** is the largest of these, with a wide stony seafront and a diverting museum that focuses imaginatively on the human and natural history of the region. You can get a close-up view of rural Devon in the unspoiled village of **East Budleigh**, a couple of miles inland and sharing with Budleigh Salterton an association with Walter Raleigh, and at **Otterton**, reachable on a riverside walk from Budleigh. Back on the coast, a mile east of Otterton, the beautifully sited beach at **Ladram Bay** is the biggest crowd-puller hereabouts.

Working east along the coast, **Sidmouth** is the most appealing of east Devon's seaside resorts, an elegantly aged Regency town with considerable architectural charm. Like Exmouth, it gets pretty lively in summer, not least when the annual **Sidmouth International Festival** takes over. There are cliff-backed beaches to either side of town, and the coast path provides an ideal way to reach more isolated stony strands, such as **Branscombe**, a secluded hamlet with a monumental church. Further east, **Beer**, though overcrowded in high season, is an immediately likeable village with an intriguing network of subterranean caverns to explore just outside. Across the bay, **Seaton** marks the last of the resorts dotted along this coast, but lacks Sidmouth's venerable charm.

Inland, the agricultural heartland that has created so much of Devon's wealth has remained more or less unchanged for centuries. The unruffled rural ambience is the main reason for straying away from the sea, but the lace museum at **Honiton** makes an absorbing distraction, while **Ottery St Mary** holds one of Devon's most impressive churches, a symbol of the largesse of the local merchants.

It's easy to explore the area via **public transport**, though **train routes** are limited to the branch line from Exeter St David's to Exmouth – a lovely ride along the Exe estuary – and the less frequent service from Exeter to Honiton. The most useful **bus service** is the #57, departing every twenty or thirty minutes from Exeter's bus station and running through Exmouth, Budleigh Salterton and Sidmouth. Beer and Seaton are linked to Sidmouth by the #899 service, while the #340 (#379 on Sun) provides frequent connections between Sidmouth and Honiton.

Topsham

Frequent buses and trains connect Exeter with **TOPSHAM**, five miles south, though many prefer to arrive via the scenic route, following the canal on foot or by bike from Exeter Quay. Exeter's main port since the middle of the first century, Topsham's continuing importance was ensured when, after a quarrel with Exeter's dignitaries in 1282, the Countess of Devon built a weir across the Exe to prevent ships riding the tide up to Exeter; all cargo had to be

East Devon

Leaflets detailing the eighty-mile circular Buzzard Cycle Route, which takes in Exmouth, Honiton, Beer, Seaton and Sidmouth, are available from local tourist offices or at bike-rental shops for 75p. Other useful publications for bikers include Cycling in East Devon *(25p), which describes ten road routes (and short cuts) and* Mountain Biking in East Devon *(£1.90), outlining road and off-road trails.*

For public-transport information in east Devon, call the DevonBus enquiry line on ☎*01392 /382800 (Mon–Fri 8.30am– 5.30pm). See* Basics, p.7 *for details of bus passes.*

ACCOMMODATION PRICE CODES

Throughout this *Guide*, hotel and B&B accommodation is coded on a scale of ① to ⑨, the code indicating the lowest price you can expect to pay per night for a double room in high season. The prices indicated by the codes are as follows:

① under £40	④ £60–70	⑦ £110–150
② £40–50	⑤ £70–90	⑧ £150–200
③ £50–60	⑥ £90–110	⑨ over £200

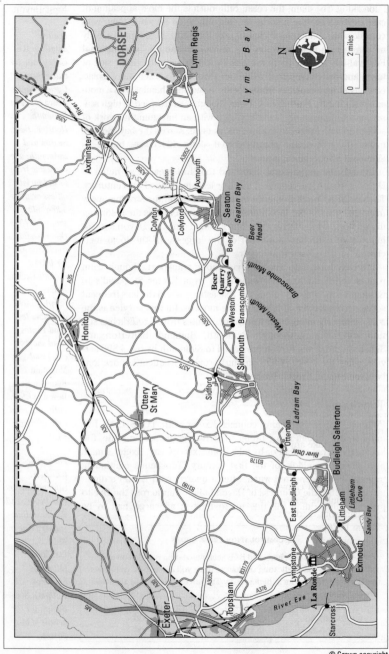

unloaded at Topsham, thus lining the pockets of the Countess and her descendants. It was not until 1566, when the country's first lock canal was built to connect Exeter directly with the estuary, that vessels were again able to dock upriver at Exeter, though Topsham continued to prosper from the expanded European and transatlantic wool markets. When the wool trade faltered at the end of the eighteenth century, Topsham was kept alive by shipbuilding and its subsidiary activities, such as chain and rope-making, until well into the nineteenth century.

The former warehouses and seventeenth-century merchants' houses along Topsham's central Fore Street and The Strand are now commuter homes and restaurants, and include good examples of the Dutch-influenced gabled architecture that was introduced by merchants trading with Holland. You can get some lively background on the town's shipbuilding and trading traditions at the **Topsham Museum** (Easter–Oct Mon, Wed & Sat, Sun 2–5pm, £1.50), 23 The Strand. Arrayed around a seventeenth-century house and former sail loft, exhibits include a model of the town as it was in 1900, a selection of local craftwork and records of families prominent in the serge-cloth trade. Twentieth-century interest is provided in the form of memorabilia of the film star Vivien Leigh, sister-in-law of the museum's founder.

Further down The Strand, the sea wall offers good bird-watching at low tide, when there are views across the reedy mud flats – look out for curlews, redshanks and, if you're lucky, the odd avocet. Closer to the centre, at the bottom of the steps behind the church of St Margaret's on Fore Street, boatyards and ships' chandlers line the riverfront. From Trout's Boatyard, Stuart Line (☎01395/222144 or ☎01395/279693 evenings and winter) run **boat trips** in the estuary, including a cruise down to Exmouth (May, June & Sept Tues, Wed & Thurs; July–Aug Mon–Fri; £3.50), departing at 11am and taking around an hour, depending on the tide; a Round Robin ticket (£6) allows you to take any of the frequent trains back.

Practicalities

Topsham offers a calmer alternative to **lodging** in Exeter. A good first call would be *Broadway House*, 35 High St (☎01392/873465; ②), a handsome red-brick Georgian house built by an Oporto merchant in 1776, with comfortable rooms and good facilities. There's a touch more luxury at the sixteenth-century *Globe Inn* at 34 Fore St (☎01392/873471; *globe@devonhotels.com*; ②), a former coaching house opulently furnished with antiques, which has half-testers and a four-poster bed (at an extra £7). Book ahead in summer.

There's a good selection of smart bistros and **restaurants** in town, but if you want somewhere less formal, the *Georgian Tea Room*, part of *Broadway House* (see above), serves a good fish pie or roast lunches (Tues, Thurs and Sun only) – and they'll make up a packed

Topsham

The town Web site www.topsham .org *has plenty of background on Topsham, and includes a directory of town traders.*

lunch or scones and cream to take away too. Otherwise, the oak-pan-elled dining room of the *Globe Inn* offers reasonably priced tradi-tional English meals alongside Caribbean and vegetarian options, and crab or prawn sandwiches from the bar. You'll also find snacks in the **pubs**, most of them stuffed with souvenirs of Topsham's sea-faring tradition; best options are the *Lighter Inn*, right by the river at the junction of Fore Street and The Strand; there are tables out-side, an open fire in winter and a restaurant upstairs. On the edge of the village, in a lovely location by the muddy River Clyst on Grove Road, the eleventh-century *Bridge Inn* is *the* place for real ale as well as soups, sandwiches and handmade Burts crisps, and you'll find occasional live **folk music** in the evenings. In summer, ferries take customers from Trout's Boatyard on the Quayside downstream to the waterside *Turf Locks Hotel* for a peaceful drink or meal (£3 return).

A La Ronde and around

From Exeter, the #57 bus stops near the turn-off for A La Ronde on the A376, from which you must walk the last half-mile.

On a hillside overlooking the Exe estuary, looking a little like some-thing out of a fairy tale, the Gothic folly of **A La Ronde** (April–Oct Mon–Thurs & Sun 11am–5.30pm; £3.40; NT) lies four miles south of Topsham and a couple of miles north of Exmouth, along a signpost-ed turn-off from the A376.

An extravagant but engaging flight of fancy dating from the 1790s, A La Ronde was the achievement of two cousins, Jane and Mary Parminter, who were inspired by a European Grand Tour to con-struct this sixteen-sided house – possibly based on the Byzantine basilica of San Vitale in Ravenna – filled with the various mementos of their travels. To these, the Parminters added a number of their own rather eccentric artistic creations, ranging from concoctions of seaweed and sand to a frieze made of game-bird and chicken feath-ers. At the top of the house, which has an enclosed octagonal hall at its centre, the gallery and staircase are completely covered in shells, which can be glimpsed from the first floor; a closed-circuit TV sys-tem lets you home in on details.

The Parminter cousins intended that the house should be inherited by their female descendants alone, but fifty years after Mary Parminter's death in 1849, the conditions of her will were bro-ken when the building was inherited by the Reverend Oswald Reichel, who became the only male owner of the house in its history. Reichel's modifications are generally considered to have been an improvement; dormer windows now admit much-needed natural light and afford superb views westward over the Exe Estuary to Haldon Hill and Dawlish Warren.

If you're taken by A La Ronde's unconventional style, it's worth heading a little further up the lane to **Point-in-View** (same hours; free), a tiny Congregational chapel with adjoining almshouses built in 1811, on the instructions of the Misses Parminter, for "four spin-sters over fifty years of age and approved character". The design is as eccentric as A La Ronde's, the minuscule chapel sporting a pyramidal roof with triangular windows, surrounded by the low almshouses and topped by a jaunty weather vane. The name derives from the motto over the entrance: "Some Point in View – We All Persue", apparently referring to the conversion of the Jews. Sunday Services are still held here 11am.

Back at A La Ronde, you can take refreshments in the excellent café, but if you're looking for something a little more special, head a mile northwest to **Lympstone**, an estuary village where Newfoundland whalers once hauled up for the winter. Here you'll find one of the region's most highly-rated **restaurants**, *The River House*, on The Strand (☎01395/265147; closed Sun & Mon), which draws in foodies from far and wide, undaunted by the expensive prices. From the upstairs dining room overlooking the Exe, you can feast on English and Mediterranean-style dishes – many of the ingredients are grown in the restaurant's own allotment.

Exmouth

At the southeastern corner of the Exe estuary, **EXMOUTH** claims to be the oldest seaside resort in Devon. Signs of its early gentility are evident in some graceful examples of Georgian architecture, but there are few surprises in the repertoire of resort attractions, and the town is primarily useful as a base for exploring the surrounding area. The place was unmentioned in history books before a Viking raiding party landed on a marauding invasion in 1001, fanning out to burn and pillage as far as Exeter. By 1200 it was the site of an important port, both sheltering and building ships, and it later became a noted smugglers' haunt. Exmouth evolved as a resort from the time of the Napoleonic wars, and the central core preserves much of the feel of that era, with its terraces rising above lawns, rock pools and two miles of **sandy beach** – a rare thing in east Devon – which, together with the stunning views across the estuary and out to sea, has confirmed the town's continuing popularity as a family destination.

The indoor covered market at 12 The Strand (Mon–Sat 9am–5pm) has fifty stalls selling anything from fish to antiques.

Though the seafront is the main focus of Exmouth, most of the finer architecture is set back from the coast concentrated on the hill known as **The Beacon**, which once accommodated such folk as the wives of Nelson and Byron – installed at 6 and 19 The Beacon respectively. This exclusive residential area was at a safe remove from the old **port** area, at the western end of town, now redeveloped as a marina with an overcrowded luxury flat development. There are still some working fishing boats in evidence, however, and it's a good place to buy fresh wet fish or to join summer **boat trips**, including estuary cruises with Stuart Line (see p.51), or a water-taxi to Dawlish Point (April–Oct; ☎07970/918418; £2.40 return). Spinnaker's Sailing Centre also rent **out sailing boats** from the harbour, for use in sea and in the lively tidal conditions of the estuary (from £40 per day; ☎01395/222551).

Exmouth

The east Devon stretch of the South West Coast Path (see Basics, p.8–9) starts from the cliffs at the eastern end of Exmouth's seafront and continues for 26 miles to the Dorset border at Lyme Regis – leaflets detailing the route are available from the tourist office.

Most visitors to Exmouth, however, are drawn to the town's **beach**, a broad sandy sweep below The Esplanade, backed by a somewhat tacky promenade and extending as far as the eastern cliffs. Swimmers should pay attention to the red warning flags, as the offshore tides can stir up strong currents. You can rent wet suits, windsurfing equipment, surf- and body-boards either from beach kiosks or from Tad Ltd on the harbour (☎01395/227007). Summer sees a lively hubbub here, but there's quite a different feel after the beach crowds have headed off, when the promenade makes a nice spot for a quiet early evening stroll. From Capel Lane and Bidmead Close (signposted at the eastern end of the seafront), you can access the level **cycle path** along the old railway track to Budleigh Salterton (see opposite); the route passes through the village of **Littleham**, where Lady Nelson is buried in the churchyard.

Practicalities

Exmouth's **train** and **bus stations** sit side by side a few minutes north of the centre of town on The Parade. The **tourist office** is on Alexandra Terrace, which runs alongside Manor Gardens from the bottom of The Beacon to the sea (Easter–Oct Mon–Sat 9.30am–5pm, plus July & Aug Sun 10am–3pm; Nov–Easter Mon–Sat 9.30am–1.30pm; ☎01395/222299; *www.exmouth-guide.co.uk*).

The most convenient **places to stay** lie between the train station and the harbour, and you'll normally pay a little extra for rooms with sea views. The pick of the row of B&Bs near the tourist office and the beach, nonsmoking *Blenheim Guest House*, 39 Morton Rd (☎01395/223123; *blenheim@beeb.net*; no credit cards; ①), offers spacious rooms and an easy-going atmosphere, but the *Barn Hotel*, further out on Foxholes Hill (☎01395/224411; ④), is more stylish. An Arts and Crafts house set in its own quiet gardens and built according to a "butterfly" design by Edward Prior, a contemporary of William Morris, it has bright, light rooms – the old nurseries on the second floor have great views – and an outdoor swimming pool and croquet lawn. At the top of The Beacon, the *Royal Beacon Hotel* (☎01395/264886; *reception@royalbeaconhotel.co.uk*; ⑤) is Exmouth's top choice if money's no object, if only for the views over the sea; rooms are suitably luxurious and there's a fine restaurant. A couple of miles west of the centre, *Prattshayes Farm* (May–Sept; ☎01395/276626) is the town's nearest **campsite**, reached on #3 bus from The Parade to the *Clinton Arms* pub in Littleham, from where it's a half-mile walk down Maer Lane. There are more campsites and other accommodation at Sandy Bay a stretch of beaches just south of here and a couple of miles east of town.

Knobblies, at the top of Exeter Road (☎01395/270182), rents mountain bikes

Though Exmouth has a surprisingly small selection of reasonable **places to eat**, you can dine well at the *Seafood Restaurant*, located just off The Beacon on Tower Street (☎01395/269459; closed Mon & Sun). The fish soups are memorable, and the seafood platter, for around £15 (minimum two people) is zesty and filling. For something more snackish, head for the *Fountain Café* on The Beacon, a cheap and friendly spot for a quick lunch, baguette or jacket potato, or settle down in one of the town's more amenable **pubs**, such as the *Deer Leap* on The Esplanade, which has a garden facing onto the sea and serves a good parsnip bake among other bar meals.

Budleigh Salterton and around

Four miles east of Exmouth along the B3178, and bounded by red-sandstone cliffs to the west and by the pebblestone ridge of the Otter estuary at its eastern end, **BUDLEIGH SALTERTON** is the apotheosis of Devon respectability. The motto on its coat of arms, "Beau Sejour" ("Have a good stay"), has been taken to heart by the legions of elderly folk who have settled here permanently, giving the place a slow, somnolent feel. Budleigh Salterton takes its name from the salterns, or salt-pans, in which monks evaporated seawater during the thirteenth century. These have long disappeared, and the town's economy has since been based on the sea. In the twentieth century, Budleigh's whitewashed cottages and houses attracted such figures as Noël Coward and P.G. Wodehouse, and it is this old-fashioned flavour which constitutes the principal charm of the place today.

The town's main road, **High Street**, is bordered at its lower end, where it becomes **Fore Street**, by a fast-flowing stream, and ends at Marine Parade, where the wide arc of beach is overlooked by one of the many nineteenth-century ornamental rustic cottages known as "cottage ornés" that are a feature of the region. Built in 1811 and sporting narrow Gothic windows, the cottage now houses the **Fairlynch Museum** (daily: Easter–Oct 2–4.30pm, plus mid-July to Aug 11am–1pm; £1), which claims to be the only thatched museum in the country. It's well worth a visit for its entertaining collection of Victorian and Edwardian costume and locally made Edwardian dolls. Geological exhibits include examples of radioactive nodules found in local cliffs, and you'll find a diverse array of historical relics in a damp, low-ceilinged "smuggler's cellar". Upstairs are beautiful examples of lace, an east Devon speciality, and there are regular demonstrations of lace-making.

The seafront below the museum still holds the wall shown in the iconic painting, *Boyhood of Raleigh*, made here by John Millais, showing a salty dog spinning a yarn to the young Walter Raleigh and his half-brother, Humphrey Gilbert, another sailor-to-be (the picture is now in London's Tate Britain gallery). The Octagon, the house where Millais stayed, stands next door to the museum. The great crescent of **beach** extending to either side from here has little of the seaside paraphernalia to be found in some of Devon's other resorts. If you're tempted to swim, you'll find the pebbles shelving quite steeply into the sea, though the currents are reasonably safe in calm weather. Tree-topped cliffs rise above the shore to the west, below which one of the oldest naturist

Budleigh Salterton

The Starcross ferry (April– Oct 10.30am– 5.30pm, plus extra crossings at 5.45pm in July and 6.15pm in Aug; £2.50 one-way, £3.20 return, bikes £1.10) runs across the estuary between Exmouth and Starcross (see p.69), and is a useful way to get to east Devon (or vice versa) without going to Exeter.

Budleigh Salterton and around

beaches in the country is hidden away. If that's not your scene, you'll find a few tiny, sheltered strips of sand by following the coast path two miles west of Budleigh to **Littleham Cove**. Following the beach to the east, you'll come across the windlass and cable still used to haul up small lobster- and crab-fishing boats at the mouth of the River Otter, **Otter Point**. A small, brackish wildlife reserve and reed bed in the Otter estuary lies on the landward side of the pebble-ridge here.

From here, you can follow the River Otter's banks for two miles to **OTTERTON**, a handsomely thatched and timbered village with a broad street and open stream running through the centre. The **Otterton Mill Centre** (daily mid-March to Oct 10.30am–5.30pm; Nov to mid March 11am–4pm; free) is the last working mill on the river, and allows you to view the flour-milling process. It doubles as a craft centre and venue for events and concerts throughout the year (call ☎01395/568521 to see what's on), but also makes a good stop for a wholesome snack or coffee. A signposted minor road leads the mile east from Otterton to **Ladram Bay**, a secluded pebbly beach sheltered by woods and beautifully eroded cliffs. Though somewhat marred by the nearby caravan site, it's a lovely spot for a swim, but gets mightily crowded in summer.

Less than two miles north of Budleigh Salterton on the B3178, **EAST BUDLEIGH** is famed for its connection with Walter Raleigh, whose father was churchwarden at the church of **All Saints** which dominates the village. Inside you can see the family's pews (the front two on the left), as well as a collection of superbly carved sixteenth-century bench ends, said to be among the oldest in the country. Each one denotes either the arms of a local family, emblems representing local trades, or animals. Though the village claims to be Raleigh's birthplace, he was in fact born one and a half miles west in the hamlet of **Hayes Barton**.

Practicalities

At the bottom of Fore Street, Budleigh Salterton's **tourist office** (Easter–Oct Mon–Sat 10am–5pm, plus July & Aug Sun 11am–5pm; Nov–Easter Mon–Thurs & Sat 10am–1pm, Fri 10am–3pm; ☎01395/445275) has lots of information on local walking and biking routes. If you want to **stay** in the town, the best choice is the *Windrush* (☎01395/442443; ③), right on the seafront with first-class views. There are a couple of other choices here, but you'll do better venturing half a mile west of Budleigh along the Knowle Road to *Clyst Hayes* (☎01395/444033; ②), a 400-year-old working farm with beams galore and fresh produce for breakfast. Nearby, on Bear Lane, there's a good sheltered **campsite**, *Pooh Cottage* (☎01395/442354; closed Oct–April), which has a heated outdoor pool. You can also camp at the *Ladram Bay Holiday Centre* at Ladram Bay (☎01395/568398), a giant development with an indoor pool, showers, a shop and a laundrette.

The Budleigh Salterton Riding School on Dalditch Lane offers horse-back rides along the coast (☎01395/ 442035).

For **restaurants**, friendly *Mario's* on Budleigh Salterton's High Street (☎01395/443330; closed Sun & Mon) serves good fish dishes and traditional Italian fare. The *Premier Restaurant* on Chapel Street does an excellent line in inexpensive, traditional fish and chips and stocks inexpensive house wines. For superb real **ice cream**, check out the *Creamery*, just opposite the museum. Budleigh's **pubs** are generally pretty staid – if you're looking for excitement, try the *Salterton Arms* on Chapel Street, where there's live jazz on Sunday evenings in winter.

Sidmouth and around

Nestled in the Sid valley six miles east of Budleigh Salterton, cream-and-white **SIDMOUTH** is east Devon's architectural aristocrat. Characterized by its terraces with castellated parapets and Gothic windows, the town was highly rated by poet and architecture buff John Betjeman – its "silvery, pink and creamy" facades inspired him to extol "Devon Georgian" as "the simplest, gayest, lightest, creamiest Georgian of all". Sidmouth boasts nearly five hundred listed buildings, largely dating from the first forty years of the nineteenth century, when the town became popular among the upper classes after the Duke of Kent retired here in 1820; his family, including his daughter, the future Queen Victoria, moved into Woolbrook Glen, now the *Royal Glen Hotel*. What had previously been a very low-key fishing village subsequently enjoyed the fashionable patronage of such figures as the Grand Duchess Helene of Russia, sister-in-law of the tsar, and the Empress Eugénie, wife of Napoleon III.

Echoes of Sidmouth's regal connections survive today in the old-fashioned personalized service in the outfitters and stores which line the pedestrianized centre around High Street, and its continuation, Fore Street. This shopping street leads to The Esplanade, where most people end up to promenade among the deck chairs and benches which, in summer, are almost permanently occupied by people contemplating the gravelly **beach** below. Here and elsewhere in the town, wrought-iron balconies with curved canopies rise above the numerous hanging baskets and lavish flower displays which have helped make Sidmouth a multiple winner of floral awards. Though the town beach makes absorbing viewing, the best area for bathing is west of the centre at **Jacob's Ladder**, a stretch of gently shelving shingle, sandy at low tide, that's backed by crumbly red cliffs and overlooked by lush gardens and a tearoom housed in a clock tower.

The town itself holds little of specific interest, its attractions best appreciated on a leisurely amble. You can see some of Sidmouth's finest architecture along Fortfield Terrace, York Terrace and Coburg Terrace, all west of Fore Street, where the dignified white facades with covered balconies are fronted by lawns and flower beds. One curiosity near the parish church on Church Street is the **Old**

*You can get a
fuller picture
of the town's
historical and
architectural
heritage on the
free two-hour
walking tours
which leave
from the Sid
Vale Heritage
Centre on
Church Street
(Easter–Oct
Tues & Thurs
10.15am).*

*The #899 bus
(Mon–Sat)
connects
Branscombe
with Sidmouth
and Seaton
(see p.61).*

Chancel, a private house standing tall and turreted beside the bowling green. It's a bizarre concoction, made up of parts rescued from the church when the latter was remodelled in 1860, the work of a local antiquary who was appalled at what he saw as the desecration of the old building. To the original chancel, which retains its Perpendicular window, he added living quarters for himself and his family, resulting in a typically Victorian pastiche of medievalism.

Around Sidmouth, the main attraction is the **coast path**, which climbs steeply eastwards up Salcombe Hill, along cliffs that give sanctuary to a range of birdlife. You'll find plenty of places to pause for a swim or a picnic, but the best beaches are at **Weston Mouth**, about two and a half miles east of Sidmouth's Esplanade, and **Branscombe Mouth**, a couple of miles further on, where the grassy cliffs and wide, secluded stony shores are protected by the National Trust. You can also reach these beaches on signposted footpaths from the inland hamlets of **Weston** and Branscombe, themselves accessible on minor roads from Sidmouth. One of the region's loveliest villages, **BRANSCOMBE** is especially worth a wander, with thatched cottages strung along a meandering valley. In a sheltered spot below the road, the surprisingly large twelfth-century church of **St Winifred**, with its prominent Norman tower, has an unusual triple-decker pulpit from the eighteenth century and fragments of medieval wall painting. There are a couple of good pubs nearby (see opposite), and the *Sea Shanty* tearooms, once a coalyard, provides welcome refreshment right on the beach.

Practicalities

Sidmouth's **tourist office** (March & April Mon–Thurs 10am–4pm, Fri & Sat 10am–5pm, Sun 10am–1pm; May–July & Sept–Oct Mon–Sat 10am–5pm, Sun 10am–4pm; Aug Mon–Sat 10am–6pm, Sun 10am–5pm; Nov–Feb Mon–Sat 10am–1.30pm; ☎01395/516441; *www.sidmouth.gov.uk*) is on Ham Lane, off the eastern end of The Esplanade behind the lifeboat station. It sells pamphlets about the many walks in the area, and the *Blue Plaque Guide* (£2) which documents the town's historic houses. You can **rent bikes** from W.V. Fish, 71 Temple St (☎01395/512185), or Sidmouth Cycles, 110 High St (☎01395/579786).

Accommodation and eating

Sidmouth has **accommodation** to suit all pockets. One of the most stylish choices is *Woodlands Hotel*, a few minutes' walk up Station Road from The Esplanade at Cotmaton Cross (☎01395/513120; *www.woodlands-hotel.com*; ③); a large cottage orné typical of the region, with antiques in the roomy bedrooms, a conservatory and gardens. Closer to The Esplanade, *Cranmere*, 2 Fortfield Place (☎01395/513933; no credit cards; ①) is a plainer and cheaper Edwardian guesthouse with a homely atmosphere and most rooms en suite. At the bottom of this same lane, *Fortfield Hotel* (☎01395/512403; *www.fortfield-hotel.demon.co.uk*; ⑨) is at the more elite end of the scale, a spacious Edwardian pile overlooking the cricket and croquet grounds and the sea. There's an indoor pool, and the nautically themed Norske bar pays tribute to the owners' Norwegian roots. If these central options are booked up, try *Kyneton Cottage*, in a quiet location in its own grounds a mile or so back from The Esplanade at 87 Alexandria Rd (☎01395/513213; *june@kyneton.freeserve.co.uk*; no credit cards; ②). Rooms are pleasantly furnished, and substantial breakfasts are served.

All **campsites** are located east of Sidmouth, along or off the A3052; none are served by public transport, so you'll need to take a taxi or tackle the uphill walk if you don't have your own transport. The nearest is *Salcombe Regis Camping and Caravan Park* (☎01395/514303; *info@salcombe-regis.co.uk*; closed Nov–Easter), a mile and a half away and within view of the sea, with level pitches and good general facilities including a shop.

With most of the hotels and guesthouses serving evening meals, there's not a great choice of **restaurants** in Sidmouth. However, you can get very reasonable seafood and vegetarian salads at *Brown's Bistro* on Fore Street (closed Sun); the inexpensive *Mocha Restaurant* on The Esplanade (☎01395/512882) also offers first-rate fish lunches, and opens in the evenings in July and August. For **snacks**, *Osborne's* on Fore Street offers teas, milkshakes and light meals.

Two hundred yards from the seafront, on Old Fore Street, the *Old Ship* and *Anchor* **pubs** provide excellent bar meals and suppers as well as a range of ales, but if you're looking for a more local feel, try the *Radway* on the corner of Salcombe Road, which also serves bar meals. **In Branscombe**, the ivy-clad *Mason's Arms* serves fresh crab and spit-roast specialities, while the fourteenth-century *Fountain Head* has a good range of meals and snacks as well as real ale.

Sidmouth International Festival

Held over eight days at the beginning of August, The **Sidmouth International Festival**, with its diverse range of musicians, characterful venues and excellent locale, is widely considered to be one of the country's best **folk festivals**. Over 600 folk and roots acts from around the world, as well as dance and theatre companies, take over venues from the Arena Theatre to various pubs and parks, while punters are accommodated in a capacious campsite outside Sidmouth with shuttle buses to the centre laid on. **Ticket prices** range from £29 per day to £56 for the weekend or £140 for the whole week, with an £8 per night supplement for camping (£40 for the week). Tickets for individual performances are also available on the day, but it's always worth booking early. For more details, visit the festival Web site (*www.mrscasey.co.uk/sidmouth*), or call the box office (☎01296/433669) or the tourist office (see opposite).

Beer and around

Seven miles east of Sidmouth, and two miles east of Branscombe, the fishing village of **BEER** is one of the gems of the Devon coast. Its allure derives largely from its location, huddled in a narrow cove between gleaming white headlands, with a gargling stream running through its centre within a deep conduit that's lined with tubs of flowers. Hardly surprisingly, the village has become a tourist honeypot in recent years, and you're best off skipping it altogether in high summer when the place is bursting at the seams. Free of congestion, however, it still manages to work its charm, with the core of the village seemingly unchanged from the time when it was a smugglers' eyrie, the local inlets used by such characters as Jack Rattenbury, whose famous exploits were chronicled in his 1837 book *Memoirs of a Smuggler*. Lace-making was a more legitimate local industry, though there is precious little left apart from the specimens in the gift shops which, along with antique shops, potteries and galleries, crowd the main Fore Street. At the bottom of this, Beer's attractive shingle **beach** is dotted with painted wooden bathing huts and walled by the white cliffs which provided shelter for the local fishing fleet. Vessels are still winched up here, alongside the odd-looking rubber conveyor-belt mats laid across the stones to provide easy walking. If you're taking a dip, be aware that the shore shelves steeply under the water.

*The name Beer
has nothing to
do with the
drink, but is a
corruption of
the old English
word* bearu
*meaning small
wood.*

A mile or so west of the village, the signposted **Beer Quarry Caves** (daily: Easter–Sept 10am–6pm; Oct 11am–5pm; last entry 1hr before closing; £4.25) are the main attraction hereabouts, allowing visitors to penetrate deep into the rock. The quarries, which include vast chambers and narrow tunnels, were worked continuously from Roman times until 1900, and the extracted **Beer stone** has been used in countless Devon churches and houses, and also went into the construction of Exeter and Winchester cathedrals as well as Westminster Abbey, St Paul's Cathedral and the Tower of London. Its chief virtues are its malleability when newly quarried (it hardens on exposure) and its smooth texture, combining to make it an ideal medium for monuments, screens and tracery. A walking tour of the complex takes an hour or so (bring a sweater); guides lead you through a chapel 200ft underground and point out the etched signatures of quarrymen going back to the year of Queen Victoria's accession. The enormous scale of the excavations seems all the more remarkable when you consider that it was all created by hand; old mining tools and pieces carved by medieval masons are on display in a small exhibition near the entrance.

Back on the coast, the **cliff path** can be followed on either side of Beer, soaring above stony beaches. To the south, the path climbs for a mile up to **Beer Head**, a majestic 426ft vantage point at the most westerly end of the south coast's white cliffs. From here, you have the choice of sticking to the clifftop or descending to an area known as **Hooken Undercliff**, the result of a landslip in 1790 and now a thickly grown wilderness that provides sanctuary for birds and other wildlife as well as a means of accessing the beach.

Following the coast path eastwards from Beer, a smooth stroll of less than a mile brings you round Seaton Bay to the resort of **SEATON**. With its useful harbour, the town was strategically important to the Romans and subsequently to the Saxons and Danes, who launched inland invasions from this deep inlet. Fishing was always important here, but the town's character today stems from its development as a spa and holiday destination after the railway arrived in 1868. It's not a particularly inviting place nowadays, the mile-long pebbly beach backed by a promenade that mutates from a placid, slow-moving haven at its western end to a much gaudier affair to the east, where there's a large and dominating sea wall. However, there are some attractive gardens interspersed between Seaton's Victorian and Edwardian architecture, which can be viewed from the much-touted **Seaton Tramway**, running from the terminus on Harbour Road (adjacent to the tourist office) to the villages of **Colyford** and **Colyton** two miles north (£5 return; 25min). It's touristy but still a pleasant ride through the verdant Axe valley: a variety of trams dating back to 1906 are in use; most are open-topped but enclosed versions operate in bad weather.

Beer and around

Beer attracts huge crowds during Regatta Week, in mid-August, accompanied by such shenanigans as barrel-rolling down Fore Street, and during the mid-October annual Rhythm and Blues Festival.

Practicalities

Information on Beer and Seaton can be obtained at Seaton's **tourist office** in the main car park on Harbour Road (April–Oct Mon–Sat 10am–5pm, plus July & Aug Sun 1.30–5.30pm; Nov–March Mon–Fri 10am–2pm; ☎01297/21660; *www.eastdevon.net/tourism/ seaton*).

Accommodation in Beer is usually full in summer, when early booking is strongly advised. The best-value B&B is *Bay View* on Fore Street (☎01297/20489; closed Nov–Easter; no credit cards; ①), whose comfortable rooms overlook the sea. One hundred yards from the beach on the same street, the *Dolphin Hotel* (☎01297/21542, no credit cards; ①) offers a quirky antique atmosphere, with every surface covered with Victorian pictures, old posters and crazy mirrors, and bedrooms decorated with Victorian furnishings. East Devon's only **youth hostel** is situated on a hillside half a mile northwest of Beer, at Bovey Combe (☎01297/20296; *www.yha.org.uk*; closed Nov–March); beds cost £10.85. To get there, walk up Fore Street as far as the Townsend Garage and turn off the signposted track on the right. Guests get day-access to a kitchen and lounge. **Campers** will find *Beer Head Caravan Park* (☎01297/21107; closed Nov–March) beautifully sited and easily reached along Common Lane, by the *Anchor Inn* at the bottom of Fore Street. If you want to **stay in Seaton**, opt for *Beach End* (☎01297/23388; closed Nov–March; ②), a bright and roomy

For more on the Seaton Tramway, call ☎01297 /20375 or log on to www.tram.co.uk

Honiton

Across Seaton Bridge and the Axe estuary, the coast stretches six hilly miles beyond Axmouth to Lyme Regis in Dorset, a bracing route for walkers with another chance to see an area of undercliffs.

Edwardian B&B on Trevelyan Road, at the far end of The Esplanade on the eastern edge of town.

If you're looking for somewhere **to eat in Beer**, you can't do better than *Simon the Pieman* for award-winning pasties, pies and pâtés, while *Bumbles* is a bistro which offers crab sandwiches and cream teas during the day – both are on the main Fore Street. *Ducky's Café*, shaded under umbrellas on the beach, gives excellent value for its generous snacks, while the *Anchor Inn*, further down Fore Street, has a garden for beer and snacks and is probably the best place for local reasonably priced fish suppers; make sure to book in high season (☎01297/20386). **In Seaton**, the *Fisherman's* pub on Marine Crescent serves tasty food all day, and has sea views and an open fire in winter.

Honiton

Most easily reached by public transport on the #340 bus from Sidmouth or by train from Exeter, the market town of **HONITON** is the biggest centre in inland east Devon. Once an important coaching stop on the London to Exeter road, with as many as thirty-five coaching inns, it was also famed as the most rotten of the parliamentary "rotten boroughs", when the purchasing of votes was commonplace among the small electorate – a practice stopped by the 1832 Reform Act. A couple of disastrous fires in the eighteenth century destroyed most of the town's medieval fabric, replacing it with the fine redbrick Regency houses visible today, solid evidence of the prosperity enjoyed by the local merchants from the local wool industry in the seventeenth and eighteenth centuries, and later from **lace** (see box, opposite). More recently the town has become an important centre of the antiques trade, accounting for its thirty-odd quality antiques shops. The best days to visit are Tuesday and Saturday, when general **markets** throng the broad High Street; the cattle market on Silver Street also takes place each Tuesday.

In the High Street, Honiton's chief attraction is **Allhallows Museum** (April–Sept Mon–Fri 10am–5pm, Sat 10am–1.30pm; Oct Sat 10am–1.30pm; £2; *www.cyberlink.co.uk/allhallows*), housed in the oldest building in town, a fourteenth-century chapel later used as a schoolroom and dining hall and now holding three galleries stuffed with examples of the fine lace with which Honiton is synonymous. It's a comprehensive, informative and well-presented collection, and sections on other aspects of the town's history will appeal to those immune to the fascinations of lace. Prehistoric artefacts are displayed in the **Murch Gallery**, including the bones of the Honiton Hippos, which date back some 100,000 years and were found during the construction of the town's bypass. There are also absorbing exhibits relating to other local industries such as pottery, cream-making and whetstone-making. Lace-lovers should make a beeline for the **Norman Gallery**, which shows examples of Honiton lace

Honiton Lace

Lace has been made in Honiton and the surrounding area for over 400 years. The industry originated in the sixteenth century when Flemish refugees introduced the craft, and escalated in importance when parliament forbade the import of foreign-made lace at the end of the seventeenth century. Requiring as much as ten hours to produce one square inch, the product was much in demand throughout this period and provided employment for half of the town's population. Merchants paid the lacemakers – mainly women and girls – to work at home, and then either sold the finished product in their shops or sent it on to London and beyond. It was primarily used as costume lace – for collars, cuffs, edgings and wedding veils – and was chosen to embellish Queen Victoria's wedding dress in 1839 (at a cost of £1000); the christening gown made for her eldest son, the future King Edward VII, in 1841, is still used by the Royal Family today.

Although there's been no commercial production since the beginning of the twentieth century, many locals still make lace as a hobby and some will produce it to order. If you want to buy a sample, check out the Honiton Lace Shop at 44 High St, which will also sell you everything you need to do it yourself.

from 1630 onwards, and the **Nicoll Gallery**, displaying the tools of the lace trade and illustrating its history. **Lace-making demonstrations** take place here daily from June to August, less regularly in September and October.

Practicalities

Honiton's **tourist office** in Lace Walk Car Park (mid-March to mid-Sept Mon–Fri 10am–4pm, Sat 10am–1pm; mid-Sept to mid-March Mon–Sat 10am–1pm; ☎01404/43716) can supply information about local walks and cycle routes. **Bikes** can be rented from Cycle, 1 King St (☎01404/47211; *www.cycle1.co.uk*).

The town has a paltry choice of **accommodation**, with the cheapest places tucked away at the west end of High Street. *Oaklands* on Exeter Road (☎01404/442182; no credit cards; ①) is an unpretentious, good-value and homely B&B, while the *Red Cow Inn* at 43 High St (☎01404/47497; ①) has a 1930s character, basic rooms and good lunches. There are better places outside town, such as *Roebuck Farm* (☎01404/42225; no credit cards; ①), a working dairy farm in the village of Weston, one mile north of Honiton off the A30 in the Exeter direction (call ahead for directions), where you'll find an old-fashioned flavour and great value, and *Wessington Farm*, a couple of miles northwest of town on the A373, in the village of Awliscombe (☎01404/42280; *asummers@farming.co.uk*; no credit cards; ①), which has cosy rooms and great views over the Otter Valley. The only **campsite**, *Otter Valley Park* (☎01404/44546; closed Oct to late March), lies a mile from the centre, right by the bypass off the A30.

*The huge
Honiton
Agricultural
Show takes
place annually
on the first
Thursday in
August, offer-
ing diverse
entertain-
ments as well
as numerous
animals, prize
marrows and
giant runner
beans to
admire.*

You needn't wander further than the High Street for a choice of **eating options**. Among the inns, the *Red Cow* (see overleaf) offers a more upmarket atmosphere and wider menu for its bar meals than most, while bustling *Dominoes Bistro* at 178 High St, extravagantly decorated with murals, cherubs and other Parisian frippery, offers an eclectic range of reasonably priced dishes, including tasty home-made pâté, mussels and vegetarian options, and there's occasional live music in the evening.

Ottery St Mary

Five miles southwest of Honiton, **OTTERY ST MARY** sits on the banks of the River Otter in a lovely valley that runs to the sea at Budleigh Salterton (see p.55). The river was eulogized by **Samuel Taylor Coleridge** ("Dear native brook! Wild streamlet of the West!"), who was born here and whose father was local vicar from 1760 until 1781. (Ottery was also the occasional home of William Makepeace Thackeray, who set his novel *Pendennis* here). The predominantly Georgian town fans out from a medieval central hub, now comprised of elegant seventeenth-, eighteenth- and nineteenth-century houses. The street names – Jesu Street, Paternoster Row, Amen Court – evoke its ecclesiastical heritage, and the main reason for visiting today is the church of **St Mary**, sprawling on a steep hill, Cornhill, overlooking the centre of town, and displaying extravagant dimensions for such a small place. It was the work of Bishop Grandisson of Exeter, who in 1335 bought the existing church, then owned by Rouen Cathedral, and rebuilt it using Exeter cathedral as his model, copying such features as the idiosyncratic positioning of two towers over the main transept; the weathercock atop one tower is reputed to be the oldest *in situ* in Europe. In the richly decorated interior, the eye is drawn to the magnificent roof bosses and the bright colours of the roof ribs, screens and stonework, the result of a restoration in 1977 to how the original medieval colours are thought to have

---

Tar Barrelling in Ottery St Mary

If possible, try and time your visit to Ottery to coincide with Guy Fawkes Day, November 5, when instead of fireworks, the ancient ritual of **Tar Barrelling** takes place. The practice is thought to have originated in the seventeenth century with the aim of ridding the streets of the devil. Each pub sponsors a wooden barrel, which is soaked in tar for about three days before the event; women and children have smaller versions, men the larger. The barrels are then set alight and carried on the back through the town until the flames die down. The evening starts with the smallest barrels, with the last and biggest specimen carried around the square at midnight. A huge bonfire is lit at the lower end of town, a funfair adds to the merriment, and the drink flows freely, with ambulances at the ready to attend to any of the twenty-thousand-odd crowd who happen to get in the way of a flaming barrel.

looked. The Dorset aisle, added in the early sixteenth century, boasts intricate fan-vaulting and corbel heads showing images of an owl, an elephant and the pagan figure of the Green Man. Look out, too, for the astronomical clock in the south transept, one of the oldest still in working order, possibly dating from Grandisson's reconstruction.

Practicalities

Ottery's **tourist office** is at 10b Broad St, downhill from the church off Silver Street (April to early Nov Mon–Fri 9.30am–4.30pm, plus July & Aug Sat 10am–1pm; late Nov to March Tues & Fri 9.30am–4.30pm; ☎01404/813964). There are some good **accommodation** choices, such as the Georgian *Normandy House* (☎01404/811088; ③), with cosy, fully-equipped rooms – some looking towards the church – a good bistro, and a quiet terraced garden to relax in. The soothing all-white rooms at *Chanter's Lodge* in Hind Street (☎01404/815925; no credit cards; ①), on the northern outskirts of town, are part of a natural-health centre, and there are oils on hand in the rooms for relaxing baths. One and a half miles south of town on the Sidmouth Road, *Fluxton Farm Hotel* (☎01404/812818; ②) is a lovely sixteenth-century farmhouse with en-suite rooms looking onto spacious gardens which hold a putting green and accommodation for 40-odd cats – for human guests, bookings are not accepted between Monday and Thursday in winter.

You can **eat** well in the elegant *Normandy House Bistro* (see above; closed Sun–Tues), which uses vegetables from its own garden for its Mediterranean-influenced menu, or in the *Tumbling Weir*, which offers moderately priced, more traditional English dishes, with a good selection of seafood and game. For inexpensive lunches or teas try *Seasons* at 9 Silver St (closed Sun & Mon), where all cakes and pastries are home-made.

Bikes can be rented from Browns Motorcycles, 89 Mill St (☎01404/ 813853); as there's only limited stock, it's wise to book ahead.

Travel details

Trains

Exmouth to: Exeter (Mon–Sat every 30min, Sun hourly; 30min).

Buses

Beer to: Branscombe (Mon–Fri 4 daily, Sat 2 daily; 15min); Exeter (Mon–Sat 5 daily; 1hr); Seaton (Mon–Fri hourly, Sat 7 daily; 10min); Sidmouth (Mon–Fri 8 daily, Sat 4 daily, Sun 3 daily; 35min).

Branscombe to: Beer (Mon–Fri 5 daily, Sat 3 daily; 15min); Sidmouth (Mon–Fri 4 daily, Sat 2 daily; 20min).

Budleigh Salterton to: Exeter (every 20min; 1hr); Exmouth (every 20min; 16min); Sidmouth (Mon–Sat 3 daily; 1hr).

Exmouth to: Budleigh Salterton (Mon–Sat every 20min, Sun 2 hourly; 15min); Exeter (every 20min; 35min); Sidmouth (Mon–Sat hourly, Sun 3 daily; 50min); Topsham (every 20min; 16min).

Honiton to: Exeter (Mon–Sat 6 daily, Sun 3 daily; 55min); Ottery St Mary

(Mon–Sat 6 daily, Sun 3 daily; 15min); Seaton (Mon–Sat 4 daily; 45min); Sidmouth (Mon–Sat 8 daily, Sun 3 daily; 40min).

Ottery St Mary to: Exeter (Mon–Sat 1–2 hourly, Sun 3 daily; 40min); Honiton (Mon–Sat 6 daily, Sun 3 daily; 10min); Sidmouth (Mon–Sat 5 daily; 30min).

Seaton to: Beer (Mon–Fri hourly, Sat 7 daily; 10min); Exeter (Mon–Sat 6 daily; 1hr 5min); Honiton (Mon–Sat 4 daily; 45min); Sidmouth (Mon–Fri 9 daily, Sat 4 daily, Sun 5 daily; 30–45min).

Sidmouth: Beer (Mon–Fri 7 daily, Sat 4 daily, Sun 3 daily; 20–35min); Branscombe (Mon–Fri 5 daily, Sat 3 daily; 20min); Exeter (Mon–Sat every 30min, Sun hourly; 40min); Exmouth (Mon–Sat hourly, Sun 3 daily; 50min); Honiton (Mon–Sat 7 daily, Sun 3 daily; 30min); Ottery St Mary (Mon–Sat 5 daily; 35min); Seaton (Mon–Fri 9 daily, Sat 4 daily, Sun 6 daily; 30–45min).

Topsham to: Exeter (every 20min; 20min); Exmouth (every 20min; 25min).

Chapter 3

South Devon

S outh of Exeter, the wedge of land between Dartmoor and the sea is one of Devon's most picturesque, a rich agricultural region that backs onto a hugely diverse range of coastal resorts. **Dawlish** and **Teignmouth** have retained a sober, small-scale appeal, while the holiday industry is intense around **Tor Bay**, a ten-mile stretch curving between the two promontories of Hope's Nose and Berry Head. Torbay is also the collective name for the towns of **Torquay**, **Paignton** and **Brixham**; of these, the first is the standard-bearer, and, with its marina and long seafront offering sparkling views across the bay, is the one which most closely measures up to the **"English Riviera"** moniker optimistically attached to Torbay by its PR wizards.

Inland of the Torbay conurbation, things get much quieter around **Totnes**, a historic riverside town which makes an agreeable base for exploring the whole region. From here you can take boats or buses eight miles downstream to the classic estuary town of **Dartmouth**, a great place to eat fish and explore the river mouth on foot. There are some enticing beaches hereabouts, particularly those at **Start Bay** to the southwest, where a wildlife reserve and the rocky headland of **Start Point** deserve lengthy exploration on foot.

The intensely rural region of the **South Hams** extends southwest of the River Dart as far as Plymouth, cleft by a splay of rivers flowing off Dartmoor. At the mouth of the Kingsbridge estuary, the attractive sailing resort of **Salcombe** makes the best base for trips around the estuary and the dramatic coast on either side of it, from where there's a fairly good chance of spotting dolphins or basking sharks out to sea. To the west, the coast path gives access to some choice beaches dotted around **Bigbury Bay**.

Trains from Exeter to Plymouth run down the coast as far as Teignmouth before striking inland for Totnes – to get to Torbay, you may have to change at Newton Abbot. For the hinterland and points south and west along the coast, you can rely on a network of **buses** from Torquay and Totnes, and the latter is also linked to Dartmouth by **river ferries**.

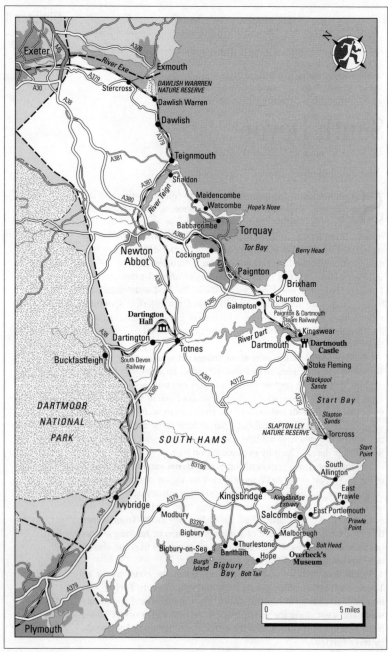

© Crown copyright

Dawlish, Teignmouth and Torbay

South of Exeter, train passengers are afforded good estuary views, while road-users following the A379 touch the shore only at the small village of Starcross and, south of the estuary mouth, at **Dawlish**, a modest resort of Regency and Victorian buildings with a low-key appeal; most of the interest for beach buffs or naturalists, however, lies north of town at **Dawlish Warren**, on the mouth of the Exe estuary. Four miles south, the river port of **Teignmouth** provides a livelier take on seaside atmosphere.

Making the most of the bay's sheltered climate and exuberant vegetation, **Torbay** is the main tourist mecca in these parts, and accordingly holds the thickest concentration of **accommodation**. Despite the "Riviera" tag, the area has a quintessentially English feel, dotted with golf courses and pervaded by a blend of traditional gentility and knockabout seaside atmosphere. The jewel in the tiara, **Torquay** has the strongest echoes of some balmier southern shore, even without the endless strings of fairy lights which are *de rigueur* hereabouts, and is lent a dynamic edge by the full-on club culture which has recently established itself. **Paignton**, on the other hand, has been assigned the role of a rather bland family resort, while **Brixham** is a genuine fishing port enlivened by arcades and fish-and-chip shops. The best **beaches** are found at the northern end of Tor Bay, notably the cliff-backed strands at **Anstey's Cove** and **Babbacombe**.

Connected to the main Exeter–Plymouth line by a branch line from Newton Abbot, Torbay is the centre of a good network of **public transport**, with frequent local buses connecting its various parts.

For more on bus passes, see Basics, p.7.

The Starcross Ferry provides easy access across the Exe Estuary from Starcross to Exmouth in East Devon; see p.35 for details.

Dawlish, Teignmouth and around

A couple of miles south of the Exe estuary, small and sedate **DAWLISH** is a typical Devon seaside resort that was favoured by nineteenth-century holiday-makers, but today pales in comparison to the flashier resorts further south. The sand and shingle town **beach** runs alongside a granite railway viaduct built by Brunel, and though the passing trains contribute occasional excitement, you'll find more seclusion at the broader, cliff-backed beach at **Coryton Cove**, a few minutes' walk south. The best bathing, however, is around the mouth

*The opening
hours of the
Dawlish
Warren inter-
pretation cen-
tre can be
irregular in
winter.*

*Fast currents
make all
swimming
around the
mouth of the
Teign risky,
though
Teignmouth's
main beach is
safe enough.*

*On
Wednesdays
between May
and
September,
Shaldon resi-
dents don eigh-
teenth-century
garb to com-
memorate an
attack at the
hands of the
French in
1690; stalls sell
trinkets and
food, and there
are free enter-
tainments in
the evening.*

of the Exe estuary, where dune-backed sands slope gently down to the sea at **DAWLISH WARREN**. Caravan parks have colonized large portions of the area, but you only need walk a few hundred metres north or south to find a little more solitude. To the north, a sandy spit jutting into the estuary holds the **Dawlish Warren National Nature Reserve**, harbouring a range of wildfowl and wading birds as well as a huge variety of flowering plants, mosses, liverworts and lichens (see Contexts, p.323). You can get some background at the **interpretation centre** (April–Sept daily 10.30am–5pm; Oct–March Sat & Sun 10.30am–5pm), but the best way to take it all in is by joining a two- to three-hour **guided walk** conducted by the reserve's wardens. These usually take place twice a week in summer, and once a month in winter; to check days and times, consult the list at the interpretation centre or call ☎01626/863980.

Three miles down the coast from Dawlish at the mouth of the Teign, **TEIGNMOUTH** (pronounced "Tinmuth") is a larger, more graceful affair. On the seafront, to either side of the pier that once segregated male and female bathers, the narrow, unexceptional bathing beach is backed by **The Den**, a tidy swath of lawns and flower beds interspersed with tennis courts, bowling greens and miniature golf courses. Overlooking the gardens are some of the town's most elegant Georgian and Victorian villas, several dating from the town's evolution as one of Devon's first seaside resorts at the end of the eighteenth century. Until that time, the town was primarily concerned with the export of granite – transported downriver from Dartmoor – from its port in the estuary just south of The Den. There's still a thriving **harbour** here, and this estuary side of town is the most interesting part, with a clutter of boats moored in the river and fishing vessels hauled up onto the pebble **Back Beach**, where the water is too oily to invite taking a dip. From here, you can cross the estuary to **SHALDON** via a passenger **ferry** (80p, bikes free), which operates from 8am to 6pm during the week and from 9am at the weekends, with the last service posted up on a board at the departure point; crossings are also increased throughout the summer. If you're driving, take the road bridge further upstream. A daintier and more sequestered version of Teignmouth, sheltered under the Ness headland, Shaldon is often bypassed by the seasonal crowds, but the tidy labyrinth of lanes off The Strand and Middle Street invite a brief wander, and the steep slopes of the Ness (reached from Marine Parade) offer excellent estuary views. Below the promontory, you can reach a cliff-backed strip of sand via a tunnel bored through the rock by a local landowner in the early nineteenth century. The beach is cut off at high tide.

Practicalities

Frequent #85 and #85a **buses** connect Exeter with Dawlish, Dawlish Warren, Teignmouth and Torquay, both Dawlish and

Teignmouth are served by **trains** on the Exeter–Paignton branch line, with centrally located stations, and Dawlish Warren is served by the main London–Penzance line. Dawlish has a **tourist office** in the gardens behind the viaduct (Mon–Sat 9am–1pm & 2–5pm, plus July & Aug Sun 9am–1pm & 2–5pm; ☎01626/863589), while Teignmouth's is directly behind the pier (June–Sept Mon–Sat 9.30am–5.30pm, Sun 10.30am–3.30pm; Oct–May Mon–Sat 9am–1pm & 1.45–5pm; ☎01626/779769). Both have information on town walks, water sports and the like, and can supply maps and accommodation lists.

If you choose to **stay in Dawlish**, head for the quietly elegant rooms at *Walton Guest House*, a Georgian building five minutes from the seafront on Plantation Terrace (☎01626/862760; no credit cards; ②). **Teignmouth** has a much greater choice, ranging from spacious, well-equipped rooms at the centrally located *Seaway Guest House*, 27 Northumberland Place (☎01626/879024; *www.welcome.to/seaway*; ①), to the much fancier *Thomas Luny House*, an impressive Georgian villa on Teign Street, near Back Beach (☎01626/772976; no smoking; no credit cards; ⑤); it's beautifully furnished, with books and flowers in the rooms, and has an enclosed garden. The nearest **campsite** to Teignmouth is the *Coast View Holiday Park*, a half-mile outside Shaldon on the main A379 south (☎01626/872392; closed Nov–Easter). In a sheltered spot half a mile from the sea at Dawlish Warren, *Leadstone Camping* (☎01626/872239; *www.leadstonecamping. co.uk; closed mid-Sept to mid-June*) offers the most appealing site in the area.

For **food and drink**, Teignmouth's alleys unearth atmospheric old pubs such as the *Ship Inn* on Queen Street, overlooking the harbour, while the *Harbour Lights* opposite provides an alternative to pub food, with seafood salads and other snacks on the menu. At Shaldon, the quaint *Ferryboat Inn* on The Strand provides excellent liquid or solid sustenance and has a terrace offering harbour views.

Torquay and around

Five miles south of the Teign estuary mouth, **TORQUAY** owes much of its appeal to its combination of hills and extensive palm-planted seafront from which views take in the whole of Tor Bay. The sheltered location and comparatively clement weather were factors in its elevation from a group of fishermen's cottages to an important naval base during the Napoleonic Wars, and Napoleon himself was a visitor – though without setting foot on land – when he was held for seven weeks aboard the HMS *Bellerophon* in Tor Bay following his defeat at Waterloo. Torquay then became a fashionable haven for invalids – among them the consumptive Elizabeth Barrett Browning, who spent three years here 1839–41 – a process accelerated by the extension of the railway from Newton Abbot in 1848. In more recent times the town has been associated with crime-writer Agatha Christie

The only place for bike rental in the area is at Dawlish Warren, from Breaking Wind on Beach Road (☎07970/183299).

(see box on p.76) and the fictional TV hotelier Basil Fawlty, whose jingoism and injured pride perfectly encapsulate Torquay's forced adaptation to the demands of mass tourism.

The Mediterranean myth as promoted by the tourist bosses doesn't stretch very far today, and evaporates altogether on a Friday or Saturday night when the town centre is stalked by bands of under-20s and the streets are awash with drink (usually having already passed through the body). However, even if you're not taken in by the clichés, nor particularly thrilled by the prospect of

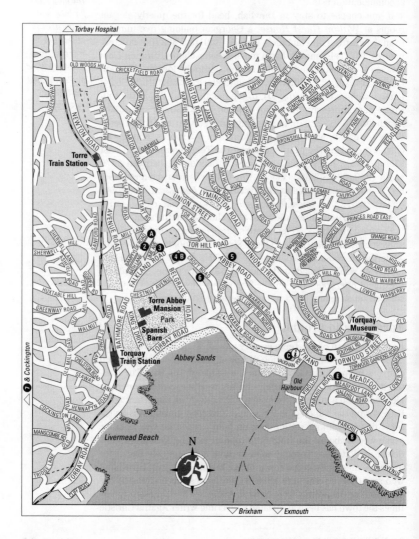

boisterous bars, Torquay has a subtle appeal, especially away from the seafront and commercial centre. The hilly residential areas reveal creamy villas on quietly elegant streets, with greenery and sea views all around, and the town also offers south Devon's two best **museums**, one located within Torbay's most noteworthy historical building, **Torre Abbey Mansion**. Activity enthusiasts will find the full range of waterskiing, surfing and sailing facilities at nearby coves and **beaches**, many of which are reachable via pleasant coastal walks.

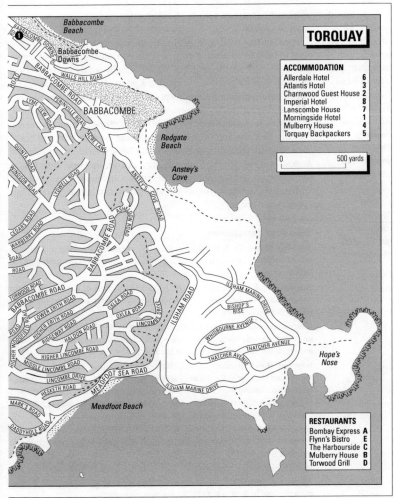

TORQUAY

ACCOMMODATION

Allerdale Hotel	6
Atlantis Hotel	3
Charnwood Guest House	2
Imperial Hotel	8
Lanscombe House	7
Morningside Hotel	1
Mulberry House	4
Torquay Backpackers	5

0   500 yards

RESTAURANTS

Bombay Express	A
Flynn's Bistro	E
The Harbourside	C
Mulberry House	B
Torwood Grill	D

© Crown copyright

Arrival, information and accommodation

Torquay's main **train station** lies a mile west of the centre on Rathmore Road, while another stop, Torre Station, lies a mile further north at the top of Avenue Road. Most **buses** stop at the Old Harbour, including the #X80 connecting with Totnes and Plymouth, the frequent #12 and #12A service linking Torquay with Paignton and Brixham, and the hourly #X46 **bus** between Exeter and Torquay. The **tourist office** is also at the Old Harbour, on Vaughan Parade (late May to Sept Mon–Sat 9.30am–6pm, Sun 10am–6pm; Oct to late May Mon–Sat 9.30am–5.15pm; ☎0906/680 1268), and can provide the full gamut of maps, accommodation and transport listings and wads of information on local attractions and entertainments.

Torquay has dozens of **accommodation** choices, but you'll still need to book in advance during peak season. Most of the hotels nearest the sea are large and glitzy places, usually wildly expensive and often booked by groups, but there's a good selection of reasonably priced places concentrated on specific streets in the higher reaches of town. The friendly, independent *Torquay Backpackers* **hostel**, 119 Abbey Rd (☎01803/299924) is fully equipped with washing and cooking facilities and even a sauna. Private doubles (①) and bunkbeds (£8) are available, but you should book well ahead in July and August. Outside town, you can stay nearer the best beaches at Babbacombe, a mile north of the centre, or enjoy rural peace at Cockington, a mile to the west. Both places are linked by good bus services to Torquay.

The best of Torquay's summer festivals are week-long Aquaculture in July, featuring concerts, theatre, films and comedy, and, in August, the Torbay Royal Regatta, the Festival of Street Music (mainly Brazilian samba) and the Riviera Jazz Festival. Contact the tourist office for further details of all these events.

Hotels and guesthouses

Allerdale Hotel, Croft Rd ☎01803/292667. A pleasantly situated Victorian mansion with an extensive, well-kept garden and views over the town and Tor Bay. ③.

Atlantis Hotel, 68 Belgrave Rd ☎01803/292917. Best of the bunch on this row, with a flower-bedecked front garden and spacious, though fairly ordinary, rooms. No credit cards. ①.

Charnwood Guest House, 8 Bampfylde Rd ☎01803/293879. Bright rooms, low rates, friendly management and set in a quiet terrace packed with B&Bs and small hotels, between Belgrave Rd and the train station. ①.

Imperial Hotel, Parkhill Rd ☎01803/294301. One of Devon's swankiest hotels, and the model for the *Majestic* in Agatha Christie's novels, this sumptuous palace dating from the 1860s has all the aristocratic trimmings and loads of period atmosphere. The Palm Court Room makes a grand setting for afternoon tea, overlooking the whole bay. ⑧.

Lanscombe House, Cockington ☎01803/606938. Solid old country house above a tea-garden in this preserved village, with thoroughly comfortable and spacious rooms. ②.

Morningside Hotel, Babbacombe Downs, Babbacombe ☎01803/327025. The nicest of a row of hotels in Babbacombe with views over the bay, just minutes from the beach. Rooms are chintzy but spacious. ③.

Mulberry House, 1 Scarborough Rd ☎01803/213639. Four light and airy rooms above an excellent restaurant (see p.78) with antique pine furnishings, crisp bed-linen and "all-body" showers in the attached bathrooms. No smoking. ③.

The town

Torquay is liveliest around the **Old Harbour**, where the quayside shops and cafés attract a mêlée of idling crowds during the day. The marina here is packed with pleasure craft, and in the summer, stalls advertise **boat trips** as far as Dartmouth and the Dart river (£8) and Exmouth (£7). To the south, limestone cliffs sprinkled with white high-rise hotels and apartment blocks separate the harbour area from Torquay's broad main beach, **Abbey Sands**, good for chucking a frisbee about but too busy in summer for serious relaxation. The beach takes its name from **Torre Abbey**, founded in 1196 and the chief power in these parts until it was razed by Henry VIII in 1539. Only the gatehouse, tithe barn, chapter house and tower survived, and now form part of the **Abbey Mansion** (Easter–Oct daily 9.30am–6pm, last admission 5pm; £3), a seventeenth- and eighteenth-century construction tucked out of sight behind the ornamental gardens adjoining the beachside Torbay Road. It currently holds the mayor's office and, in a suite of period rooms, the municipal galleries, containing a fine collection of silver, glass, sculpture and minutely detailed marine paintings by Thomas Luny, who lived and worked in Teignmouth, as well as a small but eclectic choice of twentieth-century art – a refreshing modern interlude among all the antiques. Other highlights include a series of Pre-Raphaelite window designs by Edward Burne-Jones and proof copies of William Blake's haunting illustrations for the Book of Job. Lastly, a small, wood-panelled room devoted to Agatha Christie (see box, overleaf) holds her typewriter and various photos.

Near the Christie room, a corridor leads to the well-preserved old **Gatehouse**, a square crenellated structure best appreciated from outside. You have to leave the main building anyway to see the handsome brick **Spanish Barn** just beyond it, named after the 397 Spanish prisoners captured from one of the Armada warships and held here in July 1588. Beautifully restored, it's now used for free exhibitions and occasional concerts and plays. On the north side of the house are the minimal remains of the abbey and cloisters; more enticing are the sultry Palm and Cactus houses, which provide useful heat and shelter in bad weather.

In contrast to the finery of Abbey Mansion, **Torquay Museum**, a few minutes uphill from the harbour at 529 Babbacombe Rd (Easter–Oct Mon–Sat 10am–4.45pm, Sun 1.30–4.45pm; Nov–Easter Mon–Fri 10am–4.45pm; £2), holds more down-to-earth but no less absorbing local miscellany, with displays on everything from natural history to life during World War II. However, most visitors are here primarily for the large space devoted to **Agatha**

www.the englishriviera .co.uk *contains information on the whole Torbay area.*

Torre Abbey grounds are free and always open; the palm and cactus houses are open daily from 9am to 3pm.

Torquay and around

Torbay's tourist offices dole out a free pamphlet which details all the local Christie connections, including a walking trail with a "murder mystery" to solve along the way.

Christie (see box above), which provides a detailed review of her life and achievements from the earliest photos of the young Agatha Miller, sister Madge, dog and "Nursie", to her writing career, represented by manuscripts, book covers and other items relating to TV and film adaptations. Apart from anything, the room is an absorbing retrospective of upper-class Torquay in the twentieth century.

Around Torquay

Between April and October a bus service (marked "Cockington") operates every 20min between Torquay's seafront (opposite the Torbay Hotel) and Cockington.

A mile west of Abbey Mansion, Torbay suddenly turns deeply rural at the showcase village of **COCKINGTON**. Though frequently overrun by crowds of strolling tourists, it's worth a brief stop if you can stomach the chocolate-box imagery, the result of an over-zealous preservation programme dating from the 1930s. There's more than a whiff of artifice, but the core of the original Saxon village can still be discerned, and the only completely modern building you'll see is the *Drum Inn*, concocted by Lutyens in 1934 in traditional thatched style as part of a much larger development project which never materialized. The main crowd-puller is **Cockington Court**, whose picturesquely landscaped grounds lie uphill to the left from the crossroads at the centre of the village. This much-remodelled house now holds a complex of craft studios and souvenir shops, and there's a glass-blowing workshop and an organic garden in the grounds; you're free to wander round. More interestingly, a grassy mound next to the house holds the parish church of **St George and St Mary**, a good-looking thirteenth to fourteenth-century red sandstone construction whose interior has a triple barrel-vaulted ceiling and a Renaissance pulpit, though the intricate wooden screen is recent. The surrounding parkland of woodland walks and lakes makes ideal picnicking country. There's also a **café** in the main building, or you can have a full meal or just a drink at the *Drum Inn*. Off Cockington Lane, *Lanscombe House* serves tea and sandwiches in its garden and also has accommodation (see p.74) – an option you might consider in order to see Cockington at its best, once the coach parties are gone.

To get to Cockington, follow Cockington Lane, a sign-posted right-hand turn-off from Torbay Road just south of the train station, which follows a stream for just under a mile through woods and meadows.

Many of Tor Bay's finest **beaches** are accessible via boats departing from the Old Harbour (see p.75), and some are also reachable on foot from here. If you're walking, follow the footpath signposted to the right from Parkhill Road (itself just southeast of the marina) round the coast and through Daddyhole Plain, a large grassy chasm in the cliff caused by a landslide that's locally attributed to the devil ("Daddy"). Path and road converge on the sea wall at **Meadfoot Beach**, traditionally the more "select" of Torquay's beaches, where Agatha Christie bathed in her youth. The pebble-and-sand strip, most of which is covered at high tide, is backed by a road with cafés and shops where you can rent boats and pedalos; Riviera Diving and Watersports (☎01803/607135) offers waterskiing, diving and windsurfing lessons and equipment rental.

Continuing east, the coast path winds to the end of Hope's Nose, the northern point of Tor Bay, and connects with Marine Drive for a while before heading north to a couple of tiny, sheltered, shingle-and-rock beaches, **Anstey's Cove** and **Redgate Beach**; both offer good bathing, but you may be jostling for elbow-room in summer. Another half mile along the coast path brings you to **Babbacombe Beach**, a long sand-and-shingle expanse where there's a pub, the *Cary Arms*, and an outdoor beachside café selling drinks, bacon baps and the like. The shallow bay provides ideal conditions for diving, and you can arrange **scuba and diving** courses with Divers Down, which operates from the café here in summer, and also has an office at 139 Babbacombe Rd, Babbacombe (☎01803/327111; *www.diversdown.co.uk*).

You can arrange horse riding with Cockington Riding Stables (☎01803/ 606860), just beyond the Drum Inn.

You can also reach Babbacombe beach water-taxis from Torquay's Old Harbour (£3.50 single or return), which carry on to **Oddicombe Beach**, a few minutes' walk north round the bay. Slightly more developed, this arc of sand and stone offers floats, pedalos and motor boats for rent, as well as deckchairs and free changing cabins. Northwards, you can press on a mile or two to the more secluded sand-and-shingle beaches in cliff-backed coves at **Watcombe** and

Maidencombe, both also reachable on bus #85 from the centre of Torquay. Alternatively, a **cliff railway** (Easter–Sept 75p single, £1.25 return; last departure alerted by a bell at 5.25pm, or 5.55pm in July & Aug) can carry you from Oddicombe Beach to the top of the cliffs and the village of **BABBACOMBE**. Now really a suburb of Torquay (to which it's linked by buses #32, #85 and #100), it's a peaceful place with lofty views over the sea, and a choice of hotels and tea-gardens.

Eating, drinking and nightlife

Torquay's **restaurants** are of a surprisingly high standard, many serving fresh fish brought in from nearby Brixham. A selection of **pubs**, some also serving food, are listed separately alongside **clubs**. As things change fast on the nightlife scene, it's best to call ahead before you visit, or consult the free monthly events mag *What's On Southwest*.

Restaurants

We've given telephone numbers only for restaurants where you need to book a table in advance.

Bombay Express, 98 Belgrave Rd. Calling itself the southwest's "first and only original Balti House", this smart and cheerful place is also good for takeaways. Bring your own bottle. Moderate.

Flynn's Bistro, 14 Parkhill Rd ☎01803/213936. Central but quiet place serving good French provincial cuisine, with a small garden for alfresco dining in summer. Closed lunchtime and Sun. Moderate.

The Harbourside, Vaughan Parade. A handy place next to the harbour for a sit down and a snack. Coffees and cakes, plus hot meals and baguettes. Inexpensive.

Mulberry House, 1 Scarborough Rd ☎01803/213639. One of the best restaurants in south Devon, where the menu is colour-coded according to its cholesterol content. Imaginative dishes might include fresh lasagne, ragout of Devon lamb and fish tart. No smoking. Closed Mon & Tues. Moderate.

Torwood Grill, 10 Torwood St. Convenient place near the Harbour specializing in both fresh fish and steaks – prime Devon rump, sirloin and fillet. There are some vegetarian dishes and a good choice of wines and coffee liqueurs. Good-value set-price menus. Moderate.

Pubs and clubs

Claire's, 41 Torwood Ave ☎01803/211097. Popular venue for a range of dance grooves, with big-name and resident DJs in two rooms. Fri & Sat, also Wed & Thurs in summer.

Devon Arms, 29 Park Hill Rd. Tucked away in an alley near the Harbour, and quiet enough during the day, this pub can get loud and lively later on.

Hole in the Wall, Park Lane. Torquay's oldest pub, where you can drink or snack on meat and vegetarian dishes at benches on the flower-festooned cobbles; inside, there are model ships and a piano for the occasional sing-song.

The Monastery, The Knighthouse, Torwood Gardens Rd ☎01803/292929. Set in a converted church, this is probably the best of all Torquay's clubs for the dedicated dancer, but no alcohol is served. Sat only, plus a "foreign students night" every evening in July and Aug.

The Piazza, 5–6 Braddons Hill Rd West ☎01803/295212. Ex-assembly hall that's now a throbbing pub and club with comedy on Monday, live music on Thursday evening and Sunday afternoon, and DJs on Fridays and Saturdays.

Rocky's, Rock Rd, off Abbey Rd ☎01803/292279. Small, welcoming and long-established gay club. Nightly in summer, Wed–Sun in winter.

Valbonne's, Higher Union St ☎01803/290458. Varied music aimed at a smart casual crowd; jeans are only allowed on Mondays (student night). Mon, Thurs, Fri & Sat.

Venue, Torwood Street ☎01803/213903. Foam parties and mainstream dance tracks for a young crowd. Open Wed–Sat.

Listings

Bike rental Simply the Bike, 100 Belgrave Rd (☎01803/200024).

Bus information ☎01803/664500.

Car rental Hertz is located in the train station (☎01803/294786); local operators include A.J. Blacker, 141 Newton Rd (☎01803/400808), and Laburnham on Laburnham St (☎01803/292300).

Hospital Torbay Hospital, on Newton Rd (☎01803/614567) has an Accident and Emergency department.

Police South St ☎01803/841312.

Taxis Torbay Cab Company (☎01803/213521) has a stand by the Pavilion. Star Taxi (☎01803/315000) and Babbacombe Cabs (☎01803/326450) are also reliable.

Tours For local open-top bus tours (£4.25) and sightseeing trips to Plymouth and Dartmoor (£8–12), contact Wallace Arnold, Harbourside (☎01803/211729).

Paignton

Three miles south of Torquay, and not so much a rival as a poor relation, **PAIGNTON** lacks the gloss – and the pretentions – of its neighbour. Its beach, pier, arcades and other seaside amusements identify it as a family resort, though it is somewhat spoiled by the torrents of traffic flowing through. From The Esplanade, a couple of hundred yards east of the main shopping centre, lawns back on to the rather uninspiring, level pink sands of the main town **beach**. At its southern end, a small harbour nestles in the lee of the aptly named Redcliffe headland, quite a lively spot in summer with restaurants and boat tours, while to the south, the wide, shell-specked **Goodrington Sands** are the best spot for a paddle or a dip, backed by a low sea wall and a long strip of park.

A mile inland on Totnes Road, **Paignton Zoo** (daily: summer 10am–6pm; winter 10am–dusk; £7.50) is the town's most famous attraction, its 75 acres holding a Big Cat Forest (featuring endangered Asiatic lions and Sumatran tigers), a Wetland Experience and an aviary, all with hands-on displays. There's loads to see and the various habitats are imaginatively presented; the giant Reptile Tropics glasshouse, a hot and humid home for lizards, snakes and plants, is especially impressive.

Paignton

Paignton's other main attraction, **Oldway Mansion** (Mon–Sat 9am–5pm, plus Sun 2–5pm in summer; free), lies half a mile west of the town beach off Torquay Road, surrounded by lush parkland. Built by the US sewing machine tycoon Isaac Merritt Singer (1811–75), it's mostly occupied by council offices today, but owes much of its gaudily Neoclassical appearance to a 1904 restoration by Isaac's son Paris. He lived here with his mistress, the American dancer Isadora Duncan, who was famously strangled when her scarf tangled in the wheels of the car she was driving (the 1969 biopic *Isadora*, starring Vanessa Redgrave, was filmed here). The house is surrounded by an Italian garden and croquet lawn (the latter overlooked by two hilarious stone sphinxes with the heads of society ladies), while the round, red-brick Rotunda to one side once held a swimming pool, but is not now accessible. Indeed, the only trace of past glory viewable inside – and the main reason to be here – is the mansion's eye-poppingly sumptuous marble stairway, modelled on one at the palace of Versailles. It's dominated by a reproduction of a painting by Jacques-Louis David, showing Napoleon's coronation of Josephine at Notre Dame, that's said to be the largest replica of an oil painting in the world.

If you want to know more about Oldway Mansion, join one of the guided tours available on weekdays in summer 10am–1pm (£1).

Just off the staircase, the small exhibition of early Singer sewing machines is worth a glance, displayed alongside a grandfather clock cleverly modelled on Paignton's parish church, and photos and other mementos of the house's history, including photos of Isadora Duncan.

Paignton is the northern terminus of the **Paignton & Dartmouth Steam Railway** (daily June–Sept, with reduced service in April, May, Oct & Dec; ☎01803/555872; £6.10 return), which runs from the main Queen's Park train station near the harbour to Kingswear (see p.87). The accent is on Victorian nostalgia, with railway personnel in period uniforms, but even without the trappings it's a nice way to view the countryside. The line connects with Goodrington Sands before veering inland and alongside the Dart estuary, and you could make a day of it by buying a Round Robin ticket (£9.90), which also covers the ferry connection from Kingswear to Dartmouth (see p.85–88), the trip up the Dart to Totnes, and the bus from there back to Paignton.

Practicalities

Paignton's bus and train stations are opposite each other off Sands Road, five-minutes' west of the harbour. On The Esplanade, the Apollo cinema building doubles as the **tourist office** (Easter to mid-Sept daily 9.30am–6pm; mid-Sept to Easter Mon–Sat 9.30am–5pm; ☎0906/680 1268). If you want to **stay** around here, the best option is the *Riviera Backpackers Hostel*, near the sea at 6 Manor Rd (☎01803/550160), offering bunks at £8.50 (no credit cards). There are also several B&Bs on this road, though all suffer from traffic noise. For a quieter night, try *St Weonard's Hotel*, 12 Kernou Rd (☎01803/558842; ①), a small, family-run place a couple of minutes' walk from the seafront off Polsham Road, with neat, mostly en-suite rooms.

The harbour area has a few **pubs and restaurants**, including the inexpensive *Harbour Light*, where fresh fish and chips can be enjoyed within view of the boats, and the nearby *Pier Inn*, serving ales and more seafood platters in a friendly environment. The book-stall at the train station has Torbay's only **luggage deposit** (☎01803/554528; Mon–Sat 6.45am–5pm, Sun 8am–5pm; £1 per bag), and there's a **bike rental** shop, Colin Lewis Cycles, at 7 Manor Rd (☎01803/553095).

Boat tours from Torquay's Old Harbour call at Paignton and Brixham (£3.50 single or round trip).

Brixham

From Paignton, it's about five miles round the bay to **BRIXHAM**, the smallest and prettiest of the Torbay trio. Fishing has always been Brixham's lifeblood; at the beginning of the nineteenth century, it was the major fish market in the West Country, and it still supplies restaurants as far away as London. Among the trawlers moored up on the quayside is a full-size reconstruction of the **Golden Hind** (daily: March–June & Sept–Oct 9.30am–4.30pm; July & Aug 9.30am–9pm; £1.50), the surprisingly small vessel in which Francis Drake circumnavigated the world in 1577–80 – it has no connection with the port, however. From the quayside, steep lanes and stairways thread up to the older centre around Fore Street, where the bus from Torquay pulls in. At the top of Fore Street, the small **Brixham Heritage Museum**, housed in the old police station on New Road (April–Oct Mon–Fri 10am–5pm, Sat 10am–1pm; mid-Feb to March Mon–Sat 10am–1pm; £1.50; *www.brixhamheritage.org.uk*), provides an entertaining and instructive review of the town's maritime past, with displays of sail-making, tools and navigation aids. There's also some background on the Reverend Henry Francis Lyte (1793–1847), the first incumbent of the church of All Saint's in nearby Church Street and the author of the famous hymn *Abide with Me*. The tune rings out from the church's carillon each day at 8pm.

You can explore the coastline around Brixham on various boat tours; book at the Brixham Belle kiosk on the quayside (☎01803/214202).

From the harbour, it's a thirty-minute walk east to the promontory of **Berry Head**, along a path winding up from the *Berry Head House Hotel*. Fortifications built during the Napoleonic wars are still standing on this southern limit of Tor Bay, which is now a conservation area attracting colonies of nesting seabirds and affording fabulous views across the bay.

Practicalities

Brixham's **tourist office** (June to mid-Oct Mon–Sat 9.30am–6pm, Sun 10am–6pm; mid-Oct to May Tues–Sat 9.30am–5.15pm; ☎0906/680 1268) is on the quayside; **accommodation** lists are posted on the door when the office is closed. The best places

Brixham

SOUTH DEVON 81

overlook the harbour along King Street; try the *Harbour View Hotel* at no. 65 (☎01803/853052; no credit cards; ②), where all rooms are en suite but small. Two doors down, the classier *Quayside Hotel* (☎01803/855751; *www.quaysidehotel.co.uk*; ④) offers a little more space and has two bars and a restaurant. The reputedly ghost-ridden *Smugglers' Haunt* near the museum at Church Hill (☎01803/853050; *www.smugglershaunt-hotel-devon.co.uk*; ③) is creaky and cramped, but useful if everywhere else is full. Dorm beds cost £10 at *Maypool* **youth hostel** (☎01803/842444; closed Nov–March, also Sun April & Sept–Oct), four miles away outside the village of Galmpton; buses #12 or #12A, and the Paignton & Dartmouth Steam Railway (see p.80) take you as far as the village of Churston, from where it's a two-mile walk. The landscaped and fully-equipped *Hillhead* campsite (☎01803/853204; closed Nov–Easter), two and a half miles south of Brixham on the Kingswear road (bus #22 or #200), has a heated outdoor pool.

As for **eating**, Brixham offers fish and more fish, from the stalls selling cockles, whelks and mussels on the harbourside to the *Yardarms* (☎01803/858266; closed lunch time except weekends in summer), on Beach Approach off the quayside, one of Brixham's top choices for seafood; vegetarians are also catered for. Right on the quayside, the *Sprat & Mackerel* offers staple **pub** snacks, but for a more relaxed pint, head for the low-beamed *Blue Anchor* on Fore Street, which offers coal fires and real ales.

Totnes, Dartmouth and the South Hams

Known as the **South Hams**, the area between the Dart and Plym estuaries holds some of Devon's comeliest villages and most striking coastline. The chief towns of the region are all on rivers: **Dartmouth**, the most touristy but still unspoiled; **Totnes**, further up the Dart and lately a centre for therapists and crystal-gazers; and **Salcombe**, near the mouth of the Kingsbridge estuary, a pretty, steep and narrow-laned centre for seafaring folk. Dartmouth and Totnes in particular have preserved numerous relics of their medieval past – for example the slate-hung facades for which this part of south Devon is known – which help to draw the tourists, though there is nothing like the same holiday atmosphere of the Torbay area.

Outside the towns, the South Hams is a hilly patchwork of fields. The area enjoys a sheltered, mild climate (a "hamme" is a sheltered place in Old English) which encourages subtropical plants as well as the vines which produce the famous Sharpham wine. But the real beauty resides in the rocky and ever-changing sixty miles of **coastline**, making for highly scenic but occasionally exhausting walking country, particularly west of Salcombe; tourist offices can equip you with leaflets on **walks and cycling** on off-road routes. Totnes is the best centre for **train and bus connections** – most of the X80 buses from Paignton and Torquay to Plymouth make a stop here, and it's on the main Exeter–Plymouth line – while Dartmouth and Kingsbridge (which has frequent connections to Salcombe) have bus services to all other South Hams villages. First Western National (☎01752/402060) operates buses between Totnes and Kingsbridge, and run a useful Coast Path Hoppa Bus to the beaches in summer. Tally Ho! (☎01548/853081) operates an hourly service between Kingsbridge and Salcombe (Mon–Sat).

Totnes and around

Five miles inland of Torbay, **TOTNES** has an ancient pedigree, its period of greatest prosperity having taken place in the sixteenth century, when this inland port (on the west bank of the River Dart) exported cloth to France and brought back wine. Some evocative structures from that era remain, but Totnes has mellowed into a residential market town today, its warehouses converted into gentrified flats. The arcaded High Street and secretive flowery lanes have attracted some tourist overflow from nearby Torbay, but so far its allure has survived more or less intact – enough, anyway, to attract the **New Age** candles-and-crafts crowd in recent years, accounting for the town's numerous vegetarian and wholefood cafés.

Totnes centres on the long main street that starts off as Fore Street, where the **Elizabethan Museum** (April–Oct Mon–Fri 10.30am–5pm; £1.50) occupies a four-storey period house at no. 70. Packed with an entertaining assortment of domestic objects and furniture that reveal how wealthy clothiers lived at the peak of Totnes's success, it also holds a room devoted to local mathematician Charles Babbage (1791–1871), whose "analytical engine", programmed by punched cards, was the forerunner of the computer. Fort Street, and its High Street continuation, hold a number of other Elizabethan houses in an equally good state of preservation, many having acquired later facades and often a handsome covering of slate tiles. Look out for the mustard-yellow, late eighteenth-century "Gothic House", just down from the museum; and 28 High St, overhung by curious grotesque masks.

Fore Street becomes the High Street at the white and castellated **East Gate**, a heavily retouched medieval arch. Beneath it, Rampart Walk trails east along the old town walls, curling round the fifteenth-century church of **St Mary**, where an exquisitely carved stone rood screen stretches the full width of the red-sandstone building. Behind the church, the colonnaded eleventh-century **Guildhall** (April–Sept Mon–Fri 10.30am–1pm & 2–4.30pm; £1), originally the refectory and kitchen of a Benedictine priory, now houses the town's Council Chamber, which you can see together with the former jail cells and the courtroom, and a table used by Oliver Cromwell in 1634.

On Tuesday mornings from May to September, traders don Elizabethan costumes for a charity market in Marketplace, off High Street.

Totnes and around

At the top of High Street, Castle Street leads to **Totnes Castle** (April–Sept daily 10am–6pm; Oct daily 10am–5pm; Nov–March Wed–Sun 10am–1pm & 2–4pm; £1.60; EH), the town's oldest monument. It's a classic Norman structure of the motte and bailey design, with a simple crenellated keep atop a grassy mound reached along a winding path. Not much else remains other than this shell, but it's a panoramic spot, offering wide views of the town and Dart valley.

Totnes presents a very different face at river level, around Totnes Bridge, at the bottom of Fore Street. At the highest navigable point on the **River Dart** for sea-going vessels, the quaysides here, such as Steamer Quay (a right turn over the bridge), see constant activity, with boats arriving from and leaving for European destinations. North of Totnes Bridge, a riverside walk leads eventually to Dartington, first passing, near the railway bridge half a mile north of the bridge, the terminus of the **South Devon Railway**. Between April and October (but also on some other dates throughout the year; call ☎01364/642338 for details), steam trains depart from here four to eight times daily on a half-hour ride to Buckfastleigh (see p.105), on the edge of Dartmoor. The trip, costing £6.50 return, takes you past some glorious scenery, and there's a stop at **Staverton**, where there's an inn and access to the riverside path.

Between Easter and October, cruises to Dartmouth depart daily from Steamer Quay.

A walkable couple of miles north out of Totnes, both rail and river pass near the estate of **Dartington Hall** (☎01803/863073; *www.dartingtonarts.co.uk*), an arts and education centre set up in 1925 by US millionairess Dorothy Elmhirst and her husband. You can walk through the sculpture-strewn gardens, which contain an immaculately kept tiltyard and terraces, at any time and – when it's not in use – visit the fourteenth-century Great Hall, originally built for Richard II's half-brother John Holand and rescued from dereliction by the Elmhirsts. As well as the constant programmes of films, plays, concerts, dance and workshops, an annual **literature festival** takes place here in mid-July, featuring big-name writers, and there is a summer festival of mainly **classical music** from late July through to late August.

The Cider Press Centre at Dartington Hall (Easter to late Dec Mon–Sat 9.30am–5.30pm, Sun 10.30am–5.30pm; free) retails Dartington Crystal and an assortment of upmarket crafts.

Practicalities

Totnes is served by regular **trains** on the Exeter–Plymouth line, which stop at the station on Station Road, at the end of Castle Street. The **tourist office** is in the Town Mill, off The Plains at the bottom of Fore Street, near the Safeway car park (July & Aug Mon–Sat 9.30am–5pm, Sun 10am–2pm; Sept–June Mon–Sat 9.30am–5pm; ☎01803/863168). It has a small local-history exhibition upstairs, and hikers can pick up leaflets on the seventeen-mile **Dart Valley Trail** linking Totnes with Dartmouth. **Bikes** can be rented at Hot Pursuit, 4 Fore St (☎01803/865174), whose staff can advise you on good routes.

Totnes has good **accommodation** options, though these aren't always straightforward to track down. A comfortable central choice is the *Elbow Room*, opposite the castle car park on North Street (☎01803/863480; no smoking; no credit cards; ②), a converted cottage and cider press with quiet, tastefully furnished rooms. Just over the river from The Plains, the relaxed *Old Forge*, Seymour Place (☎01803/862174; no smoking; ③) is a working medieval forge with modernized rooms, a secluded walled garden and good vegetarian breakfast options. Right on The Plains, the *Royal Seven Stars Hotel* (☎01803/862125; ③) has solid, old-fashioned comforts but fairly plain bedrooms with or without bathrooms. Finally, *Dartington Youth Hostel* (☎01803/862303; closed Oct–March, and Mon & Tues April–June), two miles outside Totnes and reachable via the #X80 Torquay–Plymouth bus (get off at Shinner's Bridge, from where it's a half-mile walk) is idyllically situated next to the River Bidwell. Dorm beds in a modern chalet cost £9.25.

You don't need to stray off the Fore Street/High Street axis to find somewhere to eat. Most places are fairly laid-back, with varying degrees of sophistication. *Rumours*, 30 High St (☎01803/864682), has a buzzy atmosphere and is good for a coffee or a full meal – either English or Mediterranean, including pizzas. Vegetarian and vegan food and organic wines are offered at *Willow*, 87 High St (☎01803/862605; no credit cards; closed evenings Sun–Tues & Thurs), with an Indian menu on Wednesday night and live music on Friday night. Across the road at 98 High St, the plant-filled *Rickshaws* (☎01803/866171; closed daytime, Sun & Mon; no credit cards) serves Asian and Indonesian food. For a drink, it's worth a trip to the top of the town where the *Kingsbridge Inn*, 9 Leechwell St (off Kingsbridge Hill) is the venue for live music and poetry readings.

Dartmouth and around

Seven miles downstream of Totnes and a mile in from the sea, **DARTMOUTH** has thrived since the Normans recognized the potential of this deep-water port for trading with their home country. The maritime connection is still strong today: fishing and freight are among the town's main activities, and officers are still trained at the imposing red-brick Royal Naval College, majestically sited on a hill behind the port.

Tightly packed on the River Dart's western bank, and rising steeply above it, Dartmouth enjoys a wonderful setting unspoiled by the excessive traffic that mars other south Devon towns. A number of lopsided but well-preserved old buildings add to the congenial atmosphere – the timber-framed **Butterwalk**, just behind the enclosed boat basin at the bottom of Duke Street, the town's central thoroughfare, is one of the most askew. Overhanging the street on eleven granite columns, the four-storey construction, richly decorated with woodcarvings, was built in the seventeenth century for a local merchant. It now holds shops and the small **Dartmouth Museum**

(Mon–Sat: April–Oct 11am–5pm; Nov–March noon–3pm; £1.50), mainly devoted to maritime curios. The highlight is the King's Room, with its original wood panelling and plaster ceiling, and displays of model sailing ships alongside delicate ivory models of Chinese craft and a man of war constructed from bone by French prisoners. Mementos of **Thomas Newcomen** (1663–1729), "Ironmonger of Dartmouth" and inventor of the world's first successful steam piston, can be seen in the Holdsworth Room. Used to pump water out of mines, Newcomen's creation was an essential aid to Devon's miners, and was a forerunner of James Watt's steam engine. An original Newcomen engine is on view in **The Engine House**, annexed to Dartmouth's tourist office in gardens backing onto the quayside (Easter–Oct Mon–Sat 9.30am–5.30pm, Sun 10am–4pm; Nov–Easter Mon–Sat 10am–4pm; £1.50); you can see the great rocking beam in action.

On Tuesday and Friday mornings, stalls selling food, gifts and household items take over Market Square, just north of Duke Street.

Across Duke Street, the fourteenth-century **St Saviour's** church was rebuilt in the 1630s, when timberwork from the captured flagship of the Spanish Armada was incorporated in the gallery. There's a finely carved fifteenth-century stone pulpit and wooden screen, and, on a door leaning up inside the south porch, some superb medieval ironwork depicting the elongated lions of Edward I and the tree of life, remounted here at the time of the rebuilding. Behind St Saviour's, Higher Street holds several notable buildings: the tottering, timber-framed **Cherub Inn**, dating from 1380, and, at no. 3–5, the larger and more ornate **Tudor House**, a handsome grey-beamed building with oriel windows, whose facade dates (despite its name) from 1635. Equally impressive, on the parallel Lower Street (at no. 28), is timber-framed **Agincourt House**, built by a merchant after the battle for which it is named, then restored in the seventeenth century and again in the twentieth.

Lower Street leads down to **Bayard's Cove**, a short cobbled quay lined with well-restored eighteenth-century houses, where the Pilgrim Fathers put to shore en route to the New World. A twenty-minute walk south of here along the river takes you to **Dartmouth Castle** (April–Sept daily 10am–6pm; Oct daily 10am–5pm; Nov–March Wed–Sun 10am–1pm & 2–4pm; £3.50; EH), one of two fortifications on opposite sides of the estuary (the other is Kingswear Castle) built at the end of the fifteenth century. The larger and more complete of the two, Dartmouth Castle was the first in England to be constructed specifically to withstand artillery, but was never tested in action and remains in an excellent state of preservation. You're free to wander as you please, taking in the various examples of weaponry on display and historical notes. If you don't relish the return walk, you can take a ferry back to town; these depart every fifteen minutes or so from the creek below the castle (Easter–Oct; £1).

Around Dartmouth

Beyond Dartmouth Castle, it's a thirty-minute walk round the estuary mouth to **Start Bay**, home to the best swimming in these parts; it's also reachable by road via the A379 from Dartmouth. Three or four miles south of town and a 45-minute walk from the castle, past the pretty hilltop village of Stoke Fleming, **Blackpool Sands** is easily the most popular of the bay's beaches, an unspoilt cove flanked by steep, wooded cliffs. There's a car park, refreshments and other facilities on hand. Past here, road and coast path descend to another good but much less sheltered swimming spot, **Slapton Sands** – three miles of shingle used during World War II by US navy and infantry divisions for rehearsing the D-Day landings. Behind the beach, the lagoon of the **Slapton Ley nature reserve** (unrestricted access; free) supports herons, terns, widgeon and – rarest of all – great crested grebes. The only development around here is at **Torcross** on the lagoon's southern end, where there's a selection of B&Bs and restaurants, and a memorial to the 639 US servicemen killed when German E-boats succeeded in breaching the coastal defences here in 1944; alongside is a Sherman tank that sank in 1944 and was recovered forty years later, its black and oily appearance giving the impression that it has only just been dredged up from the mud.

Torcross is connected with Dartmouth, Kingsbridge and Plymouth by the #93 bus.

Of the other obvious excursions from Dartmouth, the easiest is to board a ferry across the river to **KINGSWEAR**, terminus of the Paignton & Dartmouth Steam Railway (see p.80): choose between the **Lower Ferry**, which departs from below Lower Street, or, less than a mile upriver, off North Embankment, the **Higher Ferry**. The village itself has little of interest beyond its pubs, but you can follow the path south along the estuary past the remains of Kingswear Castle (now a conference centre) to the World War II gun battery at the estuary mouth. If you fancy spending longer on the water, you can book **cruises** (summer only) at kiosks on Dartmouth's quay; River Link's (☎01803/834488) trip up the River Dart to Totnes (75min; £6.20 return) is the best way to investigate the deep creeks and view the various houses on the slopes above, among them the **Royal Naval College** and **Greenway House**, birthplace of Walter Raleigh's three seafaring half-brothers, the Gilberts, and later rebuilt for Agatha Christie (see box, p.76).

From Torcross, coast-walkers can continue south down to Start Point, from where the coast path continues west to Prawle Point (see p.90), Devon's southernmost headland.

Practicalities

Dartmouth is connected to Totnes and Torquay by **bus** #X89. The **tourist office** is opposite the car park just off the quayside, north of Duke Street (Easter–Oct Mon–Sat 9.30am–5.30pm, Sun 10am–4pm; Nov–Easter Mon–Sat 10am–4pm; ☎01803/834224; *www.dartmouth-information.co.uk*).

Dartmouth's best **accommodation** is at the top of steep hills, where you'll appreciate the exquisite views over the river, but if you're baggage-laden, you'll find a good range lower down on

Victoria Road (the continuation of Duke St), notably *The Middle House* at no. 16 (☎01803/833935; no credit cards; ②), which offers two large, colourful en-suite rooms. Further up, nonsmoking *Sunnybanks*, 1 Vicarage Hill (☎01803/832766; *www.sunnybanks.com*; no credit cards ②), has plushly furnished, individually decorated rooms, mostly en suite. If it's views you're after, however, head uphill to *Avondale*, 5 Vicarage Hill (☎01803/835831; no credit cards; ②); it's friendly, spacious and elegantly furnished. Down by Bayards Cove, and with lovely views over the quay, pink-fronted *Hedley House*, 37 Newcomen Rd (☎01803/832885; ④) has antique furnishings and friendly owners. For something a little different, consider the *Res Nova Inn* (☎07770/628967; no credit cards; may close in winter), a barge moored in mid-river that's run by a friendly couple who will ferry guests to and from town. Comfy cabins – one en suite, costing £10 more – cost £25 for a single berth, £45 for a double. The area's most appealing **campsite**, *Leonard's Cove* (☎01803/770206; closed Nov–Easter), lies a couple of miles south of town near Stoke Fleming and Leonard's Cove itself.

If you're travelling from Torbay to Dartmouth (or vice versa), you can save time and a long detour through Totnes by using the frequent ferries crossing the Dart's estuary at Kingswear (50p single, £2 for cars with passengers), from 7am to around 10.45pm (ferries normally stop an hour later on Friday and Saturday and in summer). Service is continuous.

Dartmouth has acquired a certain renown for its **restaurants**, of which the town has a prolific number, including some good fast-food and snack stops. In the best places, fish is top choice, but it doesn't come cheap, for example at the port's most celebrated eaterie, *The Carved Angel*, 2 South Embankment (☎01803/832465; closed Sun eve, all Mon & Jan to mid-Feb), which also excels in game in winter and has views over the riverfront. If you're daunted by the prices and formality here, try its more casual offshoot, *The Carved Angel Café*, 7 Foss St (☎01803/834842; no smoking; closed Sun & Jan). The moderately priced menu lacks the sparkle of its parent, but there are some great soups, light suppers and puddings. The *Res Nova Inn* (see above; Thurs–Sun, plus daily in July & Aug) also serves delicious fish suppers. For breakfasts (until 2pm), coffees and snacks, the *Café Alf Resco* on Lower Street (closed Mon & Tues) is inexpensive, with outdoor tables, while the *Crab Shell* at 1 Raleigh St – an alley between Fairfax Place and the riverfront – dispenses generously stuffed and genuinely tasty crab sandwiches to take away, among other rolls and sandwiches (open Easter–Oct only, mid-morning to mid-afternoon; no credit cards).

Salcombe

Almost at the mouth of the Kingsbridge estuary, about twelve miles southwest of Dartmouth, **SALCOMBE** is Devon's southernmost resort, an endearing place whose steep and narrow lanes are mobbed with holiday-makers in summer. There is still some fishing activity, but Salcombe is primarily a sailors' town, with the calm waters of the estuary strewn with small craft and several boatyards on the shore. The entrance to the harbour is overlooked by the ruined **Fort Charles**, a Civil War relic that injects a touch of romance amid the villas and hotels.

There's enough to amuse in simply strolling up the main Fore Street, at the bottom of the town, or wandering among the mix of pink, green and white cottages interspersed with ships' chandlers that overlook the deep, clear estuary waters. On Market Street, off the north end of Fore Street, it's worth taking a look at the nautical mementos displayed in the **Salcombe Maritime Museum** (April to late Sept 10.30am–12.30pm & 2.30–4.30pm; £1). It's small but jam-packed with information about local wrecks, plus gold coins and other items retrieved from the seabed, and paintings of the brigantines, barques and schooners that set sail from here. A working model boat illustrates various sailing manoeuvres, which you can try out at first hand.

If you're inspired by the museum, or if you just want to explore the estuary and coasts, ask at the quays below Fore Street about **boat rental** – anything from a dinghy to a schooner is available. Whitestrand Boat Hire (☎01548/844475) on Whitestrand Quay arranges **cruises**, fishing trips and will rent out boats. If **surfing** or **waterskiing** is your thing, make for Splash Centre on the sheltered and popular beach at South Sands, a mile south of Salcombe's centre (☎01548/843843).

Practicalities

Bus #92 connects Salcombe with Plymouth and Kingsbridge, while bus travellers from Exeter, Dartmouth and Totnes will have to change at Kingsbridge onto the hourly #606. Salcombe's **tourist office** is just above the museum on Market Street (April–June & Sept–Oct Mon–Sat 9.30am–1pm & 2–5pm, July & Aug Mon–Sat 9.30am–1pm & 2–5.30pm; Nov–March 10am–1pm & 2–4pm; ☎01548/843927; *www.salcombeinformation.co.uk*).

Most of Salcombe's **accommodation** is above Fore Street, and affords wonderful estuary views. Near the car park on Shadycombe Road, *The Old Porch House* (☎01548/843750; no credit cards; ②) is the oldest house in Salcombe, but has modern facilities amid the brass ornaments and hanging tankards. Lower down, there's a less grand but also very comfortable (nameless) B&B round the corner from Fore Street at 7 Courtenay St (☎01548/842276; no credit cards; ①): ask for the balcony room, which has stunning views. The nearest **campsite**, *Ilton Farm*, is one and a half miles west of town just off the Malborough road, and on the #606 bus route (Easter to late Oct; ☎01548/842858).

If you're hankering for fish, Salcombe's **restaurants** should satisfy. Seafood tops the menu at *Spinnaker's* (☎01548/843408; closed Sun & Mon, Dec & Jan), a moderately priced place that shares a building with the *Salcombe Hotel* on Fore Street, overlooking the river. The long-established *Terrapins* (☎01548/842860; closed weekdays Nov–Easter) on Buckley Street (just above Victoria Quay) also has moderate prices and serves good lamb and duck as well as fish.

Between Easter and September, from 9.45am until 5.30pm or 6pm, the South Sands ferry (☎01548/ 561035; £1.70 single) sails every half-hour from Salcombe's Whitestrand Quay to South Sands beach, a mile south of the centre, from which it's a ten-minute uphill walk to Sharpitor and the Overbecks Museum (see overleaf)

Around Salcombe

The coastline **around Salcombe** offers some superb walking. From Ferry Steps, accessible from Fore Street below Whitestrand Quay, a regular passenger ferry (April–Sept 8am–7pm continuous service; Oct–March 8am–5.30pm hourly; 85p) crosses the narrow estuary channel to **East Portlemouth**, from where you can follow the coast path past the craggily photogenic Gammon Point to Devon's most southerly tip, **Prawle Point**, about five-miles' walk in all.

Ttimings for the Salcombe–East Portlemouth ferry can vary according to weather and demand.

A couple of miles south of Salcombe, along the western side of the estuary, it's a pleasant walk to the hamlet of **Sharpitor** (also reached by minor roads signposted from Salcombe); here, an elegant Edwardian house holds the excellent **Overbecks Museum** (April–July & Sept Mon–Fri & Sun 11am–5.30pm; Aug daily 11am–5.30pm; Oct Mon–Thurs & Sun 11am–5pm; £4.10; NT). It's mainly dedicated to natural and local history, but also displays such curios as a polyphon – a nineteenth-century jukebox – and a "rejuvenating machine". This, like many of the artefacts, was created by the house's former resident Otto Overbeck, a research chemist and eccentric inventor who believed that everyone could live to the age of 350. The museum building has wonderful estuary views and is surrounded by a luxuriant **subtropical garden** (daily 10am–8pm or sunset if earlier), where plants range from Japanese banana to flax; the museum entry ticket admits you to the garden, but if you only want to see the latter, you pay a reduced fee (£2.90).

A mile south of Sharpitor, **Bolt Head** marks the western end of the Kingsbridge estuary, and the start of a magnificent, moderately challenging six-mile, three-hour hike to the massive cliffs of **Bolt Tail**. Along the way, you'll see shags, cormorants and other marine birds swooping above the ragged coast, and wild thyme and sea thrift underfoot. West of Bolt Tail, **Bigbury Bay** is dotted with sandy beaches offering first-class, sheltered **swimming**. The nearest, **Hope Cove**, is nestled in the lee of Bolt Tail, and holds the tiny hamlets of **Inner Hope**, backed by fishermen's cottages and pubs, and **Outer Hope** to the north, surrounded by cliffs and with a slipway serving as a small harbour. The infrequent #162 bus connects Hope Cove with Kingsbridge and, two miles further up the coast, with **THURLE-STONE**, a thoroughly thatched village of pink-washed cottages. Backed by rolling farmland and a sprawling golf course, **Thurlestone Sands** is highly rated for its water quality and for **surfing**. At its southern end, you can explore the rock pools around the spectacular arched rock to which the village owes its name, which means "holed rock" in Old English.

Just under two miles further west, the area's most popular family beach lies on the opposite side of the Avon (pronounced "Awn") estuary at **BIGBURY-ON-SEA**, reachable in summer by a ferry between the hamlets of Bantham (a mile upstream) and Cockleridge – or by wading the river at low tide. Drivers will have to take the long way round, making a left turn off the A379. The village is modern and brash, but the level sands and sheltered waters are great for sunbathing and windsurfing, and visual interest is provided by **Burgh Island**, a few yards out to sea, dominated by a grand Art Deco hotel. You can walk to this tiny islet at low tide, or, more fun, jump on the high-rise tractor-like vehicle (50p; last ride 11.30pm) that operates when the tide is in. There's public access to most of the green and rocky promontory, whose shores are mostly lined with low cliffs, and there's a nice old pub if you're not dressed up for the hotel (see below).

Around Salcombe

Practicalities

For **information** on the Salcombe surrounds, head to the tourist office in town (see p.89). Public transport is pretty scarce on this eastern side of the Kingsbridge estuary, where the summer-only #159 connects East Portlemouth, East Prawle, Start Point and Kingsbridge.

Many of the **accommodation** options in the area are somewhat pricey, but include some excellent choices, such as the small and stylish *Henley Hotel* (☎01548/810240; ④) on Folly Hill in Bigbury, reachable by bus #87 from Modbury, which is on the #93 route from Salcombe. Three miles east of East Portlemouth and a couple of miles north of Prawle Point, the relaxed *South Allington House* (☎01548/511272; nonsmoking; ③) offers good-value rural accommodation, with quiet and comfortable rooms and croquet in the extensive gardens. If you're flush, you may be tempted by one of the area's luxury establishments, such as the clifftop *Gara Rock Hotel* at East Portlemouth (☎01548/842342; *www.gara.co.uk*; ⑤) which has splendid rooms, a pool, tennis courts and great views. On Burgh Island, the *Burgh Island Hotel* (☎01548/810514; ⑨) is a dazzling display of period style, with a stained-glass dome and sumptuous furnishings. Even rich guests need to book well ahead to stay here. At the opposite extreme, there's an idyllically situated **youth hostel** on the upper floor of Overbecks Museum in Sharpitor (☎01548/842856; closed Nov–March, Sun in April–June, and Sun & Mon in Sept–Oct), where dorm beds cost £10. **Campers** should head for the popular *Sun Park*, a level, grassy field with good facilities and caravans just up from the beach at Soar Mill Cove, midway between Bolt Head and Bolt Tail (☎01548/561378; Easter to late Oct).

The area's **pubs** are the best choice for inexpensive **meals**: at Thurlestone's *Village Inn*, dishes include poached chicken stuffed with haggis, and ostrich. Just below the *Burgh Island Hotel*, the weathered, old *Pilchard Inn* offers rolls and pies in its tiny blackened-stone bars. For a glimpse of how the stars prefer their hotels, you could always content yourself with a cream tea at the *Burgh Island Hotel* or a cocktail in the 1920s-style bar or in the lovely garden – the only restriction is on sandy shoes.

Travel Details

Trains

Dawlish to: Exeter (2 hourly; 20min); Newton Abbot (1–2 hourly; 12min); Plymouth (hourly; 55min); Teignmouth (hourly; 5min); Torquay (hourly; 25min).

Newton Abbot to: Exeter (1–3 hourly; 25min); Paignton (hourly; 20min); Plymouth (hourly 40min); Teignmouth (hourly; 10min); Totnes (2 hourly; 15min); Torquay (hourly; 15min).

Paignton to: Exeter (hourly; 1hr); Newton Abbot (hourly; 20min); Torquay (hourly; 5min).

Teignmouth to: Dawlish (2 hourly; 5min); Exeter (2 hourly; 25min); Newton Abbot (1–2 hourly; 6min); Plymouth (hourly; 50min); Torquay (hourly; 20min).

Torquay to: Dawlish (hourly; 30min); Exeter (hourly; 55min); Newton Abbot (hourly; 15min); Paignton (hourly; 5min); Teignmouth (hourly; 20min).

Totnes to: Exeter (2 hourly; 40min); Newton Abbot (2 hourly; 15min); Plymouth (1–2 hourly; 30min).

Buses

Brixham to: Kingswear (every 20min; 20min); Paignton (every 12min; 22min); Torquay (every 12min; 40min).

Dartmouth to: Kingsbridge (7 daily; 1hr); Plymouth (6 daily; 2hr 5min); Torcross (hourly; 30min); Torquay (4 daily; 1hr 25min); Totnes (6 daily; 40min).

Kingswear to: Brixham (every 20min; 20min).

Paignton to: Brixham (every 12min; 22min); Torquay (every 12min; 26min); Totnes (every 20min; 20–30min).

Salcombe to: Kingsbridge (Mon–Sat hourly; 25min); Plymouth (2 daily; 1hr 35min).

Torquay to Brixham (every 12min; 40min); Dartmouth (4 daily; 1hr 25min); Exeter (Mon–Sat hourly, Sun 5 daily; 55min); Paignton (every 12min; 26min); Plymouth (hourly; 1hr 50min); Totnes (1–2 hourly; 40min).

Totnes to: Dartmouth (6 daily; 40min); Kingsbridge (hourly; 45min); Paignton (every 20min; 20–30min); Plymouth (hourly; 1hr 10min); Torquay (1–2 hourly; 40min).

Chapter 4

Dartmoor

The longer one stays here the more does the spirit of the moor sink into one's soul, its vastness, and also its grim charm. When you are once out upon its bosom you have left all traces of modern England behind you, but on the other hand you are conscious everywhere of the homes and the work of the prehistoric people. . . . If you were to see a skin-clad, hairy man . . . fitting a flint-tipped arrow on to the string of his bow, you would feel that his presence there was more natural than your own.

Arthur Conan Doyle, *The Hound of the Baskervilles*

Covering the sweep of country between Exeter and Plymouth, **DARTMOOR** is southern England's greatest expanse of wilderness, some 365 square miles of raw granite, barren bogland, grassland and heather-strewn moor. Things weren't always so desolate, though, as testified by numerous remnants of scattered Stone Age settlements, and the ruined relics of nineteenth-century quarrying and tin-mining industries. Today, desultory flocks of sheep and groups of ponies are virtually the only living creatures you'll see wandering over the central regions of the National Park, with solitary birds – buzzards, kestrels, pipits, stonechats and wagtails – wheeling and hovering high above.

For many, the most appealing parts of Dartmoor are the emptiest, uncrossed by roads and miles from the nearest villages. These are mainly in the northern and southern reaches, appearing as bare tracts on the map, and characterized by tumbling streams and high tors chiselled by the elements. This chapter, however, necessarily focuses on the specific attractions which, for the most part, are concentrated on the periphery of the national park, though the central east–west belt has both villages with accommodation and some famous beauty spots, making viable starting points for walks into the core of Dartmoor.

The original Dartmoor Forest – a royal hunting zone in Saxon times – has largely disappeared, with only about eleven percent of the moor nowadays defined as woodland. Since the fourteenth century, the area has been owned by the Duchy of Cornwall, but public

You'll find lots of useful background and practical information relating to Dartmoor at www.dartmoor-npa.gov.uk (the National Park site), www.dartmoor.co.uk and www.dartmoor-guide.co.uk

Dartmoor

As availability can be extremely restricted in high season, it's always advisable to book accommodation ahead if you want to stay on the moor.

Dartmoor has several camping barns, for which it's wise to book ahead, particularly at weekends; call the barns directly at the numbers supplied in this chapter, or contact the Camping Barns Reservations Office (☎01200/ 420102; camp barnsyha@ enterprise.net).

access is almost unlimited today, provided certain guidelines are followed: parking overnight in unauthorized places is prohibited; vehicles are not allowed further than fifteen yards from any road, and, though camping is permitted out of sight of houses and roads, fires are strictly forbidden. The main limitation to free access are the Ministry of Defence **firing ranges** that, much to the irritation of locals and visitors alike, take up significant portions of the northern moor, an area that contains Dartmoor's highest tors and some of its most famous beauty spots. The ranges are marked by red-and-white posts; when firing is in progress, red flags or red lights signify that you cannot enter. As a general rule, assume that if no warning flags are flying by 9am between April and September, or by 10am from October to March, there is to be no firing on that day. Firing-range schedules are posted in the *Dartmoor Visitor* and other local newspapers, on village notice boards and in tourist offices.

Walking, of course, is the main reason to be on the moor. Ranging from short and simple jaunts to more challenging treks over long isolated stretches of rugged uplands, a thick web of **trails** crisscross what many regard as the country's most inspiring wilderness. On the whole, the gentler contours of the southern moor provide less strenuous rambles, while the harsher northern tracts require more skill and stamina. Seasoned hikers might also link up with some of the longer-distance walks, for example the Tarka Trail, Templer Way and the Two Moors Way. We've outlined some of the best hikes in this chapter, but more detailed information is widely available, from specific Dartmoor walking guides (see Contexts, p.300–331) to pamphlets and other publications on sale at tourist offices. You could also join a guided walk; an extensive programme of options, varying from two (£2.50) to six hours (£4.50), is listed in the free *Dartmoor Visitor* newspaper. Walks are free if you produce a bus ticket; for booking and information call ☎01822/890414. Tourist offices can also provide information on **letterboxing**, a Dartmoor institution which has seen a phenomenal growth in recent years (see box on p.114).

Though many walks are signposted or waymarked with painted stones, **map-reading** abilities are a prerequisite for all but the shortest of walks, and a good deal of experience is essential for longer distances – search parties seeking hikers gone astray are not uncommon. The single sheet 1:25,000 Ordnance Survey Outdoor Leisure map no. 28 is an impressively detailed piece of mapping, giving copious information down to field boundaries. Another fine way to experience Dartmoor is on **horseback**; numerous stables are dotted over the moor, and we've mentioned the best in the text.

Getting around

Although Buckfastleigh is connected by steam trains with Totnes, and Okehampton has a seasonal rail link with Exeter, you'll have to

9 4

THE GUIDE: CHAPTER 4

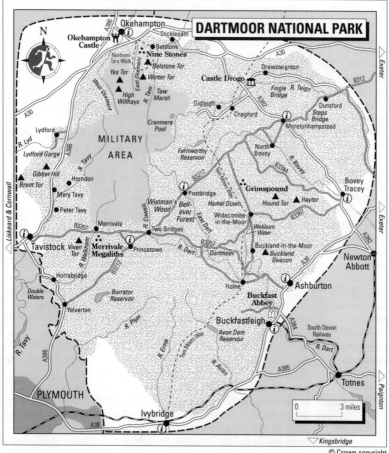

rely on a rather sketchy bus network for **public transport** within the moor. A Transmoor **bus** service (#82) operates between Exeter and Plymouth, with stops at Two Bridges and Princetown; it runs on weekends only for most of the year, but there are at least three daily services from late May to the end of September. From Exeter, the #359 (seven daily Mon–Sat) runs to Moretonhampstead, on the northeast side of the moor, while National Express coaches and smaller companies based in Cornwall serve Okehampton. There are regular buses from Okehampton to Tavistock via Lydford, while buses #98 (Mon–Sat) and #172 (daily, summer only) link Princetown with Tavistock, itself connected by frequent buses to Plymouth. Apart from these, there's little except once-weekly runs to remote villages.

*Information,
from firing
schedules and
walking routes
to pony-
trekking, is
available from
National Park
Visitor Centres
and from
information
points in
smaller
villages. All the
area's tourist
offices stock
the free
Dartmoor
Visitor newspa-
per, with use-
ful info on
accommoda-
tion, events
and listings of
facilities for
people with
disabilities.*

ACCOMMODATION PRICE CODES

Throughout this Guide, hotel and B&B accommodation is coded on a scale of ① to ⑨, the code indicating the lowest price you can expect to pay per night for a double room in high season. The prices indicated by the codes are as follows:

① under £40	④ £60–70	⑦ £110–150
② £40–50	⑤ £70–90	⑧ £150–200
③ £50–60	⑥ £90–110	⑨ over £200

The speed limit throughout Dartmoor is 40mph, and **drivers** should beware of ponies, sheep and other livestock straying onto the roads, particularly in early autumn, when they find it the warmest place to be. If you hit an animal, or come across an injured one on the road, contact the police on ☎0990/777444.

The central moor

Running diagonally across the moor, the B3212 and B3357 provide easy access to **central Dartmoor**, and as a consequence the area attracts plenty of visitors. Many are drawn by some of the region's loveliest scenic spots, including tumbling brooks and ancient forest, and you would do well to see these places outside the peak periods, when you can still find a degree of isolation. Inevitably, most of the tourist comings and goings are focused on **Princetown**, the only village of any size and a strictly functional place that's home to the national park's main information centre. You're unlikely to want to spend much time in Princetown, but what this dull collection of grey buildings lacks in beauty is amply compensated for by the epic splendour of the surrounding country, accessible on paths or from points within a short drive. The main priority, however, is to get away from the roads. From **Two Bridges**, three miles northeast and the meeting point of two rivers, you can venture forth into **Wistman's Wood**, a hoary survival of the old forest that once covered much of the moor. Further up the B3212, **Postbridge** holds one of Dartmoor's picturesque clapper bridges, and marks the start of a superb riverside route which winds south from here through **Bellever Forest** to where the East and West Dart rivers combine at **Dartmeet** – also reachable via the B3357 from Two Bridges.

*For bus
enquiries, call
☎01752/
222666
(Western
National) or
☎01392/
382800 (Devon
Bus). For all
transport
enquiries, try
also ☎0870/
608 2608.*

Princetown
PRINCETOWN owes its growth to the presence of Dartmoor Prison, whose grim spirit seeps into the place; some of the drab grey-stone buildings – like the parish church of St Michael (now closed) – were even built by French and American inmates at the beginning of the nineteenth century. The unprepossessing appearance and somewhat oppressed air of the village, not improved by the tall TV mast towering above it on North Hessary Tor, does not

invite much lingering, though you'll find most of the facilities you'll need along its main drag, Tavistock Street, which heads northwest from The Square (site of the tourist office and the intersection with the B3212). Half a mile up Tavistock Street from here, **Dartmoor prison** was just one of the schemes instigated by Thomas Tyrwhitt, appointed auditor for the Duchy of Cornwall in 1786 and responsible more than anyone for developing the moor's central territory. After the failure of his grandiose project for turning this part of the moor into a cereal-growing prairie, he began work on the prison in 1806, and two years later it was home to 2500 captured French soldiers, and later still to American prisoners from the 1812 war. The prison brought unprecedented commercial activity to this empty heart of the moor, and the weekly market held within its confines attracted traders from throughout the region. After closure in 1816, the prison reopened in 1850 to take the overload from other British jails; it later held conscientious objectors from World War I and, in 1921, IRA prisoners. Nowadays it houses about 600 inmates and remains one of the country's most unpopular penal institutions, having witnessed several riots over the years, the latest of which led to refurbishment in 1990.

You can learn much more about life inside, and view escape tools as well as a mock-up of a cell at the **H.M. Prison Dartmoor Museum**, 150yd from the main prison gate (Tues–Sat: April–Oct 9.30am–4.30pm; Nov–March 9.30am–12.30pm & 1.30–4.30pm; closes 4pm Fri; last entry 30min before closing; £2) – probably not what you came to Dartmoor to find, but a thought-provoking diversion when weather conditions preclude outdoor pursuits.

Practicalities

Reams of information on the whole moor are available at the main **National Park information centre**, housed in the old *Duchy Hotel* on the village's central green (daily: April–Oct 10am–5pm; Nov–March 10am–4pm; ☎01822/890414; *www.dartmoor-npa. gov.uk*).

Princetown itself has a good selection of inexpensive **accommodation**, including the two pubs in The Square: basic, pastel and floral rooms in the *Railway Inn* (☎01822/890232; ①); or bright and pine-furnished in the slate-hung *Plume of Feathers* (☎01822/890240; ①), which claims to be the oldest building in town, dating from 1795. The latter also has two quality bunkhouses with two, four or ten beds per room (£5.50–£6.50; book well ahead), as well as a **campsite**. *Lamorna* (☎01822/890360; no credit cards; ①) is a clean and friendly B&B fifty yards from the tourist office on Two Bridges Road, with a view of the prison, while on Tavistock Road, two hundred yards from the centre, *Duchy House* (☎01822/890552; no credit cards; ①) has fairly ordinary rooms brightened up by colourful quilts. For **meals**, both pubs provide staple bar-food; the *Plume of Feathers*, with open fires and exposed

The central moor

The Dartmoor Sunday Rover Ticket (£5) allows unlimited travel on any Sunday between late May and mid-September, and also gives discounts on attractions and free access to guided walks. Call ☎01392/382800 for booking or further information.

Dartmoor Prison Museum's hours are subject to change; before you visit, ring ahead to check on ☎01822/890305.

Princetown's National Park Centre closes for one week in early March for annual refurbishment.

beams, serves up a good bread and butter pudding, and live bands
play on Sundays.

Two Bridges

A couple of miles northeast of Princetown, at the intersection of the
B3212 and the B3357, **TWO BRIDGES** represents Dartmoor's centre point. Only one of its bridges now remains, a five-span clapper
which crosses the River Cowsic in the middle of the village (the other
originally crossed the West Dart), and there's little else here now
other than a hotel (see below), useful for rest and refreshment before
or after a wander in the vicinity. The favourite excursion is to head
for the misshapen dwarf oaks of **Wistman's Wood**, a mile or so north
via a marked bridlepath that leads along the river from the car park
opposite the *Two Bridges Hotel*. Cluttered with lichen-covered boulders and a dense undergrowth of ferns, it's an evocative relic of the
original Dartmoor Forest. The gnarled old trees once lay on the "lych
way" – a route for transporting the dead to Lydford (see p.115),
where all inhabitants of Dartmoor Forest were buried until 1260 –
and the woods are reputed to have been the site of druidic gatherings, a story unsupported by any evidence but which feels quite plau-
sible in this solitary spot.

The *Two Bridges Hotel* (☎01822/890581; ⑤) makes a luxurious
place either to **stay**, with its leather sofas and Jacobean four-poster,
or to sample the home-brewed Jail Ale in the bar. More reasonably
priced accommodation can be found at the family-run *Cherry Brook
Hotel* (☎01822/880260; closed mid-Dec to early Jan; ③), an unpretentious and somewhat characterless country place a couple of miles
northeast, set back from the B3212 Postbridge road. The **food** is the
best thing here; nonresidents can book ahead for a delicious meal
made with local produce for about £16.50.

Along the East Dart: Postbridge to Dartmeet

Three miles northeast of Two Bridges, the largest and best preserved
of Dartmoor's **clapper bridges** crosses the East Dart river at **POST-
BRIDGE**, an otherwise nondescript hamlet to which it gives its
name. Used by tin-miners and farmers since medieval times, these
simple structures consist of huge slabs of granite supported by piers
of the same material. This one, standing tall over the water alongside
the main road bridge, makes a great starting-point for **walks** up and
down the East Dart. Northward, along a riverside path on the eastern
side of the road bridge (turn immediately left into the field), you can
hike as far as **Fernworthy Reservoir** (about three miles), surrounded by woodland and lying in the midst of a number of stone circles
and stone rows. South of Postbridge, you can take an easier option
by following the broad track (turn left at the cattle-grid by the
Bellever turning) through **Bellever Forest** to the open moor beyond.
This dense working forest, planted with sitka spruce, Japanese larch

and other conifers, has provoked the ire of many conservationists over the years, as do all the other plantations of non-indigenous trees on Dartmoor. But as the true native trees of these parts – the dwarf oak and mountain ash – are few and far between nowadays, the woodland at least provides some variety from the otherwise bare landscape, and is inhabited by deer, as well as tree pipits and night-jars in the newer parts, and buzzards, sparrowhawks, dippers, ravens and tawny owls in the most mature sections; crossbills and siskins also breed here. Waymarked circular routes loop through the forest, starting from a forestry car park by the river (reached on the road from Postbridge); one finger-posted path brings you up to the open moorland around **Bellever Tor** (1453ft), from which there are out-standing views in all directions.

Beyond the Bellever Forest, four miles south of Postbridge, the East and West Dart rivers merge at **Dartmeet** after tortuous journeys from their remote sources. A place of rocky shallows and the full range of river-crossings – stepping-stones over the West Dart, a humpback bridge and the remains of a clapper bridge over the East Dart – this beauty spot is a magnet for crowds, but the valley is mem-orably lush and you don't need to walk far to leave the car park and ice-cream vans behind.

Practicalities

Postbridge has a useful **tourist office** in the main car park near the bridge (April–Oct daily 10am–5pm; ☎01822/880272). If you want to stay in the area, the *East Dart Hotel* (☎01822/880213; *www.eastdart.force9.co.uk*; ②), a nineteenth-century coaching inn at the northern edge of the village, offers warm rooms and dishes out snacks and more substantial meals such as kiln-baked salmon, local lamb and rabbit pie. The *Lydgate House Hotel*, signposted off the

---

Dartmoor ponies

There have been **ponies** on Dartmoor since the Bronze Age: small of stature, strong and hardy, they were traditionally used as working and pack animals, and at the end of the nineteenth century supplied the coal mines of Somerset and South Wales. With the decline of mining, and the fall in demand for horsemeat for which the ponies were also prized, num-bers have dwindled from 30,000 at the end of World War I to less than 3000 today. Of those remaining, few survive of the original hardy stock, as much cross-breeding has taken place over the years. Contrary to popular belief, Dartmoor ponies are not wild, merely unbroken; all have an owner and sport a brand, cut or tag to indicate who they belong to. During the "drifts" – round-ups which take place each September and October – the ponies are herded into yards, grouped according to ownership and sold on.

As they can bite and kick you should steer clear of the ponies, and above all don't feed them – it encourages them to approach traffic, and is against the law.

B3212 half a mile southwest of Postbridge (☎01822/880209; *www.lydgate-house.fsnet.co.uk*; ⑨; closed Dec–Feb), offers Victorian-style rooms and easy access to Bellever Forest. A couple of miles south of Postbridge, Bellever **youth hostel** (☎01822/880227; closed Nov–March) supplies a welcoming log fire, dorm beds for £10, meals and a wealth of information on the moor as well as outdoor activities from climbing to letterboxing (see box on p.114) – book ahead for all – and **bike rental**. Half a mile down the road to Widecombe from Postbridge, and reachable on the Transmoor #82 bus, there's a **camping barn** at Runnage Farm (☎01822/880222); bunk beds cost £3.95, and there are camping facilities alongside.

The eastern and southeastern moor

Though gentler and more populous than other parts, **Dartmoor's eastern and southeastern** sections also contain some of the most spectacularly scenic terrain. The towns along the edge of the moor, such as **Bovey Tracey**, have most of the accommodation, but it's the country west of here that holds most interest, in the shape of walking routes and specific sights – not least the various prehistoric remains dotted around (many of them accessible by road). High up in the heart of eastern Dartmoor, **Widecombe-in-the-Moor** has immense charm, its tall, granite church tower set against a magnificent backdrop of high moorland. The village also makes a great base for hikes around two of the moor's most popular attractions: the wind-whittled rockpile of **Haytor**, and **Grimspound**, a well-preserved Bronze Age settlement. South, the equally picturesque villages of **Buckland-in-the-Moor** and **Holne** make good stops for a pint, but you'll have to press on three or four miles east to **Ashburton** for a better choice of accommodation. Further south, **Buckfastleigh** also has a range of B&Bs, but its limited attractions are largely ignored by the tourist coaches which pull in up the road at **Buckfast Abbey**.

Ashburton and Buckfastleigh are regularly connected by #39 and #X39 **buses** running between Exeter and Plymouth, and Buckfastleigh is also the terminus of the **South Devon Railway**, which runs steam trains down to Totnes (see p.83). Buckland and Holne are linked to Ashburton by the #672 (Wed only), and Holne also has the #893, running to Buckfastleigh and Ashburton once weekly (also Wed).

Bovey Tracey

Despite the steep wooded valleys surrounding **BOVEY TRACEY** (pronounced "Buvvy"), built at a crossing over the River Bovey on the eastern edge of the moor, the village has an open, spacious feel. Drifting lazily through the town, the stream contributes to its leisurely air, and its capacious tea shops make this a favourite stopoff point for coach parties. For limited entertainment on a wet day, you could do worse than head for the **House of Marbles** (Mon–Sat 9am–5pm; free), a shop off the roundabout on Newton Road where gigantic marbles whizz down convoluted tracks and you can view the machine that made the world's biggest marble; glass-blowing demonstrations take place between Easter and September.

Most of the pubs and shops are concentrated along Fore Street, which leads up from the **tourist office**, a wooden chalet on Station Road (March–Sept Mon–Sat 9.30am–5.30pm, Sun 10am–1pm & 2–4.30pm; Oct Mon–Sat 10am–4pm, Sun 10am–12.30pm & 2–4pm; ☎01626/832047). A little further up and adjoining the river, the *Riverside Hotel* (☎01626/832293; ①) was where Oliver Cromwell surprised Royalist troops at the time of the Battle of Bovey Heath in 1645; it now has comfortably modernized **rooms**. The *Old Thatched Inn* on Station Road (☎01626/833421; ②) has plenty of beamy atmosphere and quiet, snug rooms. You can **eat** here too, with pizzas a speciality in the evenings. Housed in the stone mill next to the *Riverside*, the *Devon Guild of Craftsmen* offers inexpensive meals cooked with cider and other local ingredients – farm cider is also served at the welcoming *King of Prussia Inn* at the top of Fore Street.

Widecombe-in-the-Moor and Haytor

Six miles west of Bovey Tracey on the B3387, in a hollow amid high, granite-strewn ridges, **WIDECOMBE-IN-THE-MOOR** is a candidate for most-visited Dartmoor village. Its church of **St Pancras**, dubbed the "cathedral of the moor", provides a famous local landmark, its pinnacled tower dwarfing the fourteenth-century nave whose spacious interior boasts a barrel roof with vigorously carved and painted roof bosses depicting a Green Man, a pelican and, above the communion rail, rabbits – the emblem of the tinners who funded the building. The village's other claim to fame is as the

> *Tom Pearse, Tom Pearse, lend me your grey mare,*
> *All along, down along, out along, lee.*
> *For I want for to go to Widdicombe Fair,*
> *Wi' Bill Brewer, Jan Stewer, Peter Gurney, Peter Davey,*
> *Dan'l Whiddon, Harry Hawk,*
> *Old Uncle Tom Cobbleigh and all.*
> *Old Uncle Tom Cobbleigh and all.*
>
> Widdicombe Fair (traditional song)

inspiration for the traditional song, *Widdicombe Fair* (see box, above), a celebration of the event which has been held in the village since at least the nineteenth century. The ballad, published in 1880, relates the journey of Uncle Tom Cobbleigh and companions to the fair, and its popularity was a major factor in sparking Widecombe's high tourist profile. The fair is still held annually on the second

*Shilstone Rocks
Riding and
Trekking
Centre
(☎01364/
621281), just
outside
Widecombe,
offers horse
riding; to get
there, take the
turning after
the Old Inn,
with the church
on the left – the
stables are at
the first
junction on the
left.*

*Walkers from
Widecombe-in-
the-Moor to
Grimspound
should take the
Natsworthy
road past the
Old Inn, turn-
ing left at the
playing fields
(signposted
Grimspound)
and following
the track
across open
moorland at
the top. The
long uphill
climb is
rewarded by a
superb
panorama.*

Tuesday of September, but is now primarily a tourist attraction, with a funfair.

About two and a half miles east of Widecombe and reached along the B3387 (itself paralleled for part of the way by a footpath), the dramatic and much frequented **Haytor** (1490ft) makes an excellent vantage point over the open moor, the views south sometimes extending as far as the coast. The granite quarries here were worked in the nineteenth century, providing material for the British Museum and the original London Bridge, which now resides in Arizona after being purchased by a US businessman.

Practicalities

There's a park **information centre** (April–Oct daily 10am–5pm; ☎01364/661520) in the lower car park at Haytor. You'll find a good range of inexpensive **accommodation** within and around Widecombe. Opposite the post office and set in a lovely garden, *The Old Rectory* (☎01364/621231; *rachel.belgrave@care4free.net*; no credit cards; ①) has spacious, elegant rooms, antiques, a shared bathroom with a view and a jacuzzi. Next to the post office, *Manor Cottage* (☎01364/621218; no credit cards; ①) has an inglenook fireplace in the dining room and a garden where breakfast can be taken; three-course home-cooked meals are also served for around £12, or you can pick up a packed lunch. Six hundred yards south of the church on the Ashburton road, *Little Meadow* (☎01364/621236; no credit cards; ①; closed late Oct to Feb) is a Canadian-style chalet with wicker furniture made by the owner in the rooms. You can **camp** at *Cockingford Farm*, one and a half miles south of Widecombe (☎01364/621258; closed mid-Nov to mid-March).

Widecombe's busy fourteenth-century *Old Inn* attracts the crowds for its traditional pub **food**, but the small, unspoilt and old-fashioned *Rugglestone Inn*, just south of the village, is quieter and serves up very reasonably priced meals such as hot salted brisket in a roll and lamb and chicken hot-pots; there's a nonsmoking room as well. For a cream tea, sit in a blue Lloyd loom chair at the capacious, touristy *Café on the Green*.

Grimspound and Hound Tor

North of Widecombe-in-the-Moor, a four-mile hike on marked tracks across **Hamel Down** (or a three-mile drive along the minor road connecting the village with the B3212) takes you to the Bronze Age village of **Grimspound**. The site lies below Hameldown Tor, about 200yds from the road – heading north, look out for a small lay-by on the left and granite steps leading off on the right. Inhabited some three thousand years ago, when Dartmoor was fully forested and enjoyed a considerably warmer climate than it does today, this is the most complete example of the moor's prehistoric settlements, its

Dartmoor's hut circles

Wherever you tread on Dartmoor, you're likely to chance upon one of the
5000-odd Bronze and Iron Age **hut circles** that pepper the landscape. Some
are freestanding, others in groups, enclosed by circular stone walls or by
the walls of fields. The walls of the huts – whose granite bases constitute
most of what remains today – would once have supported timbers leaning
in to a central post, the conical roof covered with gorse, heather or reed.
Many were probably only used seasonally by shepherds and farmers bringing their livestock to the higher grounds in summer, while others may have
been permanent homes; some sites show evidence of corn-grinding, spinning and cheese-making, and, occasionally, pits dug in the ground as ovens.
One of the biggest concentrations of hut circles can be found on **Buttern
Hill**, northwest of the hamlet of Gidleigh, two miles west of Chagford, but
the dwellings at Grimspound are in far better shape.

comparative remoteness helping to protect it from plundering. A
stone wall nine feet thick surrounds the twenty-four circular huts
scattered within the four-acre enclosure, several of which have
raised bed-places, and you can see how the villagers ensured a constant water supply by enclosing part of a stream with a wall. South
across the valley, you'll spot the relics of old tin workings, once a
common sight hereabouts.

Grimspound is thought to have been the model for the Stone Age
settlement in which Sherlock Holmes camped in *The Hound of the
Baskervilles*, and **Hound Tor** (1360ft), an outcrop three miles to the
southwest, was supposedly the inspiration for Conan Doyle's tale.
According to local legend, phantom hounds were sighted racing
across the moor here to hurl themselves on the tomb of a hated
squire after his death in 1677. Just southeast of the tor, you can see
the remains of a **medieval village**, now no more than a collection of
low walls enclosing patches of grass, lapped on all sides by a sea
of bracken.

There's nowhere to stay in this unutterably bleak tract of moorland, but around a mile and a half northwest of Grimspound, the isolated *Warren House Inn* offers warm, firelit comfort (the fire has
been kept in for over 150 years), and good, inexpensive food: local
sausages, cheese and home-made pies. To get here, turn left when
you get onto the B3212 from the Grimspound road.

Buckland-in-the-Moor and Holne

A couple of miles south of Widecombe, **BUCKLAND-IN-THE-
MOOR** is one of the prettiest of the cluster of moorstone-and-
thatch hamlets on this eastern side of Dartmoor. Though surrounded by open country, the scattered village lies enveloped within thick woods in the winding Webburn valley. At its western end,
the restored fourteenth-century church of **St Peter** is the main
point of interest, with a medieval rood screen painted on both sides

and a good Norman font – the clock on its castellated tower has "MY DEAR MOTHER" replacing the numbers on its face. It was a gift to the parish from the local lord of the manor William Whitley in 1939, who had earlier been responsible for inscribing two slabs of granite with the Ten Commandments on top of **Buckland Beacon**, a mile east of the hamlet on the Ashburton road, in celebration of the defeat of the new Prayer Book in 1928. They're still there today, and the view from this high point is rated as one of Dartmoor's best.

From the village, the Webburn Water river trails south to join the Dart after a mile and a half, accompanied for part of the way by the road. Another mile or so south, the village of **HOLNE** is also enclosed on three sides by wooded valleys. The vicarage here was the birthplace of **Charles Kingsley**, author of such Devon-based tales as *Westward Ho!*, who is commemorated by a window in the village church. You'll also see a whimsical epitaph on the grave of Edward Collins, landlord of the next-door *Church House* inn until 1780. This timbered old pub was built three hundred years before that, and Oliver Cromwell is said to have stayed here; it still offers good meals and characterful **accommodation** (☎01364/631208; ②). On the edge of Holne, on the route of the Two Moors Way (see box on p.112), there's a **camping barn** with good facilities (☎01364/631544), backing onto a small camping field.

Ashburton

Three miles east of Holne, but thankfully bypassed by the A38, **ASH-BURTON**, a pleasing ensemble of slate-hung buildings with projecting first storeys and oriel windows, preserves an unpretentious but well-to-do air. One of Dartmoor's four **Stannary towns**, where tin was brought to be assayed and taxed, it was also an important centre of the wool trade during the Middle Ages, when nine cloth mills were at work. There's a more leisurely feel to the place these days, inviting a stroll among the antique shops, cafés and stores full of the accoutrements of country living. The oldest buildings here reflect Ashburton's former mercantile wealth, most strikingly the fifteenth-century parish church of **St Andrew**, a few yards from the centre along West Street, marked out by its lofty tower and sporting a typical Devon barrel (or cradle) roof with fine bosses. Turning left from West Street onto Lawrence Lane brings you to the fourteenth-century **St Lawrence Chapel** (May–Sept Tues & Thurs–Sat 2.30–4pm; free). Originally the private chapel of a former bishop of Exeter, it became a school before the Reformation, and remained such until 1938. Relics of the school are on show today, but more impressive is the delicate pendant plasterwork around the walls, placed here when the chapel was largely rebuilt around 1740. It is also the meeting place of the **Court Leet**, a judicial court of Saxon origin, where the Portreeve – the local market official and representative of the monarch (now an honorary position) – is still sworn in, along with his entourage of ale tasters, bread weighers, pig drovers and tree inspectors, on the fourth Tuesday in November.

Practicalities

Ashburton's **tourist office** (Mon–Sat 9.30am–1pm & 1.30–5pm; ☎01364/653426), part of the town hall on North Street, has information on the moor and on **accommodation**, of which the town has a fair selection. Top choice is the relaxed and stylish eighteenth-century *Roborough House*, 85 East St (☎01364/654614; no credit cards; ②), where breakfast is taken in the big kitchen. Down the hill, East Street has a couple of cheaper options: the *Red Lion Inn* (☎01364/ 652378; no credit cards; ①) has some cosy rooms above the bar, while the *Old Coffee House*, 27–29 East St (☎01364/652539; nonsmoking; ①), offers one en-suite room with a comfortable private sitting room. The *Ashburton Caravan Park* at Waterleat, a mile and half west of town, provides a shady riverside spot for **camping** (☎01364/652552).

For an imaginative, moderately-priced **meal**, head for informal but elegant *Agaric*, 30 North St (☎01364/654478; closed Mon & Tues). At the modish *Café Green Ginger*, 26 East St (closed Sun & Wed afternoon, plus Mon in winter), you can take breakfast, a snack lunch or cream tea in the conservatory, the walled garden or in front of the fire.

Buckfastleigh and Buckfast Abbey

Given its somewhat lacklustre air, it's hard to believe that **BUCK-FASTLEIGH**, three miles southwest of Ashburton on the A38, was once Devon's most important wool-manufacturing town, and a major staging post between Plymouth and Exeter. You'll find useful facilities here, but little to detain you other than a surprisingly engaging nostalgia-fest in the form of the **Valiant Soldier** on Fore Street (April–Oct Mon–Sat 10.30am–4.30pm, last entry 4.15pm; £2.50). Having called last orders for good in the 1960s, the pub remained untouched until its recent sympathetic restoration, which has retained all the bric-a-brac of a working-man's taproom during the 1940s and 1950s, when a pint of mild cost 1s 4d. Against the backdrop of anaglypta wallpaper, the back rooms and first-floor display a collection of old biscuit boxes, while a bakelite radio broadcasts "Mrs Dale's Diary" and a black-and-white television shows beauty queens of the 1950s. The attic has been re-created as it was when rediscovered, with a hoard of clobber going back to the turn of the twentieth century.

Most of the tourist traffic, however, converges a mile north of Buckfastleigh, where the River Dart weaves through a wooded green valley to enter the grounds of **Buckfast Abbey**. This imposing modern monastic complex occupies the site of an abbey which was founded in the eleventh century by Canute, abandoned two hundred

Buses #88, #165, #170 and #171 run to the abbey from Buckfastleigh.

Buckfast Abbey's church and grounds are open daily 5.30am–7pm; the museum and shop open May–Oct Mon–Sat 9am–5.30pm, Sun noon–5.30pm; Nov–April Mon–Sat 10am–4pm, Sun noon–4pm; free.

years later, refounded, and finally dissolved by Henry VIII. The present buildings were the work of a handful of French Benedictine monks who consecrated their new abbey in 1932, built in a traditional Anglo-Norman style which follows the design of the Cistercian building razed in 1535. It's a pretty clinical exercise, however, which doesn't invite much lingering, though there are good examples of the monks' renowned proficiency in the art of **stained-glass windows**. The vivid slabs of red, blue and yellow glass in the chapel and the huge corona of lights in front of the high altar are at their best in daylight, though for atmosphere, come to the candlelit compline here at 9pm.

Stained-glass production helps to keep the community funded, along with the honey, handicrafts and tonic wine on sale here – a flourishing trade which has inspired the locals to dub the place Fastbuckleigh. An **exhibition** outside the abbey church takes you through the process of making the stained glass, and also explains the abbey's history by way of information boards, and glass cases containing life-size dummies of handsome young monks taking a pause from their building labours. In the grounds, re-created Physic, Sensory and Lavender gardens make for a peaceful wander.

Practicalities

South Devon Railway steam trains leave from Buckfastleigh station, a mile east of town, on their journey alongside the River Dart as far as Littlehempston station at Totnes (mid-May to mid-Oct daily; check for rest of year; ☎01364/642338); a return ticket costs £6.50.

Buckfastleigh's **tourist office** is situated at the Valiant Soldier (Easter–Oct Mon–Sat 10.30am–4.30pm; ☎01364/644172). There's only one **accommodation** option in town: the basic *Kings Arms Hotel* on Fore Street (☎01364/642341; ①), which has a big bathroom and lively bars below. Better choices cluster around the abbey, the nearest being large, modern and orderly *Shyrehill*, 500yds west of the abbey on Grange Road (☎01364/642819; nonsmoking; ①). South on the Buckfastleigh road, most of the bedrooms in the eighteenth-century *Abbey Inn* (☎01364/642343; nonsmoking; ②) face the River Dart, while a few yards further down this road and over the roundabout on Dart Bridge Road, sofas, paintings and antiques combine to create an amenable atmosphere at *Dart Bridge Manor* (☎01364/643575; no credit cards; ①); free salmon fishing is also offered.

For inexpensive daytime **eating**, try the *Singing Kettle Tea Rooms*, 54 Fore St (closed Sun); it's strong on puddings, and also opens on Friday and Saturday evenings. On Plymouth Road, the continuation of Fore Street, the *White Hart* is renowned for its lunchtime pies and exotic, inexpensive evening specials; big flagstones and a log fire contribute to the congenial air. The *Abbey Inn* (see above) has a terrace right on the river for a bar snack, and a restaurant for something more substantial such as venison with pease-pudding.

The northern and northeastern moor

Although huge swaths of Dartmoor's **northern reaches** are often off-limits due to military shenanigans, there is a wealth of rugged grandeur here that's well worth seeking out. Few roads cut into the wildest parts, though plenty of tracks radiate out from the biggest town, **Okehampton**, itself a good place to hole up when bad weather sets in, with an absorbing museum. There's another cluster of villages and sights in the northeastern section of the moor, where the main centre is **Moretonhampstead**, but you'll probably be more drawn to smaller and prettier places such as **Chagford**, which also has a good choice of accommodation. North of the A382, near Drewsteignton, **Castle Drogo** is one of the last English houses planned on the grand scale, and its extensive grounds give access to some excellent walks along the Teign, taking in picturesque **Fingle Bridge**.

While Okehampton enjoys good **public transport** connections with Exeter and towns further west, services between Okehampton and Moretonhampstead are few and far between. Service #173 from Exeter is the most convenient for Moretonhampstead, Chagford and Castle Drogo.

Okehampton

The main centre on Dartmoor's northern fringes, straddling the two branches of the River Okement that merge here, **OKEHAMPTON** is an unexceptional working town lacking much of the grace or pretensions of many Devon market towns. Like other towns of similar size, Okehampton was dependent on the wool trade in medieval times, and also benefited from its position on one of the principal routes to Exeter, now the A30. Some fine old buildings survive from this period, among them the prominent fifteenth-century granite tower of the chapel of **St James** at the east end of Fore Street. Along with its continuation West Street, Fore Street forms the town's main thoroughfare, lined with shops and banks. Across from the seventeenth-century town hall, a granite archway leads off West Street to the **Museum of Dartmoor Life** (Easter–Oct Mon–Sat 10am–5pm, also June–Sept Sun 10am–5pm; Nov–Easter Mon–Fri 10am–4pm; £2), an excellent overview of habitation on the moor since earliest times. Laid out over three floors, it's a low-key but informatively labelled collection which includes such long-disappeared agricultural equipment as a threshing machine and a 1922 Morris Cowley farm pick-up on the ground floor. Upstairs is devoted to the various industries of the moor – notably tin streaming and quarrying – and the railway, though the serried ranks of domestic bric-a-brac on the top floor command more attention – look out for the pump made to keep newly-dug graves dry.

Loftily perched above the West Okement River on the south side of town, **Okehampton Castle** (April–Sept daily 10am–6pm; Oct daily

Skaigh Riding Stables (☎01837/ 840917; closed Oct–Easter) or Eastlake (☎01837/ 52513) offer horse riding in the Okehampton surrounds; both are east of town in the Belstone/Stickle path area.

10am–5pm; £2.50; EH) is the shattered hulk of a stronghold laid waste by Henry VIII; its ruins include a gatehouse, Norman keep and the remains of the Great Hall, buttery and kitchens. No shot was ever fired in anger from the granite and shale walls, and even during the Civil War both Royalists and Roundheads found themselves garrisoned here at different times. From the castle, woodland short walks and picnic spots invite a gentle exploration of what was once the deer-park of the earls of Devon.

Free audio-guides are a good means of getting some background on Okehampton Castle.

Practicalities

Okehampton is well connected by **bus** with Exeter (#X9 and #X10), Plymouth (#860) and Torbay (#X80), and is also a stop on National Express coach routes to Bodmin, Newquay and Penzance. Between May and September, an old goods line provides the town with a useful Sunday **rail** connection to Exeter via Crediton. Okehampton station is a fifteen-minute walk up Station Road from Fore Street. The **tourist office** (Easter–June & Oct Mon–Sat 10am–5pm; July–Sept daily 10am–5.30pm; Nov–Easter Mon, Fri & Sat 10am–5pm; ☎01837/53020) is near the museum, signposted next to the *White Hart* on West Street.

Facilities in Okehampton are listed on the extensive Web site www.okehampton devon.co.uk

Okehampton's best **accommodation** options lie a short walk from the centre of town. The extensive views, conservatory and outdoor heated pool outweigh the disadvantage of noise from the main A30 at *Heathfield House*, the old stationmaster's residence on Klondyke Road above the station (☎01837/54211; *www.tgibbins.freeserve. co.uk*; no credit cards; nonsmoking; ①–②; closed Nov–Easter); a £20 four-course evening meal (including wine) is offered. More economically, try the basic *Meadowlea*, lower down at 65 Station Rd (☎01837/53200; no credit cards; ①), or, in the opposite direction, the comfortable and spacious *Upcott House* on Upcott Hill, half a mile north of Okehampton's centre (☎01837/53743; no credit cards; ①). Six miles north of Okehampton on the Hatherleigh road and right on the Tarka Trail, *Higher Cadham Farm* (☎01837/851647;*www.internetsouthwest.co.uk/highercadham*; ①) is more remote, yet is still a popular spot for its oak-beamed ambience; some rooms are in a refurbished cowshed. It's signposted past the church at Jacobstowe.

Bike rental is available from Okehampton Cycles (☎01837/ 53248) at the Bostock Garden Centre, a quarter-mile north of the centre of town on North Road.

A converted goods shed at the station, Okehampton's **youth hostel** (☎01837/53916; *www.okehampton-yha.co.uk*; closed Dec–Jan) offers bunks for £11 in rooms that house four or six people; many are en suite. The small *Yertiz* **campsite** (☎01837/52281), three-quarters of a mile east of Okehampton on the B3260, is accessible by buses #X9 and #X10 from Exeter, #174 and #179 from Moretonhampstead and #180 from Widecombe; it's also signposted from the A30.

In the centre of town, tucked away behind the museum in Fairplace Terrace, the *Coffee Pot* (daytime only, plus evenings June–

A walk around Dartmoor's northern tors

This varied seven-mile, three-hour circular walk from Okehampton skirts the east of the MoD's Okehampton Range, brings you within view of the highest points on the moor, then plunges into the recesses of the East Okement River, before rounding Belstone Common and returning north to Okehampton via the village of Belstone. It's not overly arduous, though there are steep stretches along a variety of terrain, for which a compass and the Outdoor Leisure 1:25,000 map are essential.

From Okehampton, follow signs for Ball Hill and the East Okement Valley from the Mill Street car park near the centre. After half a mile, the track meets up with the right bank of the East Okement River, and soon after passes under the graceful arches of the **Fatherford Viaduct**, which carries the Exeter–Okehampton railway. South of here, the signposted path threads through the East Okement Valley, which slopes for about a mile through Halstock Wood, above and alongside the East Okement River, with weathered boulders and lovely cascades along the way. Cross the river at **Chapel Ford** using either the ford, stepping stones or footbridge here. It's a picturesque spot that makes a nice picnic-stop.

Once you've crossed, walk up the eastern bank of the East Okement for five hundred yards before following the path through an opening in the hedge, leaving the valley to head towards **Winter Tor**, just over a mile due south of the ford. At the tor, carry on up to the top of the ridge, from which a splendid panorama unfolds, with Dartmoor's highest peaks of **Yes Tor** (2028ft) and **Willhays Tor** (2039ft) visible about three miles southwest. To the east the great bowl of **Taw Marsh** can be seen.

Follow the rock-strewn ridge northwards to the pinnacles of **Belstone Common**. Between **Higher Tor** and **Belstone Tor**, you'll pass **Irishman's Wall**, the vestige of an attempt to enclose part of the moor against the wishes of the locals, who waited until the wall was nearly complete before gathering to push the structure down. Carry on heading north, descending sharply towards the **Nine Stones** cairn circle, seven hundred yards below Belstone Tor. This Bronze Age burial ground was popularly held to be the petrified remains of nine maidens turned to stone for dancing on Sunday (there are in fact twelve stones). Some 250yds north, a track leads northeast to the village of Belstone, half a mile away. From Belstone's post office, follow the road signed "Okehampton Indirect" for about half a mile northwest; you can then either carry on right back to town or turn left just beyond the private Cleave House onto a track which descends to the East Okement River, and return northwards along its bank to Okehampton.

Sept) is a cheap retreat for breakfasts, coffees and **meals**. Across West Street in Red Lion Yard, *Le Café Noir* (closed Sun) is good for inexpensive lunches, from salads and couscous to bangers and mash. A red-tiled, candlelit basement close to St James Chapel off West Street, *Cellars Bistro* (closed Sun), makes a good spot for a moderately-priced evening meal.

Moretonhampstead

At the intersection of the B3312 and the A382, which cuts across the northeastern wedge of the moor, **MORETONHAMPSTEAD** is an essentially unspoilt market town that makes an attractive entry point from Exeter – and, incidentally, shares with Woolfardisworthy (near Bideford) the honour of having the longest single-word place-name in England. Apart from its arcaded stone **almshouses** in Cross Street, dated 1637, the town is not particularly noteworthy architecturally, though it has a range of facilities that make it a useful base for stoking up or staying overnight.

Local **information** is handled by a small tourist office at 10 The Square (Easter–Oct daily 10am–1pm & 2–5pm; Nov–Easter Fri–Sun 10am–noon & 2.30–4.30pm; ☎01647/440043). Moretonhampstead's good choice of **accommodation** includes, at the western edge of the village, the friendly *Old Post House* on Court Street (☎01647/440900; *www.theoldposthouse.com*; no credit cards; non-smoking; ①); walkers are welcomed and packed lunches are available. At 33 Court St, the large Victorian *Cookshayes* (☎01647/440374; no credit cards; ①; closed Nov–Feb) is furnished in an old-fashioned country-hotel way and offers good home cooking. Three miles northeast of Moretonhampstead and right on the boundary of the National Park, one of Dartmoor's three **youth hostels** stands just 150yds away from **Steps Bridge** (☎01647/252435; closed Sept–March, also Thurs April–June) – buses #359 (not Sun) and #82 stop nearby. Its woodland setting overlooking the Teign Gorge makes it a popular overnight stop for hikers, but facilities are limited and there's self-catering only; beds cost £8.50. If you're staying locally, you can find food and drink at the *Steps Bridge Inn* at the bridge and the *Royal Oak* in **Dunsford**, a mile north.

The beamed *Gateway Tearooms* at 17 The Square in Moretonhampstead (closed Tues Oct–Easter) offers inexpensive daytime **eating**; the home-made cakes are worth sampling, and there's clotted cream to take away. On Cross Street, the *Ravensmoor* (closed Mon) offers some exotic choices such as pitta bread and tzatziki alongside more traditional cucumber sandwiches and Sunday lunches.

Chagford

Moretonhampstead has a historic rivalry with neighbouring **CHAG-FORD**, a Stannary town that also enjoyed prosperity from the local wool industry. Accessible on #173 bus between Exeter, Moretonhampstead and Bovey Tracy, it stands on a hillside overlooking the River Teign, with a pointy "pepperpot" market house at its centre that's thought to have been modelled on the Abbot's Kitchen at Glastonbury. To one side, the fine fifteenth-century church is surrounded by thatched-roofed houses, pubs and hotels.

Of these, the *Globe* on the High Street (☎01647/433485; *www.the-globe.org.uk*; ②), is the most characterful place to **stay**, with large rooms filled with books; however, its position right opposite the church means front rooms are subject to all-night tolling from the church clock. The thatched, nonsmoking eighteenth-century *Lawn House* (☎01647/433329; no credit cards; ②; closed Nov–Feb), away from The Square on Mill Street, is a quieter choice. There's a top-quality **restaurant**, the *Mill House* (☎01647/432244; closed Sun and lunchtime Mon & Tues) almost next door at 22 Mill St; the evening menu, featuring such dishes as poached quails and bouillabaisse, is very pricey, but there's a pretty good two-course set menu lunch for around £15. Chagford's pubs all offer much cheaper meals, and the *Courtyard*, just below The Square, has croissants, pies, salads, samosas and organic fruit and wholefoods, which you can eat in the small yard, and a formidable breakfast is served on Sunday mornings.

Castle Drogo and Fingle Bridge

The #173 bus (Mon–Sat) runs between Exeter, Moreton-hampstead and Bovey Tracey, while the #174 (Sun only) serves Moreton-hampstead and Okehampton.

Three miles north of Chagford, the twentieth-century granite extravaganza of **Castle Drogo** (house: April–Oct Mon–Thurs & Sat–Sun 11am–5.30pm; March Wed–Sun guided tours only, telephone ☎01647/433306 for times; £5.60; grounds: daily 10.30am–dusk £2.80; NT) occupies a stupendous site above the Teign gorge. It was built by grocery magnate Julius Drewe who, having retired at the age of 33, unearthed a link that suggested his descent from a Norman baron (Drogo), and set about creating a castle befitting his pedigree. Begun in 1910 to a design by Sir Edwin Lutyens, the original project was never completed (the money ran out in 1930), but the result was still an unsurpassed synthesis of medieval and modern elements. With six-foot walls in the main complex, the rooms are cold and austere (130 electric fires were installed to heat the place), with bare unplastered walls. The living rooms are furnished for the most part with tapestries and other items bought wholesale from a bankrupt Spanish financier. Look out for the forerunner of Subuteo in the library and the chic 1930s fashions hung on a rail in the bedroom upstairs. Immaculately clipped yew hedges surround the huge circular croquet lawn (you can rent mallets and balls if you fancy a game) and recur throughout the sunken garden, shrubbery and herbaceous border. Below the terraced gardens, paths lead down to where the River Teign burrows through the gorge, surrounded both by coppiced oakwoods – where you might spot the odd fallow deer – and bare heath, making a nice contrast for a prolonged amble.

From the eastern end of the grounds, follow Hunter's Path, higher up, or Fisherman's Path, by the riverside (both well signposted) to one of Dartmoor's most noted beauty spots, **Fingle Bridge**, a little over a mile east. This simple granite structure over the Teign, with buttresses recessed for packhorses to pass, lies in the midst of woodland that's carpeted with daffodils and bluebells in spring and is a haven for birdlife all year round. Walking westwards along the riverbank path from the bridge, you might have the luck to spot a kingfisher or any of the three types of woodpecker that frequent these

The Two Moors Way

The major walking route linking North and South Devon, the **Two Moors Way** stretches for nearly a hundred miles between Ivybridge on Dartmoor to Lynmouth (see p.144) on Exmoor's coast. The walking is good: much of the Dartmoor stretch follows a disused tramway, then switches to the Abbot's Way, the ancient path between Buckfast and Tavistock Abbeys, before passing through Holne (usually regarded as the first overnight stop), Widecombe-in-the-Moor, Chagford and Castle Drogo. There are also link paths to other routes, for example the Tarka Trail, the Templer Way (a granite tramway from Haytor to Teignmouth) and the Exe Valley Way.

The best **maps** to use are 1:50,000 Ordnance Survey Landranger maps 202, 191, 181 and 180; the Outdoor Leisure map of Dartmoor, no. 28, is also useful. If you want to walk all or part of the Two Moors Way, you should first contact the **Moors Way Association**, which can provide information about accommodation and a packhorse service for luggage-carrying along the route; send 50p in an SAE to Coppins, The Poplars, Pinhoe, Exeter EX4 9HH. The official guide from the association costs £3, or invest in either of the two fuller guides both titled *The Two Moors Way*, by John Macadam (Aurum, £12.99), which includes 1:25,000 Ordnance Survey Maps, and by James Roberts (Cicerone Press, £5.99). The tourist office at Ivybridge (April–Oct Mon–Fri 9am–5pm, Sat 9am–4pm, Sun 10am–3pm; Nov–March Mon–Fri 9am–5pm, Sat 9am–4pm; ☎01752/897035), situated at the start of the Two Moors Way next to the River Erme on Leonard's Road, can also supply plentiful **information** on the route and accommodation options.

shaded green pools in which trout, salmon and even otters frolic. At the bridge, the *Angler's Rest* pub is a handy spot for a drink, and has an adjoining **restaurant** and terrace fronting the river.

Tavistock and the western moor

More rugged and less picturesque than its other sections, **Dartmoor's western side** is also less permeated by tourism. With few obvious attractions in the neighbourhood, the moorland here has an emptier and more desolate tone. The only significant centre is **Tavistock**, an unspoilt, well-heeled town on the A386 Plymouth–Okehampton road, which holds a good range of accommodation – Thursday is a good time to stay over, to catch Friday's Pannier Market. There are fabulous walks to be made all around the town – south to **Double Waters** or northwards to forbidding **Brent Tor** and **Gibbet Hill**. You could also explore these tracts from **Lydford**, a quiet place with a small castle standing at one end of the deep **Lydford Gorge**, a gushing torrent enclosed by thick woodlands. East of Tavistock, the B3357 leads after four miles to **Merrivale**, site of the **Merrivale Megaliths**, two long, stone rows that make up one of the moor's finest prehistoric sites.

The #86 is the most useful **bus route**, travelling between Plymouth and Okehampton via Lydford and Tavistock.

Tavistock and around

On the western extremity of the moor, but just ten miles north of Plymouth, **TAVISTOCK** has its own very separate identity, partly the result of having been the seat of the most powerful abbey in the West Country during the Middle Ages. After the abbey's dissolution by Henry VIII, the town continued to prosper as a tin and wool centre, but it owes its distinctive Victorian appearance to the building boom that followed the discovery of copper deposits in the vicinity in 1844. The granite, cobbled and crenellated Bedford Square serves as the centre of the town, and is reckoned to be one of the country's finest examples of Victorian ensemble building. Behind the town hall here, the bustling **Pannier Market** has been a Friday fixture since 1105, though the present-day market buildings are nineteenth-century. On other days, craftwork, antiques and collectables are traded, making for an interesting wander. Stalls spill out from the main building, and you can usually pick up some bargains among the offerings from farmers or the Women's Institute. Tavistock is also associated with another of Dartmoor's markets, **Goose Fair**, a sprawl of stalls which take over Plymouth Road, southwest of the square, on the second Wednesday of October. You may well see some geese among the motley wares on sale, and a funfair sets up for the occasion.

Plymouth Road runs parallel to the River Tavy and, between them, to the **Tavistock Canal**, built in the early eighteenth century to carry copper ore to Morwellham Quay (see p.131), five miles away. Richly bordered with pampas grass, the towpath now provides a lovely stroll of up to one and a half miles before it disappears underground. Another fine walk is along the **viaduct** that bestrides the town to the north (walk north from Bedford Square, then turn right at Station Rd). It once carried a train track and now affords marvellous views over town and moor.

More ambitious excursions starting from Tavistock will bring you onto moorland. North of town, a four-mile lane wanders up to **Brent Tor**, 1130ft high and dominating Dartmoor's western fringes. Access to its conical summit is easiest along a path that gently ascends through the gorse that covers its southwestern side, and leads to the small church of St Michael at the top. A dark, granite structure with a squat tower, surrounded by a scattering of gravestones, it surveys a lonely scene. Bleak, treeless moorland extends in every direction, wrapped in silence that's occasionally pierced by the shrill cries of stonechats and wheatears. You'll see **Gibbet Hill** (1158ft) looming over Black Down a couple of miles eastwards; it's said to be where criminals were left to die in cages during the Middle Ages.

Practicalities

Tavistock's well-equipped **tourist office** is housed in the town hall on Bedford Square (April–Oct Mon–Sat 9.30am–5pm, plus late July & Aug Sun 9.30am–5.30pm; Nov–March Mon–Tues & Fri–Sat

10am–4.30pm ☎01822/612938). Among the **accommodation** options, a good choice in the centre of town is the Georgian *Eko Brae* (☎01822/614028; no credit cards; ①) at 4 Bedford Villas, a continuation of West Street which runs parallel to Plymouth Road off Bedford Square; the plant-filled rooms are decorated in soft pastels, and there's a sunny patio. Also on West Street but much more luxurious, *Browns* (☎01822/618686; ⑨) is a swish cream- and brown-liveried hotel with embossed French radiators, Delabole slate floors and Egyptian cotton bedding. About half a mile east out of Tavistock off the B3357 Princetown road, the excellent-value *Mount Tavy Cottage* (☎01822/614253; *www.mounttavy.freeserve.co.uk*; ①) is set in a lush garden roamed by chickens and guinea fowl, and offers pristine white bed linen, freestanding baths and organic breakfasts. For a complete splurge, you can't fault the *Horn of Plenty* (☎01822/832528; *www.thehornofplenty.co.uk*; ⑦/⑧), signposted at Gulsworthy Cross, three miles west of Tavistock off the A390. Rooms are richly furnished with antiques, service is impeccable yet without airs, and there's a stunning garden and panoramic views. The nearest **campsite** is *Higher Longford Farm* (☎01822/613360), two miles north of Tavistock on the B3357 and reachable on bus #172.

Bikes can be rented from Tavistock Cycles, Paddons Row, Brook Street (☎01822/ 617630).

Inexpensive **eats** can be had at *Monterey Jacks*, 15 West St (closed Sun lunch), a Western-style restaurant incorporated into the more traditional *Cornish Arms* pub, or opposite at *Steps* (closed Sun), which does pasta and pizza as well as beef cobbler and lamb chops. Prices are steeper at *Neil's Restaurant* (☎01822/615550; *www.neils-restaurant.co.uk*; closed daytime), 27 King St, off West Street, where fresh local ingredients are the basis of the Continental menu; booking is essential. Right on the canal the *Wharf* theatre and **arts centre** (☎01822/611166) puts on year-round films and entertainment varying from Chinese opera to Abba tributes.

Dartmoor's Letterboxes

The pursuit of **letterboxing** – a sort of treasure hunt with a rubber stamp as the prize that's unique to Dartmoor – originated in 1854 when hardy walkers started a tradition of leaving their calling cards in a jar at Cranmere Pool near the head of the West Okement river, then one of the most inaccessible points on the northern moor. In 1937, a stone "letterbox" was erected over the spot, and the practice was adopted at other tors. The "letterboxes" gradually multiplied, and today, there are around 4,000 of them. Each contains the rubber stamp and inkpad that are the key elements of this early form of orienteering. The popularity of letterboxing has much to do with the fact that it needs no organization or set starting point, however, organized walks with a competitive bent also take place occasionally: tourist offices can provide trail leaflets and schedules for forthcoming events.

Lydford

Seven miles north of Tavistock, **LYDFORD**'s unassuming appearance gives little hint of its eventful history as a Saxon outpost against the Celts, and one of Alfred the Great's four principal settlements in Devon, founded for defence against the Danes. Traces of the Saxon fortifications – an earth rampart – can still be seen on either side of the main road at the northeastern end of the village, but the Saxon castle was completely destroyed by the Danes in 997. The best-preserved monument is the sturdy but small-scale **Lydford Castle** (unrestricted access; free), a square Norman keep that, until 1800, was used as a prison for offenders against the Stannary, or Tinners' Law, with the Stannary Court on the first floor. The justice administered from here had a fearsome reputation throughout Dartmoor, as described by a local poet in the seventeenth century: "I oft have heard of Lydford Law/How in the morn they hang and draw/And sit in judgement after."

The #86 bus service connects Lydford with Tavistock and Okehampton.

The chief attraction here, though, is **Lydford Gorge** (daily: April–Sept 10am–5.30pm; Oct 10am–4pm; Nov–March 10.30am–3pm; £3.60; NT); the main entrance is a five-minute walk downhill from the village. Overgrown with thick woods, the one-and-a-half-mile gorge is an idyllic place, alive with butterflies, spotted woodpeckers, dippers, herons and clouds of insects, though you'll usually be sharing it with plenty of other visitors. A circular **walk** starts off high above the River Lyd, dropping down to the hundred-foot **White Lady Waterfall**, and returning along the opposite bank to the foaming whirlpools of the Devil's Cauldron, near the main entrance. The full course would take you roughly two hours at a leisurely pace, but there's a separate entrance at the south end of the gorge if you only want to visit the waterfall. In winter months, when the river can flood, the waterfall is the only part of the gorge open to the public (between November and March).

The Lydford Gorge café at the main entrance is open between April and October.

Back in the village and right next to the castle, the picturesque *Castle Inn* offers beautifully decorated **accommodation** in low-ceilinged, oak-beamed rooms (☎01822/820242; *castleinnlyd@aol.com*; ⑥). On a less grand scale, the family-run *Moorlands* (☎01822/820229; no credit cards; ①; closed Nov–Easter), 300yd from the A386 on the Lydford turning, retains original painted-wood panelling in the bedrooms. You can take a drink or snack in the *Castle Inn*'s firelit sixteenth-century bar, or a meal in the first-class **restaurant** – curries and game feature – but you can spend less and eat just as well at the slightly twee *Dartmoor Inn* (☎01822/820221; closed Sun eve & Mon), on the A386 opposite the Lydford turning. Tasty baguettes and set lunches are available during the day, and there are moderately-priced Mediterranean-inspired dinners for which you should book at weekends.

Horse riding in the area is on offer at the Lydford House Hotel (☎01822/ 820321), 500yd from the A386.

Merrivale

Five miles east of Tavistock, the River Walkham crosses the B3357 at **MERRIVALE**, a hamlet which amounts to little more than the

The #98 (not Sun) and #172 buses connect Merrivale with Tavistock and Princetown; just three miles north-west, the latter is a good alternative if you don't want to return to Tavistock (see p.96).

large *Dartmoor Inn*, where you can get basic meals and refreshments. At 1000ft, Merrivale commands views extending – on a very clear day – as far as the Eddystone Lighthouse in Plymouth Sound.

The spot's main claim to fame, however, is its proximity to one of Dartmoor's most spectacular prehistoric sites, the **Merrivale Megaliths**, an easy half-mile walk west and just a few yards from the B3357. This double row of upright stones, dating from any time between 2500 BC and 750 BC, form a stately procession for 850ft across the bare landscape. Probably connected with ancient burial rites, the rows are known locally as "Potato Market" or "Plague Market" in memory of the time when provisions for plague-stricken Tavistock were deposited here. Halfway along the southern row, a stone circle surrounds a cairn over a cremation pit, and blocking stones, kistvaens (rough granite box tombs) and hut circles complete the complex.

Various tracks from here offer a choice of rewarding **hikes**, for instance along the western slopes of the Walkham valley, where the sphinx-like pinnacle of **Vixen Tor** (1040ft), a mile to the southwest, crouches above the barren moor, presenting resemblances ranging from an old man's face to various animals. A mile and a half northeast of Merrivale, **Great Mis Tor**, at 1765ft affords more inspiring views and has a distinctive rock basin, Mistorpan, also known as the Devil's Frying Pan. However, as this lies within a firing area, you'll need to check on accessibility.

Travel details

Trains

Okehampton to: Exeter (late May to mid-Sept Sun 5 daily; 40min).

Buses

Ashburton to: Bovey Tracey (Mon–Sat 8 daily, Sun 6 daily; 15min); Buckfastleigh (Mon–Sat 2–3 hourly, Sun 8 daily; 10–15min); Buckland-in-the-Moor (Wed 1 daily; 50min); Widecombe-in-the-Moor (late May to late Sept Mon–Sat 2–3 daily, Sun 4 daily; 20–35min).

Bovey Tracey to: Ashburton (Mon–Sat 8 daily, Sun 6 daily; 15min); Chagford (Mon–Sat 5 daily; 45min); Moretonhampstead (Mon–Sat 5 daily; 35min).

Buckfastleigh to: Ashburton (Mon–Sat 2–3 hourly, Sun 8 daily; 10–15min).

Chagford to: Bovey Tracey (Mon–Sat 5 daily; 45min); Moretonhampstead (Mon–Sat 5 daily; 15min).

Lydford to: Okehampton (Mon–Sat hourly, Sun 2–7 daily; 20min); Tavistock (Mon–Sat hourly, Sun 2–7 daily; 25min).

Moretonhampstead to: Bovey Tracey (Mon–Sat 5 daily; 30min); Chagford (Mon–Sat 5 daily; 15min); Okehampton (Mon–Sat 1 daily, late May to late Sept also Sun 8 daily; 50min); Postbridge (late May to late Sept Mon–Sat 3 daily, Sun 5 daily; late Sept to late May Sat & Sun 3 daily; 25min); Princetown (late May to late Sept Mon–Sat 3 daily, Sun 5 daily; late Sept to late May Sat & Sun 3 daily; 30–45min); Widecombe-in-the-Moor (Sun 2 daily; 35min).

Okehampton to: Lydford (Mon–Sat hourly, Sun 7 daily; 20min);
Moretonhampstead (Mon–Sat 1 daily, late May to late Sept also Sun 8 daily;
50min); Tavistock (Mon–Sat hourly, Sun 2–7 daily; 45min).

Postbridge to: Moretonhampstead (late May to late Sept Mon–Sat 3 daily, Sun
3–5 daily; 25min); Princetown (late May to late Sept Mon–Sat 3 daily, Sun 5
daily; late Sept to late May Sat & Sun 3 daily; 15min).

Princetown to: Moretonhampstead (late May to late Sept Mon–Sat 3 daily, Sun
5 daily; late Sept to late May Sat & Sun 3 daily; 30–45min); Postbridge (late
May to late Sept Mon–Sat 3 daily, Sun 5 daily; late Sept to late May Sat & Sun
3 daily; 20min); Tavistock (Mon–Sat 9 daily, late May to mid-Sept also Sun 3
daily; 25min); Widecombe-in-the-Moor (late May to mid-Sept Mon–Sat 2 daily;
1hr)

Tavistock to: Lydford (Mon–Sat hourly, Sun 7 daily; 25min); Okehampton
Mon–Sat hourly, Sun 2–7 daily; 45min); Merrivale (Mon–Sat 9 daily, late May
to late Sept also Sun 3 daily; 15min); Plymouth (Mon–Sat 2–3 hourly, Sun
hourly; 50min); Princetown (Mon–Sat 9 daily, late May to mid-Sept also Sun 3
daily; 25min).

Widecombe-in-the-Moor to: Ashburton (late May to late Sept Mon–Sat 2–3
daily, Sun 4 daily; 20–35min); Moretonhampstead (Sun 2 daily; 35min);
Princetown (late May to mid-Sept Mon–Sat 2 daily; 1hr).

Chapter 5

Plymouth and around

A s the largest city in Devon and Cornwall, **Plymouth** has a very different feel to anywhere else in the region. There could be no greater contrast to the snug villages a short distance away in the South Hams, or the miles of wilderness in nearby Dartmoor, than the city's urban sprawl or the immensity of Plymouth Sound, with its docks and naval base. Nonetheless, Plymouth is an essential component of the Devon's seafaring identity, and the city's maritime traditions are most obvious when you're gazing down onto the Sound from historic **Plymouth Hoe**. While much of modern Plymouth is off-puttingly ugly, the **Barbican** and **Sutton Harbour** are as compact and unspoiled as any of the West Country's medieval quarters, and the city's **National Marine Aquarium** holds one of the country's finest marine collections.

Moreover, Plymouth serves as a lively base for day-trips to the handful of attractions that surround the city. The nearest of these is the wooded Rame promontory across the Sound, where formal gardens give onto a wild coastline at **Mount Edgcumbe**, and **Cawsand** and **Kingsand** preserve their villagey character; all three within easy distance of the only decent swimming spot here-abouts, **Whitsand Bay**. Further out lie a ring of elegant country houses with both aesthetic appeal and historical resonance. Most dazzling of these is **Saltram House**, an aristocratic pile to the east of the city containing a wealth of work by Robert Adam and Joshua Reynolds. If you find the overstated decor here indigestible, you

---

ACCOMMODATION PRICE CODES

Throughout this *Guide*, hotel and B&B accommodation is coded on a scale of ① to ⑨, the code indicating the lowest price you can expect to pay per night for a double room in high season. The prices indicated by the codes are as follows:

① under £40	④ £60–70	⑦ £110–150
② £40–50	⑤ £70–90	⑧ £150–200
③ £50–60	⑥ £90–110	⑨ over £200

may get more out of two Tudor mansions north of Plymouth – **Buckland Abbey**, former home of the mariners Drake and Grenville, and **Cotehele**, a rich repository of tapestries, embroideries and sixteenth-century furnishings. On a more upbeat note, **Morwellham Quay** is a surprisingly well-done heritage site reliving the history of this nineteenth-century copper-shipping port on the River Tamar, comprising an extensive open-air museum of industrial archeology.

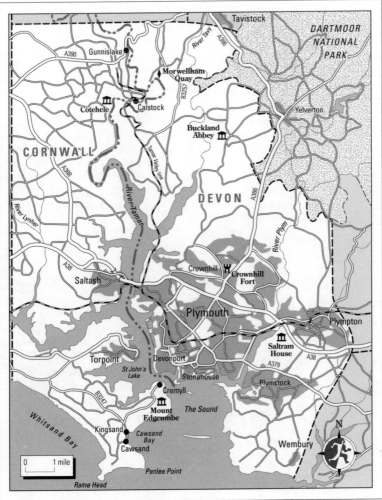

© Crown copyright

Plymouth

Though dominated by mediocre architecture and beset with heavy traffic along the inner ring roads that slice ruthlessly through its residential and shopping neighbourhoods, **PLYMOUTH** has gone to great lengths to preserve its surviving older buildings and boost its tourist profile. However, there's little harmony between its appealing historic core and the dreary modern city, and if it weren't for some absorbing newer attractions, you could easily bypass the place altogether. At all events, it would be difficult to spoil the glorious vista over **Plymouth Sound** – the basin of calm water at the mouth of the combined Plym, Tavy and Tamar estuar-

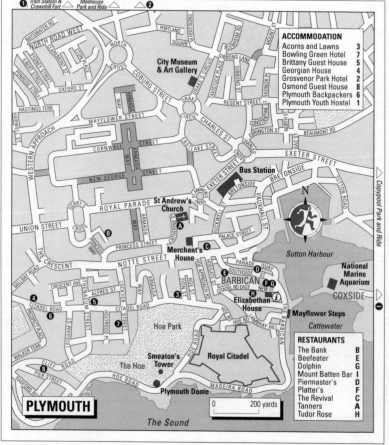

ACCOMMODATION

Acorns and Lawns	3
Bowling Green Hotel	7
Brittany Guest House	5
Georgian House	4
Grosvenor Park Hotel	2
Osmond Guest House	8
Plymouth Backpackers	6
Plymouth Youth Hostel	1

RESTAURANTS

The Bank	B
Beefeater	E
Dolphin	G
Mount Batten Bar	I
Piermaster's	D
Platter's	F
The Revival	C
Tanners	A
Tudor Rose	H

© Crown copyright

ies – from the high grassy expanse of **Plymouth Hoe**, itself largely unchanged since Drake played his famous game of bowls here before joining battle with the Armada. The best preserved remnants of the medieval town lie in a compact area within a short walk of the Hoe, down by **Sutton Harbour** and around the Elizabethan warehouses and inns of the adjacent **Barbican**, where the tight network of lanes have recently become the focus of high-spirited nightlife and a gamut of seafood restaurants. Just across from the Barbican, the **National Marine Aquarium** is Plymouth's premier draw, a modern complex housing a diverse aquatic population in imaginatively reconstructed watery habitats. Elsewhere in the city, the only unmissable item is the Victorian **Crownhill Fort**, whose honeycomb of vaults and tunnels offers a far more compelling alternative to a tour of the **Royal Citadel**, down by the water.

Some history

Plymouth grew from the "littel fishe towne" of Sutton, a site at the mouth of the River Plym owned by the monks of Plympton Priory. The growing importance of its sheltered deep-water anchorage during the Hundred Years War against France led to the amalgamation of Sutton – freed from monastic rule in 1439 – with other settlements in the estuary, and the town, under its present name, became the first in England to receive a charter by Act of Parliament. Plymouth also prospered as a result of the silting up of the River Plym upstream, making the port an important outlet for wool shipments; its wealth in Tudor times is attested by the grand houses surviving from that era in and around the city. Alongside its natural attributes, the town owed its leading role as a naval base to the fact that it was home to such great mariners as **Hawkins** and **Drake**. The royal fleet was stationed here during the wars against Spain, and it was from here that Drake sailed to defeat the Spanish Armada in 1588. **Raleigh** and **Grenville** launched their failed attempts to colonize Virginia from Plymouth, and thirty-two years later Sutton Harbour was the last embarkation point of the **Pilgrim Fathers**, whose New Plymouth colony became the nucleus of the English settlement of North America.

Plymouth sided with the Parliamentarians during the Civil War, consequently enduring a two-year siege by Royalist troops, and Charles II prudently commanded the **Citadel** to be built after the Restoration to safeguard against future anti-Royalist eruptions. The construction of the **Royal Naval Dockyard** at the end of the seventeenth century, in what's now the Devonport area, ensured the city's continuing importance. Cook and Darwin both sailed from here in later eras of discovery, and the town's prestige was further enhanced by the building of the **Royal Albert Bridge** in 1859, spanning the Tamar at Saltash to connect Devon with Cornwall by rail – the last engineering feat of Isambard Kingdom Brunel. Plymouth's Victorian street-plan was obliterated by heavy bombing during **World War II**, and the subsequent rebuilding, while undeniably ambitious, failed to inject much style or grace into the city centre. Plymouth has not shed its links with the sea, however: the naval presence is still strong, and the Devonport dockyards continue to be a bulwark of the local economy.

Arrival and information

If you're driving from Cornwall, you pay £1 to use the Saltash road bridge or Torpoint ferry (it's free the other way).

Easily reached by road or rail from Exeter, Plymouth has good public-transport connections with all the major centres of the West Country, and to the towns and villages of Cornwall's southern coast. The **train station** is north of the centre off Saltash Road; from here, bus #25 leaves every fifteen minutes for the central Royal Parade, Sutton Harbour, the Hoe and the Citadel. The **bus station** (☎01752/222666) on Bretonside, just over St Andrew's Cross from Royal Parade, is much more central, and has **left-luggage lockers** (maximum 24 hours). **Drivers** will find parking difficult, as car parks fill quickly; however **park and ride** schemes operate between Monday and Saturday from Copypool, to the east of the city off the B3416 near the Marsh Mills roundabout, and from Monday to Friday at Milehouse, near the Plymouth Argyle football ground, just north of the train station on the A386. **Rail and ride** schemes also operate from Ivybridge, Liskeard and Gunnislake stations.

A Guide Friday bus tour (late April to Oct; £5.50; ☎01752/ 667721; www .guidefriday .com) is an excellent way to familiarize yourself with the city; tickets are available on board or from the kiosk on Royal Parade, and give discounts to several Plymouth attractions.

The main **tourist office** is just off Sutton Harbour at Island House, 9 The Barbican (April–Oct Mon–Sat 9am–5pm, Sun 10am–4pm; Nov–March Mon–Fri 9am–5pm, Sat 10am–4pm; ☎01752/304849). There is another office at Marsh Mills Roundabout on the A38, east of the city (same times; ☎01752/266030).

Accommodation

Befitting its size, Plymouth has a wide range of **accommodation**, though the many conventions and events taking place here year-round mean that rooms can still be scarce. If you want to be near the sights, your best choice is the row of B&Bs edging the Hoe on Citadel Road, but if you prefer to stay close to the train station, you won't be more than a twenty-minute walk from the Hoe and Barbican areas in any case. Continental **ferry** passengers might want to be nearer the docks in the Millbay district, on the western side of the city.

Hotels and B&Bs

Acorns and Lawns, 171 Citadel Rd ☎01752/229474. One of a terrace of competitively priced B&Bs off the eastern side of Plymouth Hoe, offering good-value, florally decorated rooms and vegetarian breakfasts. No credit cards. ①.

Bowling Green Hotel, 9–10 Osborne Place, Lockyer Street ☎01752/209090; *www.bowlinggreenhotel.co.uk*. Smart and friendly, with leather sofas and bright, pine-furnished bedrooms overlooking the Hoe. ②.

Brittany Guest House, 28 Athenaeum St ☎01752/262247. More stylish than the similar establishments in the area, this easy-going place offers kippers for breakfast and use of a private car park (a bonus around here). ②.

Georgian House, 51 Citadel Rd ☎01752/663237. A good choice on this strip, with large-patterned anaglypta wallpaper and friendly owners. Bikes welcome. Closed Dec. ②.

Grosvenor Park Hotel, 114 North Rd East ☎01752/229312. Convenient for the train station, and great value, with secure parking and evening meals on request. ①.

Osmond Guest House, 42 Pier St ☎01752/229705; *mike@osmondgh. freeserve.co.uk*. Cheerful choice close to the Great Western Docks, with bright-red walls and a pick-up service from the bus and train stations. ①.

Hostels

Plymouth Backpackers, 172 Citadel Rd ☎01752/225158; *www.backpackers.co.uk*. Relaxed place on the hotel strip near the Hoe and Royal Parade. There's a free minibus pick-up service if you ring ahead, and laundry, bar and Internet access. Dorms are £10, and there are some simple double rooms (not en suite; ①). No credit cards.

Plymouth YHA, Belmont House, Devonport Rd ☎01752/562189; *www.yha.org.uk*. Lovely Georgian house with a grand dining room, separate self-catering facilities and dorm beds for £11. Walk a quarter-mile along Devonport Rd from Devonport train station, or catch a bus from the centre (Citybus #18A, #26, #33 or #34, or First Western National #15, #15A or #81).

A Day Explorer ticket (£3.40), available on buses or from the bus station, gives unlimited travel on First Western National services in the city.

The City

A broad grassy esplanade studded with reminders of the city's great events, **Plymouth Hoe** is a stirring spot to start a tour of the city. Resplendent in fair weather, the Hoe (from the Saxon "high place") can also attract some pretty ferocious winds, making it an unappealing prospect in wintry conditions. The seaward views, however, are glorious, taking in **Drake's Island** in the centre of the Sound; a fortification, then a prison and now owned by the chairman of Plymouth Argyle FC. Approaching from the city centre, you'll pass a distinctive tall, white **naval cenotaph** and smaller monuments to the defeat of the Spanish Armada and to the airmen who defended the city during the wartime blitz, alongside a rather portly statue of **Sir Francis Drake** gazing grandly out to the sea. Appropriately, there's a bowling green back from the brow of the Hoe.

In front of the war memorials, the red-and-white striped **Smeaton's Tower** (due to reopen spring 2002; call ☎01752 /603300 for times and ticket prices) was erected as a lighthouse in 1759, on the treacherous Eddystone Rocks, fourteen miles out to sea. When replaced by a larger beacon in 1882, it was reassembled here, where it gives the loftiest view over Plymouth Sound. Below the tower, the **Plymouth Dome** (April–Sept daily 9am–6pm;

Useful Plymouth-related Web sites include www .plymouth .gov.uk, a council site listing hotels, restaurants and entertainments; www.plymouth explore.co.uk, which is selective but more expansive; and www.plymouth city.co.uk, which has general info and links.

Oct–March Tues–Sun 9am–5pm, last admission 1hr before closing; £4.10) provides a slick audiovisual history of Plymouth and the lives of local heroes such as Drake and the *Mayflower* Pilgrims, with models and reconstructions – it's best tackled on a wet afternoon.

Tickets for Royal Citadel tours can be picked up at the Plymouth Dome, the tourist office or from the citadel itself before the tour.

On the seafront east of the Hoe, Plymouth's **Royal Citadel** (tours May–Sept at 2.30pm; £3; EH), an uncompromising fortress constructed in 1666 to intimidate the populace of the only town in the southwest held by the Parliamentarians in the Civil War, is still partly in military use. The ninety-minute guided tour of the grassy ramparts, seventeenth-century Governor's House and the 1845 **Royal Chapel of St Katherine** is informative and cannon buffs will be in their element; the views over Plymouth and the Sound are superb.

Sutton Harbour and the Barbican

North of the Citadel, the old town's quay at **Sutton Harbour** is still used by Plymouth's sizeable trawler fleet and is the scene of a boisterous early-morning fish market. The **Mayflower Steps** here, opposite the tourist office, commemorate the sailing of the **Pilgrim Fathers** in 1620; a nearby plaque lists the names and professions of the 102 Puritans. Captain Cook's voyages to the South Seas, Australia and the Antarctic also set sail from here, as did the nineteenth-century ships that transported thousands of convicts and colonists to Australia; Francis Chichester also embarked from and returned to Sutton Harbour on his round-the-world solo jaunt aboard *Gipsy Moth IV* in 1966–67.

In summer, the Mayflower Steps are the embarkation point for a direct motor launch to the village of Cawsand (see p.129), which departs every two hours or so from 10.30am (£2 single) when conditions permit; check here or at the tourist office.

Nowadays, the harbour is the starting point for **cruises** – mostly April to October only – ranging from one-hour tours around the Sound and Devonport naval dockyard (£4) to a four-hour cruise up the Tamar to the Cornish village of Calstock. For **fishing trips**, contact Fish 'n' Trips (☎07971/208381): two and a half hours cost £8, or you can join a four-hour mackerel expedition for £12.

The **Barbican** district, which edges the harbour to the south, is the heart of old Plymouth, with shops and restaurants lining the main Southside Street. The parallel New Street holds seventeenth-century warehouses and some of the oldest residential buildings, among them the **Elizabethan House** (April–Sept Wed–Sun 10am–5pm; £1), a former captain's dwelling that retains most of its original architectural features, including a lovely spiral staircase with what's probably a disused ship's mast for the central newel post and a rope for the rail. The three floors are crammed with fine sixteenth- and seventeenth-century furniture and textiles, including such items as a child's chair and a geometrically patterned spice cabinet in the dining room. The attic bedrooms hold a pair of grand beds, an oak-carved canopied tester and a Brittany box bed with sliding door, decorated with winged cherubs.

The National Marine Aquarium

Cross the footbridge by the Mayflower Steps over Sutton Harbour to reach Plymouth's newest exhibit, the grand **National Marine Aquarium** (daily: April–Oct 10am–6pm; Nov–March 10am–4pm; £6.50; *www.national-aquarium.co.uk*). Exhibits are on three levels, arranged according to habitat: an escalator takes you to the upper level (a moorland stream), then you zizzag your way down to river estuary, shore and shallow sea, ending up in coral seas and the shark theatre. The most popular exhibits are Europe's largest collection of seahorse species, the colourful reefs – look out for the extraordinary frog fish waving its tentacles – and the sharks, though these, as yet immature, are eclipsed by the stately diamond-like lookdown jacks which parade in shoals. Guides are on hand to answer questions, and talks and presentations take place throughout the day. Feeding-times – carried out by divers – are particularly worth catching: currently 11am on Monday, Wednesday and Friday for the sharks, and daily at 2.30pm (winter) or 3pm (summer) for the deep reef.

Aquarium tickets allow re-entry for one day (make sure your hand is stamped before you leave); buying in advance from the tourist office will save you queuing.

Merchant's House Museum and St Andrew's

Across Notte Street from the top of Southside Street, the handsome timber-framed **Merchant's House Museum** at 33 St Andrew's St (April–Sept Tues–Fri 10am–1pm & 2–5.30pm, Sat 10am–1pm & 2–5pm; £1) dates back to 1608 when it was lived in by William Parker, a merchant, privateer, mayor of Plymouth and probably the master of the *Mary Rose*, which victualled Francis Drake's fleet when it sailed against the Armada. Preserving its original architecture, it's now an engrossing collection of relics from Plymouth's past. Each of the three floors follows a historical theme: the Victorian schoolroom can be quickly passed through, but the photographs documenting the wartime blitz are enlightening, and the reconstructed prewar pharmacy on the third floor, resplendent with variously coloured bottles, invites a linger, and you can also see the old Barbican ducking stool.

Behind the museum, off Royal Parade, the city's chief place of worship is **St Andrew's** (Mon–Sat 9am–4pm), a reconstruction of the original fifteenth-century building that was almost completely destroyed by a bomb in 1941. Occupying the role of the Anglican cathedral which Plymouth (strangely) never had, the church has always been at the heart of the city's life: local boy William Bligh, of *Mutiny on the Bounty* fame, was baptized here, and the entrails of the navigator Martin Frobisher are buried here, as are those of Admiral Blake, the Parliamentarian who died as his ship entered Plymouth after destroying a Spanish treasure fleet off Tenerife. However, the real draw are the six stained-glass windows designed by John Piper, who was also responsible for the more famous stained glass in Coventry Cathedral. Luridly coloured in deep reds and blues, and incorporating symbols from the scriptures – the central east window shows the elements air, earth, fire and water – the windows, installed in 1958, are a radical departure from the norm, and have raised plenty of hackles among traditionalists.

City Museum and Art Gallery

To the north of St Andrew's Cross at Drake's Circus, the **City Museum and Art Gallery** (Tues–Fri 10am–5.30pm, Sat 10am–5pm; free) is a small but engaging collection that's worth an idle hour or two, especially for its paintings and changing exhibitions. The Art Gallery has a particularly good collection of modern British paintings which form the basis of rotating exhibitions, including works by artists of the Newlyn and St Ives schools such as Stanhope Forbes, Peter Lanyon, Patrick Heron, Bryan Pearce and Alfred Wallis. Amongst the rather random items in the permanent museum displays, the fine eighteenth-century Plymouth porcelain in the China Connection room is worth seeking out, but the most absorbing section is **Tales from the City** on the ground floor, an imaginative review of Plymouth citizens' lives over the past century, which covers everything from birth to death via shopping and housing. Photographs and tape recordings tell the stories – you sit at a school desk to hear classroom memories, at a bus seat for tales of transport, and a cinema seat for film reminiscences.

Crownhill Fort

Plymouth's best example of military architecture – and a worthwhile excursion for anyone keen to get off the main tourist circuit – lies four miles north of the centre, in the Crownhill district. Easily accessed from the A386, the sixteen-acre site of **Crownhill Fort** (April–Oct daily 10am–5pm; £3.75; *www.crownhillfort.co.uk*) was designed by E.F. Du Cane, who was also responsible for Wormwood Scrubs prison in London, and was built between 1863 and 1872 as one of the "Palmerston forts" – intended to defend the country from a fancied French invasion – when it represented the cutting edge of military design. It was kept on by the army until 1986 and subsequently fully restored to its original design, surrounded by a ditch and hefty earth ramparts. The impressive, Norman-style granite entrance leads to a gravel parade ground; from here, you've free access to a deep warren of passages that lead off to the scattered gun emplacements and barracks restored to both Victorian and 1940s usage. Look out for the Moncrieff counterweight "disappearing" gun, the only one of its type in the world, which fires and then disappears by sinking into the ground. If you can, time your visit for when this, along with other cannonry here, is fired by an artillery unit in the uniform of the 1890s (usually on the third weekend in the month; call ☎01752/793754 to check for times).

The frequent buses #40, #41 and #44 run to Crownhill from Royal Parade (outside the Pizza Hut) – get off at Budshead service station.

Eating and drinking

Plymouth is well-served with **eating and drinking** establishments, of which you'll find a particularly eclectic range in and around the Barbican quarter.

The Bank, Old George St. Originally designed as a bank, this pub retains its opulent mahogany ambience and is popular with the business crowd. Potato skins and baguettes as well as standard main meals are on offer, and live bands play on Thursdays.

Beefeater, Southside St ☎01752/224305. Chain restaurant with mediocre food but a terrific atmosphere. The restored Refectory Room– part of the one-time Blackfriars monastery – is one of Plymouth's oldest buildings, with timbered roof and original features, and also claims to be the last stopover of the Pilgrim Fathers. Moderate.

The Dolphin, Southside St. Long-established fishermen's pub in the Barbican that's busy with seafarers in the morning and boisterous at night. Simple lunchtime snacks are available.

The Mount Batten Bar, Lawrence Rd, Mount Batten. Reachable by water taxi from the Mayflower Steps, this large venue with wrought-iron pillars has a good choice of snacks and meals and live bands at weekends. Upstairs, the more formal *Shaw's Restaurant* (☎01752/405500) has a good range of international dishes; window seats get booked up quickly, especially for Sunday lunch. Inexpensive–Moderate.

Piermaster's, 33 Southside St ☎01752/229345. Plain and elegant fish restaurant that's supplied straight from the nearby harbour. Closed Sun. Moderate–Expensive.

Platters, 12 The Barbican ☎01752/227262. Very popular, down-to-earth place where diners are surrounded by a plaster relief illustrating the life of a guppy fish. Food (mainly fish) is not bad either. Moderate.

The Revival, 58 Notte St. Mexican/Italian/American diner with lots of jazzy ambience, offering lunches for under a fiver and a Sunday carvery. Inexpensive–Moderate.

Tanners, Prysten House, Finewell St ☎01752/252001. Set in Plymouth's oldest building, this blends flagstones and New Agey painted walls, and offers alfresco dining in summer. The dishes are also a mixture, a sort of West Country *à la Mediterranée*. Booking is essential (2–3 weeks ahead for weekends). Evenings only. Closed Mon & first 2 weeks in Jan. Moderate–Expensive.

Tudor Rose, 36 New St. Good for daytime traditional food such as cottage pies, and summer teas in the garden. Inexpensive.

We've given telephone numbers only for restaurants where you need to book a table in advance.

Nightlife and entertainment

Nightlife in Plymouth, from theatre-going to clubbing, has become very lively in recent years. The Theatre Royal on Royal Parade (☎01752/267222) stages **plays**, **opera**, **ballet and musicals** throughout the year, and houses the Drum, a more intimate venue for drama and musicals. The Barbican theatre, on The Barbican itself (☎01752/267131), stages more avant-garde performances. Plymouth Pavilions on Millbay Road (☎01752/229922) is the major venue for pop, rock and classical **concerts** and comedy, while

*Monthly free
listings
magazines* tdb,
twenty4-seven
and What's On
Southwest *are
worth consult-
ing for up-to-
date entertain-
ment informa-
tion.*

informal live-music sessions are held at the *China House* pub at Coxside. One of the liveliest venues, the *Candy Store* at 103 Mayflower St (☎01752/220077) has regular indie gigs and stays open until 4am for **dancing**, when UK garage and US house are aired. *The Cooperage* at 114 Vauxhall St (☎01752/229275; *www.pmc.uk.net*) and the *Dance Academy* (☎01752/220055; *www.danceacademy.co.uk*) at 121 Union St also play club sounds until 5am at weekends, while *Destiny*, at Barbican Leisure Park, Coxside (☎01752/255057), plays old and new dance classics, usually for over-21s. New places are popping up all the time on Southside Street; *Bar Rhumba*, with a cocktail bar and a large dance floor, is the current hotspot.

Listings

Car rental Hertz, Sutton Rd, Coxside ☎01752/207207; Rent-a-Car, 8 The Octagon, off Union St ☎01752/601000; Thrifty, 22–28 Cattedown Rd ☎01752/210021.

Hospital Derriford Hospital, Derriford (☎01752/792511), four miles north of the centre, has a 24hr casualty unit.

Internet access You can log on for £5 per hour at *City Café*, 32 Frankfort Gate (Mon–Sat 9am–6pm; ☎01752/221777).

Laundrette K.R. Endacott, 55 Notte St (☎01752/223031).

Post office St Andrew's Cross (Mon–Sat 9am–5.30pm).

Taxis There are ranks at the train station, as well as at Raleigh St (off Derry's Cross) and The Barbican. You can also call Armada Cabs ☎01752/666222; Central Taxis ☎01752/363638; Plymouth Taxis ☎01752/252525; and Taxifast ☎01752/222222.

Around Plymouth

The various sights **around Plymouth** provide a welcome antidote to the urban bustle, and all are within an hour's journey of the city. One of the best local day-excursions is to **Mount Edgcumbe**, where woods and meadows lie within easy reach of some fabulous sand. You can get here by ferry from Plymouth, or walk up from the villages of **Cawsand** and **Kingsand**, once notorious smuggling bases and nowadays reachable by boat from the Mayflower Steps. Just outside the city to the east, the aristocratic opulence of **Saltram House** offers contrasting refinement, the ornate Georgian mansion stuffed with fine art and furniture in rooms designed by the great Robert Adam. There's a compact cluster of attractions a few miles further out to the north of Plymouth, in the Tavy and Tamar valleys. On the edges of Dartmoor, Drake's old residence at **Buckland Abbey** has more of the flavour of a museum than a historic home, and has souvenirs relating to the sea dog and to his rival and predecessor in the house, Richard Grenville. A few miles northwest of here, you should set aside at least half a day to visit the various parts of **Morwellham**

The west front of Exeter Cathedral, Devon

Jacob's Ladder, Sidmouth, Devon

Devon landscape

Brixham, Devon

Salcombe, Devon

Hound Tor, Dartmoor, Devon

Tin mine, Dartmoor, Devon

Dartmoor pony, Devon

C. PARKER/AXIOM

Clovelly, Devon

JOHN MILLER

Lynmouth, Devon

Quay, once the country's greatest copper port and now thronging with coach parties, but well worth seeing nonetheless for its riverside works and mine shafts. Nearby, **Cotehele** is the best of the houses to be seen around Plymouth, tastefully preserved and full of curiosities redolent of the Tudor era.

It's most likely that you'll be basing yourself at Plymouth: the only alternative **accommodation** would be at Cawsand or Kingsand, on the Mount Edgcumbe peninsula, or at Tavistock (see p.112), from which the places north of Plymouth can easily be visited. From Plymouth, **public transport** connections can be tricky: you'll need to change buses at Tavistock or else take a train on the Tamar Valley Line from Plymouth, boarding a bus at Gunnislake or Calstock stations, or walking from there: details are given below.

Mount Edgcumbe and around

Situated on the Cornish side of Plymouth Sound and visible from the Hoe, **Mount Edgcumbe** is a winning combination of Tudor house, landscaped gardens and acres of beautiful rolling parkland alongside the sea, with access to coastal paths. Though the house (April–Sept Wed–Sun 11am–4.30pm; £4.50) is a reconstruction of the Tudor original that was gutted by incendiary bombs in 1941, the predominant note inside is eighteenth-century, with authentic Regency furniture in the elegantly restored rooms. Paintings (including works by Joshua Reynolds), sixteenth-century tapestries and items of Plymouth porcelain hold mild appeal, but the real interest lies in the enticing **park** (unrestricted access; free), which includes immaculate gardens divided into French, Italian and English sections – the first two a blaze of flowerbeds adorned with classical statuary, the last an acre of sweeping lawn shaded by exotic trees. The park covers the whole eastern side of the Rame peninsula, which juts into the estuary to the southwest of Plymouth, and holds a section of the South West Coast Path (see box, on p.138), which you can join at the quayside at Cremyll, on the peninsula's northeastern tip. Whether following the coast path or roaming at random within the park, you'll come across some singularly beautiful spots around here, the landscaped wooded walks making the best of the estuary and sea views.

You can reach Mount Edgcumbe by car from Plymouth, taking the **Torpoint chain ferry** (£1) from Devonport (well signposted) to Torpoint and driving round the peninsula, but it's a lengthy route. It's far quicker on the passenger **ferry** to Cremyll, which leaves at least hourly (£1) from Admiral's Hard, a small mooring in the Stonehouse district of the city (reachable on buses #33 and #34 from outside the Guildhall). Walkers also have the option of a longer but more scenic route by taking the ferry to **CAWSAND**, an old smugglers' haunt a couple of hours' pleasant hike from the house; weather permitting, a direct motor launch sets off from the Mayflower Steps between the end of May and early September (£2). Cawsand's narrow lanes of colour-washed or

*From
Cawsand or
Kingsand, you
can follow the
coast path
south around
the peninsula
for sweeping
views of
Plymouth
Sound and the
open sea from
the headlands
of Penlee Point
and Rame
Head.*

red-stone cottages descend to a quay and beaches in a protected bay. Until 1830, the Devon/Cornwall border divided the village from **KINGSAND**, just a few minutes' walk north up the coast and marked by its Institute clock tower right on the sea. Both villages lie just a mile east of the extensive sands of **Whitsand Bay**, the best bathing beach in the area, accessible from the B3247. Reached by paths snaking down from the cliffs, the four miles of flat sands get long ranks of rollers with the wind blowing from the southwest, but as the currents can be strong, swimmers should take care not to go too far out.

Practicalities

Staff at Cawsand's post office (Mon & Wed–Fri 9am–1pm & 2–5.30pm, Tues 9am–1pm, Sat 9am–12.30pm; ☎01752/823280) can fill you in on **accommodation** in the twin villages. Kingsand's *Halfway House* on Fore Street (☎01752/822279; *halfway@ eggconnect.net*; ③) is one good possibility, decorated in Victorian style with quietly elegant rooms and a big central fireplace. In Cawsand, the large plate-glass windows of the *Cawsand Hotel* on The Bound (☎01752/822425; ②) face right on to the sea. For **meals**, the *Halfway House* does a good line in fresh fish (it's best to book), and the *Smugglers Inn* on The Square makes an unpretentious stop for inexpensive snacks or pub grub.

Saltram House

House April–Sept Sun–Thurs noon–5pm; Oct Mon–Thurs and Sun noon–4pm; garden Feb–March Sat & Sun noon–4pm; April–Oct Sun–Thurs 10:30am–5:30pm; house and garden £6, garden only £3; NT.

Three miles east of Plymouth, just south of the A38, the grand, white eighteenth-century **Saltram House** is Devon's largest country house, and attracts quite a scrum of visitors. If you're a fan of Neoclassical exuberance, you'll be in your element, and even if you're not, there are individual elements here which will appeal. To get any details of the items on display, however, you'll need to pick up a guidebook (£2.99), as labelling is minimal where it exists at all.

*You'll find
plenty of
additional
information
on Mount
Edgcumbe,
Cawsand and
Kingsand at
www
.crabpot.co.uk*

The original Tudor building received its dramatic Georgian makeover at the hands of the Parker family, local bigwigs who numbered **Joshua Reynolds** among their acquaintances. Born nearby in Plympton and a master at the local grammar school, Reynolds was a regular guest at the hunting, shooting and gambling parties held here, and left several works scattered around the house, including fourteen portraits of the family. Saltram's showpiece, however, is the double-cube **Saloon** designed by Robert Adam, supposed to be the perfect embodiment of a classically proportioned room of the era. A fussy but exquisitely furnished room dripping with gilt and plaster, it's an eye-popping sight, set off by a huge Axminster carpet especially woven in 1770. This and other rooms here featured in the 1995 film of *Sense and Sensibility*, in which the house served as Norland Park In Jane Austen's novel.

Other high points include works by the eighteenth-century Swiss portraitist Angelica Kauffman – one a likeness of her friend and mentor Reynolds – in the staircase hall, where you'll also see George Stubbs' *The Fall of Titan*. The first floor is rich in chinoiserie – wallpaper, mirror paintings and Chinese Chippendale, and there is much Chippendale furniture elsewhere too. You have to exit the house to visit the **Great Kitchen**, where the chopping block has been so worn down as to resemble a saddle. The scale of entertaining can be judged by the hundreds of items of copperware on display here, alongside such curiosities as glass cockroach-catchers, which would be filled with beer to entice the offenders.

Saltram's landscaped **park** provides a breather from this riot of interior design, with garden follies and riverside walks, though it's somewhat marred by the proximity of the road.

Around Plymouth

You can get to Saltram on the hourly #22 bus (Mon–Sat only) from Royal Parade to Cot Hill, from where it's a ten-minute signposted walk.

Buckland Abbey

April–Oct Mon–Wed & Fri–Sun 10.30am–5.30pm; Nov–Dec & mid-Feb to March Sat & Sun 2–5pm; last admission 45min before closing; house & grounds £4.60, grounds only £2.40; NT.

Eight miles north of Plymouth via the A386, **Buckland Abbey** stands right on the edge of Dartmoor (see Chapter 4) close to the River Tavy. In the thirteenth century, this was the most westerly of England's Cistercian abbeys, and was converted after its dissolution to a private home by the privateer Richard Grenville (a cousin of Walter Raleigh), from whom the estate was acquired by Francis Drake in 1581. Though it remained Drake's home until his death, the house – a stone Tudor construction with an ungainly central tower – reveals few traces of his residence, as he spent most of his retirement years plundering on the Spanish Main. There are numerous maps, portraits and mementos of his buccaneering exploits on show, however, most famous of which is **Drake's Drum**, said to beat a supernatural warning of impending danger to the country.

The house displays various other relics of the Elizabethan seafaring era and a gallery of model ships, though most eye-catching are the architectural embellishments in the oak-panelled **Great Hall**, dated 1576 but previously the nave of the abbey. One end of the room sports a frieze of holly and box interspersed with allegorical scenes, musicians and sheila-na-gigs (women in less than decorous attitudes), and there's fine ornamental plasterwork on the ceiling.

To get to Buckland by bus, take the #83, #84 or #86 to Tavistock from Plymouth's bus station, changing at Yelverton to the hourly #55 minibus (Mon–Sat only).

Morwellham Quay

Daily: Easter–Oct 10am–5.30pm; Nov–Easter 10am–4pm; last admission 2hr before closing; £8.90 in summer, £5 in winter; *www.morwellham-quay.co.uk*.

Three miles northwest of Buckland Abbey, and ten miles north of Plymouth via the A386 and the B3257, the sleepy, narrow river at **Morwellham Quay** makes it difficult to believe that this was once a

Sir Francis Drake

Born around 1540 near Tavistock (see p.112), **Francis Drake** began his
seafaring career at the age of thirteen, working in the domestic coastal
trade before taking part in the first English slaving expeditions between
Africa and the West Indies, led by his Plymouth kinsman John Hawkins.
Later Drake was active in the secret war against Spain, raiding and looting
merchant ships in actions unofficially sanctioned by Elizabeth I. In 1572 he
became the first Englishman to sight the Pacific, and soon afterwards, on
board the *Golden Hind*, became the first one to **circumnavigate the
world**, for which he received a knighthood on his return in 1580. The following year Drake was made mayor of Plymouth, settling in Buckland
Abbey (see p.131 overleaf), but was back in action before long – in 1587 he
"singed the king of Spain's beard" by entering Cadiz harbour and destroying 33 vessels that were to have formed part of Philip II's **Spanish Armada**.
When the replacement invasion fleet appeared in the English Channel in
1588, Drake – along with Raleigh, Hawkins and Frobisher – played a leading role in wrecking it. The legend that he took his time in finishing a game
of bowls on the Hoe before setting sail is most probably due to the fact that
he was conversant with the tides and could gauge his time. The following
year he set off on an unsuccessful expedition to help the Portuguese against
Spain, but otherwise most of the next decade was spent in relative inactivi-
ty in Plymouth, Exeter and London. Finally, in 1596 Drake left with
Hawkins for a raid on Panama, a venture that cost the lives of both captains.

   Though Drake has come to personify the Elizabethan Age's swashbuck-
ling expansionism and patriotism, England's naval triumphs were as much
the result of John Hawkins' humbler work in building and maintaining a
new generation of warships as they were of the skill and bravery of their
captains. Drake was simply the most flamboyant of a generation of reck-
less and brilliant mariners who broke the Spanish hegemony on the high
seas, so laying the foundations for England's later imperialist pursuits.

hive of activity at the heart of Devon's mineral-producing area.
Morwellham first came to prominence as a port in the twelfth century, when tin, silver, lead ore and arsenic (a by-product of the mines)
were exported. Its main commodity, however, was copper, used in
Tudor times for cannons and throughout the Napoleonic wars for
copper-bottoming of sailing ships. During the reign of Queen
Victoria, it was the country's greatest copper port, and in the early
and middle years of the nineteenth century, when the River Tamar
outdid the Mersey in the number of its ships, it was said there was
enough arsenic piled up on the quays to poison the world. Today, the
site has been sensitively restored to its 1860s glory as a working
quay, equipped with warehouses, lime kilns and a giant water-wheel,
and there are enough diversions to provide a good half-day's entertainment.

   Though firmly on the coach- and school-party track, the site has
largely escaped falling into terminal tackiness. The costumed atten-
dants are down-to-earth and knowledgeable, and a big-screen video
provides interesting background. The entry ticket includes a

tramway ride into the copper mine, and visits to the mining museum and a "gypsy camp", though most are content with wandering around the quay and overhead tramways and poking around in the cottages, and blacksmith's and cooper's workshops, where there are daily demonstrations and lots of hands-on activities. Other attractions include a ketch restored to its 1909 appearance, and a wildlife area with bird-watching hides.

From Plymouth, **getting to the site** by public transport is a two-stage process: from the bus station at Bretonside, take services #83, #84 or #86 to Tavistock, where you change onto the #185 (Mon–Sat), #188 (Sun only) or #187 (May–Sept Sun only) run to Morwellham.

Cotehele

House April–Oct Mon–Thurs, Sat & Sun 11am–5pm, Oct closes 4.30pm; mill April–June and Sept Mon–Thurs, Sat & Sun 1–5.30pm, July & Aug daily 1–6pm, Oct Mon–Thurs, Sat & Sun 1-4.30pm; garden daily 11.30am–dusk; £6.20 for all three, or £3.20 garden and mill only; NT)

Nestled in the wooded and exotically planted Tamar Valley, two miles west of Morwellham and ten miles northwest of Plymouth, **Cotehele** is one of the best preserved and least altered medieval houses in the country. Built largely between 1485 and 1539, it remained in the Edgcumbe family for six hundred years, though their residence at Mount Edgcumbe (see p.129) from the end of the seventeenth century meant that Cotehele remained mostly unmodified, preserving its tranquil Tudor character. Exhibits – chiefly a fascinating collection of needlework, tapestries, weaponry and vigorously carved seventeenth-century furniture – are arranged in an interlinked group of granite, slate and sandstone buildings around three courtyards. It's best to visit on a bright day, if you can, as there's no electricity indoors – a fact which has aided the remarkable state of preservation of the many textiles.

Each of the rooms displays something that grabs the eye. The fine arch-braced **Hall**, with its bare lime-ash floor, has a rare set of folding mid-eighteenth-century chairs, still with their original leather, while the **Old Dining Room**, hung with Flemish tapestries, leads to the chapel in which you can see the earliest domestic clock in England, dating from 1485 and still in its original position. The rooms on the first and second floor are embroiderers' heaven: Jacobean floral crewelwork in the white bedroom; delicate seventeenth-century bed hangings, stumpwork and an eighteenth-century bedspread in the south room; gros point in **King Charles's Room**, and Victorian patchwork in **Queen Anne's Room**. Don't miss the grenade-like Victorian glass fire-extinguishers on the lower landing and, on the upper, the carved Welsh bed-head from 1532, replete with a hunting and hawking frieze and a scaly angel expelling Adam and Eve from the Garden of Eden.

Practicalities

To get to Cotehele by **public transport**, you can take a Tamar Valley Line train (May to late Sept only) from Plymouth to Calstock, from where you can walk the one and a half miles to the house (the route is signposted) or catch one of the frequent ferries from Calstock to Cotehele's quay (Easter to late Sept; £2 single, £3 return). From Plymouth's bus station, take buses #83, #84 or #86 to Tavistock, where you change onto the #79 (Mon–Sat) to get to Cotehele; the same service also runs past Gunnislake train station. On Sundays from late May to late September, a Dartmoor Sunday Rover Ticket (£5) will cover you for the Plymouth-to-Calstock train journey and the connecting #190 bus (Sun only) from Calstock to Cotehele, and for the return trip. **By road**, you have to negotiate the narrow but well-signposted lanes leading off the A390 to Cotehele.

If you want to **stay** in the area, the *Rifle Volunteer Inn* at St Ann's Chapel (☎01822/832508; ①), just over the Cornish border on the A390, is a restored former mine-captain's house with stylish bedrooms and a **restaurant** (Mon–Sat dinner only, Sat & Sun lunch and dinner) offering great views over the Tamar Valley and inexpensive curries, pastas and Mediterranean-influenced food; booking is essential at weekends. On Cotehele's quay, the cosy *Mount Edgcumbe Arms* provides teas and inexpensive **meals**.

Travel details

Trains

Plymouth to: Bristol (Mon–Sat 1–2 hourly, Sun every 1–2 hours; 2hr); Calstock (summer 5–7 daily, winter Mon–Sat 5-7; 35min); Exeter (Mon–Sat 1–2 hourly, Sun every 1–2 hours; 1hr); Gunnislake (summer 5–7 daily, winter Mon–Sat 5–7; 45min); London (Mon–Fri every 30min, Sat & Sun hourly; 3–4hr); Penzance (Mon–Sat 1–2 hourly, Sun every 1–2 hours; 2hr); St Austell (Mon–Sat 1–2 hourly, Sun every 1–2 hours; 1hr).

Buses

Plymouth to: Ashburton (Mon–Sat 9 daily, Sun 6 daily; 50min); Exeter (1–2 hourly; 1hr 10min); Okehampton (Mon–Sat hourly, Sun 2 daily; 1hr 45min–2hr); Saltram (hourly; 15min); Tavistock (Mon–Sat every 20min, Sun hourly; 45min–1hr); Yelverton (Mon–Sat every 20min, Sun hourly; 35min).

Chapter 6

Exmoor

A high, bare plateau sliced by wooded combes and splashing rivers, **Exmoor** presents a very different aspect to Dartmoor, the southwest's other national park. Though it boasts tracts of wilderness every bit as forbidding, Exmoor is smaller, with greater expanses of farmland breaking up the heath, and owes its distinctiveness mainly to the proximity of the sea, from which mists and rain-storms can descend with alarming suddenness. Though most of the park is privately owned – including about ten percent held by the National Trust – provision is made for walkers and others via a network of public paths, and the National Park Authority's programme of **guided walks** (see box on p.147) ensures that walkers of all abilities can get out onto the moor. Exmoor's coastal section is the most easily accessible part of the moor for visitors, with the A39, which runs parallel to the sea, providing an easy link to the alluring small towns and villages around here. The traditional seaside resort of **Minehead** is the biggest centre, but the town's main appeal is its range of accommodation, which makes it a useful base for excursions onto the moor, and its proximity to the well-preserved medieval village of **Dunster** and its impressive castle. Minehead also marks the start of the **South West Coast Path**, which offers the best way to get acquainted with Exmoor's seaboard.

Working west along the coast, the string of coastal villages west of Minehead – including **Porlock**, **Lynmouth**, **Lynton** and **Oare** – make up part of what's known as "**Doone Country**", an indeterminate area that includes some of Exmoor's wildest tracts, and which is now inextricably tied to R.D. Blackmore's tale, *Lorna Doone*. Surprisingly soon after its publication in 1869, this romantic melodrama, based on the outlaw clans inhabiting these parts in the seventeenth century, established itself as part of Exmoor's mythology, and remains so today despite the fact that the book is now hardly read. From Lynton, you can discover the appeal of Doone Country exploring such places as the **Valley of the Rocks**.

Since Exmoor has a geographical unity which ignores county boundaries, this chapter includes much that lies within Somerset. The Brendon Hills, east of the A396, are officially part of the National Park, but this area is quite distinct from Exmoor and so is not covered.

For details of guided walks, Land Rover safaris and adventure sports on Exmoor, see p.147.

Exmoor

You'll find useful information on accommodation and other services, as well as background on the moor, at www.exmoor nationalpark .gov.uk and www.exmoor tourism.org

Public transport on Exmoor

There are fairly regular **bus** connections between Exmoor's main centres and along the coast, but services to small inland villages are pretty sporadic. From late May until the end of September, the most useful lines are the **#285**, looping between Minehead, Dunster, Wheddon Cross, Exford and Porlock (Mon–Fri only), and the **#295** connecting Dulverton with Lynton via Tarr Steps and Exford (Mon–Fri only); alternatively, the **#398** runs throughout the year (Mon–Sat) between Minehead, Exford, Winsford, Dulverton and Tiverton. On the coast, the **#300** (daily in summer, Sat & Sun only in winter) connects Minehead with Lynton and Ilfracombe three times daily, extending as far as Taunton on one of its journeys, and the **#38** runs four times daily between Minehead and Porlock (Mon–Sat only). All services are much reduced in winter, and few buses run on Sundays at any time. Simonsbath is not presently served on any route.

You can **flag down** a bus anywhere on the moor, providing it is safe for it to stop. If you're planning to make good use of the buses, consider buying a money-saving Explorer pass, valid for one day (£5.70) or three days (£9.50); both can be bought on board the buses, or direct from the operator, Southern National (☎01823/272033).

Inland Exmoor lacks any main road running through it, though you'll almost certainly make use of the B3223, B3224 and B3358, which traverse the moor in an east–west direction and which provide access to some of the best walking country. By basing yourself at **Dulverton**, on the moor's southern edge and site of the park's main information office, or at **Exford**, at the centre of the moor, you'll be well-placed for some of the choicest areas, including such celebrated beauty spots as **Tarr Steps** and the moor's highest point of **Dunkery Beacon**. Though these rank among the most popular destinations, you'll generally find yourself alone on the moor, but you can expect much more coming and going at weekends, when groups of hikers, photographers and hunting and shooting folk descend (incidentally taking up much of the region's accommodation). Be warned that winter, especially, is the time when you'll run into the **organized hunts** for which Exmoor is notorious – at least until the law on hunting with dogs is changed.

Drivers should beware of sheep straying over Exmoor's roads, including the relatively fast coastal A39; after dark you may even find them lying down on the tarmac.

ACCOMMODATION PRICE CODES

Throughout this *Guide*, hotel and B&B accommodation is coded on a scale of ① to ⑨, the code indicating the lowest price you can expect to pay per night for a double room in high season. The prices indicated by the codes are as follows:

① under £40	④ £60–70	⑦ £110–150
② £40–50	⑤ £70–90	⑧ £150–200
③ £50–60	⑥ £90–110	⑨ over £200

THE GUIDE: CHAPTER 6

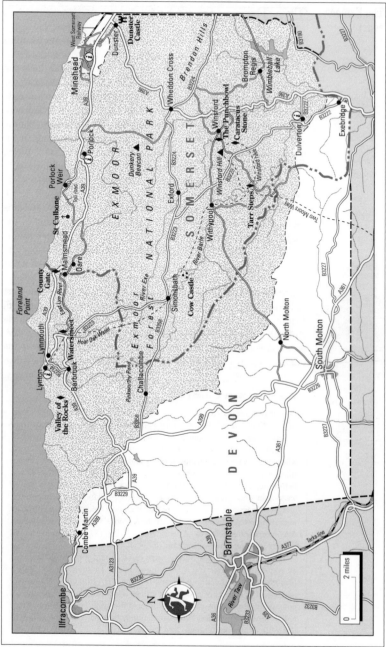

© Crown copyright

The Exmoor coast

The thirty-odd miles between Minehead and Combe Martin form
England's highest section of **coastline**, with cliffs rising to 1420ft.
With gentle upper slopes, the hogbacked hills still make for some
fairly strenuous hiking if you're following the **South West Coast
Path**, but long stretches of woodland add variety to an already
extremely diverse landscape. The narrow, stony strips of beach here
don't compare with those in other parts of the West Country, but the
sea is still the central attraction, with a constantly changing shoreline and an unchanging view across the Bristol Channel to the Welsh
coast. Tracking the top of the coast and slightly behind it, the A39
frequently affords sublime sea views, especially between Porlock and
Lynmouth.

Minehead, Somerset's chief resort, lacks much atmosphere but is
useful for its transport links and proximity to Exmoor and to the
medieval wool-town of **Dunster**, whose prominent hilltop castle is
well worth taking in. **Porlock** has a stronger flavour of Exmoor and
makes a more attractive base for excursions to places such as **St
Culbone**, a deeply hidden church in the woods west of the village,
and around the Doone Country south of Oare and Malmsmead. West
of Foreland Point, there are more terrific walks to be enjoyed from
Lynton and **Lynmouth** – sibling villages which occupy a niche in the
cliff wall with woodland and moorland on all sides. Two of the easiest excursions present Exmoor's most contrasting faces: west to the
dramatic **Valley of the Rocks** and inland to **Watersmeet**, where two

---

The South West Coast Path

The longest footpath in Britain, **the South West Coast Path** begins its journey at Minehead, where a signpost points the way to Poole, Dorset (630
miles). Some degree of planning is essential for any walk of more than half
an hour along the Path, and nowhere more so than on Exmoor's coast,
where the weather can change abruptly and you can be exposed to driving
rain, not to mention disorienting mists. Make a reliable **weather** check
before departing by calling the tourist office nearest to the area you're
walking in, and carry waterproofs and rations; solid footwear is important,
and a compass and good maps are essential: once you've strayed onto the
high, featureless moors, one blasted heath looks very similar to another.
Accommodation needs to be considered too: don't expect to arrive late in
the day and find a bed – even campsites can fill to capacity.

The relevant Ordnance Survey **maps** can be found at most village shops
en route; for Exmoor you'll need the all-in-one Outdoor Leisure Map 9
(1:25,000) or the Landranger maps 180 and 181 (1:50,000). Many local
newsagents, bookshops and tourist offices also stock books or pamphlets
containing route plans and details of local flora and fauna. Aurum Press
and the South West Coast Path Association both publish walking **guides** to
the route – for more on these, see Basics, p.8.

of the moor's rivers merge. Nine miles west, **Combe Martin** marks the edge of the moor and the end of one of the toughest sections of the coastal walk.

Minehead and Dunster

There's little to recommend spending much time in the Somerset port of **MINEHEAD**, though its jaunty promenade and wide sandy beach still preserve some residue of the town's Victorian character. The more genteel **Higher Town** on North Hill holds some of the oldest houses, and offers splendid views across the Bristol Channel. Steep lanes link the quarter with **Quay Town**, the harbour area at Minehead's western end, where a few fishing vessels still operate. You'll get to see something of both neighbourhoods if you're here for the **South West Coast Path** (see box, opposite), which begins on Quay Street about 500yd before the harbour – a brown sign near *Sacha's* restaurant points up some steps to North Hill, from where the path is waymarked.

Minehead lies three miles northwest of the area's major draw, the classic old village of **DUNSTER**. An important cloth centre that reached its peak of wealth in the sixteenth century, it prospered under the protection of **Dunster Castle** (castle April–Sept Mon–Wed, Sat & Sun 11am–5pm; Oct Mon–Wed, Sat & Sun 11am–4pm; grounds April–Sept daily 10am–5pm; Oct–March daily 11am–4pm; house and grounds £6, grounds only £3; NT), whose towers and turrets dominate the village's broad High Street. The site was once a Saxon frontier post against the Celts, and was rebuilt by the Normans, but almost nothing of these earlier constructions survived the thorough pasting the building received during the Civil War. Inherited by Lady Elizabeth Luttrell in 1376, the property remained in her family for six hundred years until the National Trust took over in the 1970s. The castle had already become something of an architectural showpiece following the drastic remodelling it received around 1870, to which it owes its present castellated appearance, though this is an effective disguise for what is essentially a stately home, predominantly Jacobean within.

Dating back to 1420 and flanked by a pair of squat towers that formed part of the Norman construction, the formidable battlemented **gatehouse** smacks of authenticity. Beyond the gatehouse, the irregular design of the main building reflects the various changes it has undergone over the years. The highlights of the interior, however, are all seventeenth-century: most obvious is the grand oak and elm **staircase**, magnificently carved with hunting scenes – a recurrent theme throughout the house. Alongside the stag's heads, numerous portraits of the Luttrells gaze across the rooms, including one showing the sixteenth-century John Luttrell wading Triton-like across the Firth of Forth. Much of the furniture and artwork is sixteenth or seventeenth century, such as the odd "thrown" chairs of ash, pear-

Minehead is the terminus of the West Somerset Railway, which has steam and diesel trains running up to eight times daily from April to October (plus some dates in Dec) as far as Bishop's Lydeard, some twenty miles away. Call ☎01643/ 707650 for a talking timetable, or ☎01643/ 704996 for other enquiries.

You can rent bikes from Pompy's, behind Minehead station on Mart Road (☎01643/ 704077).

*For details of
the summer
drama
productions
staged in
Dunster
Castle's
grounds, call
☎01985/
843601.*

wood and oak in the Inner Hall, and the rare **gilt-leather hangings** in the upstairs Gallery, which vividly depict the story of Antony and Cleopatra. Outside, it's well worth a stroll round the sheltered terraced **gardens**, where oranges and lemons have been growing since 1700. Mimosas and palm trees add to the subtropical ambience, and paths lead down to the River Avill.

Below the northern gateway of the castle, Dunster village makes a pleasant place for a wander before or after a tour of the house. In the High Street, the octagonal **Yarn Market**, dating from 1609, is the most evocative of a handful of relics of the village's wool-making heyday, its hefty oak rafters in the cone-shaped roof rising above a bare space. From the southern end of the High Street, it's just a few steps to one of the area's finest churches, **St George**, on the corner of Church Street. Originally a Norman priory church, it has a fine bossed wagon-roof and a magnificent rood screen from about 1500, said to be the longest in the country. Among the tombs of various Luttrells, look out for a group at the top of the south aisle which includes the alabaster floor slab inscribed to Elizabeth Luttrell, from 1493. The sloping chest here is thought to be unique, and was probably used by the Benedictine monks of the priory in the fifteenth century. Behind the church, the sixteenth-century **Tithe Barn** stands opposite a circular dovecote from the same period, kept by the monks – the only people allowed to keep doves as they damaged farmers' crops.

A few yards beyond St George on West Street, turn down Mill Lane to reach the three-hundred-year-old **Dunster Water Mill** (July & Aug daily 10.30am–5pm; April–June, Sept & Oct Mon–Thurs & weekends 10.30am–5pm; £2.10; NT), still used commercially for milling the various grains which go to make the flour and muesli sold in the shop. There isn't a great deal to see or do here once you've absorbed the mysteries of milling and viewed the small array of agricultural tools, but the riverside café and garden make a good spot for refreshment. A path along the Avill from the mill soon brings you to **Gallox Bridge**, a quaint packhorse bridge from the eighteenth century.

Sprouting out of the woods at the northern end of Dunster's High Street, the hilltop **Conygar Tower** is a folly dating from 1776, worth the brief ascent from The Steep for the excellent views. There are also longer walks from here, for which you can get route maps from the tourist office: **Grabbist Hill**, a mile or so west from the village via a path that starts near the school opposite St George's, or eastwards for about a mile to the sandy and rocky **Dunster Beach** – not great for swimming but with a long foreshore that makes an appealing spot for a picnic.

Practicalities

Minehead's **tourist office** is off The Parade at 17 Friday St (April–June, Sept & Oct Mon–Sat 9.30am–5pm; July & Aug Mon–Sat

9.30am–5.30pm, Sun 10am–1pm; Nov–March Mon–Sat 10am–4pm;
☎01643/702624). In Dunster, the **Exmoor Visitor Centre**
(Easter–Oct daily 10am–5pm; Nov–Easter Sat & Sun 11am–3pm;
☎01643/821835), by the main car park at the top of Dunster Steep
(follow the High St round to the north), has information on **guided
walks on Exmoor**, and also houses a free exhibition focusing on the
peculiarities of the moor, with hands-on activities and background on
the local wool and timber industries and conservation issues.

The **West Somerset Railway**, which curves eastwards into the
Quantocks, terminates at Minehead station at the south end of The
Esplanade, and also stops at Dunster, though the station here is a
mile out, near Dunster Beach; from Minehead, you're better off using
the frequent **buses #15, #28, #39 and #305**.

There isn't a great choice of **restaurants** in Minehead. Drinks and
bar meals are best at the *Ship Aground* (see overleaf); for coffees,
quiches and pasties head for *Mother Leakey's Parlour*, on Quay
Street near the harbour. Right by the steps leading to the coast path,
the *Harbour House Tea Rooms* has teas, cakes and outside seating.
You'll find tearooms on every corner **in Dunster**, but *The Tea
Shoppe* at 3 High St (☎01643/821304; open Fri, Sat and Sun lunch
only in winter) is also a good restaurant, specializing in local game;
you can also get bar snacks or full meals at the atmospheric *Luttrell
Arms*, right by the Yarn Market.

Accommodation

Though Dunster has heaps more character, Minehead's **B&Bs** are
more varied and less expensive. Midway between the two places, and
signposted from the village of Alcombe, **Minehead youth hostel**
(☎01643/702595; closed Sept–March) sits in a secluded combe on
the edge of Exmoor; dorm beds cost £10. Buses #28 and #928 from
Minehead, Dunster and Taunton stop a mile away at Alcombe. You
can **camp** near the coast path at the *Camping and Caravanning
Club Site* (☎01643/704138; Easter–Sept), a mile north of
Minehead, above Higher Town on North Hill. No buses pass near, but
you can save the uphill hike by taking a taxi from the rank on The
Parade, near the main bus-stop.

Avill House, 12 Townsend Rd, Minehead ☎01643/704370. Just up from the
tourist office, this budget B&B has plain rooms with or without private bath,
and some with distant sea views. No credit cards. ①.

Dollons House, 10 Church St, Dunster ☎01643/821880; *www.corn-
flowerblue.com*. Neat, nonsmoking rooms above a gift shop, with en-suite
showers or bathrooms. ③.

The Gables, 33 High St, Dunster ☎01643/821496. Attractive nonsmoking
rooms under the eaves, with spacious bathrooms. ③.

Kildare Lodge, Townsend Rd, Minehead ☎01643/702009. Five-minutes' walk
from the tourist office, this reconstructed Tudor inn was designed by Barry
Parker, a pupil of Edwin Lutyens, and strongly influenced by him. It has a
courtyard, garden and comfortable "period" rooms. ③.

Luttrell Arms, 32–36 High St, Dunster ☎01643/821555. Opposite the Yarn Market, this ancient inn is dead pricey but oozes historical charm. Rooms with four-poster beds, such as no. 14 with its cosy little reading room, cost an extra £25, but make the others look dull in comparison. ⑦.

Ship Aground, Quay St, Minehead ☎01643/702087. Some of the clean, quiet rooms at this quayside pub near the start of the coast path have a harbour view. ②.

Porlock and around

The real enticement of **PORLOCK**, six miles west of Minehead, is its extraordinary position in a deep hollow, cupped on three sides by Exmoor's hogbacked hills. The thatch-and-cob houses and dripping charm of the village's long High Street, with its succession of hotels, cafés, antique shops and stores selling outdoor gear, have led to invasions of tourists, some of whom are also drawn by the place's literary links. According to Coleridge's own less than reliable testimony, it was a "man from Porlock" who broke the opium trance in which he was composing *Kubla Khan*, while the High Street's beamed *Ship Inn* prides itself on featuring prominently in the Exmoor romance *Lorna Doone* and, in real life, having sheltered the poet Robert Southey, who staggered in rain-soaked after an Exmoor ramble.

Once you've wandered the High Street, and taken in the mildly diverting collection of photos and portraits on Porlock and Exmoor's past at the **Doverhay Manor Museum**, at its eastern end (Mon–Fri 10am–1pm & 2–5pm, Sat 10am–noon & 2.30–4.30pm; free), there's little else to keep you in the village. However, from the western end of the High Street, you can walk or drive the two miles west over reclaimed marshland to the tiny harbour of **PORLOCK WEIR**, whose sleepy air gives little inkling of its former role as a hard-working port trafficking with Wales. With its thatched cottages and lovely stony foreshore, it's a peaceful spot, giving onto a bay that enjoys the mildest climate on Exmoor.

*From Porlock,
two easy miles'
walk west
along the
South West
Coast Path
brings you to
St Culbone,
which claims
to be the small-
est church in
the country.*

West of Porlock, the A39 climbs 1350ft in less than three miles – cyclists and drivers might prefer the gentler and more scenic toll road (cars £2, bikes 50p), travelling mainly through woods, to the direct uphill trawl. Just before the Devon–Somerset border at County Gate, the hamlet of **OARE** has another minuscule church, famous in the annals of Lorna Doonery as being the scene of the heroine's marriage, and where she was shot. R.D. Blackmore's grandfather was rector here, and it's likely that the author derived much of the inspiration for his border tale from the local stories told to him on his visits. The area around is the heart of "**Doone Country**", with the valleys of Lank Combe and Hoccombe Combe and Badgeworthy Water suffused with echoes of Blackmore's fictional Doone Valley. If you want to explore the area, head three-quarters of a mile west to the hamlet of **Malmsmead**, from where you can follow the Badgeworthy Water river upstream; Porlock tourist office can supply a detailed route. Between Malmsmead and Oare, the **Field Centre** in the Oare Village Hall (May to mid-July early Sept Wed & Thurs 1.30–5pm; mid-July to Aug Tues–Thurs 1.30–5pm; free) provides everything you might want to know about the natural history of the area. Pictures, posters, tapes and slide projections illustrate the local fauna and flora, there's a picnic area outside by the pond, and volunteers will point out items of interest on guided walks from late May to mid-September. To reach the Field Centre, you can follow a scenic half-mile path from the car park at County Gate, but it's quite steep and might seem a long way back. Driving there is more convenient: the car park behind the well-marked Lorna Doone Farm in Malmsmead is just 200yd away.

Practicalities

Porlock's **tourist office** is at West End, at the western end of the High Street (March–Oct Mon–Sat 10am–6pm, Sun 10am–1pm; Nov–Feb Mon–Fri 10.15am–1pm, Sat 10am–2pm; ☎01643/ 863150; *www.porlock.co.uk*). The best **accommodation** is on the High Street, where the conspicuous *Lorna Doone Hotel* (☎01643/ 862404; ②) offers three sizes of rooms with private bath and TV. Further along, next to the Flare garage, the wooden-porched *Cottage* is smaller, quainter and a little pricier (☎01643/862687; ③), while the thatched *Myrtle Cottage* (☎01643/862978; *bob. steer@talk21.com*; ③) offers more of the same – small en-suite rooms and parking facilities, in a traditional setting. Porlock's central **campsite**, *Sparkhayes Farm* (☎01643/862470; closed Nov–March), is signposted off the main road near the *Lorna Doone*.

Porlock has a handful of good **eating** options for snacks or complete meals. On the corner of Sparkhayes Lane and the High Street, the *Countryman* has sofas round a stove and serves steaks, grills and seafood dishes (☎01643/862241; moderate), though between November and March, it's open from Friday evening to Sunday lunchtime only. You can pick up good snacks at *Lowerbourne House*, a tearoom and bookshop with useful local information posted up, and at the yellow-walled *Whortleberry*, which serves whortleberry jam on its muffins and tea-cakes – both are on the High Street (both open on weekends only in winter). In **Porlock Weir**, open crab sandwiches are a lunchtime favourite at the oak-beamed *Ship Inn* by the harbour.

Lynton and Lynmouth

Nine miles along the coast from Porlock, on the Devon side of the county line, the Victorian resort of **LYNTON** perches above a lofty gorge with splendid views over the sea. Encircled by cliffs that left the village pretty isolated for most of its history, Lynton struck lucky during the Napoleonic wars when frustrated Grand Tourists unable to visit their usual continental haunts discovered a domestic piece of

The Exmoor coast

Swiss landscape here. Coleridge and Hazlitt trudged over to Lynton from the Quantocks, but the greatest spur to the village's popularity was the 1869 publication of *Lorna Doone*, which resulted in swarms of literary tourists discovering this part of Exmoor. Most of the present-day visitors are similarly attracted by the natural beauty of the place, while the existence of a number of walks radiating out from here onto Exmoor and along the coast are a major bonus, and you might well be tempted into a prolonged stay.

Lynton's imposing **town hall** on Lee Road epitomizes the Victorian–Edwardian accent of the village. It was the gift of publisher George Newnes, who also donated the nearby **cliff railway** (March to mid-July & mid-Sept to Nov daily 9am–7pm; mid-July to mid-Sept daily 9am–10pm; £1) which connects Lynton with Lynmouth, five hundred feet below. The device is an ingenious hydraulic system, its two carriages counterbalanced by water tanks which fill up at the top, descend, and empty their load at the bottom. **LYNMOUTH** itself lies at the junction and estuary of the East and West Lyn rivers, in a spot described by Gainsborough as "the most delightful place for a landscape painter this country can boast". Shelley spent his honeymoon here with his sixteen-year-old bride Harriet Westbrook, making time in his nine-week sojourn to write his polemical *Queen Mab* – two different houses claim to have been the Shelley's love-nest – and R.D. Blackmore, author of *Lorna Doone*, stayed in **Mars Hill**, the oldest part of the town, whose creeper-covered cottages are fringed by the cliffs behind the Esplanade.

Lynmouth's peace was shattered in August 1952 when nine inches of rain fell onto Exmoor in 24 hours and the village was almost washed away by **floodwaters** raging down the valley. Huge landslips carried hundreds of trees into the rivers, all the bridges in the area were swept away, houses were demolished and 34 people lost their lives. There are numerous reminders of this disaster around the village, the most vivid being the boulders and other rocky debris still strewn about the **Glen Lyn Gorge** (daily: Easter–Oct exhibition 10am–5pm; £3; Nov–Easter 9am–dusk £2), a steep wooded valley through which the destructive torrent took its course. Entered from the main road at the back of the village, the gorge has a deeply tranquil air which makes it difficult to imagine the fury of that stormy night. The walks and waterfalls upstream make ideal picnic spots, and there are also displays on the uses and dangers of water-power, including a small hydroelectric plant which provides electricity for the local community.

Summer boat trips offered at Lynmouth's harbour by Exmoor Coast Boat Cruises (☎01598/753207) are an excellent way to view birdlife on the cliffs; excursions last from one hour (£5) to a four-hour sailing to Porlock Weir and back (£7.50).

Practicalities

The area's main **tourist office** is in Lynton's town hall on Lee Road (summer daily 9.30am–5.30pm; winter Mon–Sat 10am–4pm; ☎01598/752225), while Lynmouth has a **National Park Visitor Centre** by the harbour (April–Oct daily 10am–5pm, closes 6pm in Aug; ☎01598/752509).

Lynton has the better choice of inexpensive **B&Bs**. *The Turret*, 33 Lee Rd (☎01598/753284; ①), is one of the cheapest options in the row of accommodation lining this street. It's run by a friendly Scot and has six spacious rooms, four of them en suite including the turreted room at the top. More centrally, whitewashed *St Vincent* (☎01598/752244; *keenstvincent@lineone.net*; ①) on Castle Hill has spacious, tastefully-decorated rooms and a tea-garden. The *Lynhurst*, Lyn Way (☎01598/752241; *lynhurst@demon.co.uk*; ③), is a few minutes' walk farther out, but has striking views over the valley. Lynton **youth hostel** (☎01598/753237; closed Nov–Feb) occupies a homely Victorian house about one mile inland from the centre, signposted off Lynbridge Road; beds cost £10. In **Lynmouth**, the most inspiring place to stay is *Harbour Point*, a B&B right on the harbour at 1 The Esplanade (☎01598/752321; no credit cards;②; closed Oct–April) – the slightly pricier Turret and Balcony rooms are the best choices here. A more upmarket option is the smart *Shelley's Hotel* right next to the Glen Lyn Gorge (☎01598/753219; ④), where you can sleep in the room supposed to have been occupied by the poet – he apparently left without paying his bill.

Everything from teas and coffees to hot baguettes, trout and Madagascar Duck is served at the *Green House*, a large **restaurant** on Lee Road in Lynton, while *Lily May's* at 1 Castle Hill is more intimate and has ratatouille and battered cod on the menu – both places are inexpensive–moderate. In **Lynmouth**, the *Village Inn* on Lynmouth Street does inexpensive fish and steak dishes as well as vegetarian options, though you'll find the classiest food at the *Rising*

The Exmoor coast

There's a post office and a branch of Lloyds Bank on Lee Road in Lynton.

Walks from Lynton and Lynmouth

The major year-round attraction in these parts is **walking**, not only along the coast path but inland. Most trails are waymarked, and you can pick up walkers' maps of the routes from the tourist office or Park Visitor Centre. One of the most popular walks is about two miles eastward along the banks of the River Lyn to Watersmeet (see overleaf), itself the starting-place for a myriad of trails; from Lynmouth, the path starts near the *Rocklyn Riverside Tea Garden*. Another undemanding expedition takes you west out of Lynton along the North Walk, a mile-long path leading to the **Valley of the Rocks**, a steeply curved heathland dominated by rugged rock formations. The poet Robert Southey summed up the raw splendour he found here when he described it as "the very bones and skeleton of the earth, rock reeling upon rock, stone piled upon stone, a huge terrific mass". At the far end of the valley, herds of wild goats range free as they have done here for centuries.

Lynmouth is the best starting point for coastal walks. East, you can reach the lighthouse at **Foreland Point**, a little over two miles away, via a fine sheltered shingle beach at the foot of Countisbury Hill – one of a number of tiny coves that are easily accessible on either side of the estuary – while the route west towards Combe Martin (see overleaf) traces some of Devon's most majestic and unspoiled coastline.

You can rent bikes from Biketrail at 19 Queen St, Lynton (☎01598/7539 87; www .biketrail.co.uk).

Sun (expensive), a pub and hotel down by the harbour serving classic English and European dishes.

Watersmeet and around

From Lynton, you can drive or walk the one and a half miles east along
the course of the East Lyn River to where it's joined by Hoar Oak Water
at **Watersmeet**. This otherwise tranquil, wooded spot can be transformed into a roaring torrent after a bout of rain, and the water that is
usually crystal-clear is stained brown with moorland peat. Drivers can
leave vehicles at a car park (50p per hour) off the A39, and follow the
path down through oak woods to the two slender bridges where the
rivers merge. On the far side of the bridges and the only building in
sight, **Watersmeet House** (April–Sept daily 10.30am–5.30pm; Oct
daily 10.30am–4.30pm; free) is a fishing lodge owned by the National
Trust that opens as a shop and restaurant in summer, with a veranda
where you can take teas, salads and soups, and a small exhibition of
photos of the 1952 Lynmouth floods in the back.

*Drivers or bik-
ers bound for
Lynton and
Lynmouth
from the west
– or leaving
for the west –
can cut their
mileage by
turning off the
A39 onto the
B3234, which
joins
Lynmouth
with Barbrook,
along the
course of the
West Lyn River
- a road which
misses out
Watersmeet.*

Watersmeet is surrounded by signposted **paths**, many of which
were established as donkey tracks when the local charcoal and tanning industries flourished in the nineteenth century. One three-quar-
ters-of-a-mile route from the bridge takes you south up Hoar Oak
Water to **Hillsford Bridge**, the confluence of Hoar Oak and Farley
Water, while Fisherman's Path leads east along the East Lyn river,
climbing and swooping through the woods above one of the river's
most dramatic stretches. Another marked route strikes off from
Fisherman's Path after only a few hundred yards, zigzagging steeply
uphill to meet the A39, about a mile north of Watersmeet and 100yd
east of the *Sandpiper Inn*. Opposite the pub, a path leads a quarter-
mile north to meet the coast path and gives access to **Butter Hill**
which, at nearly 1000ft, affords stunning views of Lynton, Lynmouth
and the north Devon coast. You can pick up pamphlets with full
details about all the various routes at Watersmeet House.

Combe Martin

At the western edge of Exmoor's seaboard, **COMBE MARTIN** has little of the spirit of the moor but has some diversions that merit an
hour or two of your time. Sheltered in a fertile valley, the village is
famous for its straggling main street, which follows the combe for
about a mile down to the seafront, and holds the unusual *Pack of
Cards* inn, supposed to have been built by a gambler in the eighteenth century with his winnings from a card game. Originally pos-
sessing 52 windows (some were later boarded up), it has four storeys
– decreasing in size as they get higher – each with thirteen doors, and
chimneys sprouting from every corner.

Displays at the **Combe Martin Museum**, 4 Kingsley Terrace (June
to mid-Sept Sun–Fri 1.30–4pm, 11am–4pm during school summer

holidays; £2) illustrate local silver-mining, lime-quarrying, agriculture, horticulture and maritime history, but the **Motorcycle Collection**, next to the main car park on Cross Street (late May to Oct daily 10am–5pm; £2.90) is far more engaging. Unashamedly nostalgic, it displays over sixty motor-bikes, scooters and rare examples of motorized "invacars" (for people with disabilities) from the 1920s to the 1970s against a background of old signs, petrol pumps and other garage memorabilia, all drenched in old world atmosphere.

Head straight down the High Street to reach Combe Martin's **beach**, a good swimming spot which is sandy at low tide, with rock pools and secluded bays on either side. A spectacular stretch of coast extends east of Combe Martin, notably round Wild Pear Beach to Little Hangman and Hangman Point, part of the **Hangman Hills**. The waymarked path is signposted off the north end of the car park behind the *Foc's'le Inn* – it's a gruelling route, involving a two-mile uphill slog, with no refreshments to hand, to the great gorse-covered headland of **Great Hangman** (1043ft). The payback is the incredible panorama, occasionally taking in glimpses of the Gower peninsula in Wales. From here you can retrace your steps back or complete a circle by veering inland round Girt Farm and west down Knap Down Lane to Combe Martin, the whole well-marked circuit adding up to about six miles.

You can find out more details on this route and others at the **Exmoor Visitor Centre** at Seacot, Cross Street (April–Sept daily

---

Organized activities on Exmoor

One of the best ways to enjoy the full range of outdoor activities on Exmoor is as part of an organized group. Park visitor centres can supply a full list, but the most appealing options include the partly off-road **Land Rover tours** to view Exmoor ponies, red deer and other wildlife run by Barle Valley Safaris (☎01643/851386 or 01398/323699), which leave from the *Exmoor House* hotel car park near the *Bridge Inn* in Dulverton, and are bookable at the Old Blacksmiths Gallery on Bridge Street; another equally good operator offering the same thing, Exmoor Safaris (☎01643/831229) start their tours at *White Horse* in Exford, where you can also book. Excursions with both companies last two to three hours and cost around £12. For **canoeing**, **kayaking** and other **adventure pursuits**, contact Mountain Water Experience ☎01548/550675; *www.mountainwaterexp.demon.co.uk*), while the Exmoor Outdoor Activity Group (☎01643/862816) is a loose association of operators offering everything from riding to falconry, fly-fishing and climbing.

The National Park Authority and other local organizations have also put together a programme of **guided walks**, graded according to distance, speed and duration and costing £2–3.50 per person depending on the length of the walk. For more details, and for specific schedules, contact any of the Park Visitor Centres or phone the National Park base at Dulverton (☎01398/323665).

10am–5pm, closes 7pm in Aug; Oct 10am–1pm; ☎01271/883319). The best place to **stay** is *Saffron* House on King Street (☎01271/883521; ②), a few minutes from the beach and with its own heated pool. The *Foc's'le Inn* off Cross Street is top choice for a **drink** and snack, with sea views from its outdoor benches.

Inland Exmoor

Watered by 325 miles of river and crossed by over 600 miles of public footpaths and bridleways, the upland plateau of inland Exmoor reveals rich swaths of colour and an amazing diversity of wildlife. The cheapest and best way to appreciate the grandeur of the moor is on foot, and endless permutations of **walking routes** are possible along a network of some six hundred miles of footpaths and bridleways. **Pony trekking** is another option for getting the most out of Exmoor's desolate beauty, and stables are dotted throughout the area. Whether walking or riding, bear in mind that over seventy percent of the National Park is privately owned and that access is theoretically restricted to public rights of way; special permission should certainly be sought before doing anything like camping, canoeing or fishing.

There are four obvious bases for excursions. **Dulverton**, in the southeast, makes a good starting-point for visiting the seventeen-span medieval bridge at **Tarr Steps**, about five miles to the northwest. You could also reach the spot from **Winsford** via a circular

---

Exmoor wildlife

The establishment of the National Park has done much to protect Exmoor's diverse **wildlife**, from dormice and fritillaries to ravens and buzzards. The management of the coastal heath that makes up most of the terrain has allowed certain species of birds to thrive, while the gorse covering large parts of it has especially favoured the diminutive blue Dartford warbler and the orange-breasted stonechat. Most celebrated of the moor's mammals, though are **Exmoor ponies**, a unique species closely related to prehistoric horses. Most commonly found in the treeless heartland of the moor around Exmoor Forest, Winsford Hill or Withypool Common, these short and stocky animals are not difficult to spot, though fewer than twelve hundred are registered, and of these only about two hundred are free-living on the moor. You probably won't get close to them, but if you do, don't try to feed them, and bear in mind that their teeth have to be sharp to tear up the tough moorland plants. Much more elusive are the **red deer**, England's largest native wild animal, of which Exmoor supports the country's only wild population. Over the centuries, hunting has accounted for a drastic depletion in numbers, but red deer have a strong recovery rate – about 2500 are thought to inhabit the moor today, and their annual culling by stalking as well as hunting is a regular point of issue among conservationists and nature-lovers.

walk which takes in the prehistoric **Wambarrows** on the summit of Winsford Hill, and the ancient **Caratacus Stone**. On the B3224, **Exford** would make a useful base for the heart of the moor, and further west, **Simonsbath** is an excellent starting point for hikes, despite holding only a couple of hotels – Dulverton and Exford have most of inland Exmoor's **accommodation**.

Dulverton

On Exmoor's southern edge, **DULVERTON** holds the National Park Authority's headquarters, which should be your first port of call if venturing onto the moor. The village is grouped around the parallel Fore Street and High Street which run between the River Barle and the parish church on a hill, but most of the action takes place around Fore Street – shops, pubs and the **Exmoor Visitor Centre** (daily: April–Oct 10am–1.15pm & 1.45– 5pm; Nov–March 10.30am–3pm; ☎01398/323841), which shares premises with the public library at no. 7. The centre has information on the whole moor and, at the back, a small exhibition on life on Exmoor with a video-screening showing aspects of moor-management. Behind the visitor centre, the **Guildhall Heritage Centre** (Easter–Oct daily 10am–4.30pm; free) has an extensive museum of the village as it was 100 years ago, including an art gallery and a reconstructed cottage, as well as annual exhibitions which are often made up of images from the Exmoor Photographic Archive.

Land Rover safaris leave from Dulverton; see box on p.147 for details.

There's a post office and a branch of the NatWest bank with a cashpoint on Fore Street.

With the moor beckoning, you're unlikely to want to linger long in the town itself, but Dulverton does hold a wide spread of **accommodation**, convenient if you plan on doing some walking. First choice has to be *Town Mills* (☎01398/323124; no credit cards; ①), a Georgian millhouse in the centre of the village with good-size pine-furnished bedrooms, in which breakfast is taken at the time of your choosing. If other central options are full, or you hanker after beams and four-posters, try the pricier *Lion Hotel* in Bank Square (☎01398/ 323444; ③), where the best rooms are 9 and the slightly larger 11, both with a nice prospect over the street. Nearer the moor, signposted two and a half miles north of town on the B3223, extensive *Highercombe Farm* (☎01398/323616; ②) has spacious and comfortable rooms. One mile north of Dulverton, past the *Rock House Inn*, there are two **camping barns** at Northcombe Farm, each one accommodating up to fifteen people at £4.50 per person per night, with cooking facilities and hot showers but no linen, and there's also a camping field (☎01398/323118 or 01258/857107).

You can rent bikes in Dulverton from Lance Nicholson, 9 High St (☎01398/ 323409).

For **food**, head for *Crispin's*, opposite the chemist at 26 High St (☎01398/323397), which offers moderately priced meals including a flavoursome vegetarian stroganoff; there's a vine-covered garden for fine weather, but it's usually busy so booking is advisable. The *Lion Hotel* is good for bar food. On Fore Street, *Lewis's Tea Rooms* serves snacks and a range of **cream teas**, best of them the Somerset

Dulverton is
connected by
bus #307 to
Barnstaple
and Taunton,
and by #398
to Tiverton
and
Minehead.

Cream Tea, with freshly made sandwiches and cake. Three miles south, at Exebridge, the *Starlight Express* is a restaurant in a converted railway carriage (☎01398/324028). Steaks and oven-roasted duck breast are the specialities, served in individual compartments; in winter, unless you book, the restaurant is only open Friday and Saturday evenings and Sunday lunchtime.

Tarr Steps and around

Nestling in the deeply wooded Barle valley five miles northwest of Dulverton, the **Tarr Steps** clapper bridge is one of Exmoor's most tranquil spots. Many prefer to walk here (from Dulverton Bridge, simply follow the riverside track upstream); by road it's a left turn from Dulverton's Fore Street, and another left five miles along the B3223. If you're driving, leave your vehicle in the car park and walk the final 500yd downhill, or else you can follow a tributary of the Barle to the bridge signposted from the car park.

Positioned next to a ford, the ancient **bridge** is said to be the finest of its type in Britain, constructed of huge gritstone slabs that are fixed onto piers by their own weight – which can be as much as two tonnes. Over 180ft long with seventeen spans, it's normally about a metre above water-level – much lower than when originally built due to the river silting up. Floodwaters now frequently cover the bridge, often causing damage – all but one of the slabs were washed away on the night of the 1952 Lynmouth deluge (see p.144). When this hap-

West Anstey
Farm
(☎01398/
341354), a
couple of miles
west of
Dulverton,
offers moor-
land horse-rid-
ing, including
one- and two-
day treks, and
lessons.

A walk from Tarr Steps

Tarr Steps makes a great destination on foot from Dulverton or Winsford (a route is detailed on pp.151 and 152), and you can extend the walk by combining it with this exhilarating five-mile circular walk which also takes in Winsford Hill, near Winsford. It's not excessively challenging, and you should be able to complete the circuit in around four hours.

Follow the riverside path upstream from Tarr Steps, turning right after about half a mile along Watery Lane, a rocky track that deteriorates into a muddy lane near Knaplock Farm. Stay on the track for three-quarters of a mile until you reach a cattle-grid, on open moorland. Turn left here, cross a small stream and climb up **Winsford Hill** for the 360-degree moorland views and the group of Bronze Age burial mounds (see p.152). If you want a refreshment stop, descend the hill on the other side to the village of Winsford (see opposite).

A quarter-mile due east of the Barrows, via any of the broad grassy tracks, the ground drops sharply by over 200ft to the **Punchbowl**, a bracken-grown depression resembling an amphitheatre. Keep on the east side of the B3223 which runs up Winsford Hill, following it south for a mile until you come across the **Caratacus Stone** (see p.152), just by Spire Cross. Continue south on the east side of the road, cross it after about a mile, and pass over the cattle grid on the Tarr Steps road, from which a footpath takes you west another one and a half miles back to the river crossing.

---

pens, however, the stones seldom travel far, and they are now numbered for easy repair; they're also protected by upstream cables that help to arrest flood debris charging down.

The bridge's age has been much disputed, with some claiming prehistoric origins, apparently backed up by the Bronze Age tracks found converging on the crossing, and its name, derived from the Celtic *tochar* meaning causeway. But there's no proof of a previous construction to this one, the earliest record of which is from Tudor times. Most now agree that, like the clapper bridges on Dartmoor, it is likely to be medieval. According to legend, however, the bridge was made by the devil as a place to sunbathe. The Prince of Darkness vowed to destroy any creature attempting to cross, and when a parson was sent to confront him he was met by a stream of profanities. When the abuse was returned in good measure, the devil was so impressed he allowed free use of the bridge.

The ancient **woodland** around Tarr Steps largely consists of sessile oak – formerly coppiced for tan bark and charcoal production – and a sprinkling of beech, but you'll also see a mix of downy birch, ash, hazel, wych-elm and field maple, often with a thick covering of lichen. The hazel coppice forms an important habitat for dormice, and you may spot red deer on the riverbanks. Birds breeding hereabouts include redstart, wood-warbler and pied fly-catcher, and you'll probably catch sight of dippers, grey wagtails and kingfishers. There is a choice of **walks** to embark upon, either onto Winsford Hill (see box, opposite); upstream of the river as far as Withypool (4 miles); or downstream to Dulverton. The visitor centre at Dulverton can equip you with itineraries for the two waymarked circular walks starting from Tarr Steps, of 1.5 miles and about four miles length.

Above the Steps, *Tarr Farm*, a sixteenth-century riverside inn, restaurant and tearoom provides an excellent spot to contemplate the river, and also serves good moderately-priced evening **meals**, for which you should book (☎01643/851507; closed Sun evening and Mon–Wed evenings in winter). Specialities include fish, local lamb and venison steak, and there's a long wine list.

Winsford

Five miles north of Dulverton, and signposted a mile west of the A396, **WINSFORD** – birthplace of the renowned Labour politician Ernest Bevin – lays good claim to being the moor's prettiest village. A scattering of thatched cottages ranged around a sleepy green, Winsford is watered by a confluence of streams and rivers – one of them the Exe – giving it no fewer than seven bridges. Once you've admired the village's obvious charms, the best plan is to abandon it in favour of the surrounding countryside. The obvious walking excursion from the village is the climb up **Winsford Hill**, a heather moor cut through by the B3223 that's reached on foot by taking the Tarr Steps road past the *Royal Oak*; turn off onto the moorland where it turns sharp left after about three-quarters of a mile. About the same distance further west, the hill's round 1400-foot summit is invisible until you are almost there, but once you're at the top, your efforts are repaid by views as far as Dartmoor, and you can clamber around three Bronze Age burial mounds known as the **Wambarrows**. A mile southeast of the summit, near the turning for Tarr Steps, the B3223 runs close to the **Caratacus Stone**, an inscribed monolith thought to date from between 450 and 650 and referred to in medieval documents as the Longstone. It is easily found, thanks to the comic "bus shelter" canopy built over it in 1906. The damaged inscription on the greyish-green monolith, four feet high, reads "Carataci Nepos" – that is, "kinsman of Caratacus", the last great Celtic chieftain who was defeated by the Romans in 46 AD.

The walking route from the Caratacus Stone to Tarr Steps is detailed in the box on p.150.

The *Royal Oak* (☎01643/851455; *www.royaloak-somerset. co.uk*; ⑤), a rambling, thatched old inn on Winsford's village green, is the obvious place for drinks, snacks and full restaurant **meals**, and also offers comfortable but pricey **accommodation**; rooms in the modern annexe are cheapest. Fifty yards beyond the pub on Halse Lane, the nonsmoking *Karslake House* (☎01643/851242; ④; closed Feb–March), has more reasonable rates and pleasantly furnished rooms – all with shower, some with toilet – and a relaxed but expensive restaurant serving exquisite meals. One mile to the north of the village, *Larcombe Foot* (☎01643/851306; no credit cards; ②; closed Dec–Feb) overlooks the Exe and has footpath access to the moor. Further along Halse Lane, *Halse Farm* **campsite** (☎01643/851259; *www.halsefarm.co.uk*; closed Nov to mid-March) is not very well sheltered but lies right on the edge of the moor and is convenient for walkers.

Exford

At an ancient crossing-point on the River Exe, **EXFORD**, four miles northwest of Winsford, preserves an insular air, its sedate cottages and post office ranged around a tidy village green. A part of the Royal Forest of Exmoor from Saxon times until the early thirteenth century, Exford prospered as a junction for packhorse trains carrying wool and cloth. During the nineteenth century, it grew as a **sporting cen-tre** and today, as the base of the Devon and Somerset Staghounds, local life is intimately involved with the **hunt**, particularly during the long season, which lasts from early August to late April. The village is also popular with walkers for the hike to **Dunkery Beacon**, Exmoor's highest point at 1700ft; a four-mile hike to the northeast, the route is clearly marked along a track which starts from Combe Lane, just past the post office (turn right at the end of the playing fields). The bridle-way here eventually becomes a rough track, which winds slowly round to the summit of the hill – a steady uphill trudge. A substantial cairn sits at the top, from where a majestic vista unfolds, with lonely moorland all about and the sea usually visible.

Meets of the Devon and Somerset Staghounds are advertised in the local press, as are the hunt's puppy and horse shows, point to point races and other summer events.

It's common for the various hunters and walkers, not to mention the shooters and fishers, who frequent these parts, to fill all of Exford's relatively wide range of **accommodation**. Sporty types are most evident in the two large inns that dominate the village: the impressively timbered and ivied *White Horse Hotel*, by the bridge, which has smallish but comfortable rooms (☎01643/831229; ⑥), and the more upmarket *Crown Hotel* (☎01643/831554; *www.gratton.co.uk/crown*; ⑥), with dark furnishings and large bathrooms. A friendly, nonsmoking vegetarian and vegan B&B, *Exmoor Lodge* (☎01643/831694; *www.exmoorlodge.co.uk*; ①) is a considerably cheaper alternative, with small, plain rooms with or without private bath, and lots of local information on hand. The village also holds Exmoor's main **youth hostel**, a large, gabled Victorian house near the centre (☎01643/831288; closed Nov to mid-Feb;). Most rooms have four to six beds (£11), and there are two doubles (①). Two and a half miles northwest of Exford, beyond Edgcott, *Westermill Farm* (☎01643/831238) provides a tranquil **campsite** in grass paddocks on the banks of the Exe. There are free hot showers and waymarked walks over the 500-acre farm.

Inland Exmoor

Horse riding can be arranged at Stockleigh Stables (☎01643/ 831166), half a mile north of the village.

Hunting on Exmoor

For many, outdoor sports on Exmoor means hunting and shooting, practices which have been at the heart of local communities for centuries. Shooting mainly takes place between September and January, but **hunting** can go on all year – though mostly in winter – and plays a large part in the lives of many of Exmoor's inhabitants. Socially too, the institution is central, since most hunts have full calendars of events throughout the year. Simultaneously, though, many locals **oppose hunting** – and not just because of the cruelty: the two reasons most often cited are the damage caused to farmland and gardens by dogs and horses, and the chaos created by the hunt followers – many of them city-folk – whose frantic cross-country mass manoeuvrings can block up roads and show scant regard for either countryside or property. The National Trust's ban on stag-hunting on its land has added more fuel to the debate, since it has virtually ended the practice in many places.

The true number of local opponents to the hunt will never be known – few want to risk taking a stand in Exmoor's close-knit communities – but the voice of hunt supporters is loud and clear: "**Endangered Exmoor**" stickers are evident everywhere, in support of the eponymous organization which campaigns primarily for the preservation of hunting, while the **Countryside Alliance** pro-hunting lobby also has strong support. The latter's claim that 16,000 jobs will be lost if hunting with hounds is banned has been countered by much lower estimates, but it cannot be denied that Exmoor's economy – more than most other hunting areas in Britain – is particularly dependent on hunting, chiefly in villages such as Exford, which holds the kennels and stables of the Devon and Somerset Staghounds and where a large proportion of the population are employed in activities connected with the hunt. If you're looking for a quiet time in these parts, you're best off keeping your views on the matter to yourself, since feelings run high.

Exford's two inns provide the village's main **restaurants**: the *Crown Hotel* has delectable but quite expensive dishes such as baked fillet of salmon and shank of lamb, while the *White Horse* has more basic meals popular with walkers, hunters and hostellers. Next to the *White Horse*, the *Exmoor House Hotel* has a snack menu and does sandwiches and cream teas in its converted Methodist chapel, and there's a traditional Sunday carvery. Both the inns offer afternoon teas, and the *Crown* sells farmhouse sandwiches to take away.

Exmoor Forest and Simonsbath

Exmoor Forest is one of the moor's wettest and boggiest zones; waterproofs are essential whatever the weather, and you should take note of local weather reports.

At the centre of the National Park, **Exmoor Forest** is the barest part of the moor, scarcely populated except by roaming sheep and a few red deer – the word "forest" denotes simply that it was formerly a hunting reserve. In the middle of the area, and just over five miles west of Exford on the B3223, the village of **SIMONSBATH** (pronounced "Simmonsbath") consists of little more than a couple of hotels, a pottery and a sawmill at a crossroads between Lynton, Barnstaple and Minehead on the River Barle. The village was home to Midlands ironmaster John Knight, who purchased the forest in 1819 and, by introducing tenant farmers, building roads and importing sheep, brought systematic agriculture to an area that had never before produced any income. The Knight family also built a wall round their land – parts of which can still be seen – as well as the intriguing dam at Pinkworthy (pronounced "Pinkery") Pond, part of a scheme to harness the headwaters of the River Barle, though its exact function has never been explained.

Paths radiate from Simonsbath across epic moorland, for which park visitor centres can supply walking itineraries. One easy waymarked route starts from opposite the *Exmoor Forest Hotel* and leads through Birchcleave Wood, running more or less parallel to the Barle for a couple of miles to **Cow Castle**, site of an old hillfort, and four miles further to Withypool. In the opposite direction, you can follow the River Barle upstream from Simonsbath for about four miles to the dark, still waters of **Pinkworthy Pond** – keep a lookout for red deer drinking here in summer. If you don't want to walk all the way, the B3358 passes within a couple of miles of the lake.

The old-fashioned *Exmoor Forest Hotel* (☎01643/831341; *helen@exforest.freeserve.co.uk*; ②) offers uninspiring **accommodation**, and has space for free **camping**; the bar here is good for a drink if you're not put off by the stag's heads, guns and other hunting paraphernalia on the walls. You'll find much bigger and better rooms at the *Simonsbath House Hotel* (☎01643/831259; ⑤), former home of the Knights and now a cosy bolt-hole offering seven agreeably plush rooms, all en suite, and wonderful views of the raw moorland. The expensive **restaurant** here is worth visiting for its excellent local venison and trout, but for coffees, crusty rolls and lunches, head for *Boevey's* (open daytime only, closes Dec–Jan), in a converted barn next door. A couple of miles southwest of the village on the Brayford road, the *Poltimore Arms* at Yarde Down is a classic country **pub**, serving excellent food including vegetarian dishes. Alternatively, at Challacombe, a hamlet five miles west on the edge of Exmoor, the *Black Venus* is a traditional place with real ale and excellent food.

Travel details

Trains

Minehead to: Bishops Lydeard (April–Oct 3–8 daily; 1hr 15min); Dunster (April–Oct 3–8 daily; 6min).

Buses

Combe Martin to: Barnstaple (hourly; 1hr); Ilfracombe (hourly; 25min); Lynmouth (summer 3 daily, winter Sat & Sun 3 daily; 55min); Lynton (3–5 daily; 40min); Minehead (summer 3 daily, winter Sat & Sun 3 daily; 1hr 30min); Porlock (summer 3 daily, winter Sat & Sun 3 daily; 1hr 15min).

Dulverton to: Exford (Mon–Sat 1–2 daily; 40min); Minehead (Mon–Sat 7 daily; 55min–1hr 15min); Winsford (Mon–Sat 1–2 daily; 30min).

Dunster to: Dulverton (Mon–Sat 6 daily; 45min); Minehead (1–2 hourly; 10min); Winsford (Sun 2 daily; 40min).

Exford to: Dulverton (Mon–Sat 2 daily; 35min); Minehead (Mon–Sat 1–2 daily; 40min); Porlock (Sun 2 daily; 15min); Winsford (Mon–Sat 2 daily; 10min).

Lynmouth to: Minehead (summer 3 daily, winter Sat & Sun 3 daily; 40min); Porlock (summer 3 daily, winter Sat & Sun 3 daily; 25min).

Lynton to: Barnstaple (Mon–Sat 10 daily; 55min); Combe Martin (3–5 daily; 35min); Ilfracombe (3–5 daily; 50min); Minehead (summer 3 daily, winter Sat & Sun 3–5 daily; 55min); Porlock (summer 3 daily, winter Sat & Sun 3 daily; 40min).

Minehead to: Combe Martin (summer 3 daily, winter Sat & Sun 3 daily; 1hr 25min); Dulverton (Mon–Sat 6 daily; 55min); Dunster (1–2 hourly; 10min); Exford (2 daily; 40min–1hr 15min); Lynton (summer 3 daily, winter Sat & Sun 3–5 daily; 55min); Porlock (Mon–Sat 7–9 daily, Sun 3 daily; 20–25min); Porlock Weir (Mon–Sat 7 daily; 30min); Taunton (hourly; 1hr 10min); Winsford (2 daily; 50min).

Porlock to: Combe Martin (summer 3 daily, winter Sat & Sun 3 daily; 1hr 15min); Exford (Sun 1 daily; 1hr 30min); Lynton (summer 3 daily, winter Sat & Sun 3 daily; 40min); Minehead (Mon–Sat 7–9 daily, Sun 3 daily; 20min); Porlock Weir (Mon–Sat 7 daily; 5min).

Winsford to: Dulverton (Mon–Sat 2 daily; 20min); Dunster (Mon–Sat 1–2 daily; 40min); Exford (Mon–Sat 1–2 daily, Sun 2 daily; 10–25min); Minehead (2 daily; 50min–1hr); Porlock (Sun 2 daily; 40min).

Chapter 7

North Devon and Lundy

E xtending east from Exmoor to the Cornish border, the **north Devon** region encompasses a motley range of landscapes from banal beach resorts to picture postcard villages and savagely windlashed rocks. Apart from a few pockets of more intense activity, it's a tranquil, unhurried region, less touristy than Devon's southern coast. The chief town, **Barnstaple**, at the end of the branch-line from Exeter, is a good place to get started from, with extensive transport connections and a range of hotels and restaurants, though its low-key appeal doesn't invite much lingering. From here it's an easy run to some of Devon's best beaches, at **Croyde**, **Woolacombe** and **Saunton Sands**, all hugely popular with surfers. **Ilfracombe**, on the other hand, is a traditional tourist resort with strong Victorian trappings; to the east, the hilly stretch of coast as far as Exmoor (see Chapter 6) provides a strenuous but stimulating hiking route.

Enjoying a fine site on the Torridge River, the robust working town of **Bideford** is mainly a transit centre, with some decent accommodation and bus connections to all the towns on the bay. Easiest to reach is **Appledore**, sheltered in the mouth of the Torridge estuary. Inland, **Great Torrington** makes a good destination for walkers or bikers following the **Tarka Trail** (see box, opposite), which passes through some of the region's loveliest countryside. West of Appledore, **Westward Ho!** has a magnificent swath of sand to compensate for the ugly holiday developments. The coast along the fur-

You'll find a wealth of information on north Devon at www .northdevon.co. uk. For transport information in the region, call ☎0870/ 608 2608 or consult the Web site www .devon-cc.gov .uk/devonbus

---

ACCOMMODATION PRICE CODES

Throughout this *Guide*, hotel and B&B accommodation is coded on a scale of ① to ⑨, the code indicating the lowest price you can expect to pay per night for a double room in high season. The prices indicated by the codes are as follows:

① under £40	④ £60–70	⑦ £110–150
② £40–50	⑤ £70–90	⑧ £150–200
③ £50–60	⑥ £90–110	⑨ over £200

thest reaches of Bideford Bay is dominated by cliffs, where the tourist honeypot of **Clovelly** clings to the steep slope amid thick woods. If you're put off by the crowds and artifice, follow the bay round to stormy **Hartland Point** at Devon's northwestern corner. This intensely rural area is pretty much off the beaten track, and offers some bracing cliff walks as well as the more temperate appeal of Hartland Abbey. For remoteness, though, you can't get much further out than **Lundy Island**, a patch of wilderness in the middle of the Bristol Channel that makes a great bolt-hole for a night or two, and affords tremendous views of England, Wales and, westwards, the Atlantic Ocean.

Barnstaple

At the head of the Taw estuary, **BARNSTAPLE** has been north Devon's principal town since at least Norman times, but reveals surprisingly little of great age or interest. Remote from the power-centres of the south coast, its role as one of north Devon's rare ports was largely lost when the river silted up in the nineteenth century, preventing large ships from docking; smaller vessels still dock to load up

---

The Tarka Line and the Tarka Trail

Rated by some as one of the finest pieces of nature writing in the English language, Henry Williamson's *Tarka the Otter* (1927) has been enthusiastically appropriated as a promotional device by north Devon's tourist industry. As parts of the book are set in the Taw valley, it was perhaps inevitable that the Exeter to Barnstaple rail route – which follows the Taw for half its length – should be dubbed the **Tarka Line**, while Barnstaple forms the centre of the figure-of-eight traced by the **Tarka Trail**, which tracks the otter's wanderings for a distance of over 180 miles, the route marked by an otter's-paw symbol. For walkers and cyclists, it's a brilliant way to get around as well as get a close-up look at the estuary's wildlife. To the north, the trail penetrates Exmoor then follows the coast back along the cuttings and embankments of the old Barnstaple–Ilfracombe rail-line, and passes through Williamson's home village of **Georgeham** on its return to Barnstaple. South, the path takes in Bideford, following the disused rail line to Meeth and continuing as far as Okehampton, before swooping up via Eggesford, the point at which the Tarka Line joins the Taw valley.

The twenty-three miles of the trail that follow former rail lines are ideally suited to **bicycles**, and there are rental shops at Barnstaple (see p.160), Bideford (see page 166) and Great Torrington (see p.167). Bikes can be carried free on Tarka Line trains (but only one per carriage). Tourist offices give out leaflets detailing individual sections of the trail, and the best overall books are *The Tarka Trail: A Walker's Guide* (Halsgrove Books: £4.95), and Terry Gough's more detailed *The Tarka Trail: Exploring the Old Rail Routes by Cycle and Foot* (Past and Present Publishing; £7.99). Both titles are available from tourist offices or bookshops.

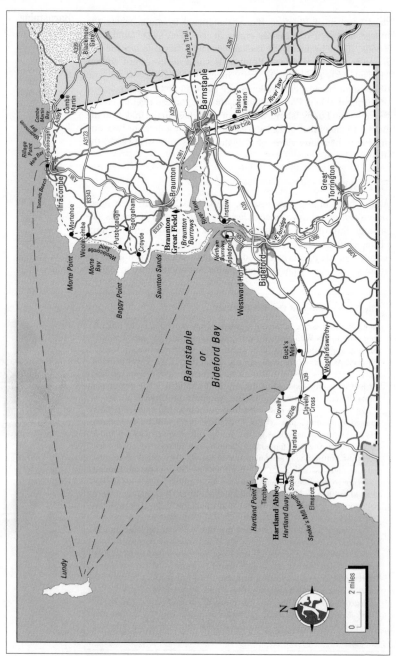

© Crown copyright

THE GUIDE: CHAPTER 7

with sand (used for ballast). The local Taw and Torridge rivermouths have also provided large quantities of the red clay used in the famous **pottery** that has been produced in the Bideford and Barnstaple area since the thirteenth century, and was exported to Wales, Ireland, Northern Europe and the New World by the early seventeenth century. The status of the local **Barum ware** enjoyed a further boost when it received Queen Victoria's patronage in 1885, but pottery-making has nothing like the same importance nowadays. The town's centuries-old role as a marketplace for local foodstuffs, however, is perpetuated in the daily bustle around the huge timber-framed **Pannier Market**, off the pedestrianized High Street, the model for many other similar structures in north Devon towns. The market offers crafts (Mon & Thurs), antiques (Wed) and general goods and fresh local produce (Tues, Fri & Sat). Alongside it runs **Butchers Row**, its 33 archways still holding mainly identical butcher's shops.

Between the High Street and Boutport Street, which curves round to meet the High Street at its southern end, a grassy area holds Barnstaple's **parish church**, with its curiously twisted "broach" spire – octagonal, rising from a square tower – and the fourteenth-century **St Anne's Chapel**, an oddly-shaped, part-battlemented building converted into a grammar school in 1549 and later numbering John Gay, author of *The Beggar's Opera*, among its pupils; it's now closed to the public. At the end of Boutport Street, the lively miscellany of militaria and pottery at the **Museum of North Devon** (Tues–Sat 10am–4.30pm; £1, free Sat 10am–noon) is well worth taking in. The ground floor illustrates local wildlife, focusing on the ecosystems of North Devon's estuaries and coastline, but there's more gripping material upstairs, where a room is devoted to Barum ware, the colourful work created by C.H. Brannam's studio, featuring lurid lizard and fish designs in greens and ochre-reds. You can also see examples of sgraffito design, a traditional north Devon technique achieved by scratching through the slip to show the red clay underneath. Other first-floor rooms display war memorabilia – uniforms, flags, guns – connected to the Devonshire regiment and the Royal Devon Yeomanry, formed two centuries ago to protect the coast from Napoleon.

The museum lies alongside the Taw, where footpaths make for a pleasant riverside stroll, with the florid and colonnaded **Queen Anne's Walk** – built as a merchants' exchange in the eighteenth century – providing some architectural interest. The **Tarka Trail** runs past it on its route along the riverbank.

Practicalities

Barnstaple's **train station** is on the south side of the Taw, a five-minute walk from the centre, where the **bus station** sits between Silver Street and Belle Meadow Road. Nearby, the town's well-informed **tourist office**, opposite Butchers Row on Boutport Street (May–Sept Mon–Sat 9.30am–5.30pm; Oct–April Mon–Sat 9.30am–

5pm; ☎01271/375000; *www.barnstaple.co.uk*), covers the whole north Devon area as well as the Devon side of Exmoor.

Of the numerous places to **stay** in town, two of the cheapest lie five hundred yards south of Long Bridge (the main crossing over the Taw), both smart and well-equipped places: *Nelson House*, 99 Newport Rd (☎01271/345929; no credit cards; ①), backing onto Rock Park and the river, has shared toilets (though two of the three rooms have private showers), while around the corner on Victoria Road, the more capacious *Ivy House* (☎01271/371198; no credit cards; ①), has good-size rooms with and without private bathrooms. A little further out, on Landkey Road – a continuation of Newport Road – the first-rate *Mount Sandford* (☎01271/342354; no credit cards; ②) is packed with flowers both inside and in the lovely garden, which each of the spacious en-suite rooms overlooks. Most central of all, near the museum at the end of Boutport Street, the plush Victorian *Royal and Fortescue Hotel* (☎01271/342289; *www .royalfortescue.co.uk*; ②) is rather formal but has some surprisingly cheap room-only rates and a decent restaurant.

You can rent bikes from Tarka Trail Cycle Hire at the train station (☎01271/ 324202). Riverside Cycle Hire, a quarter-mile northwest of town in the Pottington Industrial Estate (☎01271/ 325361), is conveniently placed for the Tarka Trail's northern section towards Braunton.

Among the best budget **restaurants** in town, the traditional *Old School Coffee House* on Church Lane, near St Anne's Chapel, serves morning coffees, teas and light lunches including pies and toasted sandwiches. At 70 Boutport St, the coolly modern *PV* (closed Sun) offers dishes such as poached salmon and the vegetarian Louisiana Green Gumbo in its moderately-priced upstairs restaurant; the ground floor, which doles out coffees and snacks during the day, becomes a wine bar in the evening. *La Viennetta* at 27 Boutport St (☎01271/325531; closed Sun & Mon) has a range of inexpensive Italian staples, while *Jalapeño Peppers* (closed Sun) on Maiden St (off the end of the High St) has Mexican platters from fajitas to "red-hot chilli bullets". For gourmet dining, head a mile south of the centre to the nonsmoking *Lynwood House*, on Bishops Tawton Road (☎01271/343695; *www .lynwoodhouse.co.uk*), which serves a moderate set lunch, and expensive but choice seafood suppers.

The *Cornerhouse* **pub**, on the corner of Boutport Street and Joy Street, is somewhat spoiled by the fruit machines, but still has a traditional working atmosphere, and the tiled back room is quieter. On Silver Street, off Boutport Street, *Shooters* pub has a **club** attached for dancing – Tuesday is comedy night. You can drink juices and coffees at *surfdotcom*, an **Internet café** at 4 Market St (£1 for 15–20min).

Croyde and around

Eight miles west of Barnstaple, village gentility collides with youth culture at **CROYDE**, a cosy huddle of cottages alongside a leat, or channelled stream, that empties into the sea half a mile away at **Croyde Bay**. Backed by grassy dunes, the firm, sandy beach here has retained its secluded, undeveloped appeal, despite its recent incarnation as a major **surfing** venue. Drivers can park to the north of the sands at the bottom of Moor Lane, an equally good spot from which to explore the **Baggy Point** headland at the top of Croyde Bay, where the vertical cliffs are inhabited by nesting birds, and, from September to November in particular, a swirl of gannets, shags, cormorants and shearwaters. In clear weather, you can see round Bideford Bay to Hartland Point, while nearer at hand lies the flat silhouette of Lundy straight out to sea.

South of Croyde, surfing is also much in evidence at **Saunton Sands**, a very long strand magnificently exposed to long ranks of breakers. Extending behind the beach are the substantial sand dunes and mud-flats of **Braunton Burrows**, a three-mile-long nature reserve interwoven with walking trails, from which you can view the aquatic birdlife. The coastal path cuts right across, and you can also make an easy detour along quiet signposted lanes to get here from the Tarka Trail, which passes through **BRAUNTON**, three miles inland. This sizeable village is notable mostly for **Braunton Great Field**, a 340-acre area to the west of the Velator level-crossing that's one of the few remaining open-field systems surviving in the country. It's still strip-farmed according to medieval methods, the strips divided by grass balks, or ridges.

Practicalities

Bus #308 travels from Barnstaple via Braunton and Saunton to Croyde, which has the area's best choice of **places to stay**, many of them lining St Mary's Road, beside the leat. At no. 16, *Parminter* (☎01271/890030; ③) is a fine flagstoned cottage with large rooms in the loft and young, friendly owners. On the other side of the road, at the end of an impressive drive, *Croyde Manor* (☎01271/890350; *www.croyde-bay.com/manor.htm*; ②) is the classiest B&B, a Georgian country house with four-posters in each of its immaculately furnished rooms, and huge shared bathrooms. Nearest the beach – but only just – *Bridge Cottage* at 2 St Mary's Rd (☎01271/890589; ②) is a simple B&B with shared bathrooms. Five-minutes' from the centre of Croyde, and signposted just before *The Thatch* pub, *Bay View Farm* is a grassy caravan and **camping** site (☎01271/890501; closed Nov–Easter). You'll find more rough-and-ready facilities and cheaper prices in the more tent-friendly *Orchard* (☎01271/ 890422), a small field behind the post office on Hobbs Hill, usually open all year.

Right across St Mary's Road from *Bridge Cottage*, **tea and scones** are to hand at *May Cottage Tearooms*, while further up (opposite *Parminter*), *LA's* is an all-American down-home diner with burgers, Cajun chicken, and "sanwiches" (both places are closed Sun in winter). For **pubs**, choose between *The Thatch*, a surfers' hangout at the centre of the village on Hobbs Hill, or *The Manor*, a coaching inn at the back end of St Mary's Road, also popular. A full range of bar snacks is available at both.

Croyde and around

A useful Web site for accommodation and other facilities, including surf reports, is www.croyde-bay.com

You can rent bikes from Otter Cycle Hire on Station Road, Braunton (☎01271/ 813339).

You can rent surf equipment from stalls on Croyde's beach in summer. Tuition is supplied by Surf South West, in the Burrows Beach car park (☎01271/ 890400; www.surfsouth west.com*). For the latest on local surf conditions, call ☎0891/ 007007 or ☎0906/566 2020 (50p per minute), or visit* www .croyde-surf -cam.com

Woolacombe and around

North of Baggy Point, the pick of the beaches in **Morte Bay** is **Putsborough**, quieter and less crowded than **Woolacombe Sand**, the broad expanse stretching northward from here, which is very popular with surfers and families alike at its far end. Though splendidly positioned at the bottom of a valley, **WOOLACOMBE** lacks much charisma, amounting to little more than a collection of hotels, villas and retirement homes – things do get animated in summer, but there's a rather drab feel at other times. The beach, of course, is the main attraction, and the surrounding coastline holds equal appeal. At its northern end, Morte Bay is bracketed by **Morte Point**, an area of grass and gorse that's good for walking, below which stretches a rocky shore whose menacing sunken reef inspired the Normans to give it the name Morte Stone. A break in the rocks makes space for the pocket-sized **Barricane Beach** (signposted), famous for the tiny tropical shells washed up here from the Caribbean by Atlantic currents, and another favourite swimming spot. Walkers can take in the splendid rock contortions hereabouts by continuing a mile or so beyond Morte Point to **Bull Point**, where a lighthouse warns ships off the fractured reefs tapering away out to sea.

Practicalities

On Woolacombe's Esplanade, the **tourist office** (Easter–Sept Mon–Sat 10am–5pm, plus July & Aug Sun 10am–5pm; Oct–Easter Mon–Sat 10am–1pm; ☎01271/870553) has information on the coast from Saunton Sands to Ilfracombe.

Running downhill to the sand, Beach Road holds most of the **accommodation**, including *Camberley* (☎01271/870231; ②), a three-storey B&B with superb views (like every place along here) from its picture windows; guests can use the indoor pool in the next-door *Royal Hotel*. Just above the tourist office on Rockfield Road, the huge *Baggy Leap* has spacious, modern rooms with or without bathrooms and views of the whole bay (☎01271/870222; no credit cards; ②). At the opposite extreme, the turreted brown-and-white *Woolacombe Bay Hotel* (☎01271/870388; *www.woolacombe-bay-hotel.co.uk*; ⑧), at the bottom of South Street, oozes nostalgia, with a sward of lawn in front and a pool and tennis courts; ask about special low-season discounts. The nearest **campsite** is *Woolacombe Sands Holiday Park* (☎01271/870569), though with all the razzmatazz of heated indoor pool, nightly entertainments in the season and other organized amusements, you might prefer the relative peace of *North Morte Farm* (☎01271/870381), five-minutes' walk from Mortehoe village (less than a mile north of Woolacombe), and steps from the beach. Both sites open between Easter and October only.

Just behind the beach, surfies congregate in the *Red Barn*, a popular **bar** and **restaurant** with a rank of surfboards in the roof. On the

You'll find a full range of surf gear at the Second Skin Surf Shop and Hire, right next to the Red Barn.

Esplanade, *The Boardwalk* is a cool place for teas, coffees, panini and pizzas, with fresh seafood dishes in the evening.

Ilfracombe
and around

Ilfracombe and around

Five miles east of Morte Point and squeezed between hills and sea, **ILFRACOMBE** is north Devon's most popular resort. With large-scale development restricted by the surrounding cliffs and outcrops, the town is essentially little changed since its evolution into a tourist destination in the nineteenth century, after which it languished as a kind of quirky Victorian theme-park and full-on family resort. Only lately has it begun to rouse from its long slumber, and though it continues to draw elderly folk and the bucket-and-spade brigade, Ilfracombe is also starting to attract the surfer crowd and a hipper image, symbolized by the modernistic twin white chimneys of the **Landmark Theatre** on Wildersmouth Beach. Nonetheless, the resort goes into overdrive in summer, when the relentless pressure to have fun and the ubiquitous smell of chips can become oppressive – though, as the chief attractions lie in the surrounding area, this shouldn't impinge too much.

Ilfracombe does have some genuine draws, but they're best appreciated outside the peak season. The town's **harbour** still sees some low-key fishing activity, and crab and lobster are also hauled up here. The port, which is the departure-point in summer for cruises to Lundy (see p.173), coastal tours and fishing trips (bookable from kiosks here), is protected by the grassy mound of Lantern Hill. Surmounting the headland, the fourteenth-century **St Nicholas chapel**, once offered refuge to pilgrims en route to Hartland Abbey (see p.170) and was later used as a lighthouse. The only other point of interest is next to the Landmark on Wilder Road, where the **Ilfracombe Museum** (April–Oct daily 10am–5.30pm; Nov–March Mon–Fri 10am–12.30pm; £1) has a rich archive of photos and Victoriana relating to the town, and plenty of material about the local wildlife; there are giant stuffed gulls, thousands of butterflies in cases and a room devoted to the wildlife and history of Lundy.

The town's best collection of antiquities lies a mile east of the centre, off the A399 road to Combe Martin, where you can join a guided hour-long tour of **Chambercombe Manor** (Easter–Sept Mon–Fri 10am–5.30pm, Sun 2–5.30pm; £4). Although parts of this whitewashed huddle of buildings around a cobbled courtyard survive from the eleventh century, the furnishings are mostly Elizabethan and Jacobean. Highlight of the tour is a hidden chamber where a dummy recalls the body of a girl discovered here in 1865 – her dead body had been secretly sealed in the room 200 years earlier by her father who, while pursuing his wrecking activities off the coast, discovered that his daughter had been one of the victims. The four acres of lovely gardens and woods are an added incentive to visit.

Ilfracombe and around

Otherwise, the coast is the main event, not least the **beaches**. West of the centre, past Wildersmouth Bay, rocky **Tunnels Beach** takes its name from the two tunnels bored through the cliffs by Welsh miners in the nineteenth century, still the main means of access; privately-owned (erratic hours, but usually 9am–6pm; £1.10 entry), the beach has a protected rock bathing pool at low tide. Surfers will be more interested in the long west-facing strands at Woolacoombe (see p.162).

One of Devon's loveliest coastal walks extends east of town towards Combe Martin (see p.146), though it involves a stiff ascent up to the grassy heights of **Hillsborough**, about a mile from the centre, which offers a perfect prospect over Ilfracombe. Beyond, **Hele Bay**, its deep waters almost encircled by cliffs, is the first of a sequence of undeveloped coves and inlets surrounded by jagged slanting rocks and heather-covered hills. **Rillage Point** offers the occasional seal sighting, while the first-class sand beach at **Watermouth Bay**, three miles east of Ilfracombe (reachable on bus #30), is protected by yet more dramatic cliffs and rocky outcrops. Close to the shore here, the imposing castellated nineteenth-century mansion of **Watermouth Castle** (April–Oct Mon–Fri & Sun 10am–4pm; £6) is best admired from the outside unless you have kids, who will appreciate the water shows, dungeons and carousel.

Watermouth Castle's opening hours can vary, so it's wise to call ☎01271/863879 before you visit; last admission is one hour before closing.

Practicalities

Ilfracombe's **bus station** is very near the harbour on Broad Street, at the bottom of High Street and its continuation Fore Street, which themselves hold most of the shops. **Buses** between Ilfracombe and Barnstaple (#1, #2, #30 or #303), Mortehoe and Woolacombe (#31 or #303), Combe Martin (#30 or #300), and Minehead and Lynton (#300) all stop here. If you're planning to return by bus from a coastal hike, note that services can finish early and that few run on Sunday. By the Landmark Theatre on the seafront, the **tourist office** (Easter–Oct daily 10am–6pm; Nov–Easter Mon–Fri 10am–5pm, weekends 10am–4pm; ☎01271/863001; *www.ilfracombe-guide.org.uk*) can provide bus timetables as well as changing money and selling boat tickets for Lundy and other trips.

Ilfracombe has a good choice of **accommodation**, though space can be scarce in summer. One of the less expensive B&Bs is the very central *Kinvara* at 6 Avenue Rd, opposite the bandstand between the High Street and the seafront (☎01271/863013; no credit cards; ①; closed Nov–Easter); just two of its nine rooms are en suite. If you want views, try the *Cavendish Hotel* at 9 Larkstone Terrace on the western edge of town (☎01271/863994; no credit cards; ③). The 23 rooms, mostly en suite, are plain but comfortable, and the Malaysian owner rustles up exotic evening meals on request. On Highfield Road, above the High Street, the three-storey *Inglewood Guest House* (☎01271/867098; ①; closed Nov–March) offers panoramic views from most rooms and home-cooking in the evening. There's an excellent independent **hostel**, *Ocean Backpackers*, near the bus station and harbour at 29 St James Place (☎01271/867835). Beds in dorms, singles and doubles go for £9 per night, and there's a very cool restaurant (see below). The YHA hostel, *Ashmour House* (☎01271/865337; closed Nov–Feb), is above the harbour on Hillsborough Terrace, with bunk-beds for £10. If you want to stay near the beaches, try *Little Meadow* campsite at Lydford Farm (☎01271/862222; closed Oct–Easter) – connected by footpath to Watermouth Castle and the beach – or the sites around Morte Point (see p.162).

Ilfracombe's best **place to eat** is the *Atlantis*, below *Ocean Backpackers* on St James Place, specializing in international dishes, with ambient, world and jazz musical background. There's Caribbean cooking at *Level Vibes*, 63 Fore St, while *The Red Petticoat* by the harbour doles out ridiculously cheap fish and chips to the cheesy sound of 1930s music. On the High Street, *The Lantern* is a funky surfer's **café** serving salads, rolls and other snacks. Also on the High Street, the *Lamb and Leprechaun* and the *Bunch of Grapes* are two **pubs** with live music; if you want a quieter drink, head for *The George and Dragon* on Fore Street, the oldest pub in town. Have a cocktail or absinthe at *Swivel*, 155 High St, perhaps before hitting one of the town's two **clubs**, the *Colossus* on Market Street – surprisingly large, with an over-the-top interior, playing mainly house – and the less exciting *Lucky's* on High Street, playing more mainstream sounds. Both are open Fridays and Saturdays until 2am, charging £3–7.

Bideford and Appledore

Serenely spread out along the west bank of the River Torridge, the estuary town of **BIDEFORD** formed an important link in the north Devon trade network. From the Norman era until the eighteenth century, the port was the property of the Grenville family, whose most celebrated scion was **Richard Grenville**, commander of the ships that carried the first settlers to Virginia, and later a major player in the defeat of the Spanish Armada. Today, the long tree-lined quay is still the focal point of the town, and the most conspicuous reminder of its former mercantile importance still straddles the broad banks of the Torridge: the **medieval bridge**, first built in 1300, reconstructed in stone in the following century and subsequently reinforced and widened – hence the irregularity of its twenty-four arches, no two of which have the same span.

Apart from the sailings of the ferry to Lundy (see p.173), Bideford preserves few other maritime links, and you'll get a stronger taste of the sea a couple of miles downstream at **APPLEDORE**, near the confluence of the Taw and Torridge rivers. This elegant old shipbuilding port still has several working boatyards, providing one of the few north Devon industries entirely independent of tourism. With most of

On the far side of Bideford's bridge, East-The-Water holds Bideford's disused station, where a converted carriage serves as an information point for the Tarka Trail, which runs alongside the river on this side.

Bideford's traditional Pannier Market on Market Place is open Tuesdays and Saturdays for produce and crafts.

Bideford and Appledore

the yards out of sight, however, the pastel-coloured Georgian cottages and placid quayside combine to confer a deeply mellow air on the town. The easy-going atmosphere also suffuses the tiny back lanes climbing above the quay, which are worth a wander. A few minutes' walk up Meeting Street or Bude Street, the **North Devon Maritime Museum**, housed in a typically elegant villa on Odun Road (Easter–April daily 2–5pm; May–Sept Mon–Fri 11am–1pm & 2–5pm; Oct Mon–Fri 2–5pm; £1), gives an occasionally enthralling insight into the town's seafaring past. The ships' figurehead, cannon and anchors arrayed outside give a good idea of the contents within: mainly roomfuls of salvaged equipment, along with photos and models, and an assortment of oddities from shipwright's tools to mud shoes.

Practicalities

Between May and October, Tarka Cruises (☎01237/ 476191) runs one-hour estuary and river trips from Appledore (£4.50) and passenger ferries every fifteen minutes across to Instow (£1.50).

Buses #1 and #2 from Barnstaple and Ilfracombe stop on Bideford Quay. The **tourist office** is located alongside Victoria Park (Easter–June & Sept Mon–Sat 10am–5pm, Sun 10am–1pm; July & Aug Mon–Sat 10am–5pm, Sun 10am–4pm; Oct–Easter Mon–Tues & Thurs–Fri 10am–4.30pm, Wed & Sat 10am–1pm; ☎01237/477676), from which you can pick up information on Lundy (see p.171) – boat tickets to the island are available here or from the booths along the quayside.

To explore the Tarka Trail, you can rent bikes from Bideford Bicycle Hire, Torrington St (☎01237/ 424123), two hundred yards south of the bridge on the eastern riverbank (£9.50 per day).

If you want to **stay in Bideford**, seek out the friendly *Cornerhouse*, 14 The Strand (☎01237/473722; no credit cards; ①), two minutes from Victoria Park and favoured by travellers to Lundy. Further out on Northam Road, but linked to the centre by a footpath, the attractive *Mount* (☎01237/473748; *alex@laugharne1 .freeserve.com*; ②) is set in its own walled gardens, with elegant rooms and a separate lounge for guests. **Appledore**'s best B&Bs overlook the estuary on Marine Parade: try *Regency House* at no. 2 (☎01237/473689; ①), a handsome building with small palm trees and flowers outside, and magnificent views from the front rooms.

For a **meal** or a drink, head up Bridge Street from Bideford's bridge to Market Place, where the imposing, porticoed *Old Coach Inn* opposite the Pannier Market provides ales and hearty snacks, while *Praxis II* (closed Wed afternoon and Sun; no credit cards) across the square is much more up-to-date, with artworks on the walls and metal tables and chairs: it's a good place for a coffee or herb tea, and filled French sticks and vegan pasties are available during the day. In Appledore, Market Street, running parallel to the quayside, has several good **pubs** including the *Coach and Horses*, which serves meals in its garden, and the *Royal*, which has benches outside and live music every Saturday.

Great Torrington

Five miles up the River Torridge from Bideford, connected by the Tarka Trail and the A386, **GREAT TORRINGTON** is a sleepy market town surrounded by woods and by hills carpeted by gorse and bracken. Much of the place is nondescript, but the central **Square** is a handsome ensemble, with the pink Georgian facade of the long Pannier Market at one end, and a porticoed town hall.

Torrington changed hands several times during the **Civil War**, and was the scene of the last great battle in 1646, at the end of which the New Model Army under Thomas Fairfax and Oliver Cromwell occupied the town – a crucial turning-point that led, soon after, to the trial and execution of Charles I. After the battle, two hundred Royalist soldiers were imprisoned in St Michael's church, just north of The Square, where, unknown to their captors, eighty barrels of gunpowder had also been stored; somehow (for reasons never discovered) it was ignited, the ensuing explosion killing them all. In the churchyard of the rebuilt St Michael's, a large cobbled mound near the main entrance is reputed to be the burial place of the victims. The events are brought to life in **Torrington 1646** (Tues–Sat: April–Sept 10.30am–5pm; Oct–March 11am–4pm; £3.50), a permanent exhibition at Castle Hill car park, a few steps along South Street from The Square, where guides in seventeenth-century costume narrate the night of the battle and explosion and show you around the physic garden. In the Royalist encampment, you can try your hand at some of the games of the era, and try on armour.

Bus #315 runs between Barnstaple, Bideford and Torrington.

Torrington's **tourist office** is next to the exhibition centre at Castle Hill car park (Mon–Fri 10am–4.30pm, Sat 10am–1pm; ☎01805/626140). If you want to **stay** locally, try the *Tarka Country Guest House*, a double-fronted B&B at 6 Halsdon Terrace, off South Street (☎01805/623756; no smoking; ①), where the large en-suite rooms, all with TVs, are great value.

There are some enticing **restaurants** in town, among them *Browns* at 37 South St, open during the day (but closed Sun) for coffees and teas and such dishes as lamb, aubergine and apricot casserole and cashew-nut roast. You'll find a couple of decent **pubs** on The Square: the *Newmarket*, a free house with inexpensive bar meals, and the *Black Horse*, one of the oldest buildings in town (probably sixteenth-century) that was the headquarters of General Fairfax. Tarka Trailers will appreciate the *Puffing Billy*, the old station just north of the village and on the trail, now converted into an informal restaurant. On Fore Street near The Square, the *Plough Arts Centre* (☎01805/624624) has a gallery with arts and craft-work exhibitions, a lively programme of events, including roots concerts, and a café.

You can rent bikes from Torridge Cycle Hire at the old station (☎01805/ 622633).

Westward Ho!

Three miles northwest of Bideford and less then two miles west of Appledore, **WESTWARD HO!** is the only English town to be named after a book. **Charles Kingsley**'s best-selling historical romance, which he wrote while staying at nearby Bideford, was set in the surrounding country, and it wasn't long after its publication in 1855 that speculators recognized the tourist potential of what was then an empty expanse of sand and mud pounded by Atlantic rollers. The town's first villa was built within a decade, but even its early development failed to inspire much enthusiasm. Rudyard Kipling, who spent four years of his youth here (as recounted in *Stalky and Co.*), described the place as "twelve bleak houses by the shore". His presence is recalled in Kipling Terrace – the site of his school – and **Kipling Tors**, the heights at the west end of the three-mile sand-and-pebble beach.

There's a shop renting out surfing gear on Pebble Ridge Road, and lessons are available from Walking on Water (☎07974/ 082592) and Big Blue Surf School (☎01288/ 331764).

Kingsley didn't think much of the new resort when he paid a visit, and he probably wouldn't care for it now, with its spawning amusement arcades, caravan sites and holiday chalets. Once you get below these, however, the broad sandy expanse has an undeniable grandeur. Popular with kite-flyers and kite-surfers, the **beach** offers fabulous swimming and great views across Bideford Bay. Behind the sands, and protected from the sea by the long rocky foreshore and a high ridge of large pebbles, **Northam Burrows** is a flat, marshy expanse of dunes and meadows rich in flora and fauna, attracting plenty of migratory birds.

Buses #15 and #15A follow a circular route between Bideford Quay, Appledore and Westward Ho! (Mon–Sat), the #14A runs from Bideford to Appledore on Sundays.

Golf Links Road, the main route to the beach, holds most of the town's facilities. At its western end, Pebble Ridge Road has a selection of fish-and-chip shops and snack bars – try the pleasant *Pebble Ridge Tea Rooms*. The *Waterfront Inn* at the western end of Golf Links Road provides **drinking** and **meals** close to the beach, as well as spacious, modern and en-suite **rooms** (☎01237/474737; ④). A couple of doors down, you'll find cheaper B&B at *Lower Lodge* (☎01237/477496; no credit cards; ②), where the plushly overdecorated rooms share bathrooms.

Clovelly

The impossibly picturesque village of **CLOVELLY**, which must have featured on more calendars, biscuit boxes and tourist posters than anywhere else in the West Country, was put on the map in the second half of the nineteenth century by two books: Charles Dickens's *A Message From the Sea* and, inevitably, *Westward Ho!* – Charles Kingsley's father was rector here for six years. To an extent, the archaic tone of the village has been preserved by restricting hotel accommodation and banning holiday homes, but in the tourist season, when it's an obligatory stop for a regular stream of visitors, it's impossible to see past the artifice. Come out of season, however, and you'll find genuine charm – be prepared, though, for the hefty uphill slog over tricky cobbles on the way out.

Unless you're coast-pathing, the first hurdle to surmount is the horrific, oversized **Visitor Centre** (daily: summer 9am–5pm, winter 9.30am–4pm), where you are charged £3.50 for access to shops, snack bars, an audiovisual show and use of the car park (it's well-nigh impossible to leave your motor anywhere else). Walkers, cyclists and users of public transport have right of way to the village, via a gate on the right of the complex which leads onto the cobbled, traffic-free High Street. Known locally as Up-along or Down-along according to which way you are going, it plunges down past neat, flower-smothered cottages where battered sledges are tethered for transporting goods – the only way to carry supplies since the use of donkeys ceased.

At the bottom of the village, Clovelly's stony beach and tiny **harbour** lie snuggled in a cleft in the cliffs; the jetty was built in the fourteenth century to shelter the only safe port on this coast between Appledore and Boscastle in Cornwall. A lifeboat now operates from here, but a handful of fishing boats and piles of lobster baskets are the only remnants of a fleet which provided the village's main business before the herring and mackerel stocks dried up during the first half of the twentieth century. In summer, kiosks at the harbourside advertise **boat trips**, providing a good way to see the bay and coastline, as well as cruises to Lundy (see p.171): sailing time is an hour each way, and you get six hours on shore (☎01237/431405; £22.50).

Immediately below the car park, Hobby Drive is a signposted three-mile walk along the cliffs through woods of sycamore, oak, beech, rowan and the occasional holly, with grand views over the village.

Practicalities

You can reach Clovelly on bus #319, which traces a route from Barnstaple and Bideford to Hartland (not Sun). As there are few **accommodation** options in the village, you'd be wise to book ahead even in winter. Enjoying the best position in Clovelly, the *Red Lion* at the harbour (☎01237/431237; *redlion@clovelly.demon.co.uk*; ⑥) has small, crowded bedrooms but wonderful views and a friendly atmosphere. The only B&B in the village is *Donkey Shoe Cottage* at 21 High St (☎01237/431601; no credit cards; ②), whose plainly furnished rooms are bigger than you might expect from the outside. You're more likely to find availability in the mostly inexpensive guesthouses at Higher Clovelly, a twenty-minute walk up from the visitor centre. Try the *Old Smithy*, on the main road (☎01237/431202; no credit cards; ①) or, fifty yards further down, the nonsmoking *Boat House Cottage* (☎01237/431209; no credit cards; ①) – both are small and neat with distant sea views. On Burscott Lane, the modern *Fuchsia Cottage* (☎01237/431398; no smoking; no credit cards; ①) appears quite far out, but it's right in front of a track leading through fields to the lower town in about ten minutes. Cheap evening meals are served here.

Clovelly's best **eating** option is the *New Inn* on High Street, which offers pasties and teas as well as more substantial food. Down by the harbour, the *Red Lion* offers bar snacks in its Harbour Bar at the front, with locals congregating to drink in the Snug Bar at the back. Upstairs, the restaurant offers a good two-course dinner for £20.

If you can't face the uphill climb back to the top of the village, take the Land Rover which leaves every fifteen minutes or so from behind the Red Lion to the car park at the top (Easter–Oct daily 9am–5.30pm; £1.60).

Hartland and around

Four miles west of Clovelly and about three from the coast, **HART-LAND** has a quiet, insulated air, remote from the main routes of the West Country. The village has three pubs and a café to supply nourishment, but it's the coast to north and west that provide the main incentive for being here, reached – unless you're on the coastal path – along narrow, high-hedged lanes between cultivated fields. Three miles northwest, the Atlantic meets Bideford Bay at **Hartland Point**, one of Devon's most dramatic sights. A solitary lighthouse 350ft up overlooks jagged black rocks battered by the sea, and when conditions are clear, the bare horizon is interrupted only by the long, low profile of Lundy (see opposite). Seals can sometimes be seen here or a mile east of the point at **Shipload Bay**, the only sandy beach between Westward Ho! and the Cornish border. Walkers can reach it along the coastal path. By road, park at *East Titchberry Farm* (500yd before *West Titchberry Farm*), from which a signposted path leads 300yd to the beach. Erosion and subsidence here has made access difficult in recent years and the last section of steps down to the beach is missing, but it's well worth the effort of negotiating the rather tricky clamber down.

South of the headland, **Hartland Quay** is a scatter of houses around the remains of a once-busy port, financed in part by the mariners Raleigh, Drake and Hawkins, but mostly destroyed by storms in the nineteenth century. The slate in the cliffs to either side forms beautiful patterns, curving and folding in on itself, though its instability makes it inadvisable to approach the edge, climb or sit under the cliffs. The hotel here (see opposite) houses the small **Hartland Museum** (Easter–Oct daily 11am–5pm; £1), displaying various salvaged items from the dozens of shipwrecks that have taken place around this stretch of coast over the centuries. Many more must have been prevented, though, by the tower of fourteenth-century **St Nectan's** – a mile inland in the village of **Stoke** – which acted as a landmark to sailors before the construction of the Hartland lighthouse at Hartland Point; at 128ft, it's the tallest church tower in north Devon. Inside, the church boasts a finely carved rood screen and a Norman font, all covered by a repainted wagon-type roof.

Half a mile east of Stoke and about a mile west of Hartland, gardens and lush woodland surround **Hartland Abbey** (May–Sept Wed, Thurs & Sun 2–5.30pm; plus July & Aug Tues 2–5.30pm; £4.25), an eighteenth-century country house incorporating the ruins of an abbey dissolved in 1539. It's an endearing old place, displaying fine furniture, old photographs and recently uncovered Victorian murals on Arthurian themes, copied from the House of Lords. The Regency library has portraits by Gainsborough and Reynolds, and George Gilbert-Scott designed the vaulted Alhambra Corridor and outer hall. From the house, a path leads a mile through woodland strewn with bluebells and primroses to cliffs and a small bay that's sandy at low tide.

Southwards down the coast, saw-toothed rocks and near-vertical escarpments defiantly confront the waves, with spectacular water-falls tumbling over the cliffs. A mile or so south of Hartland Quay, **Speke's Mill Mouth** is a select surfers' beach – though the rocks and even fragments of wrecks lying just below the surface of the water make surfing ill-advised for anyone unfamiliar with the area. A main-ly rocky cove, it's reached by steep steps from the coast path. There's no road access, and no facilities of any kind.

Practicalities

Hartland is served by bus #319, which, starting from Barnstaple, takes in Bideford and Clovelly on its route west. Although the village's inns provide B&B **accommodation**, the best choice here is on North Street (off Fore St) at 2 Harton Manor (☎01237/441670; no credit cards; ①), where there are two congenial rooms above an artist's studio, one with a four-poster. Otherwise, the most appealing places are outside the vil-lage. Near Hartland Point, *West Titchberry Farm* (☎01237/441287; no credit cards; ①) offers simple rooms, a warm guests' lounge and evening meals (£9); to get to the farm, follow the numerous signs for Hartland Lighthouse. Though the rooms are fairly ordinary, the *Hartland Quay Hotel* (☎01237/441218; closed Nov to mid-Feb; ②) is another great place to stay due to its proximity to the sea, with spray flecking the windows on rough days. Inland of here at Stoke, *Stoke Barton Farm*, just opposite St Nectan's church (☎01237/441238; no credit cards; ①), offers spacious en-suite rooms and also has basic **camping** facilities. **Elmscott youth hostel** occupies a converted Victorian schoolhouse at Elmscott (☎01237/441367; closed Sept–March), two miles south of Stoke and about half a mile inland. It's a remote spot, and difficult to reach by public transport: take bus #319 to Hartland, from where it's a three-and-a-half-mile walk along the foot-path from the west end of Fore Street; bunks cost £10.

Places to **eat and drink** include the *Anchor Inn*, at the western end of Hartland, which gets crowded in the evenings and has a pool table and separate dining room. Also on Fore Street, the *Shamrock Café* provides decent snacks including fish and chips and teas, and *The Happy Pear* is a laid-back wholefood café and health-food shop that serves delicious hot and cold meals. The *Hartland Quay Hotel* has Wreckers' Ale on tap and mediocre bar meals.

Lundy Island

Disembarking on the windswept island of **LUNDY**, twelve miles northwest of Hartland Point, feels like arriving at the last outpost. A granite sliver three miles long and roughly half a mile wide, the island was home to an early Christian community in the fifth and sixth cen-turies, and today its twenty-odd full-time residents share it with the thousands of marine birds for which Lundy is a refuge. With no roads, one pub and one shop, little has changed since the **Marisco** family established itself here in the twelfth century, making use of the coves and shingle beaches to terrorize shipping up and down the Bristol Channel. The family's reign ended in 1242 when one of their number, William de Marisco, was found to be plotting against the king, whereupon he was hanged, drawn and quartered at Tower Hill in London.

After the Mariscos, Lundy's most famous inhabitants were **Thomas Benson**, MP for Barnstaple in the eighteenth century – mainly remembered now for using slave labour to work the island's granite quarries and for his part in a massive insurance fraud – and **William Hudson Heaven**, a clergyman from Bristol who bought the island in 1834 and established what became known as the "Kingdom of Heaven". He reopened the quarries, which are said to have provided the tough granite for the Thames Embankment in London, though they closed soon afterwards. The National Trust acquired Lundy in 1969, and it's now managed by the Landmark Trust with the aim of restoring the many relics of former habitation that are scattered around – many of them converted into holiday accommodation – and preserving the primitive character of the place. Accordingly, you won't find any new-fangled amusements to impinge on Lundy's pristine, low-tech ambience, and all electricity is cut off at 11pm each night. Returning to the mainland after a few hours here induces something close to culture shock.

You'll find pages of information on Lundy at www.landmark-trust.co.uk/lundy.html *and* www.lundyisland.co.uk

Walking is really the only thing to do here, and tracks and footpaths interweave all over the island. Inland, the grass, heather and bog is crossed by drystone walls and grazed by ponies, goats, deer and the rare Soay sheep. The shores – mainly cliffy on the south and west, softer and undulating on the east – shelter a rich variety of **birdlife**, including kittiwakes, fulmars, shags and Manx shearwaters, which often nest in rabbit burrows. The most famous birds, though, are the **puffins** after which Lundy is named – from the Norse *Lunde* (puffin) and *ey* (island). They can only be sighted in April and May, when they come ashore to mate. Offshore, **basking sharks**, which can grow to 25ft, can be seen from early July to mid-August, and grey seals can be seen all the year round.

Around the island

In spite of the lack of artificial entertainments, Lundy provides plenty of diversion, and an overnight sojourn allows you to experience the very different flavour after the day-trippers have sailed off. The few specific sights provide destinations for walks, but really, the best advice is to wander at will. The island is divided into holdings by walls cutting across its width; a fast walk from wall to wall takes about twenty minutes, and you can calculate some five or ten minutes to traverse from the cliffier western shore to the more protected east, along paths branching off to left and right of the central plateau.

Just up from the harbour on the southeastern corner of the island, **Lundy Island** **Marisco Castle** was erected by Henry III following the downfall of the Mariscos in 1244, and was paid for from the sale of rabbits – Lundy was a Royal Warren. The small keep has walls three feet thick, constructed of local granite and all inclining inwards, and was probably the main building on the island until the late eighteenth century. Rebuilt in the Civil War, it's now restored as holiday accommodation. From here, it's a few minutes' walk to the "**village**", a uniform cluster of buildings including the pub and shop. Just east of the pub stands **Millcombe House**, an incongruous piece of Georgian architecture in these bleak surroundings that was the home of William Hudson Heaven. South of the pub, the square-towered church of **St Helena** was built in 1896 by his son, Hudson Grosett Heaven, to the design of the eminent Victorian architect John Norton. Some of the loneliest parts and most dramatic landscapes of Lundy lie west of here, around the island's southern tip. Here, the **Devil's Limekiln** should be approached with care: it's a pit over a hundred yards deep, into which the sea enters from the bottom.

You are warned not to swim at the northern end of the island, where fierce currents can pull you out fast.

North of the village, Lundy's main track heads along the north–south axis of the island, across the springy turf and heather of **Ackland's Moor** to the first of the island's three dividing walls. After the first or "quarter wall", climb down a steep path to the right to see the **Quarries** – last used in 1911 – and adjacent beach. At the western end of the wall, granite steps lead down to remains of the cottages, magazine and gun-station which make up the **Battery**, dating from 1863, from which a cannon was fired every ten minutes in foggy conditions. The cannons are still there. Half a mile north of here, **Jenny's Cove** is named after a vessel reputed to be carrying ivory and gold that was wrecked here in the seventeenth century, and is the haunt of razorbills, guillemots and puffins. Despite their beauty, the rhododendrons that grow thickly around these shores are considered a pest, since they acidify the soil and prevent the growth of other foliage – the Landmark Trust (see overleaf) is always seeking volunteers to clear away the plants and assist with other conservation projects.

Practicalities

The *Oldenburg* crosses to Lundy two or three times weekly **from Bideford** between April and December, and **from Ilfracombe** between March and October. In each case, journey-time is around two hours; day-return tickets cost around £25, open returns about £40; for reservations, and to check departures (sailings are very dependent on the state of the seas, and cancellations are common) call ☎01237/470422. A quicker but extravagant alternative is the twelve-minute **helicopter** journey from Lake Heliport (☎01237/421054), near Abbotsham, between Bideford and Westward Ho! for which you'll need to fork out around £350 per round trip for up to five people, plus £40 per hour waiting time if you want to explore the island.

A cheerful hall with a balcony, whose only chilling note is supplied by the display of life-preservers from some of the ships foundered off the island's coasts, the *Marisco Tavern* is very much Lundy's focal point. The buffet lunch and local ale are good enough to discourage some trippers off the ferry from venturing any further on the island. The village **shop** has a good range of provisions, and if you're staying on the island, you can arrange to have groceries delivered.

Accommodation on Lundy can be booked up months in advance, and B&B is only available in houses which have not already been taken for weekly rentals. Since B&B bookings can only be made within two weeks of the proposed visit, this limits your options, but outside the holiday season it's still eminently possible to find a double room for £45 per night. All **bookings** must be made through the Landmark Trust's Shore Office in Bideford (☎01237/470422). Choices include the two-storey granite *Barn*, a hostel sleeping fourteen; the *Old House*, where Charles Kingsley stayed in 1849, and the *Old Light*, a lighthouse built in 1820 by the architect of Dartmoor Prison, one of the three lighthouses on the island (the other two are in use). The remotest place is the *Admiralty Lookout*, about one and three-quarter miles from the village along the main track to the north, and the only property that has no electricity; it sleeps four in bunks. A single person might find the *Radio Room* cosy; it once housed the transmitter that was the island's only link with the outside world. In all cases, furnishings are chosen to suit the individual property. There's also a **campsite** near the *Tavern* in the village, open throughout the year; it's surrounded by a protective wall but can still get pretty rain- and windswept in stormy weather.

Travel details

Trains

Barnstaple to: Exeter (Mon–Sat 7–9 daily, Sun 4 daily; 1hr 10min).

Buses

Appledore to: Barnstaple (Mon–Sat hourly, Sun 3 daily; 40min); Bideford (hourly; 15min); Westward Ho! (Mon–Sat hourly; 15min).

Barnstaple to: Appledore (Mon–Sat hourly, Sun 3 daily; 45min); Bideford (Mon–Sat every 15min, Sun hourly; 35min); Braunton (Mon–Sat every 30min, Sun hourly; 20min); Clovelly (Mon–Sat 4 daily; 1hr 5min); Croyde (Mon–Sat hourly; 35min); Exeter (Mon–Sat 6 daily, Sun 2 daily; 2hr 20min); Great Torrington (Mon–Sat 1–2 hourly, Sun 2 daily; 35min); Hartland (Mon–Sat 5 daily; 1hr 20min); Ilfracombe (Mon–Sat 3 hourly, Sun hourly; 50min); Lynton (Mon–Sat 10 daily; 55min); Plymouth (Mon–Sat 5 daily, Sun 2 daily; 3hr 5min); Tiverton (Mon–Sat 10 daily; 1hr 25min); Westward Ho! (Mon–Sat hourly, Sun 6 daily; 50min); Woolacombe (Mon–Sat 4–6 daily; 45min).

Bideford to: Appledore (hourly; 15min); Barnstaple (Mon–Sat every 15min,

Sun hourly; 45min); Braunton (Mon–Sat every 30min, Sun hourly; 1hr); Clovelly (Mon–Sat 4 daily; 40min); Exeter (Mon–Sat 5 daily, Sun 2 daily; 2hr); Great Torrington (Mon–Sat 1–2 hourly, Sun 4 daily; 20min); Hartland (Mon–Sat 5 daily; 55min); Ilfracombe (Mon–Sat every 30min, Sun hourly; 1hr 25min).

Braunton to: Barnstaple (Mon–Sat every 30min, Sun hourly; 20min); Bideford (Mon–Sat every 30min, Sun hourly; 50min); Croyde (Mon–Sat hourly; 20min); Ilfracombe (Mon–Sat every 30min, Sun hourly; 25min); Westward Ho! (hourly; 1hr); Woolacombe (Mon–Sat 5–6 daily; 15–25min).

Clovelly to: Barnstaple (Mon–Sat 5 daily; 1hr); Bideford (Mon–Sat 6 daily; 40min); Hartland (Mon–Sat 4 daily; 15min).

Croyde to: Barnstaple (Mon–Sat hourly; 40min); Braunton (Mon–Sat hourly; 20min); Saunton (Mon–Sat hourly; 7min).

Great Torrington to: Barnstaple (Mon–Sat 1–2 hourly, Sun 2 daily; 40min); Bideford (Mon–Sat 1–2 hourly, Sun 4 daily; 20min).

Hartland to: Barnstaple (Mon–Sat 6–7 daily; 1hr 15min); Bideford (Mon–Sat 5–6 daily; 55min); Clovelly (Mon–Sat 5 daily; 15min).

Ilfracombe to: Appledore (3 daily; 1hr 40min); Barnstaple (Mon–Sat 3 hourly, Sun hourly; 50min); Bideford (Mon–Sat every 30min, Sun hourly; 1hr 25min); Braunton (Mon–Sat every 30min, Sun hourly; 25min); Lynton (Mon–Sat 5 daily, Sun 3 daily; 55min); Woolacombe (Mon–Sat 9 daily; 30min).

Saunton to: Barnstaple (Mon–Sat hourly; 30min); Braunton (Mon–Sat hourly; 12min); Croyde (Mon–Sat hourly; 6min).

Westward Ho! to: Appledore (Mon–Sat hourly; 15min); Barnstaple (Mon–Sat hourly, Sun 8 daily; 1hr); Bideford (Mon–Sat hourly, Sun 8 daily; 15min); Ilfracombe (Mon–Sat hourly, Sun 8 daily; 1hr 50min).

Woolacombe to: Barnstaple (Mon–Sat 4–6 daily; 35min); Braunton (Mon–Sat 5–6 daily; 15–25min); Ilfracombe (Mon–Sat 9 daily; 25min).

Chapter 8

South Cornwall coast

There's comprehensive background on south Cornwall, as well as heaps of listings, at www .cornish-riviera .org.uk

Nearly all of Cornwall's rivers empty into the sea along the county's **southern coast**, providing a succession of estuaries which shelter the numerous small fishing ports strung along the seaboard. This combination of natural beauty and quaint old villages has ensured that the area is heavily visited, and most places are tarnished by various degrees of commercialization, but the thrilling cliff-hung coastline always provides a convenient escape, the best sections of which are only accessible on the South West Coast Path.

Tourism has certainly stamped its imprint on medieval ports such as **Looe** and **Polperro**, which are best visited out of season when they revert to the sleepy state that suits them best. The estuary town of **Fowey**, however, is big enough to transcend the summer influx, and as a working port has an agreeably self-sufficient air. West of here, **St Austell**, the capital of Cornwall's china-clay industry, lacks much intrinsic interest, but it's just a stone's throw from the unspoiled Georgian harbour village of **Charlestown**, the most appealing of the resorts on **St Austell Bay**, and the nearest stop to the jaw-dropping **Eden Project**, the region's most talked-about attraction, which finally opened in 2001. On a smaller scale, the **Lost Gardens of Heligan**, further west, are also spectacular, a salvaged Victorian garden which retains a swampy, jungle-like appearance. Close by, first impressions suggest that **Mevagissey** is just another overexploited fishing port with a strong tourist presence in summer, but it has preserved its charm more successfully than many others, and boasts some good restaurants. To the south, **Veryan Bay** is a sequestered nook mostly off the tourist track, though its gorgeous beaches are popular in summer.

Continuing west along the coast, **Carrick Roads**, the complex estuary basin which forms one of the finest deep-water anchorages in Britain, has pockets of frantic tourist activity counterbalanced by the rural calm of its creeks and muddy inlets. At its top, the county capital of **Truro** has Cornwall's best museum and one of Britain's most striking – and newest – neo-Gothic cathedrals, but the major

---

ACCOMMODATION PRICE CODES

Throughout this *Guide*, hotel and B&B accommodation is coded on a scale
of ① to ⑨, the code indicating the lowest price you can expect to pay per
night for a double room in high season. The prices indicated by the codes
are as follows:

① under £40	④ £60–70	⑦ £110–150
② £40–50	⑤ £70–90	⑧ £150–200
③ £50–60	⑥ £90–110	⑨ over £200

---

resort in these parts is **Falmouth**, at the bottom of the estuary, where
the mighty Pendennis Castle occupies a commanding site on the end
of the promontory. Its sister-fort lies across the estuary mouth at **St
Mawes**, the biggest village on the mercifully undeveloped **Roseland
Peninsula**, a blissful spot whose waterside churches are steeped in a
timeless calm.

The main **train** line to Penzance runs through Lostwithiel, St
Austell and Truro, but apart from these towns, and Falmouth and
Looe, which lie at the end of picturesque branch-lines, most of the
places in this chapter are served by buses only. On the whole you'll
find a good distribution of **accommodation** throughout the region,
though many places close in winter.

Looe

LOOE was drawing crowds as early as 1800, when the first
bathing-machines were wheeled out, but the arrival of the railway
in 1879 was what really packed its beaches. The town stands at the
mouth of the East and West Looe Rivers which meet here, the
combined stream dividing East Looe, where most of the action is,
from quieter West Looe, and crossed by a seven-arched bridge
near the main car park. On the East Looe side, the main Fore
Street runs south from the bridge, a long gaudy parade of shops
and cafés that ends at the web of narrow lanes around Buller Quay
and the harbour. If the tide's right, crossing by ferry from Buller
Quay (30p) saves you the trek round by bridge to the centre of
West Looe.

It's East Looe's long **harbour**, however, that holds all the interest.
When not beset by milling crowds, it's an absorbing place to while
away some time, its quays stacked with crates and lobster baskets,
and plenty of low-level pottering on the boats below. Moored alongside the sixty-odd fishing vessels that continue to work from here is
a small flotilla of other craft used for summer **boat trips**, for which
you sign up at boards lined up on the quayside. These days, Looe
touts itself as something of a shark-fishing centre (it's the headquarters of the Shark Fishing Club of Great Britain), so it's not surprising
that among these should be **shark-fishing expeditions** (£30 for a full
day), though a more modest two-hour mackerel quest (£7) is enough

Looe

You'll find up-to-date info on everything from walks to whist drives at www.looe.org

for most. The excitement quotient can be high on these trips, depending on the weather and the catch, but if you want to see something of the coast you're better off on a six-hour coastal voyage aboard a Cornish lugger (£23). From Buller Quay, there are also regular trips in summer to **Looe Island** (also called St George's Island), a mile or so out. Once the site of a Celtic monastery, the low, green hump, just a few hundred yards across, was bombed in World War II by Germans who mistook it for a warship, and is now a privately-owned bird sanctuary. It makes a great place for a gentle ramble: trips out cost £3 plus a £2.50 landing fee; take food and drink if you're planning a long stay as the island only has a drinks dispenser for refreshments. **River and estuary trips** are also available from Buller Quay (£3 per hour), but best of all are the guided canoe excursions available from Floating Leaf Canoes (☎01503/240566), based at Kilminorth Woods on the West Looe river (signposted); a half-day guided trip costs £15.

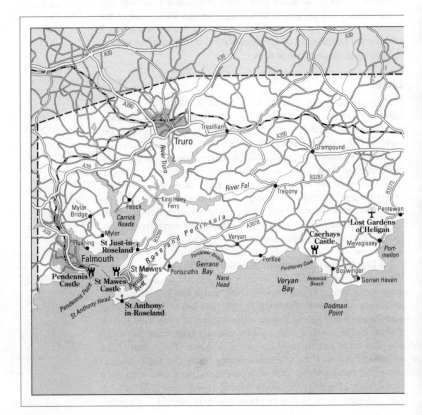

Projecting south from the harbour, Banjo Pier – named for its shape – separates the river mouth from the broad expanse of **East Looe Beach,** the handiest stretch of sand if you're looking for a place to sprawl. As the most popular of the town's beaches, with a flurry of stalls and activities advertised, it gets pretty congested; you'll find a choice of calmer and more varied strands to east and west. At the far end of the town beach, try the quieter and rocky **Second** or **Sanders Beach**, reached through a break in the rocks known locally as the Khyber Pass. More secluded and sandy beaches are accessible from here at low tide and also from the coastal path from Looe or by road. One of the best is **Millendreath**, a crescent of sand and shingle less than a mile east of Looe, backed by concrete terraces and holiday chalets but still scenic, with scattered rocks and green hills on either side; the swimming is good too. In West Looe, you can escape from the glut of holiday-makers on the long stretch of **Hannafore Beach** at the end of Marine Drive.

Looe

Guided town walks kick off from the tourist office at 11am on Thursdays (late May to Sept; £2).

© Crown copyright

Shingly at high tide, it reveals rock pools at other times, and has good views over to Looe Island.

Practicalities

Between June and September, the **Looe Valley Line** makes a scenic run along the course of the East Looe river from Liskeard, itself a stop on the main rail line from Plymouth. There are also regular **buses** from Liskeard (#73 and #73A) and Plymouth (#72 and #81A). If you **drive** in, you're best off heading for the Millpool car park at the approach to the town, as the car park near the bridge fills up quickly; alternatively, there's free parking along Marine Drive in West Looe.

The **tourist office** is at the Guildhall, halfway down Fore Street in East Looe (Easter & May to late Sept daily 10am–5pm; April & late Sept to Oct daily 10am–2pm; Nov–Easter open but unattended Mon–Fri 10am–noon; ☎01503/262072; *www.southeastcornwall.co.uk*).

The plethora of **accommodation** in town helps to keep prices down. Pick of the bunch are behind the beach in West Looe's Hannafore district: try the nonsmoking *St Aubyn's* on Marine Drive (☎01503/264351; *www.staubyns.co.uk*; ②/③; closed Nov–Easter), a large detached house adorned with tapestries and crystal. Close to the beach and harbour in East Looe, converted fisherman's cottage *Osborne House* on Lower Chapel Street (☎01503/262970; ②; closed Nov & Jan) has smallish granite-walled bedrooms and a bright restaurant below. *Sea Breeze*, a friendly three-storey B&B further up the same street (☎01503/263131; *JohnJenkin@ sbgh.freeserve.co.uk*; ①), has appealing, mostly en-suite colour-co-ordinated bedrooms.

Of the nine **campsites** in the Looe vicinity, opt for *Tregoad Farm* (☎01503/262718; *www.cornwall-online.co.uk/tregoad*; closed Nov–March), one and a half miles west of Looe via the B3253 Polperro road (and on the Coastal Hoppa bus route): it's quieter than most, with a bar/bistro and free hot showers.

The narrow streets between East Looe's quay and seafront hold a crop of **restaurants** which get very busy in summer. For moderately priced fish dishes, try the *Water Rail* on Lower Market Street (☎01503/262314; Easter–Sept closed Wed; Oct, Dec & Feb–Easter closed Sun–Thurs; closed Nov & Jan), a rose-covered smuggler's cottage complete with priest hole. In West Looe, it's worth booking at *Tom Sawyers* on Marine Drive (☎01503/ 262782) a bustling place strong on seafood and steak dishes, and especially popular on Sunday for its £6 carvery. Plainer, inexpensive fare is served at any number of places along Fore Street, among which the *Golden Guinea* is reliable for seaside nosh such as fish and chips.

Among the **pubs**, *Ye Olde Fishermans Arms* on Higher Middle Street puts on Irish music on a Thursday or Friday, while *Ye Olde Salutation* on Fore Street has sloping slate floors, a gallery of shark photos on the walls and good, cheap pub meals and snacks.

Barbican Motors on East Looe's Barbican Road (☎01503/ 262877) rent bikes, and will deliver and collect from the train station.

From mid-July to mid-September, the Coastal Hoppa bus runs four times daily from Seaton to Looe and inland to Lanreath and Porfell on Tuesday and Thursday (also Wed in school summer holidays). A ticket valid for one-day's unlimited travel costs £1.80. Call ☎01503/ 262718 for timetables.

Polperro and around

Smaller, quainter and usually even more overrun by summer visitors, **POLPERRO** is linked with neighbouring Looe, four miles east, by hourly buses #72A, #73A and #81A. From the bus stop and car park at the top of the village, milk floats disguised as trams (60p single) and horses and carts (90p single) tout for those who cannot manage the ten-minute walk alongside the River Pol to the minuscule harbour. The tightly-packed houses rising on each side of the stream present an undeniably pretty sight, little changed since the village's heyday of smuggling and pilchard fishing, but the "discovery" of Polperro has robbed it of much of its charm in season, and its straggling main street, The Coombes, is now an unbroken row of touristy shops and cafés.

For more on Polperro, visit the community Web site: www.polperro .org.

If you prefer a focused tour to a mere ramble through the village's tidy lanes, join one of the **guided walks** that start from the Village Hall, halfway down The Coombes (Tues: May–Aug 7.30pm; Sept 2.30pm). Otherwise, you can get some good background on the village at the **Polperro Heritage Museum of Smuggling and Fishing** (Easter–Oct daily 10am–5pm; £1), housed in the old pilchard factory on The Warren, to the eastern side of the harbour. Focusing on the fishing and smuggling communities that once inhabited Polperro's packed cottages, it's a pretty low-key display, but you'll unearth some intriguing photos from the 1860s among other works by Victorian artists attracted to the area, including some showing the local fishermen wearing their traditional "knitfrocks" (knitted sweaters), examples of which are also on view here.

The Polperro Fishermen's Choir holds quayside concerts on Wednesdays at 8pm during July and August.

West of Polperro, the five miles to **Polruan**, on the Fowey estuary, are among the most scenic stretches of south Cornwall's coastal path, giving access to some beautiful secluded sand beaches. Away from the coast, the B3359 leads five miles north of Polperro to **LAN-REATH**, home to one of the West Country's most engaging collections of traditional culture, the signposted **Lanreath Folk and Farm Museum** (April–Oct Mon–Fri & Sun 11am–5pm; £2.50). A higgledy-piggledy arrangement of family heirlooms and items picked up from local sales – everything from donkey shoes to a calf-resuscitator – has been stuffed into a tithe barn, along with vintage tractors that you can sit on and farming implements in the sheds outside.

Practicalities

Although Polperro deserves no more than a swift visit at the most during the busy summer months, it makes a peaceful place to **stay** for a night or two at any other time, and is a useful bolt-hole for coast walkers. The most congenial options include *Talland House* on Talland Street, an extension of Fore Street (☎01503/273176; no credit cards; ①), which has two simple en-suite cottagey rooms with painted stone walls. Close to the harbour but relatively secluded, the pricier *Old Mill House* (☎01503/272362; *www.oldmillhouse.i12.com*; ③) is a mellow pub on Mill Hill which has eight cream-coloured rooms with antique furniture. Overlooking Talland Bay a mile east of Polperro (signposted at the car park roundabout), *Great Kellow Farm* (☎01503/272387; closed Nov–Easter has a small, quiet **campsite**.

Unsurprisingly, Polperro's numerous **restaurants** tend to specialize in seafood. On The Coombes, the moderately-priced, non-smoking *Kitchen* (☎01503/272780; closed Nov–March) has delicious vegetarian options alongside the fish dishes; it's open daily from July to September, but ring to check for other months as hours can vary; booking is advisable in any case. Moderately priced seafood and local beef are the main items at the bow-fronted and beamed *Neville's*, at Little Green, off Big Green (closed Sun mid-March to Oct, Sun–Tues Nov to mid-Jan, and mid-Jan to early March; ☎01503/272459), a popular spot with locals, while *Captain Nemo's* brasserie, just by the Saxon Bridge off Fore Street and replete with nautical trappings, serves more modest salads and pastas. The small and snug *Blue Peter* **pub** on The Quay is the place to be in the evening, with jazz in the background and, on Saturday nights (except in high season) and Sunday afternoons, played live.

Fowey and around

The frequent ferries that cross the River Fowey from Polruan afford a fine first view of the quintessential river port of **FOWEY** (pronounced "Foy"), a cascade of neat, pale terraces at the mouth of one of the peninsula's greatest rivers. Having become Cornwall's major south-coast port in the fourteenth century, Fowey became ambitious enough for Edward IV to strip the town of its military capability, but it continued to thrive commercially, coming into its own as the leading port for china-clay exports in the nineteenth century. Fowey retains its strong maritime flavour today: in addition to the bulky freighters docking at the wharves north of town, the harbour is crowded with trawlers and yachts, giving the town a brisk, purposeful character lacking in many of Cornwall's south-coast ports. The town's prosperous air is reflected in its new-found status as one of the West's fastest growing property markets, with prices boosted by the infiltration of film stars and other affluent incomers settling in the locality. You can expect to see a good turn-out at Fowey's premier annual event, **Regatta Week** in mid-August, when blue blazers mingle with pony-tails around the champagne and canapés.

A sailing extravaganza with evening entertainments, combined with what is rated as one of Cornwall's best carnivals, Fowey's Royal Regatta and Carnival takes place over a week in mid-August. Call ☎01726/ 832133 for details.

Fowey's Ferries

The **Bodinnick–Fowey** car and passenger ferry (April–Oct Mon–Sat 7am–8.45pm, Sun 8am–8.45pm; Nov–May daylight hours) £1.65 for cars, 50p per passenger. The **Polruan–Fowey** passenger and cycle ferry (May–Sept Mon–Sat 7.15am–11pm, Sun 9am–11pm; Oct–April Mon–Sat 7.15am–7pm, Sun 10am–5pm) costs 70p; bikes are free.

Fowey's steep centre is dominated by the fifteenth-century church of **St Fimbarrus** prominently sited at the junction of the two main streets which run parallel to the river – Fore Street upriver and The Esplanade towards the sea. The church marks the traditional end of the ancient **Saints' Way** (see p.281) from Padstow, linking the north and south Cornish coasts. Beside St Fimbarrus, the **Literary Centre** on South Street (mid-May to mid-Sept daily 10am–5pm; free) is a small exhibition devoted to the life and work of Daphne Du Maurier, who spent her most creative years in the region around Fowey. There's also material on other writers with local connections, notably Sir Arthur Quiller-Couch and Kenneth Grahame, though much of the space is devoted to merchandising.

One of the best ways to explore the area is on one of the river and coastal **cruises** which operate between May and September from the Town Quay, below Fore Street: tickets cost £5–8 – Fowey River Steamers (☎01726/833192) are a reliable operation. More daringly, *Le Nu* (☎01726/833289) offers naturist trips as well as full- and half-day motor cruises. From the boathouse at Fowey Gallery, 17 Passage St, the continuation of North Street (☎01726/833627), you can make accompanied canoe trips (£15 per day) or self-drive motorboat rides (£35 for one person, £45 for two).

At its southern end, The Esplanade shrinks to a footpath that gives access to some exhilarating **coastal walks**. On the right, look out for the remains of a blockhouse that once supported a defensive chain hung across the river's mouth; a few minutes' walk past this will bring you to the small beach of **Readymoney Cove**. As the only town beach, it doesn't take long to get jam-packed, but you can escape along the wooded path which climbs steeply above the southern end of the cove to enjoy fine estuary views from the scanty ruins of **St Catherine's Castle**, built by Thomas Treffry on the orders of Henry VIII – little more than a wall or two remain today.

Practicalities

Fowey is most easily accessible by ferry from Polruan (see box, opposite) or twice-hourly #24 **buses** from St Austell and Par train stations. **Drivers** will find that the central car park off Hanson Drive fills up quickly; follow the Bodinnick Ferry signs for the alternative Caffa Mill car parks. A minibus (May–Sept daily continuously; Oct–April Mon–Sat hourly; 70p) shuttles from the St Fimbarrus to the main car parks from 10am until about 5pm. There's a small **tourist office** (May–Sept Mon–Fri 9am–5.30pm, Sat 9am–5pm, Sun 10am–5pm; Oct–April Mon–Fri 9am–5.30pm, Sat 9am–12.30pm; ☎01726/ 833616), in the post office building at 4 Custom House Hill (the top end of Fore St, away from the church), which can supply good local walking itineraries.

Accommodation is abundant, varied and good value, but if your visit coincides with Regatta Week in mid-August, make sure you book well ahead. Two hundred yards from the river, the sixteenth-

Growing every year, Fowey's annual Daphne Du Maurier Festival takes place for ten days in mid-May. It encompasses talks, walks and concerts as well as strictly literary fare, featuring big-name authors, poets and musicians. Call ☎01726/ 223535 for details, or visit www .cornish-riviera .org.uk/daphne .html

century *Ship* in Trafalgar Square is the best of the central pubs offering B&B (☎01726/833751; *www.staustellbrewery.co.uk*; ①); if you're lucky, you'll get the main bedroom with original oak panelling, and there's parking. From The Esplanade, climb up Daglands Road to *Seahorses* at 14 St Fimbarrus Rd (☎01726/833148; *jandh@globalnet.co.uk*; nonsmoking; no credit cards; ①; closed Oct–April), which provides bathrobes, Dutch pancakes for breakfast and stylish rooms, and has a banjo-playing owner; advance booking is recommended. The area **around Fowey** also throws up some excellent choices. About twenty-minutes' walk west of town, at the end of a lane off the B3269, *Coombe Farm* (☎01726/833123; no credit cards; ①) provides perfect rural isolation, a beach and cream teas in summer. Across the river from Fowey at Bodinnick, *Hall Farmhouse* (☎01726/870050; *hall-holidays@eclipse.co.uk*; nonsmoking; no credit cards; ①) has fresh-looking rooms and a beamed sitting room with wood-burning stove; you'll find it on the brow of the hill up from the ferry, 300yds at the end of a lane to the right.

A Georgian mansion overlooking the estuary outside Golant, three miles north of Fowey, *Penquite House* **youth hostel** (☎01726/833507; *www.yha.org.uk*; closed Nov–Jan) is set in gardens and fourteen acres of woodland, and offers dorms (which can get noisy) and smaller rooms; beds in both cost £10.85. The #24 bus passes the end of the drive at Castle Dore crossroads, from where it's a one-and-a-half-mile walk. The nearest **campsite** is at *Yeate Farm* (☎01726/870256; closed Nov–Feb), three-quarters of a mile up from the Bodinnick ferry crossing.

Fowey's **restaurants** have an excellent reputation. Among the best is the wood and wicker *Ellis's* at 3 The Esplanade (☎01726/832359; closed Sun Easter–Sept, Sun & Mon Oct & Jan–Easter), specializing in lobster, and the low-beamed *Food For Thought*, The Quay (☎01726/832221; closed Sun and Jan–Feb), which offers weekday fixed-price seafood-based menus and sumptuous puddings – both are quite formal, expensive places opening in evenings only. More casual and very popular are *Sam's*, 20 Fore St (closed Jan, and Sun & Mon in Dec & Feb), a bistro which operates a no-booking policy (be prepared to wait, or come early) and serves fish dishes including a mean bouillabaisse as well as more modest home-made burgers, and the airy and modern *Other Place*, 41 Fore St (☎01726/833636; closed Oct–April), which offers anything from lobster to fish and chips and has eighteen flavours of ice cream.

The area is also well provided with worthy **pubs**, such as Bodinnick's *Old Ferry Inn*, whose back room is hewn out of the rock, and Polruan's excellent *Lugger Inn*, with high-backed settles.

Inland to Lostwithiel

Five miles north of Fowey and reachable on train or bus #77 from St Austell and Plymouth, **LOSTWITHIEL** is an old market town and tin exporting port on the lowest bridging point of the Fowey river, with an appealing mix of comely Georgian houses and dark cobbled passageways. The main A390 passes through the centre of town along Queen Street, east of which lie Fore Street and the parallel North Street – the latter leading to the fifteenth-century granite bridge over the river, and the train station.

Tanning was a major industry in Lostwithiel until the late 1800s, so it's apt that St **Bartholomew's church** (Easter to late Sept Tues, Thurs & Fri 11am–3pm) on Church Lane (off Fore St), with its Breton-inspired octagonal spire, should be dedicated to the patron saint of tanners. Inside, the finely-carved octagonal font is worth taking a look at, but the chief reason for coming to Lostwithiel is for the imposing ruins of **Restormel Castle**, crowning a hill a mile or so north of the town (April–Sept daily 10am–6pm; Oct daily 10am–5pm; £1.80; EH). Thought to have been built by a Norman baron around 1100 to protect the port, and enlarged at the end of the thirteenth century, Restormel preserves the shale-built shell of its huge circular keep, surrounded by a deep moat. By the time of the Civil War, the castle was already in a sorry state, and Royalist forces under Sir Richard Grenville found it easy to prise it out of the hands of the Earl of Essex's Parliamentarian army in 1644, the last time when Restormel saw any service – and the last time that it was inhabited, since the Royalists abandoned it almost immediately. It's a peaceful, panoramic spot, an easy walk from Lostwithiel and good for a picnic.

Practicalities

Signposted at the northern end of town from the A390, Lostwithiel's **tourist office** (Mon–Sat 10am–5pm; ☎01208/872207) is located in the Community Centre on Liddicoat Road; there's a free car park nearby.

There are a couple of good local **accommodation** options hereabouts. Close to the castle entrance gate, *Restormel Farm* (☎01208/872484; no credit cards; ①) is an old-fashioned farmhouse with large basic rooms and a few finds from the fields displayed in the dining room. A mile northeast of town, towards Dobwalls, take a left turn at St Winnow's School to find *Peregrine Hall* (☎01208/873461; *peregrineh@aol.com*; no credit cards; ②), a former convent set in ten acres of gardens; it has lovely, large bedrooms with sofas, customized breakfasts and use of a swimming pool and multigym. Book ahead.

Lostwithiel also has a great (but expensive) **restaurant**, the unhurried, cottagey *Trewithen*, 3 Fore St (evenings only; closed Sun June–Oct, Sun & Mon Nov–May; ☎01208/872373), where dishes take inspiration from the chef's travels, on such themes as Famous French Chefs or Tastes of India; booking is essential. A less pricey option is the beamed thirteenth-century *Royal Oak* on Duke Street, good for salads and vegetarian dishes as well as wild boar.

Widely available from shops, pubs and tourist office, the monthly free Gazette details events in the Fowey, Lostwithiel, Mevagissey and St Austell area.

The Eden Project

The newest and highest-profile of South Cornwall's attractions, the **Eden Project** (daily 10am–6pm; £9.50; *www.edenproject.com*), was already a major crowd-puller before it fully opened in spring 2001. Located four miles northeast of St Austell, from which it's reachable by Truronian bus #T9 (daily, leaving every hour or so) and signposted from all roads, Eden is the inspiration of Tim Smit, the leading light behind the rescue of the Lost Gardens of Heligan (see p.189), who devised the plan to transform a disused 34-acre claypit into a centre for showcasing the crucial relationship between people and plants, in a style he described as "Picasso meeting the Aztecs". The pit is divided into three distinct areas (biomes), which consist of gigantic conservatories in the form of geodesic domes: the humid, **tropical zone**, with rainforest including teak and mahogany trees, and the warm **temperate zone**, home to groves of olive and citrus and other trees and vegetation more usually found in the Mediterranean. The third roofless biome grows plants indigenous to Britain, including many native to Cornwall, spreading out on scimitar-shaped terraces.

Eden is a constantly evolving scheme, and sculptures and imaginative hands-on activities throughout the site will be added in the coming years. Allow at least half a day for a full exploration; there's a Land Train (free) if your feet give up, and well-informed guides on hand to provide information or take you on a tour (free). On the lip of the crater, the **visitor centre** puts out the word for global sustainability by means of wacky and engaging exhibits, described by one staff member as "Heath Robinson on acid".

St Austell, Charlestown and around

Six miles west of Fowey, **ST AUSTELL** is an unprepossessing place that developed on the strength of the china-clay industry after deposits were found locally in the eighteenth century (see box, opposite). The conical spoil heaps left by the mines are still the predominant feature of the local landscape, especially on Hensbarrow Downs to the north, where the great green-and-white mounds make an eerie sight. However, the only reason to pass through St Austell itself is en route to choicer destinations nearby on the coast or inland. Two and a half miles north of town on the B3274, and connected by the #29 bus from St Austell train station and Trinity Street, **Wheal Martyn China Clay Heritage Centre** (May–Sept daily 10am–5pm; April and Oct Mon–Fri & Sun 10am–5pm; £5; *www.wheal-martyn.com*) reveals everything you ever wanted to know about the china clay industry. It's an extensive and absorbing exhibition, allowing a close-up view of how the pits were operated, with tours round the old clay workings, along with the original loco-

---

China clay

The extraction of **china clay**, or kaolin, is a Cornish success story. An essential ingredient in the production of porcelain, kaolin had until the mid-eighteenth century only been produced in northern China, where a high ridge, or *kao-lin*, was the sole known source of the raw material. In 1756, one **William Cookworthy** discovered deposits of kaolinite near Helston and subsequently in the hills west of St Austell, so kicking off the industry in Cornwall. The china clay was originally extracted to supply ceramics producers such as Wedgwood and Spode, but further uses were soon found. Among its many applications today, china clay improves the properties of paint and makes expensive prime-colouring pigments go further; it adds strength and resistance to rubber and plastics used for electrical insulation; and it's also used as an anticaking agent in fertilizers, in insecticides, and as an ingredient in medicines – notably for quelling upset stomachs.

Its most important use, though, is in **paper production**, and it remains the most widely used material after wood pulp. Still a vital part of Cornwall's economy, some 80 percent of the county's china clay is exported abroad through the ports of Fowey and Par to Western Europe (Scandinavia in particular).

---

motives and wagons used in the pits. There's also a fairly absorbing nature trail on site, so allow at least two hours to see everything.

St Austell's nearest link to the sea is at **CHARLESTOWN**, an unspoilt port that's an easy one-mile walk downhill from the centre. It's named after the entrepreneur Charles Rashleigh, who in 1791 began work on the harbour of what was then a small fishing community, widening its streets to accommodate the china-clay wagons that passed through daily. Still used until the 1990s for shipping clay, the wharves appear oversized beside the tiny jetties, and are often dressed up by elaborate old-fashioned film sets – it's a favourite location for movie-makers. The dock is now owned by the Square Sail Shipyard, and you'll usually see one of the company's three old-fashioned square riggers *in situ*.

On each side of Charlestown's dock are coarse-sand and stone **beaches** sprinkled with small rock pools, above which cliff walks lead to the beaches around St Austell Bay. Most of these are fairly mediocre, surrounded by caravan parks and holiday chalets, but if you continue on about three miles east of Charlestown, you'll come to the sheltered, sandy cove of **Polkerris**, flanked by rocks and green cliffs and sheltered by a curving breakwater. The easternmost limit of St Austell Bay is marked by **Gribbin Head**, near which stands Menabilly House, where Daphne Du Maurier lived for twenty-four years. The model for "Manderley" in *Rebecca*, the house is not open to the public, but you can see where Rebecca met her watery end at Polridmouth Cove.

Bus #26 or
#26A leaves
hourly from St
Austell's train
station to the
main car park
at the top of
Mevagissey.

Practicalities

Trains on the main Penzance line stop at St Austell station on Station Approach, in the centre of town off High Cross Street. Most buses connecting St Austell with other towns stop here too: #24 and #24A for Fowey; #31 for Charlestown; #26 and #26A for Pentewan and Mevagissey. You can pick up full transport timetables as well as general information on the area from St Austell's **tourist office** (Easter–Oct daily 10am–5pm; Nov–Easter Mon–Fri 10am–2pm; ☎01726/76333), half a mile southeast of the centre at the BP garage on Southbourne Road (the A390).

Charlestown holds the most appealing **accommodation** options, the best of which are *T'Gallants*, 6 Charlestown Rd (☎01726/ 70203; ②), a smart, elegantly furnished B&B at the back of the harbour, and *Broad Meadow House*, behind the Shipwreck Centre on Quay Road (☎01726/76636; *neildeb.broadmeadow@tinyworld .co.uk;* no credit cards; ①), which has one beautifully furnished bedroom, a large sitting room and choice breakfasts. In St Austell Bay, the nearest **campsite** is *Par Sands* (☎01726/812868; closed Nov–March), next to Par beach, with all the amenities plus ranks of static caravans.

Behind *T'Gallants*, the *Rashleigh Arms* in Charlestown puts on real ale and a standard range of moderately priced **food** with plenty of vegetarian options. If you're mobile, head for the cosy *Rashleigh Inn*, right above the jetty at Polkerris (signposted from the A3082) and a good spot for a lunch or inexpensive evening meal. On Saturdays throughout the year, plus Fridays in July and August, a pianist provides musical background which usually develops into a singsong as the night wears on.

Mevagissey and Heligan

Up to the nineteenth century, **MEVAGISSEY**, five miles southwest of Charlestown, was famed for the fast ships constructed here, and used for transporting contraband as well as pilchards. Today, the tiny port might display a few stacks of lobster pots, but the real business is tourism, with day-trippers converging on the harbour and overflowing into its surrounding labyrinth of alleys, a tight cluster of picturesquely flower-draped fisherman's cottages. Despite the crowds, the minute inner harbour – separated from the larger outer harbour by a pair of breakwaters – has an irresistible lure, a clamour of swirling gulls amid the apparatus of the small fishing fleet. Other than this, the village's only specific attraction is its **museum** (Easter–Oct daily 11am–5pm; 60p) at the end of East Quay, the road running alongside the harbour. The building has as much history as the exhibits inside: built in 1795 for the construction and repair of smugglers' boats, most of its roof beams were recycled from the revenue-dodgers' old vessels. Alongside evocative photographs and other items illustrating the history of the region is a

From
School Hill (a
continuation
of Church St),
in Megavissey,
bus #26 runs
regularly to
Heligan.

display devoted to Mr Pears, the local chemist who made his fortune from soap.

Many visitors to Mevagissey end up on the broad, sandy **Pentewan** beach, a mile to the north, much of which is dominated by a caravan site, but a much more engaging option is to head two miles north of the village via the B3273 to the awesome display of greenery at the **Lost Gardens of Heligan** (daily: late March to late Oct 10am–6pm, last entry 5.30pm; late Oct to late March 10am–5pm, last entry 4.30pm; £5.50; *www.heligan.co.uk*). At their prime in the late 1800s, the gardens later fell into neglect and have only been rescued from their ten-foot covering of brambles in the last decade, largely under the instigation of Tim Smit, of Eden Project fame (see p.186). The marvellously abundant palm trees, giant Himalayan rhododendrons, immaculate vinery and glasshouses scattered about the garden all look as if they've been transplanted from warmer climes. Near the entrance, the northern gardens contain huge flower and vegetable gardens, including pineapple pits dating from 1720, where the first pineapples in 150 years were coaxed into life a few years ago by the original manure heating system. In the garden wall, you'll see rare bee boles (holes) for skeps (straw forerunners of hives) with wooden doors. A boardwalk takes you past interconnecting ponds, through a jungle and under a canopy of bamboo, ferns and palms down to the **Lost Valley**, where there are lakes, a wild-flower meadow and leafy oak, beech and chestnut rides.

You can sample produce from the gardens at the steward's house above the jungle area, or in the *Willow* restaurant near the entrance.

Practicalities

The town's helpful **tourist office** is ensconced in Mevagissey Telecottage, a business centre at 14 Church St (Mon–Fri 9am–5pm, Sat 9am–12.30pm; ☎01726/842266; *www.mevagissey.net*). Right in the heart of Mevagissey on Cliff Street, off East Quay, the best **accommodation** option is the fifteenth-century *Fountain Inn* (☎01726/842320; *fountain_meva@hotmail.com*; ①), with bright, stylish and airy rooms, while the old *Ship Inn* (☎01726/843324; ①) nearby on Fore Street (the first road back from the harbour), offers pine bedrooms with washstands and a big, shared bathroom. Continuing 200yd up the street brings you to *Lawn House*, 1 Church Lane (☎01726/842754; no credit cards; ②; ring ahead Nov–Easter), a lovely, spacious Queen Anne construction replete with candelabra and brass beds. Handy for the Lost Gardens of Heligan (a signposted half-mile away) *Corran Farm*, St Ewe (☎01726/842159; no credit cards; ①), is a spick-and-span, tile-hung farmhouse.

Most of Mevagissey's **restaurants** specialize in fish. The large *Shark's Fin Hotel* (closed Jan) overlooking the inner harbour is worth a try, while there's a Portuguese slant to the seafood at the moderately

Mevagissey and Heligan

To get the most out of the gardens, join one of the guided tours that take place twice a day in summer (11.30am and 2.30pm; £1.50).

Between early June and mid-October a ferry runs five times (three in Oct) daily between Mevagissey outer harbour and Fowey. The return fare is £7.50.

You can rent bikes from Pentewan Valley Cycle Hire, Pentewan (☎01726/ 844242); a delivery service is available.

priced and daintily decorated *Alvorada* (Easter–Sept daily; Nov–Jan Fri & Sat only; ring to confirm for other evening openings; ☎01726/842254), one street back from West Quay at 2 Polkirt Hill. Economical lunches are served in the bars in the *Fountain Inn* and in its restaurant in the evening. With original slate floor, oak beams, and fireplaces, the bars rely on a piano as the main means of entertainment.

Veryan Bay

Curving west between Dodman Point and Nare Head, the five-mile parabola of **Veryan Bay** is barely touched by commercialism. Bounding the bay on the east, **Dodman Point** ranks as one of south Cornwall's most dramatic headlands, and has been the cause of many a wreck. From its gorse-covered heights, you can look down on a chaos of reefs and rocks, and splendid views extend westward across Veryan Bay. The promontory is topped by a stark granite cross built by a local parson as a seamark in 1896, and holds the substantial remains of an Iron Age fort, with a bulwark of earth cutting right across the point. Less than a mile west, sandy **Hemmick Beach** makes an excellent swimming spot, with rocky outcrops affording a measure of privacy. You'll find a little more commotion a mile or so west at **Porthluney Cove**, where the safe swimming tends to attract families. In a beautiful setting of wood, stream and pasture, the sandy beach is backed by the battlemented **Caerhays Castle** (house mid-March to April Mon–Fri 2–4pm; gardens mid-March to mid-May Mon–Fri 10am–4pm; house £3.50; garden £3.50; combined ticket £6), built in 1808 by John Nash. If you're here during the very limited opening period, you can join a half-hour tour of the house, mainly of interest to anyone who has seen the film *Rebecca*, which was shot here. The beautiful wooded garden is more compelling, though, displaying a world-famous collection of camellias, magnolias and rhododendrons.

Three miles further west, the minuscule and whitewashed village of **Portloe** is fronted by jagged black rocks that throw up fountains of seaspray, giving it a good, end-of-the-road kind of atmosphere. A mile inland of here, **VERYAN** itself has a pretty village green and pond, but is best known for its curious circular, white **houses** built some 200 years ago by one Reverend Jeremiah Trist, apparently to guard the village from devils, which would be unable to hide in corners; for additional protection, the thatched roofs are topped by crucifixes. Twee in places, the village has seen incursions by arts and crafts galleries, but deserves a brief visit, if only for a chocolate-box photo.

A lane from Veryan leads a mile down to **Pendower Beach**, one of southern Cornwall's cleanest swimming spots. Two-thirds of a mile long and backed by dunes, Pendower joins with the neighbouring **Carne Beach** at low tide to create a long sand-and-shingle continuum.

Practicalities

If you want a drink or a bed in Veryan, head for the *New Inn* (☎01872/501362; ②) near the pond, a friendly pub with a quiet garden, where you can feast on wholesome meals such as duck with forest mushrooms, and sleep in one of the spacious B&B rooms; alternatively, try *Elerkey Guest House* (☎01872/501261; *www.elerkey-guest-house.co.uk*; ②), a large comfortable ex-farmhouse with a spacious garden and adjoining art gallery and coffee shop; it's the first on the left after the church.

There's a great **youth hostel** (☎01726/843234; closed Nov–March, Sun April–June and Sun & Mon Sept–Oct) in a former farmhouse at Boswinger, a remote spot half a mile from Hemmick Beach; beds cost £10. Difficult to reach without your own transport, it's about a mile from the bus stop at Gorran Church Town, served infrequently by some #26 buses from St Austell and Mevagissey. Boswinger also has a **campsite**, *Sea View International* (☎01726/843425; closed Oct–Easter), in a panoramic position overlooking Veryan Bay; book ahead in July and August.

Truro

Connected to the Carrick Roads estuary by the Truro river, the city of **TRURO** developed as a protected inland port, shipping tin to Europe and copper to Wales. One of Cornwall's original stannary towns, it was a long-standing rival to Falmouth, which was never a stannary town but had a more convenient anchorage. Although the silting of the river led to Truro's decline in the seventeenth century, prosperity returned with the tin-mining boom of the 1800s, as reflected in the solid Georgian houses. The arrival of the railway in 1859 and the granting of city status in 1877 ensured that Truro has remained Cornwall's commercial and administrative centre. However, it's more of a tourist crossroads than a holiday centre, poorly equipped for accommodation and lacking enough diversion to keep you here for more than a day or two.

Arrival and information

Buses stop in the city centre at the Lemon Quay **bus station**, or near the **train station** on Richmond Hill. Truro's **tourist office** lies on Boscawen Street (Easter–May, Sept & Oct Mon–Fri 9am–5.15pm, Sat 10am–1pm; June–Aug Mon–Fri 9am–6pm, Sat 10am–5pm; Nov & Feb–Easter Mon–Thurs 9am–5.15pm, Fri 9am–5.45pm; Dec & Jan Mon–Fri 9am–4.45pm; ☎01872/274555). There are banks nearby, and the main **post office** opposite the cathedral has a *bureau de change*.

Buses #X89 and #X90 run between Falmouth, Truro and Newquay.

Accommodation

Accommodation in Truro is limited and gets overbooked in August, though you shouldn't have much problem the rest of the year. Inexpensive choices are mostly on or around Lemon Street, the long

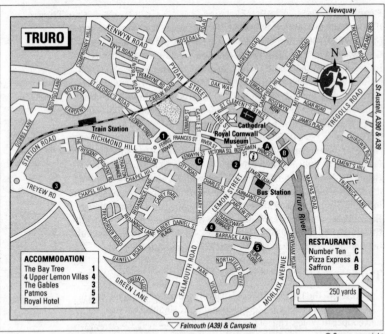

© Crown copyright

road south of the centre sloping down from the A39. The nearest **campsite** is *Carnon Downs*, three miles outside Truro on the A39 Falmouth road (☎01872/862283; closed Nov–March).

The Bay Tree, 28 Ferris Town ☎01872/240274. Neat, smartly restored Georgian house in the city centre. No smoking here, but it is permitted at the annexe round the corner at 12 St George's Rd. ①.

4 Upper Lemon Villas, Lemon St ☎01872/278018. One of a row of Georgian houses just before the tall Richard Lander monument at the top of Lemon St, this has three comfortable rooms with shared bathroom. No credit cards; no smoking. ①.

The Gables, 49 Treyew Rd ☎01872/242318. Convenient for the train station, the back rooms here have views to the cathedral; all have showers but toilets are shared. No credit cards. ①.

Patmos, 8 Burley Close, off Barrack Lane ☎01872/278018. Split-level modern house with friendly hosts; specify the larger room with views over the river if there's a choice. No smoking. No credit cards. ①.

Royal Hotel, Lemon St ☎01872/279345. Dead central and completely modern behind its Georgian facade, this casually smart, business-oriented place has a good brasserie and will appeal to anyone looking for a little more zip. ⑤.

The City

On the wedge of land separating the Allen and Kenwyn rivers, Truro's cobbled centre has plenty of interest, retaining traces of the medieval town's lanes where "kennels" or water channels still burble in the streets. There is little uniformity of style, however, most glaringly apparent at the bottom of pedestrianized Pydar Street, where the brisk modern shopping centre collides with the chronologically confused **Cathedral** (daily 8am–6pm or 7pm; suggested donation £2). Completed in 1910, this neo-Gothic confection of local granite and Bath stone is the result of architect John Loughborough Pearson's controversial decision to revert to the Early English style, rather than something more in keeping with Truro's predominantly Georgian lines. Nonetheless, it makes a powerful impact, its tall exterior sprouting dramatically from the heart of the city in a style more commonly found in France, without the sward of lawn or "close" usually surrounding English cathedrals. In fact, the building had to be shoe-horned into the available space, accounting for the skew-whiff alignment noticeable in the nave. Apart from this slight aberration, the overall effect is of orderly, clean-cut lines – a rather academic exercise in Gothic church-building which, a century later, has not noticeably mellowed or blended to any degree with the city.

With its emphatically pointed arches and elaborate roof vaulting, the airy interior is notable for its Victorian **stained-glass** windows, considered the finest collection in the country. The most impressive include the Rose window of the west front, depicting the Creation, and those in the north and south transepts. The south (right) aisle has a fine **baptisry**, with arcading and a font with pillars fashioned from Cornish serpentine. Further up on the same side, to the right of the choir, **St Mary's Aisle** is a relic of the Perpendicular church that formerly occupied the site, mostly demolished to make way for the new construction. You can see etchings of its original appearance at the back of the aisle, where there's also a copy of a letter of thanks from Charles I to the Cornish for their loyalty during the Civil War. The medieval-looking tryptich behind the altar here is the work of Frank Pearson, the son of the cathedral's architect, who completed the project after his father's death. As well as the other fragments of the original church scattered about, there are some colourful Jacobean tombs worth viewing – and, in a different vein, look out for the matchstick model of the cathedral on the south aisle: it took 1600 hours and some 42,000 matches to assemble.

If you're spending any time in the county, a visit to the **Royal Cornwall Museum** (Mon–Sat 10am–5pm; £3; *www. royalcornwallmuseum.org.uk*) on River Street provides some essential context to your travels. It's a formidable mix, and if time is tight you could confine yourself to the collection of minerals on the ground floor and the upstairs galleries holding works by local artists and members of the Newlyn School. The **main gallery** on the ground floor illustrates diverse aspects of Cornwall's past, and includes, by the stairs, a Celtic inscription found at Tintagel (see p.286), and a portrait of Anthony Payne, "the Cornish giant" of Stratton (near

Truro

Free guided tours of the cathedral take place daily at 11.30am and 2pm in summer, and 11.30am in winter. Photographic permits cost £1, video permits £3.

If you want to delve deeper into Cornwall's past and present, the Courtney Library in the Royal Cornwall Museum is an invaluable archive of manuscripts, newspapers from 1798, reference works and art books; call ☎01872/ 272205 to arrange a visit.

Bude), in the uniform of a halberdier, thought to have been commissioned by Charles II. To the right, the **Bonython gallery** is dedicated to Cornwall's natural history, while on the other side, the **Rashleigh gallery** illuminates the county's geological make-up. Its collection of specimens is internationally important and includes examples of cassiterite (the only tin mineral of economic importance), mirror-surfaced iron pyrites and copper, asbestos and, in its various mottled forms, serpentine from the Lizard peninsula. You can also learn about Delabole slate and china clay via a diorama of a china-clay pit.

For more on the arts in Cornwall, see Contexts, p.326.

Upstairs, take a glance at the **Egyptian gallery** showpieces – an unwrapped mummy and two detached feet from Roman-period mummies – on your way to the **Philbrick gallery** of Cornish art, which features some outstanding paintings by the Newlyn School, including Harold Harvey's famous *St Just Tinminers*, a jaunty group of freshly turned out miners on their way down to the pits. There's also work by Stanhope Forbes and some sentimental but occasionally striking paintings by Henry Scott Tuke: maritime subjects, a small selection of his homoerotic nudes and a self-portrait.

A flea market takes place three or four days weekly in the Hall for Cornwall, with entrances on Boscawen Street and Back Quay (days vary: see inside Hall for details), and there's a Saturday morning farmers' market in nearby Tinner's Yard.

The upstairs **balcony** shows decorative art, including Roman jewellery, Greek coins, fragments of Gothic churches and Renaissance items, including a beautiful embossed-copper dish, probably sixteenth-century Italian. Off the balcony, the **De Pass gallery** has Old Master drawings and other items from the museum's fine-art collection, while the **Link gallery** features textiles and costumes. Downstairs, the adjoining **Café Gallery** (free) has exhibitions throughout the year and also shows the Truro Art Society's Summer Exhibition in August; it makes a good place to end up the museum visit, with tables outside in summer.

Eating and drinking

A good selection of Truro's **restaurants** lie on or around Kenwyn Street, west of the centre, including *Number Ten* at no. 10 (☎01872/272363), where inexpensive wholesome dishes from around the world are on the menu alongside teas, coffees and healthy fruit drinks; you bring your own booze, and there's an outdoor eating area round the back. Elsewhere in the city, *Saffron* at 5 Quay St (☎01872/263771; closed Sun) offers inexpensive brunches and an especially good-value pre-theatre menu, as well as originally prepared fish and meat dishes. Near the tourist office on Boscawen Street, the *Pizza Express* is housed in the imposing old Coinage Hall, which sports carpets on the walls alongside portraits of George II and other notables.

On the corner of Frances Street and Castle Street, the *Wig and Pen* is a decent **pub** with bar food, real ale and jazz on Wednesdays and Fridays. Truro's Hall for Cornwall, with entrances on Boscawen Street and Quay Street, has a programme of concerts and plays throughout the year (☎01872/262466).

Listings

Banks Branches of all the main banks are scattered around Boscawen St and St Nicholas St.

Bike rental Truro Cycles, 110 Kenwyn St (☎01872/271703) offers a delivery/collection service. At Bissoe, five miles southwest of Truro, Bissoe Tramways Cycle Hire (☎01872/870341) hires out bikes for exploring the old tramways (see p.000).

Car hire Avis, Tregolls Rd (☎01872/262226); Hertz at the train station (☎01872/223638); Vospers, Station Yard, Richmond Hill (☎01872/223676).

Hospital There's a 24hr accident and emergency department at the Royal Cornwall Hospital (Treliske), Higher Town (☎01872/250000), about a mile west of the centre on the A390 Redruth road.

Internet access *The Internet Place* at 5 Frances St ☎01872/272421; *www.internet-place.co.uk*.

Taxis Call ☎0800/318708.

In summer, passenger ferries depart four times daily from Truro's quayside on a scenic river cruise to Falmouth (£5 return).

St Mawes and the Roseland Peninsula

In a secluded spot at the mouth of the Percuil estuary and across the neck of the Carrick Roads from Falmouth, **ST MAWES** is an elite cluster of cottages, villas and abundant gardens, sloping above the simple harbour. Though there's more than a hint of creeping suburbanism here, the village merits a brief stroll, not least for the splendid views of the estuary from its higher reaches. Most people, however, come for the small and pristine **St Mawes Castle** (April–Sept daily 10am–6pm; Oct daily 10am–5pm; Nov–March Wed–Sun 10am–1pm & 2–4pm; £2.70; EH), just out of sight a few minutes' walk to the north of the village. Like Pendennis Castle, across the water in Falmouth (see p.200), this was built during the reign of Henry VIII between 1539 and 1543, based on designs by the king's German military architect Stefan von Haschenberg, if not actually built by him. Both castles adhere to the same clover-leaf design, with a central round keep surrounded by robust gun-emplacements, but this is the more architecturally interesting of the pair, with three semicircular bastions surrounding the four-storey central tower, and some of the best examples of decorative stonework of all Henry's fortified works. The castle lacks much drama, however, partly on account of its immaculate condition, which it owes to its early surrender when placed under siege by General Fairfax's Parliamentary forces in 1646. The bloodless takeover eased the way for Fairfax's harder-fought acquisition of Pendennis Castle a few weeks later.

Among the examples of Tudor stone-carving and stone-dressing, look out for a Latin inscription to Henry (with a back-to-front "S") at the entrance. There are few other signs of finesse here, however, the strictly utilitarian design offering little scope for comfort or privacy for the lonely garrison, with scarcely a passage or stairway not overlooked by slits and spy-holes. Although its design was considered revolutionary at the time, it retained such medieval features as the terrifying *oubliette*, a deep, square shaft just inside the entrance on the right where prisoners were detained; it's now covered by a glass roof. The cellar kitchen and the gun installations constitute the main points of interest, though you'll learn plenty about the castle's background as well as local history with the audioguide (supplied free with the entrance ticket); otherwise, you can join one of the **guided tours** which take place every Wednesday at 2.15pm during July and August (also free). The guidebook (£2.95) represents good value if you're also planning to visit Pendennis Castle (see p.200), which it also describes.

Within easy distance of St Mawes, the backwaters of the **Roseland peninsula**, a deeply serene area of narrow lanes and idyllic waterside retreats, make an irresistible excursion. You can get a taste of it on a trip to one of Cornwall's most picturesque churches, **St Anthony-in-Roseland**, a twelfth- to thirteenth-century building reachable in fifteen minutes from St Mawes harbour by the summer-only **ferry** across the Percuil River (daily every 30min 10am–4.30pm; £1.70 return, 80p for bikes). The peninsula's rocky southern coast is well worth exploring, especially for the throngs of seabirds that nest hereabouts. St Anthony's charm is if anything eclipsed by that of a second church lying three miles north of St Mawes, **St Just-in-Roseland**, reachable on signed paths. On the shore of a creek surrounded by palms and subtropical shrubbery, with granite gravestones tumbling right down to the water's edge, the small grey church dates from 1261 but has a fifteenth-century tower. A couple of miles further north, the chain-driven **King Harry ferry** crosses the River Fal about every twenty minutes (summer Mon–Sat 7.50am–9.10pm, Sun 10am–9.10pm; winter Mon–Sat 8am–7pm, Sun 10am–5pm; £2.50 per car, foot passengers 20p), obviating the need for drivers to take a long diversion to get to Truro or Falmouth.

Regular pedestrian ferries make the twenty-minute crossing between Falmouth and St Mawes (May–Sept Mon–Sat every 30min, Sun hourly; Oct–April Mon–Sat six daily; £2.15 one-way, £2 for bikes).

Practicalities

You'll find that Falmouth has far more eating and accommodation options than St Mawes, but if you do want to **stay** here, the best budget choices are a ten-minute walk up from the seafront on Newton Road: *Little Newton Farm* (☎01326/270664; ②) and the more capacious *Newton Farm* next door (☎01326/270427; ②), both offering spacious en-suite rooms. If you're flush, you can't do better than the *St Mawes Hotel* (☎01326/270266; ⑨; closed Nov to mid-Feb); right on the seafront, it enjoys glorious views over the estuary, and has eight rooms decorated according to fishing, sailing, rugby and other themes (those with balconies cost more). There's a well-equipped **campsite** three miles north of St Mawes outside St-Just-in-Roseland, signposted off the B3289, *Trethem Mill* (☎01872/580504; closed Nov–March). The *Victory Inn* is a fine old oak-beamed **pub** just off the seafront, which also serves seafood meals.

Falmouth and around

The construction of Pendennis Castle on the western side of the Carrick Roads estuary mouth in the sixteenth century prepared the ground for the growth of **FALMOUTH**, then no more than a fishing village. The building of its deep-water harbour was proposed a century later by Sir John Killigrew, one of a mercantile dynasty that dominated local life long, and Falmouth's prosperity was assured when it became chief base of the fast Falmouth Packets in 1689, which sped mail and bullion to the Mediterranean and the Americas. In the twentieth century, however, Falmouth lost most of its Cornish character in the process of becoming a full-time tourist resort, but has latterly assumed another identity as a centre of the local **arts scene**, providing a vital antidote to the predominant eating-and-shopping tone of its main street. The castle, of course, is the chief attraction, and some good beaches and eating and sleeping choices add to the town's allure. There are also some excellent river cruises for exploring the ins and outs of the Carrick Roads, and even the twenty-minute crossing to St Mawes (see p.195) makes a great way to view Pendennis as well as St Mawes Castle and St Anthony Head.

Arrival, information and accommodation

A branch line from Truro runs daily to Falmouth (not Sun Sept–June), stopping at Falmouth Town and Falmouth Docks **train stations**, nearest the beaches and castle respectively, and equidistant from the centre. **Buses** stop on The Moor, the old town's main square at the western end of the long main street which runs almost the whole length of the harbour, variously called High Street, Market Street, Church Street and Arwenack Street. The Moor is also the site of Falmouth's **tourist office** (Easter–June & Sept Mon–Thurs & Sat 9am–5pm, Fri 9am–4.45pm; July & Aug Mon–Sat 9.30am–5.30pm, Sun 10am–2pm; Oct–Easter Mon–Thurs 9am–1pm & 2–5pm, Fri 9am–1pm & 2–4.45pm; ☎01326/312300; *www.falmouth-sw-cornwall.co.uk*).

Hotels and B&Bs

Most of the town's **accommodation** lies near the train stations and beach area; expect to pay more for places nearer the beaches. Among the overdeveloped caravan parks on the coast south of Falmouth, the nearest **campsite** is *Tremorvah Tent Park* (☎01326/318311), a grassy, terraced site about a mile outside town behind Swanpool Beach and on the coast path.

Arwenack Hotel, 27 Arwenack St ☎01326/311185. Centrally located on the busy main street, this workaday hotel in a 250-year-old building offers good value without many trimmings. No credit cards. ①.

If you're not easily embarrassed, hop on the Road Train, a Disney-type bus with commentary which runs hourly from Falmouth Moor via Falmouth Docks station to the castle and back via the beaches (June–Sept 10.20am–5.20pm). Tickets, bought on board, are £2.95 round trip, or £3.95 for all-day use.

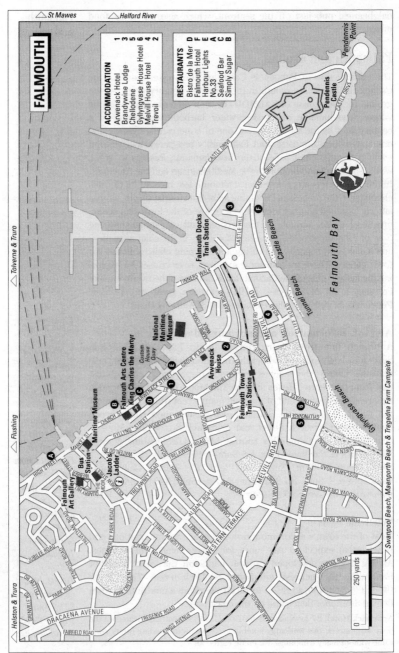

FALMOUTH

ACCOMMODATION

Arwenack Hotel	1
Brandywine Lodge	3
Chellodene	5
Gyllyngvase House Hotel	6
Melvill House Hotel	4
Trevoil	2

RESTAURANTS

Bistro de la Mer	D
Falmouth Hotel	F
Harbour Lights	E
No.33	A
Seafood Bar	C
Simply Sugar	B

© Crown copyright

Brandywine Lodge, 3 Bay View Crescent ☎01326/318709. Two upstairs rooms share a bathroom in this cosy cottage just off Castle Drive; one has its own balcony overlooking the garden. No credit cards. ①.

Chellowdene, Gyllyngvase Hill ☎01326/314950. Unusual deep-roofed building 50yd from the beach, with two excellent balcony rooms overlooking the sea; landward rooms are cheaper. No smoking, no pre-teens and no credit cards. Closed Oct–April. ③.

Gyllyngvase House Hotel, Gyllyngvase Rd ☎01326/312956. Staid but comfortable choice within its own grounds. Two minutes from the sea, some rooms have bay views and there's a restaurant. ③.

Melvill House Hotel, 52 Melvill Rd ☎01326/316645; *www.falmouth.net/melvill-house*. Run by a Franco-Scottish couple, this pink-fronted terrace house offers good value, and you can get dinner by prior arrangement. No smoking. ②.

Trevoil, 25 Avenue Rd ☎01326/314145. Behind Arwenack House and convenient for the centre, station, beaches and castle, this has eight rather cramped rooms, plainly furnished but good value. No credit cards. ①.

The town

The logical place to start exploring Falmouth is The **Moor**, the Old Town's elongated central square, now mainly used as a bus terminus and car park. From here, you can trace the **High Street** and its continuations Market and Church streets, running parallel to the harbour. The combination of cars and crowds on this long thoroughfare, crammed with humdrum shops and cafés, makes it rather a slog at times. A landmark halfway along is Falmouth's parish church of **King Charles the Martyr**, consecrated in 1662 when the town was once again able to assert its royalist allegiances. It's unusual for its round arches and huge granite Tuscan columns within, and has some good Victorian stained and enamelled glass in the north aisle, though successive alterations have stripped it of much of its character. Further up on Arwenack Street, the white-columned facade of the **Customs House** (1820) stands in front of the lively **Custom House Quay**, the spur of Falmouth's development as a port after it was built in 1670 by the Killigrews. Their home, the Tudor **Arwenack House** (not open to the public), still stands at the southern end of Arwenack Street, and is Falmouth's oldest example of domestic architecture, though only fragments of the fourteenth-century house remain following remodelling in the sixteenth and eighteenth centuries.

Falmouth's links with the sea are explored at the **Maritime Museum** at Bell's Court, at the Moor end of the High Street (Easter–Oct daily 10am–5pm; Oct–Easter Mon–Sat 10am–3pm; £2.20), which tracks the evolution of boat design with a focus on traditional local boat-building and repairing skills. Alongside the tools and other sundry items connected with these activities, there are models of oyster-punts, dredgers and a Victorian steam pinnace. It's a rather lacklustre collection at present, but will be revitalized when it transfers in

Signifying the start of the oyster-dredging season, Falmouth's three-day Oyster Festival, around Oct 7, features races in the harbour, twice-daily seafood cooking shows and oysters on offer in the Oyster Bar, all to folk and jazz accompaniment. The main venue is Custom House Quay; for more info contact the tourist offices.

For a bird's-eye view of the harbour and a panoramic perspective over Falmouth, climb the precipitous 111 steps of Jacob's Ladder, accessible from the Moor.

Ferries and cruises from Falmouth

From the Prince of Wales Pier, below the Moor, frequent **ferries** leave for St Mawes (summer Mon–Sat every 30min, Sun hourly; winter Mon–Sat 6 daily; £2.50, or £4.50 return), a 25-minute crossing between about 8.30am and 5.15pm, stopping earlier in winter, and for Truro (up to five times daily in summer; 1hr; £5.50). In summer there are also hourly crossings to the placid hamlet of Flushing, across the Penryn river (every 30min; lunch-break 12.45–2pm; last ferry 5.15pm; adults & bikes £1.20, pay on board) and there are various other **cruises** up the Fal river and other local estuaries, including the Helford River (11am and 2.30pm, £5.50); all are bookable from kiosks on the pier. Summer also sees excursions from Custom House Quay, such as an hourly service to St Mawes (not Sat). You can also hire **self-drive cabin boats** from here, which carry up to six people (£15 per hour plus £15 deposit); no sailing experience is necessary. You can arrange rental at the Quay or by calling ☎01326/212727 (evenings) or ☎07769/580147.

2002 to a purpose-built exhibition centre in a waterfront setting on Arwenack Street, with exhibits from all over the country alongside an education centre and a restaurant.

Falmouth's arts scene presents a very different side to the town, which you can investigate at Church Street's **Falmouth Arts Centre** (daily 10am–5pm; free) and **Falmouth Art Gallery** on The Moor (Mon–Sat 10am–5pm; free), both of which have small but eclectic collections of contemporary art, with regular exhibitions. There are plenty of private art galleries in town as well as open studio events, publicized on flyers, posters and at the tourist office, generally showing a more dynamic slant than much of the artwork on display at the region's other arts centre, St Ives. Round the corner from Falmouth Art Gallery, the northern end of the **High Street** continues the bohemian theme, with good restaurants, cafés and bookshops around Old Brewery Yard.

Pendennis Castle and around

Falmouth's most popular attraction, **Pendennis Castle** (daily: April–Sept 10am–6pm; Oct 10am– 5pm; Nov–March 10am–4pm; £3.80; EH), occupies the tongue of land at the eastern end of town. Standing sentinel at the entrance to Carrick Roads, it's a less-refined contemporary of the castle at St Mawes (see p.195), but the site on its own pointed peninsula wins hands down, the stout ramparts offering superb all-round views. Although now much larger and more imposing than St Mawes Castle, Pendennis was originally the same size, consisting of the circular keep and curtain wall erected by Henry VIII. Spurred to action by the Spanish Armada and the Spanish attack on Penzance in 1595, Elizabeth I added the bastioned outer defences which were to prove crucial during the Civil War a half-century later, when it

Note that the castle grounds stay open until 8pm in July and August. Falmouth-to-Truro #88 and #89 buses pass near the castle.

endured a five-month siege by the Parliamentarians that ended only when nearly half its defenders had died and the rest had been starved into submission.

The central **Keep** now holds a collection of cannonry, and its gun deck is the scene of regular re-enactments of a battle, with much cordite and noise. The structure formerly housed the garrison as well as the guns, and is joined to a domestic block which accommodated the governor, and also army officers during both world wars (accounting for the somewhat incongruous panelling in some of the rooms). An earlier brief occupant was the sixteen-year-old Prince Charles, later Charles II, probably in the upstairs bedroom. While his father was suffering defeat at the hands of the Scots, the fugitive prince was sheltered here in July 1646 before departing for the Isles of Scilly and thence to the Continent. He escaped the disastrous siege of the castle by only a few weeks.

Near the Keep, the fifteenth-century **Gunshed** has an exhibition where you can hone your Morse code and aiming abilities. In front, next to the One-Gun Battery, the Sally Port is the entrance to tunnels leading to the camouflaged **Half-Moon Battery**, first built in 1795 as a cannon platform, after which it remained the castle's most important gun emplacement for some 150 years. The battery was remodelled in the nineteenth century to hold a pair of huge "disappearing guns", which were only visible at the moment of firing before recoiling back into pits. Together with the battery on St Anthony's Head on the opposite side of the estuary, Pendennis provided Falmouth's main defence during both world wars, though the guns visible now are 1946 models. There is a good view out to sea from the **Battery Observation Post**, where sightings were taken and relayed to the battery itself; it's now restored to how it might have looked during World War II, with instruments and charts, radio equipment and taped conversations adding to the ambience.

Out on the headland, beyond the walls, **Little Dennis** is the original blockhouse built by Henry VIII, reachable from the car park on Castle Drive from outside the Castle. It's a breezily exposed point to visit at any time, with terrific views of Falmouth Bay and the estuary.

West of Pendennis Point stretches a series of long sandy bays with various **beaches** backed by expensive hotels. Bus #X89 (Mon–Sat hourly) connects Falmouth to the most popular of these, **Gyllyngvase Beach**, though neighbouring **Swanpool Beach** – accessible by cliff path from Gyllyngvase – is pleasanter, with an inland lake. Both have good facilities and boats for hire. You'll find less paraphernalia a couple of miles further on at **Maenporth**, from where there are some fine clifftop walks.

Open-air evening theatre productions are staged in Pendennis Castle grounds during August (tickets around £8). Ask at Falmouth's tourist office or call ☎01326/ 316594 for dates and details. Dress warmly, and bring folding chairs or cushions and a picnic.

Eating

Pasties, pizzas and chips are available everywhere in Falmouth. You'll find good freshly-baked **pasties** from the shop at Custom

House Quay, including vegetarian choices. The High Street has a useful **wholefoods shop** for self-caterers at no. 16 and a deli at no. 32 for fantastic baguettes and cakes, and there are a couple of relaxed healthfood **cafés** round the corner in Old Brewery Yard.

Bistro de la Mer, 28 Arwenack St ☎01326/316509. Serious fish restaurant with large cellar-room downstairs, offering a three-course set menu. Moderate.

Falmouth Hotel, Castle Beach. Nonresidents at this classic Victorian seaside palace can sample the atmosphere over a reasonably-priced cream tea, overlooking the lawns and Castle Beach. Inexpensive.

Harbour Lights, Custom House Quay. Fish'n'chips and snacks with views over the harbour, plus good sandwiches and all-day breakfasts. Inexpensive.

No. 33, 33 High St ☎01326/211944. Easy-going café/restaurant offering well-cooked dishes including seafood and vegetarian. Closed Sun.

Seafood Bar, Lower Quay Hill (also known as Quay St) ☎01326/315129. Off the main drag, below the *Panda House* Chinese takeaway, and serving the best fish in town; where thick crab soup is a winter speciality; go for lobster, crab and Helford oysters at other times. Closed lunch, and Sun & Mon in July–Sept. Moderate.

Simply Sugar, Upton Slip, 48 Church St. Cheap and hearty food including poached salmon and trout, rabbit casserole and takeaway jacket potatoes. It's unlicensed but you can bring your own wines and beers. Closed Sun, and Mon evening. Moderate.

Drinking and nightlife

The *Quayside Inn* at 41 Arwenack St is the pick of the **pubs**, with waterside tables and sizzling skillets of chicken and vegetable stir fry – note the King's Pipe outside, a brick chimney used to incinerate seized contraband tobacco. On The Moor, the classic old *Seven Stars* has a quiet atmosphere and a vicar-landlord whose family has operated the pub since 1873.

The two main **clubs** in town are *Paradox* (open Wed, Fri & Sat) at the bottom of The Moor, and *Shades* on Quay Hill, both offering mainly UK garage and nostalgia nights. As well as its four exhibition galleries, **Falmouth Arts Centre** (☎01326/2123000; *www.falmoutharts .org*) has a crowded schedule of film, drama, dance, talks, recitals and live-music events.

Listings

Banks Barclays is on The Moor; HSBC and NatWest are on Market St; Lloyds TSB is on Killigrew St and Church St.

Bike rental Bissoe Tramways Cycle Hire (☎01872/870341) at Bissoe, 15 miles north of Falmouth, signposted off the A39 at Devoran, operate a delivery and collection service to Falmouth.

Bus information Western National ☎01209/719988.

Car hire Falmouth Garage, North Parade (☎01326/313029); Selecthire, Fiesta House, Bar Rd (☎01326/319357); Millers, 5b Tregoniggie Industrial Estate (☎01326/373575).

Police Dracaena Ave ☎0990/777444.

Post office The main office on the Moor has a *bureau de change*.

Tours Coast and Country Tours operate guided minibus tours to Bodmin Moor, the Roseland and Lizard peninsulas and Land's End, with walking breaks (£24 for a day, or £16 for half-day tour). You can get tickets from the tourist office, or by calling ☎01326/211889.

Travel details

Trains

Falmouth to: Truro (10–12 daily; 25min).

Looe to: Liskeard (June–Sept 8–9 daily; 30min).

Par to: Penzance (hourly; 1hr 10min); Plymouth (hourly; 50min).

Truro to: Bristol (9 daily; 3hr 20min); Exeter (7 daily; 2hr 15min); Falmouth (10–12 daily; 25min); Liskeard (hourly; 50min); London (9 daily; 4hr 40min); Penzance (1–2 hourly; 40min); Plymouth (hourly; 1hr 15min).

Buses

Charlestown to: St Austell (hourly; 20min).

Falmouth to: Exeter (1 daily; 4hr); Helston (8 daily; 1hr); Penzance (7 daily; 1hr 45min); Plymouth (2 daily; 2hr 30min); St Austell (2 daily; 1hr 30min); Truro (Mon–Sat 2–3 hourly, Sun 1 hourly; 30–40min).

Fowey to: Par (Mon–Sat every 30min; Sun hourly; 16min); St Austell (Mon–Sat 2 hourly; Sun hourly; 40min).

Gorran Haven to: Mevagissey (4–7 daily; 25min).

Looe to: Liskeard (hourly; 20min); Plymouth (Mon–Sat 7 daily, Sun 5 daily; 1hr 20min); Polperro (hourly; 20min).

Lostwithiel to: St Austell (Mon–Sat 5 daily, Sun 4 daily; 20min).

Mevagissey to: Gorran Haven (4–7 daily; 25min); St Austell (Mon–Sat hourly, Sun 9 daily; 20min).

Polperro to: Liskeard (hourly; 55min); Looe (hourly; 20min).

St Austell to: Charlestown (hourly; 20min); Falmouth (2 daily; 1hr 30min); Fowey (Mon–Sat 2 hourly, Sun hourly; 30min); Lostwithiel (Mon–Sat 5 daily, Sun 4 daily; 20min); Mevagissey (9 daily; 25min); Newquay (hourly; 50min–1hr 10min); Par (Mon–Sat 2 hourly, Sun hourly; 15min); Truro (1–2 hourly; 40–50min).

Truro to: Bristol (1 daily; 5hr); Exeter (2 daily; 3hr 10min); Falmouth (Mon–Sat 2–3 hourly, Sun 1 hourly; 30–40min); Penzance (hourly; 1hr 45min); Plymouth (7 daily; 1hr 30min–2hr); St Austell (1–2 hourly; 40–50min); St Ives (12 daily; 1hr 15min–1hr 45min).

Ferries

Falmouth to: St Mawes (May–Sept Mon–Sat every 30min, Sun hourly; Oct–April Mon–Sat 6 daily; 20min); Truro (June–Sept 5 daily; 1hr).

St Mawes to: Falmouth (May–Sept Mon–Sat every 30min, Sun hourly; Oct–April Mon–Sat 6 daily; 20min).

Truro to: Falmouth (June–Sept 4 daily; 1hr).

Chapter 9

The Lizard and Penwith peninsulas

You'll find brief descriptions of the main villages, attractions and a few accommodation options on the Lizard peninsula's official Web site, www .thelizard.co.uk

Jutting like pincers into the Atlantic, the twin prongs of the **Lizard and Penwith peninsulas**, respectively the mainland's most southerly and westerly points, are where the land runs out. Scenically, it is one of the country's most spectacular areas, a succession of wave-pounded cliffs interspersed by a variety of superlative beaches, and encompassing wide expanses of undeveloped moorland. Additionally, the mild climate favours a range of exotic vegetation, with fiery monbretia or rich-purple foxgloves crowding every roadside, and bright geraniums and lobelia spilling from the grey granite that's the region's primary building material. Indeed granite is ubiquitous, evident everywhere from farmsteads to drystone walls, churches and castellated cliffs, though much of the Lizard is also made up of greenish-brown serpentine, a soft hydrated magnesium silicate that's sometimes mottled or spotted like a serpent's skin (hence the name) and is the staple material of craft-shop trinkets.

The **Lizard peninsula** is the less developed of the two, its mostly flat and bare interior giving way to precipitous bluffs and cliff-girt coves where it meets the sea. Most of the holiday traffic is concentrated around these rugged bays with their superb beaches – places like **Kynance Cove**, theatrically framed by rocky pinnacles and serpentine cliff walls – though of course there's always a stream of pilgrims to

---

ACCOMMODATION PRICE CODES

Throughout this *Guide*, hotel and B&B accommodation is coded on a scale of ① to ⑨, the code indicating the lowest price you can expect to pay per night for a double room in high season. The prices indicated by the codes are as follows:

① under £40	④ £60–70	⑦ £110–150
② £40–50	⑤ £70–90	⑧ £150–200
③ £50–60	⑥ £90–110	⑨ over £200

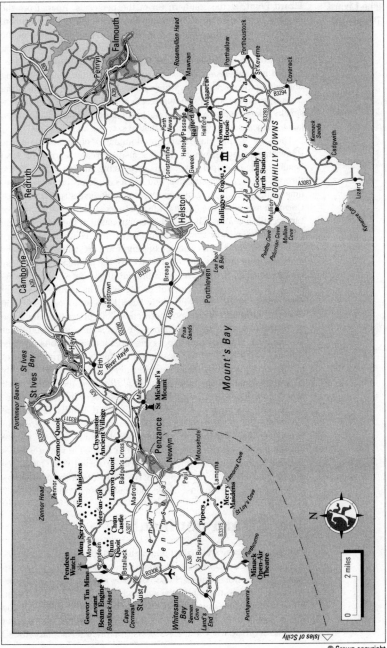

© Crown copyright

Lizard Point, at the southern tip of the peninsula. Apart from the region's chief town of **Helston** and its nearby port of **Porthleven**, where a small fishing fleet lends a slightly brisker feel, most of the spartan villages hereabouts are tiny unflustered havens buried away at the end of remote lanes, such as **Mullion Cove** and **Coverack**, suspended in a timeless tranquillity. You can reach the most appealing ones along the coastal path, which allows access to the awe-inspiring coastal scenery, though you might also consider exploring the peninsula by bike – a great way to get the best out of the network of narrow lanes connecting the villages and beaches.

The raw granite landscape predominates once more on the **Penwith peninsula**, where there is also a greater choice of sand beaches. The principal town, **Penzance**, is big enough to absorb the throngs of tourists in summer, and has a couple of first-class museums giving a fascinating insight into the geological structure of west Cornwall as well as the cultural life which existed here at the turn of the twentieth century. Many artists congregated in the neighbouring port of **Newlyn**, now the west's biggest fishing centre, where there still exists a good collection of contemporary art, while later waves of artists were attracted across the neck of the peninsula to the busy holiday town of **St Ives**, where a branch of the Tate Gallery showcases their work within earshot of the sea. The peninsula's main draw, however, lies in its dramatic coastline – an inhospitable ring of cliffs, unbroken on the northern coast, but punctuated by some of Cornwall's best sandy beaches to the south, for instance at **Porthcurno**. Most visitors bypass the most interesting bits on their way to **Land's End**, whose position at Britain's westernmost point has endowed it with a mythic significance, and also with a brashly commercialized entertainment complex. However, the jagged coast on either side has been spared, and offers some of the most rewarding coastal walking in the county. North of Land's End, **Cape Cornwall** retains its desolate air, the abandoned chimney stacks of Penwith's once-flourishing mining industry only adding to the majesty, while you can soak up the flavour of the interior at villages such as **Zennor**, whose granite integrity attracted D.H. Lawrence during World War I, or by exploring the remnants of the peninsula's prehistoric societies amidst bleak, hilly moorland.

The Lizard peninsula

The bare plateau of the **Lizard peninsula** – from the Celtic *lys ardh*, or "high point" – has plenty of primitive appeal, but you'll need to make a little effort to unearth some of the more serendipitous discoveries. If the peninsula can be said to have a centre, it is **Helston**, known for its folk museum and the centuries-old tradition of the Furry (or Flora) Dance, and a useful transport hub for buses. From here, it's a broad, treeless landscape as you follow the solitary A3083 to the southern headlands and the village known simply as **The Lizard**, at the peninsula's tip. On either side of the A3083, roads branch off westwards towards obvious attractions like **Loe Pool**, Cornwall's largest natural lake and a haven for wildlife, or remote hamlets such as **Mullion Cove**, little more than a scattering of cottages set around a thick-walled harbour. Though the neighbouring beaches of **Polurrian** and **Poldhu** are more popular with surfers, **Kynance Cove**, just south of The Lizard village, is the peninsula's most appealing place to swim. The Lizard's eastern coast is also sparsely settled, though such villages as **Coverack** attract a good deal of summer traffic for their lovely secluded settings. In contrast, the insular communities and secretive creeks of the **Helford River** have a very different tone, where pleasure boats cruise the muddy banks.

From Helston, which is linked to Penzance by the frequent Western National #2, **bus routes** into the Lizard peninsula are run by Truronian: #T1 – taking in Perranporth, St Agnes, Redruth and Truro – goes to the village of The Lizard via Helston, Porthleven and Mullion; #T2 connects the east-coast villages of St Keverne and Coverack (neither service runs on Sun in winter). The #T3 "Lizard Rambler" takes in many points along its meandering route from Helston, including Mawgan, St Keverne, Coverack, Kynance Cove and The Lizard, as well as remote stops useful for coast walkers.

Helston

Three miles from the sea at the northern end of the Lizard Peninsula, **HELSTON** is a sleepy, hilly place, very different nowadays from its former appearance when, as Hellaz, it was a busy port on the Cober river. This all changed when its sea outlet became silted up by deposits from upstream tin-workings – by around 1300 the town was cut off from the sea – which resulted in both the formation of Loe Pool (see p.209) and the frequent flooding which afflicted the town until the 1980s. These days the water-level is controlled by a sluice and culvert at Loe Bar (see p.209) and by giant tanks in the town. Despite losing its role as a port, Helston remained an important centre as a stannary town, as recalled in the name of its broad main thoroughfare, Coinagehall Street, which meets Helston's second axis, Meneage Street, at the Neoclassical **Guildhall**, itself the starting point for the town's celebrated **Furry** or **Flora Dance** (see box, overleaf).

You can learn more about the Furry Dance and other aspects of the town's history at the eclectic **Helston Folk Museum** (Mon–Sat 10am–5pm; £2), housed in former market buildings behind the Guildhall on Church Street. The long exhibition space, leading up through the old butter market to the fish and meat markets, is filled with a happy assortment of local bric-a-brac relating to local trades, and includes sections on the telegraphy pioneer Marconi and on

The Lizard peninsula

Available from Helston's tourist office, the "Discovery Trails" information pack outlines walking routes and bus connections on the Lizard.

If you're planning more than a couple of bus journeys on the Lizard in a day, consider a Day Rover ticket, costing £4.50 for unlimited travel on Truronian buses.

Helston's Furry Dance

Helston is most famous for its annual **Furry Dance** (also called Flora Dance), a complex mimetic ritual held on Flora Day, May 8 (unless this date falls on a Sun or Mon, when the procession takes place on the previous Sat). It is the high point on the town's calendar and preparations are made for it months in advance. Although it is said to commemorate an apparition by St Michael, the town's patron saint, the revelry probably predated Christianity as a spring fertility ritual, since it formerly involved a ceremony in woods close to town followed by a dance back to the centre, now commemorated by the Hal-an-Tow ceremony, the second dance of the day. Of the five separate dances, the most important is at midday, a stately procession of top-hatted men and summer-frocked women performing a solemn dance through the town's streets, gardens and even houses, led by the Helston Brass Band. The first dance begins at 7am, and is the least crowded: at 8:30am, 9:30am, noon and 5pm for the later ones, for which you should give yourself plenty of time to find a good viewing spot.

Helston's native son, **Bob Fitzsimmons** (1863–1917), the first boxer to be world middleweight, light heavyweight and heavyweight champion, and the only Briton to achieve this triple. The reconstructed Victorian classroom, with examples of canes and a leather tawse for beating children, and an upstairs section on mining and quarrying are also worth taking in. Helston lay at the centre of one of Cornwall's most intensely mined regions, and near to the biggest tin mine in the country, owned by the mighty Godolphin family, who had their town house in what is now the *Angel Hotel*, almost opposite the Guildhall on Coinagehall Street. At the bottom of this street, the arched and turreted **Grylls Monument** was erected in honour of a local banker and benefactor on the former site of Helston's castle, once guarding the Cober valley but already a ruin by 1478. Once you've done a circuit of Helston's hilly backstreets, there's little else to detain you unless you're tempted by **Flambards Theme Park** (mid April to mid-July, Sept & Oct daily 10.30am–5pm; mid-July to Aug daily 10am–6pm; £9.50), packed with various family amusements, such as a re-created Victorian village and a choice of white-knuckle rides. It's well signposted from the A394 and A3083, on the eastern side of town.

Flambards sometimes closes on Mondays and Fridays in April, May, September & October; to check, call ☎01326/ 564093

Practicalities

All **buses** stop on Coinagehall Street, including the frequent Western National #2 and #2A from Falmouth and Penzance and the #2E from Penzance; plus Truronian's #T1 from Perranporth, St Agnes, Redruth and Truro and #T4 from Falmouth. Helston holds the peninsula's only **tourist office** at 79 Meneage St (Easter–Sept Mon–Sat 10am–1pm & 2–5pm; Oct–Easter Mon–Fri 10am–1pm & 2–4.30pm; ☎01326/565431), which provides maps and accommodation lists.

St Michael's Mount, Cornwall

Robarte's tomb, Truro Cathedral, Cornwall

Pilchards in crate, Newlyn, Cornwall

Polperro, Cornwall

Botallack tin mine, Cornwall

Mousehole, Cornwall

St Mawes Castle, Cornwall

Porthmeor Beach in mist, St Ives, Cornwall

Barbara Hepworth Museum, St Ives, Cornwall

Egyptian House, Penzance, Cornwall

Sand flats near Newquay, Cornwall

Lanyon Quoit, Cornwall

Riding the waves near Gunwalloe, Cornwall

At 52 Coinagehall St, *No. 52* is a smart **B&B** with solid old furnishings in rooms to front and rear (☎01326/569334; ②); ask at the adjacent *Blue Anchor* (see below) if there's no reply. Just up the street at no. 16, the *Angel Hotel* (☎01326/572701; ②) retains some of the features from its 500-year history, including a minstrel gallery and well, though guestrooms are rather dull. For a drink or a pub snack, the *Blue Anchor* is an essential stop, a fifteenth-century monks' rest house with a series of snug flagstoned rooms, a skittle alley and a small garden; brewed on the premises, the Spingo beer is available in three strengths. If it's just a bite you're after, *Hutchinson's*, 95 Meneage St, serves award-winning fish and chips to eat in or take away.

The Lizard peninsula

You can rent bikes from Helston's Bike Services on Meneage Street (☎01326/5645 64), or Family Cycles at 7 Church St (☎01326/ 564564).

Porthleven and around

Three miles southwest of Helston on the B3304, **PORTHLEVEN** is a sizeable port that once served to ship tin ore from the inland mines. Characterless houses now ring the top of village, but the harbour, healthily packed with fishing boats, has more interest, with two sets of stout harbour walls, on the outer of which sit a brace of cannons, salvaged from a frigate, the HMS *Anson*, wrecked on Loe Bar in 1807 with the loss of 120 sailors. The guns are said to have fired at Napoleon's navy at the battle of Brest.

There are plenty of good **beaches** within easy reach of Porthleven: the best for swimming are around **Rinsey Head**, three miles north along the coast, while in the other direction, one and a quarter miles to the south, **Loe Bar** is a lovely bank of sand and shingle, accessible via the coast path from Porthleven's harbour. The Bar separates the sea from the freshwater **Loe Pool**, which extends one and a quarter miles inland, and formerly stretched much further up the valley of the River Cober towards Helston. Loe Pool is one of two places which claim to be where the sword Excalibur was restored to its watery source (the other is on Bodmin Moor; see p.304). You can make a lovely five-mile hike on a waymarked path round the creeks and woods on the lake's perimeter.

Swimming off Loe Bar is not recommended, due to the steeply shelving bottom and the strong currents.

Practicalities

Buses #2 and #2E connect Porthleven with Penzance and Helston, while the #2A and #2B run between Helston and Porthleven. One of the best **accommodation** choices here is the almost excessively picturesque *Anchor Cottage*, whose pale-pink walls overlook the beach on Cliff Road (☎01326/574391; ①); during the day you can usually contact the owners in the shop in the Bickford-Smith building just a few doors along, distinguished by its clock tower. Alternatively, two smartly furnished nonsmoking rooms are available above *Critchard's* restaurant, at Harbour Head (☎01326/562407; ②), the larger benefiting from a glorious vista for which you pay about £10 more. If you want to stay nearer Loe

From Porthleven Angling Centre (☎01326/ 561885) or Quay Clothing (☎07977/ 972174), both on Porthleven harbour, you can book fishing trips and coastal cruises to see local caves and cliff-faces.

Bar, *Dolphin Cottage* on Loe Bar Road (☎01326/562264; no credit cards; ②) occupies a grand, isolated site overlooking the sea a few minutes' north of the bar; in summer, B&B is available by the week only.

Semiformal, nonsmoking and moderately priced *Critchard's* is Porthleven's best fish **restaurant** (evenings only, closed Sun). The most congenial place for snacks is round the corner in Fore Street, where *The Galley* serves all-day breakfasts as well as healthy salads, pasta dishes and fuller evening meals. Across the harbour, *The Smoke House*, a stylish modern bar/restaurant (moderate), dishes out pastas and pizzas and lays on summer-evening barbecues with **live music**; bands also play on Sunday afternoons. If only for its position, *The Ship Inn* is the pick of the **pubs**, right on the edge of the harbour with outside seating and food.

Mullion and around

Three miles south of Helston, a right turn off the A3083 towards Gunwalloe brings you along a scenic coastal road which leads after about five miles to the inland village of **MULLION**. Here, a triangle of quiet roads encloses the fifteenth- to sixteenth-century church of **St Mellanus**, dedicated to the Breton Saint Mellane (or Malo). The short tower is partly constructed of serpentine, and the interior has some knobbly oak bench-ends showing a jester, a monk and cherubs with a chalice and barrel. Look out, too, for the dog-flap in the south door, originally for shepherds' dogs. Otherwise, the village is nothing special, but makes a useful base for the beaches and coves hereabouts.

Signposted a mile and a quarter west of the village, a scattering of picturesque cottages amid gorse- and bracken-smothered slopes look down on the gorgeous, enclosed little harbour of **Mullion Cove** – also known as Porthmellin – where a handful of fishing boats are sheltered behind thick brick jetties and rocky outcrops. Rocky strips of sand lie around the cove, but there's much better swimming at cliff-flanked **Polurrian**, a popular surfing beach less than a mile north along the coast path, and also accessible from the Mullion Cove road from Mullion. A further mile or so north, **Poldhu** is a generous expanse of sand wedged between acres of wild moorland, also accessible on the minor Mullion–Helston coast road (from Mullion, take The Commons, which turns into Poldhu Rd). If you're walking the coast path from Polurrian, you'll pass, on Poldhu's southern cliff-edge, the **Marconi Monument**, a solitary obelisk erected in 1937 to mark the spot from which the first transatlantic radio transmission was made by Guglielmo Marconi in 1901. Poldhu continued as a commercial radio station until 1922, and during World War II was a vital link between Britain and the Atlantic convoys bringing men, munitions and food.

Riding in the Mullion area is offered at Newton Farm on Polhorman Lane, a right turn off the Poldhu Road from Mullion (☎01326/240388).

From Mullion Cove, you can take fishing trips and pleasure cruises to local sea caves: you'll find the operator by the harbour during the summer months, or call ☎01326/240345 or 07974/803924.

Practicalities

There are a few good **accommodation** options **in Mullion**, including *The Old Vicarage*, at the top of Nansmellyon Road (☎01326/240509; ③); enclosed within a garden, it offers four elegant and spacious en-suite rooms. Five-minutes' walk along the Commons (at the top of Churchtown heading west towards Poldhu) and just half a mile from the sea, *Campden House* is a friendly B&B with a fuschia-filled garden (☎01326/240365; no credit cards; ①); dinners and good-value snacks are available. Next to the car park **in Mullion Cove**, *Criggan Mill*, 200m up from the sea in a peaceful narrow field (☎01326/240496), has simple, prefabricated lodges for **B&B** (②), and offers self-catering in timber lodges bookable by the week. At the other end of the scale, the palatial *Mullion Cove Hotel* (☎01326/240328; *www.mullioncove.com*; ⑨) is spectacularly situated high above the harbour, with its own diminutive outdoor pool. Nonresidents can stop here for teas, snacks in the bistro or evening drinks.

Almost all the **eating** options are in Mullion, where you'll find substantial, moderately priced fish and meat platters at *Stock's* (☎01326/240727), just down from the church on Churchtown. Also on Churchtown, the *Cottage Restaurant* (☎01326/241414) has local lobster served with chilli, and serves snacks at the attached *Forget-Me-Not Café*. Across the road from *Stock's, Hatton's* offers a glorious range of Rodda's ice cream as well as sandwiches to take away. Right by the harbour in Mullion Cove, the relaxed *Porthmellin Café* (Easter–Oct) has delicious home-made cakes, cream teas, crab sandwiches and pizzas.

The Lizard and around

Around four miles after the Mullion turn-off from the A3083, the nondescript village of **THE LIZARD** is the main centre at the peninsula's southern end. Likened by John Betjeman to "an army housing scheme given over to visitors", it holds shops and a handful of places to sleep and eat, but unless you're looking for serpentine souvenirs or refreshment, it has a strictly functional appeal. A web of footpaths radiate out from the village towards the sea, the most popular being the mile-long track, which runs parallel to the road to mainland Britain's southernmost tip, **Lizard Point**. Here, a plain lighthouse and a couple of low-key cafés and gift shops look down on a ceaselessly churning sea and a tiny sheltered cove holding a disused lifeboat station. It's all quite unspoiled, a far cry from the paraphernalia surrounding Land's End (see p.230), and the coast on either side is no less impressive, a succession of rugged chasms and caves hollowed out by the sea. The coast path leads east past the **Lion's Den**, a huge cavity in the cliffs caused by the collapse of a sea cave, to **Housel Cove**, where Marconi conducted his early radio experiments from a bungalow, still visible above a small sandy beach,

From Lizard Point, you'll often be able to see grey seals fishing out to sea, and you should look out too for basking sharks and dolphins.

The Lizard peninsula

(which can be reached by a steep cliff path). Beyond Marconi's bungalow, the prominent white, castellated building on **Bass Point** was constructed by Lloyds insurers in 1872, so that company agents could semaphore passing ships and relay news of cargoes to merchants in London; it's now a private house. Half a mile further east and north of here, **Church Cove** is the site of the lifeboat station which replaced the former one at Lizard Point. The cove lies at the end of a lane connecting to the village of **LANDEWEDNACK**, whose fifteenth-century church was the last place where a sermon was preached in the Cornish tongue, in 1674. From here it's less than a mile by road back to The Lizard.

A mile northwest of The Lizard, the peninsula's best-known beach, **Kynance Cove**, lies at the end of a toll-road (Easter–Oct £1.50, Nov–Easter free), signposted west off the A3083. In all, it's about a forty-minute walk from Lizard Point, including a final fifteen-minute clamber down steep steps to the shore. The white-sand beach is encircled by sheer 200ft cliffs in which the olive-green serpentine is flushed with reds and purples, and faces the stacks and arches of offshore islets which are joined to shore at low tide. The biggest of these, Asparagus Island, takes its name from the wild asparagus that grows there. Masses of other wild flowers adorn the rocks on every side, and the scene has an appealing wild grandeur. The water quality is excellent, though bathers should take care not to be stranded on the islands by the tide, which submerges the entire beach at its flood. There's a seasonal café here and toilets.

Swimmers should take extra special care at the beaches around The Lizard, where fierce currents and creeping tides pose serious risks.

Practicalities

Hourly #T1 **buses** link The Lizard to Mullion, Helston and Truro. The village has a good choice of **accommodation**, including the non-smoking *Caerthillian*, a comfortable bright-blue **B&B** in the centre of the village (☎01326/290019; no credit cards; ②). There are several possibilities on Penmenner Road, among them *Parc Brawse House* (☎01326/290466; no credit cards; ②), a solid, brilliant-white building with large windows in its seven rooms; it's virtually the only place in the area that allows smoking indoors, and has a restaurant. On Lighthouse Road, which leads south towards the lighthouse,

Tregollas, Britain's most southerly farm, is plainly furnished, friendly and relaxed (☎01326/290226; no credit cards; ②, closed Nov–Easter). The Lizard has little in the way of fine **restaurants**, though the inexpensive *Regent Café*, opposite the car park at the centre of the village, provides first-class fish and chips and other basic platters. The moderately priced traditional English fare at the nearby *Witchball Restaurant* (☎01326/290662) includes such dishes as fillet of lamb with apricots, as well as vegetarian choices and home-made desserts. It also offers an extremely good-value set two-course lunch on Tuesdays for £3.75 – booking is recommended. At the centre of the village, the mainland's southernmost **pub**, the *Top House*, serves lunch-time snacks and full meals, and has a few outside tables.

Goonhilly Downs and Coverack

West of the A3083 Helston–Lizard road, the lonely B3293 crosses the broad windswept plateau of **Goonhilly Downs**, where the futuristic saucers of an extensive satellite station and the nearby ranks of wind turbines are somewhat spooky intrusions. The tracking dishes appear deceptively small when seen from afar; close up they're enormous – the largest, "Merlin", is 32m in diameter. Claiming to be the world's largest satellite station, the **Goonhilly Earth Station** (Easter to late June daily 10am–5pm; late June to early Sept 10am–6pm, but Aug weekdays 10am–8pm; early Sept to early Nov daily 10am–5pm; last entry 1hr before closing; *www.goonhilly.bt.com*; £4.50) is capable of handling 600,000 phone, fax, video and data calls worldwide at any one time. You can find out more about its operations at the multimedia visitor centre, largely a customer relations exercise on the part of British Telecom, but you'll take in some pretty spectacular views as well as all the statistical gush and technological wonders on the guided tours round the site, and there are interactive displays and a film showing how satellite technology developed from ideas by science-fiction author Arthur C. Clarke.

Continuing east, the B3293 meets the coast at the fishing port of **COVERACK**, once a notorious centre of contraband. The sequestered village presents a placid picture, its thatched and lime-washed granite cottages overlooking a curve of beach which almost disappears to nothing at high tide; you'll occasionally see dolphins frolicking in the bay. At the southern end of the village, a tiny walled harbour is crammed with boats and there's a small selection of cafés and **restaurants**. Among these the *Fodder Barn* offers pizzas, baguettes and evening meals, and the *Paris Hotel* has tables outside on the grass near the harbour; opposite, the *Old Lifeboat House Seafood Restaurant* (☎01326/280899; closed Oct–Easter; moderate) serves good-value seafood specials and also has a fish-and-chips shop attached. Coverack would make an ideal **place to stay** for rest and recuperation, though the few options are frequently fully

At the harbour, the Coverack Windsurfing Centre (☎01326/ 280939) offers sessions and courses between March and November, using a range of open-sea and inland locations. Equipment is provided, and it also rents out "surf-skis" – a cross between a surfboard and a canoe.

booked. Try *Fernleigh*, on Chymbloth Way, a turn-off from Harbour Road (☎01326/280626; no credit cards; ①), which has three spacious rooms, a small garden with bay views and amiable proprietors, who can cook up a good three-course meal for £10. Down by the harbour, the *Paris Hotel* (☎01326/280258; ④) has seafront vistas on three sides and well-equipped modern rooms. The peninsula's only **youth hostel** lies 200m west of here (up School Hill, signposted opposite the harbour), and has bunk-beds for £10, panoramic views and information on windsurfing and other local activities (☎01326/280687; closed Nov–March). Outside the village, just under a mile distant, *Little Trevothan* is a quiet **campsite** with level pitches and caravans for hire (☎01326/280260; closed Oct–Easter); it's signposted on the right of the B3293 as you approach Coverack, near the St Keverne fork.

St Keverne and around

*Buses #T2
(not Sun)
and #T3
(June–Oct
only) connect
St Keverne
with Coverack,
Helston and
other points
on the penin-
sula, while the
Lizard
Rambler
bus stops at
Porthallow
three times
a day.*

Five miles north of Coverack via the B3293, the inland village of **ST KEVERNE** is the main centre for shops and facilities around these parts, centred on its pretty square. Here, the ribbed, octagonal spire of **St Akeveranus** has served as a marker for sailors over the centuries; in the adjoining churchyard are the tombs of those claimed off this treacherous stretch of coast. On the square, the *White Hart* (☎01326/280325; ①) and the *Three Tuns* (☎01326/280949; ①) pubs offer good-value **accommodation**; both have gardens and decent **restaurants**. The intimate *Poppy's Bistro*, just off the square (☎01326/280800; Tues–Sat evenings only in summer, Thurs–Sat evenings in winter), serves steaks and fresh salmon and crab.

Several mainly stony **beaches** lie within a short distance from the village, perfect for a swim if you don't mind the rocks. A mile east of St Keverne, via the road to the right of the *White Hart* (turn off along the signposted lane to the right), the nearest of these is **Porthoustock**, a stone-and-shingle strip flanked by quarry workings which faces the dreaded **Manacles** rocks, three miles offshore and the cause of numerous shipwrecks over the centuries. Alternatively, stay on the road from the *White Hart* for a couple of miles to reach **PORTHALLOW**, where there's a small grey-sand beach and a cluster of cottages around the harbour. Right on the shore here, the *Five Pilchards Inn* serves sizzling steaks and succulent, fresh-off-the-boat fish and lobster.

*Just above the
village of
Porthallow,
Porthallow
Vineyard
(Mon–Sat
11am–1pm &
2–5pm) sells
local ciders,
wines and
liqueurs, and
offers free
tastings.*

Less than a mile south of St Keverne (signposted off the Coverack road after Zoar Garage), **Roskilly's** (summer daily 10am–9pm; winter Sat & Sun 10am–dusk; free) produces some of Cornwall's best ice creams, available in fifty-odd flavours. You can purchase these, as well as yogurt ices and other goodies, in the shop and restaurant, which stays open late for barbecues in summer, and you can also wander around the surrounding ponds, glades and wetlands, created to shelter wildlife.

Along the Helford River

At the northeastern side of the Lizard peninsula, the **Helford River**, actually a drowned river valley or ria, reveals a range of different faces along its length, from sheltered muddy creeks upstream to its rocky, open mouth, all of which repay exploration on foot or by boat. On its south side, **Frenchman's Creek**, one of a splay of inlets running off the river, was the inspiration of Daphne Du Maurier's novel of the same name, and her evocation of it still holds true: "still and soundless, surrounded by the trees, hidden from the eyes of men".

The creek is reachable on a footpath (signposted uphill in front of the *Shipwright's Arms* – see below) and road from **HELFORD**, less than a mile east. Surrounded by woods and lying at the bottom of a steep and narrow lane, this agreeable old smugglers' haunt has a neat, gentrified appearance nowadays, immersed in a comfortable lethargy. Overlooking the river, the *Shipwright's Arms* is a fine spot to soak up the atmosphere and eat **pub** lunches in the garden. You can cross to Helford River's north bank by the seasonal passenger ferry (April–Oct 9am–5pm hourly, or according to demand in peak season, when it runs 8.30am–9pm; £1.50) to the hamlet of **Helford Passage**. Both Helford and Helford Passage make good starting points for riverside walks, or you can **rent boats** (£20–40 for two hours) or canoes (£7 per hour) from Helford River Boats, Helford Passage (☎01326/250770), which operates a kiosk in season in front of the *Ferryboat Inn*.

In contrast to these inland locations, the village of **MAWNAN** stands close to the mouth of the Helford River, a couple of miles east of Helford Passage, its granite church of St Maunanus set apart from the village on a height. **Rosemullion Head** juts out into Falmouth Bay about a mile northeast of here, strewn with wild flowers in spring and summer and reachable on the coast path which winds round to Maenporth and beyond to Falmouth (see p.197).

Near the westernmost reaches of the river, near the village of Mawgan (signposted from Garras), **Trelowarren House** (Easter–Sept Wed 2.15–5pm; £1.50 per car, free for non-car users) is an old Cornish manor which, since 1427, has been in the hands of the local Vyvyan family, famous for their royalist sympathies during the Civil War. Guided tours lasting an hour or so (£1.50) are led around the mainly sixteenth-century house – described by Daphne Du Maurier as "the last of England as I will ever know it" – where the highlights are the exquisite plasterwork and medieval stained glass of the Rococo Chapel. More compelling, though, are the lovely way-marked woodland walks through the estate, one leading to the late Iron Age **Halliggye Fougou**, a tunnel in an earthwork which once enclosed a settlement. Steps lead down to the stone-walled construction, several yards long and with a roof high enough that you don't need to stoop; there's little to see, but you'll need a torch as it's very dark. Another path can be followed to Tremayne Quay on the Helford

River, nearly four miles away. The estate has a café and arts studios, and a superb **campsite** within the walled gardens and orchards in the centre of the park (April–Sept; ☎01326/221637).

The Penwith peninsula

Though more densely populated than the Lizard, and absorbing a heavier tourist influx, the **Penwith peninsula** (also known as West Penwith, or the Land's End Peninsula) retains the elements which have always marked it out – craggy, wave-pounded granite cliffs and a succession of superlative sand beaches, encompassing wild, untrammelled moorland. The main town, **Penzance**, the terminus for trains from London and Birmingham and the embarkation point for the Isles of Scilly (see Chapter 10), is never overwhelmed by the weight of tourist traffic passing through and preserves a lively, unpretentious feel. Its choice of accommodation, shops and restaurants and good transport links make it an obvious starting point for forays to nearby sights: the offshore bastion of **St Michael's Mount**, the well-preserved Iron Age village of **Chysauster**, the neighbouring fishing centre of **Newlyn**, or, just beyond, the bijou **Mousehole**. On the other hand, you shouldn't be deterred from pushing on further round the coast to be nearer beaches such as **Porthcurno**, site of one of the country's most famous performance venues, the cliff-hewn **Minack Theatre**. The raw appeal of Penwith's rugged landscape is still encapsulated by **Land's End**, though the headland's commercialization leads many to prefer the unadulterated beauty of **Cape Cornwall**, four miles north. A couple of miles inland from here, **St Just-in-Penwith** is the largest village on this extreme western seaboard, though it has little to detain you. More compelling are the remnants of the mining industry around **Pendeen**, the remote prehistoric remains dotted inland of here, and the compact granite village of **Zennor**. Penwith's northern coast has few beaches to compare with its southern side, though this absence is compensated by the generous sands surrounding **St Ives**, whose tight knot of flower-filled lanes and Mediterranean ambience have long made it a magnet for artists and holiday visitors alike.

Penwith is more easily accessible than the Lizard, with a road circling its coastline and a good **bus** network from St Ives and Penzance, though transfers onto different routes can involve some lengthy waiting and services on Sundays and in winter are reduced or nonexistent. **Train** passengers to St Ives should change at St Erth, for the four-mile branch line that qualifies as one of Britain's most scenic railway tracts. Hikers have the option of walking the eight miles separating Penzance from St Ives along the old **St Michael's Way**, a waymarked pilgrim's route for which the tourist office in both these towns can provide a free route-map. Bikers can ask at the tourist offices for the free *Cycling in Penwith* pamphlet, which details eight **cycling routes** around the peninsula of 14 to 28 miles.

Penzance

Occupying a sheltered position at the northwest corner of Mount's Bay, **PENZANCE** has combined a busy working atmosphere with the trappings of the holiday industry since the rail link to London was established in the 1860s. Most traces of the medieval town were obliterated at the end of the sixteenth century by a Spanish raiding party, and the predominant style now is Regency and Victorian, most conspicuously on the broad promenade west of the harbour and in the centre. The twin axes of Market Jew Street, climbing up from the train station, and the more attractive Chapel Street, swinging back

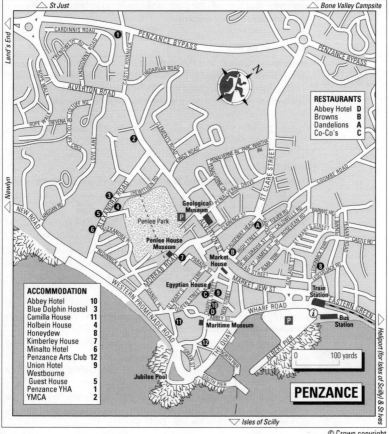

RESTAURANTS

Abbey Hotel	D
Browns	B
Dandelions	A
Co-Co's	C

ACCOMMODATION

Abbey Hotel	10
Blue Dolphin Hostel	3
Camilla House	11
Holbein House	4
Honeydew	8
Kimberley House	7
Minalto Hotel	6
Penzance Arts Club	12
Union Hotel	9
Westbourne Guest House	5
Penzance YHA	1
YMCA	2

PENZANCE

© Crown copyright

| The Penwith peninsula | downhill from its top, hold most of the shops, banks and other facilities, while the main residential area, and most of the hotel accommodation, lie west of here. |

Arrival and accommodation

Penzance's **train and bus stations** are next to each other by the seafront at the eastern end of town, also the location of the town's **tourist office** (May–Sept Mon–Fri 9am–5pm, Sat 9am–4pm, Sun 10am–1pm; Oct–April Mon–Fri 9am–5pm, Sat 10am–1pm; ☎01736/362207), which can supply information on the whole peninsula. There are some **B&Bs** nearby at the bottom of Market Jew Street, but better choices lie either on Chapel Street, or west of the centre on Morrab and Alexandra Roads. Apart from the full-time campsite listed opposite, there's one much nearer the centre open in August only, well-signposted in a field near the Tesco roundabout as you come into town off the A30; facilities are very basic, but rates are low and there are hot showers.

Hotels and B&Bs

Abbey Hotel, Abbey St ☎01736/366906. Just off Chapel St, this seventeenth-century house – now owned by former model Jean Shrimpton and her husband – offers top-class accommodation with oodles of old-fashioned comfort, superb views over Mount's Bay, a well-stocked library and a quality restaurant. ⑦.

Camilla House, 12 Regent Terrace ☎01736/363771. Just off the seafront Promenade, this flower-decked Regency B&B is convenient for the harbour and has sea views from most rooms; the top room is cosiest. No smoking. Closed Dec–Jan. ②.

Holbein House, Alexandra Rd ☎01736/332625. Cheerful, cheap and spacious B&B; breakfast is served in the bright-painted rooms. There's no single-room supplement. No credit cards. ①.

Honeydew, 3 Leskinnick St ☎01736/364206. Basic B&B at the bottom of Market Jew St, very close to the bus and train stations. No credit cards. ①.

Minalto, Alexandra Rd ☎01736/362923. Good-value middle-sized hotel with a polite, old-fashioned atmosphere, large rooms, a cocktail bar and a restaurant. A car park is available for long-term parking (for example for Scillies-bound travellers) for £1.50 a day. ②.

Penzance Arts Club, Chapel House, Chapel St ☎01736/363761. Four boldly painted rooms in this handsome, stylishly furnished building that was once the Portuguese embassy, dating from 1781. ③.

Union Hotel, Chapel St ☎01736/362319 or 0800/136885. This old coaching inn is a fine place to soak up the local atmosphere, with breakfast served in the Georgian Assembly Room. Most rooms are en suite, costing £20 more than standard rooms. ②–④.

Westbourne Guest House, Alexandra Rd ☎01736/350535. There are few surprises in this modest B&B with simple rooms, but the landlord can give you the lowdown on surfing in Penwith. ①.

Hostels and campsites

Blue Dolphin, Alexandra Rd ☎01736/363836. Probably the tidiest backpacker's hostel in the west, and one of the most welcoming. Dorm beds cost £10, and there are a couple of private rooms (①).

Bone Valley, Heamoor ☎01736/360310. The nearest campsite to Penzance lies two miles north of town, reachable on buses #11 or #11D.

Penzance YHA, Castle Horneck, Alverton ☎01736/362666; *www.yha.org. uk*. Two miles from town (call ahead for directions), this Georgian mansion has Internet access, lockers and no curfew, and serves tasty pizzas from the kitchen with free coffees thrown in. Dorm beds cost £11, and there are also private rooms (①) and camping facilities. Closed Jan.

YMCA, The Orchard, Alverton ☎01736/365016; *www.ymca.org.uk/ gallery/cornwall*. Just past Alexandra Rd, this well-equipped hostel has a gym, a large common room and pool; dorm beds cost £7.50 a night, singles are £12.50 and twins are also available (①); prices rise by up to £5 in summer.

The town

At the top of Penzance's main traffic artery, **Market Jew Street** (from *Marghas Jew*, meaning "Thursday Market"), the pillared **Market House**, dating from 1836 and now a bank, marks the centre of town, its silver dome conspicuous from miles around. In front stands a statue of **Humphry Davy** (1778–1829), the local woodcarver's son who became one of the leading scientists of the nineteenth century. A pioneer in the field of electrochemistry, he discovered six new elements including potassium and sodium, discovered the use of nitrous oxide or laughing gas for anaesthetic use in 1798, and invented the life-saving miners' safety-lamp, which bears his name and which his statue holds. A left turn immediately past it brings you to the top of the elegant **Chapel Street**, which has some of the town's finest buildings, including the flamboyant **Egyptian House**, built in the 1830s as a museum and geological repository but subsequently abandoned until its restoration thirty-odd years ago. Colourfully daubed with lotus-bud capitals – an "Egyptian" style harking back to the vogue spawned by Napoleon's campaign in Egypt in 1798 – the building currently holds holiday apartments.

At 19 Chapel St, the **Maritime Museum** (Easter–Oct Mon–Sat 11am–2pm; £2) holds a colourful collection of seafaring articles, including many items salvaged from local wrecks, all housed within a full-size section of an eighteenth-century man o' war. It's an entertaining trawl, taking in waxworks of surgeons and carpenters hard at work and models of ships showing how they were constructed. The Upper Deck has the Great Cabin, with an array of finds from the wreckage of Sir Cloudesley Shovell's fleet that foundered in the Isles of Scilly (see box, p.253), including barrels, barometers, sextants, musket flints and figureheads.

Grown-ups and landlubbers will probably get more out of the minerals and earth-related items gathered in Penzance's excellent **Geological Museum** (March to mid-Dec Mon–Fri 10am–4.30pm, also Sat 10am–1pm in Aug; £2) on Alverton Street, a continuation of Market Jew Street. The ranks of glittering specimens in the main gallery vividly bring to life the region's close dependence on its subterranean wealth – an incredibly diverse collection mostly dug out of the labyrinth of mines bored through the area. Charts illustrate the distribution of the main seams, and the museum also covers a wider frame, with videos showing how tectonics, seismic disturbances and eruptions worldwide have shaped the planet.

In contrast, the collection at the **Penlee House Gallery and Museum** (Mon–Sat: May–Sept 10.00am–5.00pm; Oct–April 10.30am– 4.30pm; *www.penleehouse.org.uk*; £2, free on Sat), on the way down towards the promenade on Morrab Road, concentrates on the art scene that flourished in Penwith at the turn of the twentieth century. The gallery holds the largest collection of the works of the Newlyn School in the country, though space constraints limit the number of works on display at any one time. Frequently sentimentalized but often bathed in an evocatively luminous light, impressionistic maritime scenes rub shoulders with portraits of Newlyn's fishing community by the likes of Stanhope Forbes and Norman Garstin – whose atmospheric masterpiece *The Rain it Raineth Every Day* is displayed here – while temporary exhibitions highlight particular artists or themes. Penlee House itself is a creamy Italianate Victorian villa from 1865, which was inherited in 1918 by Alfred Branwell, a keen horticulturalist who introduced rare trees and shrubs from China, South America and Australia into its surrounding gardens, which make a fine spot for a picnic or a snooze.

For more on the arts scene in Penwith, see Contexts, p.326.

At the bottom of Morrab Road, bulging out of the Promenade into Mount's Bay, the Art Deco **Jubilee Pool** (May–Sept daily 10am–6.15pm; £1.70, half-price after 5pm) is a tidal, saltwater (though chlorinated) open-air swimming pool, built to mark the Silver Jubilee of George V in 1935. It's a classic example of the style, and nonswimmers can stroll around as a visitor (60p) to get a closer view of the pool and bay.

Eating, drinking and nightlife

Penzance has few **restaurants** that rise above the average, though there are some reasonably priced eateries in the centre. If you're after an authentic **pasty**, head to W.C. Rowe at 71 Causeway Head; fresh fish is best bought from the Fish Boutique on the seafront near the tourist office. The town has a burgeoning **nightlife** scene, though the only permanent dance spots are *The Barn* (☎01736/365754), near the Tesco roundabout off the A30, a mile east of the centre, and *Club 2000* (☎01736/331211), opposite the tourist office, both playing mainly house music; the latter also has live **concerts** most Wednesdays. *Vibes*, in the basement of *Kublai's* restaurant at 30 Alverton St, has excellent reggae, jazz and blues, played live or by DJs, and bring-your-own-instrument nights (currently Tues), while if you're after just a quiet drink, the *Admiral Benbow* and *Turk's Head* pubs have most atmosphere (see below). In a converted chapel on Parade Street (west of Chapel St), the *Acorn Theatre* (☎01736/365520; *www.acorntheatre.co.uk*) stages concerts and theatre productions on most weekends, and also has a funky basement café (closed Sun). At the bottom of Chapel Street, Penzance Arts Club has poetry readings, small concerts and exhibitions (☎01736/363761).

Restaurants and pubs

Abbey Hotel, Abbey St ☎01736/366906. Exquisite food, an open fire and Georgian furnishings make this the ideal place to pamper yourself, offering set-price evening meals with a choice of fish. Expensive.

Admiral Benbow, 46 Chapel St. Crammed with gaudy ships' figureheads and other nautical items, this historic pub has a restaurant made out to resemble a ship's galley. Look out for the armed smuggler on the roof. Inexpensive–Moderate.

Browns, Bread St. Soups, salads, quiches and other veggie delights are available at this modern, daytime-only café/restaurant located above a gallery off Causeway Head. Closed Sunday. Inexpensive.

Co-Co's, 12 Chapel St. Congenial tapas bar that's also good for paellas and other seafood dishes, or just coffees, cakes, baguettes and beers. Closed Sun lunch. Inexpensive–Moderate.

Dandelions, 39a Causeway Head. Tiny vegetarian restaurant at the top of the shopping precinct, where you can have delicious pitta bread sandwiches as well as salads, soups and quiches. Open daytime only, closed Sunday. Inexpensive.

Turk's Head, 49 Chapel St. The town's oldest inn, reputed to date back to the thirteenth century, and a great place for a drink or a full meal, including monkfish, prawn curry and seafood tagliatelle. There's a small walled garden. Moderate.

Listings

Bike rental Try R.C. Pender & Son, Jennings St ☎01736/365366; The Cycle Centre, Knights Warehouse, Bread St ☎01736/351671, and at the Sail Loft, New St ☎01736/363665; or Pedals Bike Hire, Wharfside Shopping Centre, Wharf Rd ☎01736/360600.

Car hire Europcar Hire, Station Yard ☎01736/360356; Economy Hire, Heliport Garage ☎01736/366636.

Car parks There are car parks by the train and bus stations and tourist office, and a cheaper one off Alverton Rd (convenient for Penlee House). Travellers to the Isles of Scilly can deposit their vehicles at Avalon car park near the harbour and opposite Jubilee Pool at South Place (☎01736/364622), for about £2.50 per day, or at the *Minalto Hotel* (see p.218).

Hospital West Cornwall Hospital in St Clare (☎01736/362382) has an accident and emergency department.

Internet access The Internet Place, 28 Market Jew St (Mon–Sat 10am–6pm; ☎01736/366999; *penzance@internet-place.co.uk*) charges £1 for 10min or £5 for 1hr.

Post office The main office is on Market Jew St (Mon–Fri 9am–5.30pm, Sat 9am–12.30pm).

Surf shops Groovy Poodle, 44 Market Jew St; South Shore, Wharfside Shopping Centre, Wharf Rd.

Taxis Albert's Taxis ☎0800/074 6778; Stone's Taxis ☎01736/363400 or 364772.

Tours Bolitho Tours ☎01736/871510 and Harry Safari (call at tourist office or ☎01736/711427) arrange tours of the prehistoric, Celtic and druidic sites of the peninsula lasting about four hours (about £10 per person). You can also go on wacky one-hour "ghost tours" around Penzance (☎01736/331206; Feb–Sept; £3): walks begin at 8 or 9pm outside the bus station.

Marazion and St Michael's Mount

Five miles east of Penzance, **MARAZION** is one of Cornwall's oldest chartered towns. Its biblical-sounding moniker is in fact a corruption of the names of local markets which were traditionally held here as early as 1070: Marghas Byghan ("Small Market") and Marghas Yow ("Thursday Market"). These days, the town attracts a regular stream of visitors, including many from Penzance who come here in summer for the wide, sand beaches, though most are here for the offshore isle of **St Michael's Mount**, whose chimneys and towers are an irresistible lure to anyone travelling along the long curve of Mount's Bay. Just four hundred yards from the mainland, the promontory can be approached on foot along a cobbled causeway at low tide, otherwise by frequent small ferries from Marazion (£1 each way).

A vision of the archangel Michael to some local fishermen led to the construction of a church on this granite pile in the fifth century, and within three centuries a Celtic monastery had been founded here. The present building derives from a chapel raised in the eleventh century by Edward the Confessor, who handed over the abbey to the Benedictine monks of Brittany's Mont St Michel, another island-abbey inspired by a vision of Saint Michael, and the model for this one. The monastery complex was appropriated by Henry V during the Hundred Years War, and it became a fortress following its dissolution a century later. After the Civil War, when it was used to store arms for the Royalist forces, it became the residence of the St Aubyn family, who still inhabit parts of the castle.

Although there's no arguing with its eye-catching site, the fortress-isle has a milder, more pedestrian feel than its prototype off the Breton coast. Above the island's harbour – historically used by the fishermen of Marazion, which never possessed its own – and a restored **dairy** that formerly served a small herd of Jersey cows, it's a steep climb up the cobbled Pilgrims' Steps to the **castle** itself (April–Oct Mon–Fri 10.30am–5.30pm, last admission 4.45pm, plus most weekends April–Sept 10.30am–5.30pm; Nov–March open most weekends, call ☎01736/710507 for times; £4.50; NT). Inside, a series of surprisingly small rooms displays a wealth

Buses #2 and #2A leave Penzance bus station every thirty minutes for Marazion. Other services are the summer-only #17 (hourly) and #32 (Mon–Sat 6 daily).

of weaponry and military trophies, period furniture and a feast of miniatures and larger paintings. The highlight of the tour is undoubtedly the **Chevy Chase Room**, the former monks' refectory given a seventeenth-century makeover. Sadly unconnected to the eponymous Hollywood actor, the name refers to a medieval hunting ballad ("Chevy" is either from the Cheviot Hills or the French *chevaux*, horses), which is illustrated by a simple plaster frieze on the walls. Apart from this, the room is dominated by the royal coat of arms given by Charles II in recognition of the St Aubyns' support during the Civil War. The family is well represented in the portraits covering the walls in other parts of the castle, and in the inscriptions in the battlemented **chapel** that crowns the island's summit. The Georgian finery of the **Blue Drawing Room**, embellished with Rococo twirls and fancy plasterwork, makes a refreshing contrast to all the militaria, while the model of the house made of champagne corks in the **Map Room** also suggests less-than-martial pursuits. The castle's primary function, however, is remembered in the **Garrison Room**, where the Armada was first sighted on 30 July, 1588; the beacon fire that was lit was the first to warn the nation that the Spanish invasion had come. The full story is recounted on a video screened down by the entrance, which is also where you can find **refreshment** at the *Sail Loft* café/restaurant, though the *Island Café* beyond the harbour is a pleasanter spot, with tables outside overlooking the sea. Both places are open April–October only (and the *Sail Loft* closes Sat in Oct).

Back on the mainland, you could take a rewarding stroll around Marazion, which gets a good share of the overspill of visitors to St Michael's Mount. Unless you're tempted by the collection of photos and reconstructed police cell in the **town museum**, housed on the ground floor of the town hall on Market Place (May–Sept daily 11am–5pm; 50p), you're unlikely to want to linger in the busy main street, spoiled by the steady procession of cars and coaches crawling through. However, you'll find more tranquillity at **Marazion Marsh**, an area of wetland behind the beach on the Penzance road, where there's an RSPB reserve (always open; free). The passage of trains on the main Penzance line seems to have little effect on the wildlife here: migratory birds and residents such as Cetti's Warbler thrive, as well as do migrant dragonflies and butterflies.

Back in town, *Philps Bakery*, opposite the ferry embarkation point, is the place to go for a **snack**, with renowned pasties, while the *Marazion Hotel* in the Square has a relaxed and inexpensive restaurant, and also serves teas, coffees and cakes. The hotel wouldn't make a bad choice to stay if you're seeking **accommodation** in the area: some rooms have good views though others can be dingy (☎01736/710334; ③). The best alternative is the quiet and comfortable *Castle Gayer*, on Leys Lane (☎01736/710202; ③), superbly positioned and with a garden overlooking the sea.

The Penwith peninsula

To find out more about the history of St Michael's Mount, and to take a room-by-room virtual guided tour, check out the Web site www.stmichaels mount.co.uk

Chysauster

One and three-quarter miles from the turn-off on the B3311
Penzance–St Ives road (the route of the #16 bus) at Badger's
Cross, the Iron Age village of **Chysauster** (April–Sept daily
10am–6pm; Oct daily 10am–5pm; £1.70; EH) occupies a windy
hillside with views over Penzance. The best-preserved ancient settlement in the southwest, it dates from about the first century BC
and consists of the shells of eight stone buildings, each holding an
open courtyard from which small chambers lead off. The largest
structures are likely to have been farm dwellings, probably thatch-
roofed with walls coated with wattle and daub, while other rooms
were probably barns, stalls or stables, or even protected vegetable
gardens. Huts three, four and six are the best preserved and give
the most vivid impression of the grandeur of the dwellings, where
open hearths, stone basins for grinding corn and covered drains
have been identified.

The site was used as an open-air pulpit by Methodist preachers at
the beginning of the nineteenth century and was first excavated in
the 1860s. The surrounding heather and gorse give the place a bracing, wild feel, though it's a mystery why the original inhabitants
would have chosen such a high exposed position for their village.

Newlyn

Well protected behind two long piers immediately south of
Penzance, **NEWLYN** is Cornwall's biggest fishing port and an important market and distribution point for the catches of smaller west
Cornwall ports. The town was also the focus of Cornwall's first
"artists' colony", when a group of artists gathered here in the wake
of the painter Stanhope Forbes in the late nineteenth century. Their
work is displayed at Penlee House in Penzance (see p.220), but
Newlyn's artistic spirit is perpetuated in **Newlyn Art Gallery**, occupying a detached Victorian building on the seafront at 24 New Rd
(Mon–Sat 10am–5pm; free). Elegantly modernized within, the small
gallery concentrates on contemporary works, but its regular exhibitions often focus on local artists, giving an insight into how the local
tradition has evolved.

*For more on
the arts scene
in Newlyn and
St Ives, see
Contexts,
pp.327-328.*

You can get an inkling of Newlyn's bohemian society at the turn
of the twentieth century by delving into some of the town's more
picturesque corners away from the seafront. Off The Strand, which
backs the harbour, Orchard Place, Chapel Street and Fragdan
Place preserve a cobbled and unspoiled appearance, adorned with
flowers and palms. Off Fore Street – a continuation of The Strand –
climb Trewarveneth Street to another enclave in the higher town,
where one of the alleys was lightheartedly named Rue des Beaux
Arts by the Victorian painters who lived here (though, confusingly,
this is not the lane to the left which currently bears that name). A

smattering of present-day artists and craftspeople now inhabit the area.

Newlyn's artistic profile is dwarfed, however, by the **fishing** business, whose vitality – despite huge problems concerning falling stocks and foreign (particularly Spanish) competition – is a refreshing contrast to the dwindling activity evident in most of Cornwall's other ports. Appropriately, the town has the county's best museum of fishing in the **Pilchard Works**, on the banks of the Coombe, a stream running down to New Road (Easter–Oct Mon–Fri 10am–6pm; £2.95). Although this focuses on the pilchard – the backbone of the Cornish fishing industry for centuries (see box, below) – all aspects of fishing are lucidly explained, illustrated by models of boats, marine etchings and paintings and examples of nets and baskets. The pilchard takes pride of place, however. Maps show the fish's distribution over the years, and in a section of the Works still operating commercially, you can watch pilchards being pressed and crated in "coffins" for export to Italy (June–Oct only), and see Britain's last surviving pilchard-net-making machine.

You can sample the local catch at Newlyn's various shellfish and seafood outlets such as those opposite the Pilchard Works. Alternatively, the *Smugglers* (☎01736/331501; Nov–Easter closed Mon–Wed; moderate) is a fine seafood **restaurant** right on the

---

The Cornish pilchard industry

Actually a mature Breton sardine, the **pilchard**, or *sardina pilchardus*, has been caught, salted and pressed in Cornwall for over 400 years. Migrating annually to breed in Cornish waters between August and December, the fish were traditionally caught in **seines**, encircling nets with floats at the top and weights at the bottom. Pilchards have always found a better market abroad than in England, and in the late seventeenth and early eighteenth centuries were even shipped to the West Indies to feed slaves working on sugar plantations, the cargoes frequently paid for in rum.

Around the middle of the nineteenth century, the pilchard fishery shifted its centre from the south Cornish coast to St Ives and the Mount's Bay ports, but by the 1870s overfishing meant that the industry was already in decline. This, in turn, was largely due to the increasing use of **drift nets**, which effectively dispersed the shoals further out to sea, and to the change from sail- to steam-power and subsequently to the internal combustion engine adopted by the "drifter" boats just before World War I. By 1920 seine catches were rare, while drift-net fishing itself suffered a significant decline in the mid-1930s due to falling stocks. Nowadays, the pilchard catch is a tiny fraction of its former size, although, despite the limited demand for Cornish salted pilchards in Britain, a considerable **export** market survives in France, Spain and Italy. Italy was and remains the largest market, where *salacche inglesi* are traditionally eaten during Lent and form part of such pasta dishes as *spaghetti alla puttanesca* and *pasta con le sarde*.

---

harbourfront, where you can enjoy skate, sea-bass and shark steak while soaking up the views over Mount's Bay. For a lunchtime **snack**, *Aunty May's Pasty Company*, at the bottom of the Coombe, has a range of pasties including such "gourmet" fillings as pork and apple or chicken and tarragon. The cheapest place in town, however, is the canteen of the Royal National Mission to Deep Sea Fisherman, right by the harbour, where you can indulge in a no-nonsense fry-up. If you're here in the evening, the *Meadery*, next door to the Pilchard Works, serves extra-strong Cornish mead wines and has chicken, scampi and chips on the menu (no smoking in upstairs restaurant). As for **pubs**, the snugly beamed *Tolcarne Inn* has outdoor tables by the beach behind the art gallery, and serves inexpensive meals. The local fishing folk tend to congregate in the simple, stripped-down *Swordfish* on the harbourfront, or the *Star Inn* two doors along, both of which can get quite boisterous after the boats have come in.

Newlyn doesn't have a great choice of **accommodation**, but *Harbour Heights*, on Boase Road, leading off the harbourside Fore Street, provides simple B&B in modern and light rooms (☎01736/350976; ①).

Mousehole and Paul

Accounts vary as to the derivation of the name of **MOUSEHOLE** (pronounced "Mowzle"), three miles south of Penzance. Originally the village was named Porth Enys ("port of the island"), a reference to St Clement's Isle, a low, bare reef that faces the village a few hundred metres offshore, while its present name may have been taken from a smugglers' cave just south of town. In any case, it perfectly encapsulates the village's minuscule round harbour cradled in the arms of a granite breakwater and encircled by a compact huddle of cottages. As the village attracts more visitors than it can handle, you'd do well to avoid the peak holiday periods to explore its tight tangle of lanes, where many of the neat whitewashed or granite-grey cottages are draped with jasmine, fuschia and even cacti. Most are rented out as holiday homes in summer, giving the place rather an artificial air, though at least there is little modern development and no motor traffic.

If you're driving into Mousehole, it's best to park on the roadside before entering the village to the north; steps here lead down to a concrete path by the water which takes you directly into the village.

A stroll through Mousehole will soon bring you to Keigwin Place, just up from the harbour, and site of Mousehole's oldest house, the porched **Keigwin House** (closed to visitors). Dating from the fourteenth century, it survived the famous raid on 23 July, 1595, when 400 Spanish arquebusiers and pikemen landed in the village and set about the local inhabitants, slaying Squire Jenkyn Keigwin but sparing his house. The rest of the village and the church in nearby Paul were torched, however.

Further diversion can be had poking around the rocky foreshore north of the harbour, where there are good views across the bay to St Michael's Mount. Half a mile inland, at the top of steep Mousehole

Hill, the churchyard wall at **PAUL** holds a memorial to Dolly Pentreath, a Mousehole resident who died in 1777 – reputedly aged 102 – and is said to have been the last person to speak solely in Cornish. Whether this is true or not, the tablet has become a shrine to the death of the language, and the inscription includes a Cornish translation of a verse from the Bible.

Right on Mousehole's harbourfront, the *Ship Inn* provides a welcome refreshment stop – ales, sandwiches and other bar snacks as well as full meals in its **restaurant** (moderate). If the *Ship* is heaving, try *Lewis's Fish and Chips*, just around the corner, or the *Cornish Range*, a good fish restaurant at 6 Chapel St (☎01736/731488; closed daytime and Nov, Feb & March Mon–Wed) with a smart Mediterranean feel. Lemon sole and Newlyn crab salad feature on the menu, and cocktails are available by the glass or pitcher in summer. On Old Quay Street, the *Old Pilchard Press* is a tearoom for daytime snacks and Cornish ice creams.

Mousehole has a few **accommodation** possibilities, but you'll need to book well ahead in the summer months. Best options are the neat and tiny *White Cottage* near the harbour at 10 Fore St (☎01736/731462; no credit cards; ①), or, further up, *Trewill* at 20 Chapel St (☎01736/731067; no credit cards; ①), another diminutive granite cottage with two doubles. The *Ship* also has some cramped rooms (☎01736/731234; no credit cards; ③) – those with a view cost slightly more.

The Penwith peninsula

Buses #6A and #6B connect Mousehole with Penzance at least twice hourly.

Christmas and New Year are the best times to be in Mousehole, when the Christmas illuminations are a local crowd-puller.

Lamorna Cove and around

Four miles southwest of Mousehole, **Lamorna Cove** is squeezed between granite headlands, accessible along a deeply-wooded lane from the comfortable old *Lamorna Wink* pub – as the sign shows, it was the wink that signified that contraband spirits were available. Placid and unspoiled, the cove has a small crescent of sand that's covered at high tide, and is sheltered by a sturdy pier and backed by a disused granite quarry gouged out of the rock. The spot makes a nice starting point for exploring the coastpath: following it westwards takes you round Boscawen Point to **St Loy's Cove**, a couple of miles' hike, where *Cove Cottage* serves up teas, delicious cakes or savoury snacks, and also has one large double **room** upstairs (☎01736/810010; ④), with a fabulous panorama. There are numerous **campsites** on the coastal B3315, which runs parallel to the path, among which *Treverven*, a couple of miles south of Lamorna Cove (☎01736/810200; closed Oct–Easter), makes a good choice, with a grassy open field for pitches and lofty sea views.

If you're following the B3315, it's easy to drop in on the signposted **Merry Maidens**, a ring of nineteen stones in an open field about a mile west of the road junction for Lamorna – there's a small lay-by for parking. The rough-hewn circle is said to be all that remains of a group of local women turned to stone as a punishment for dancing on

Sunday. Half a mile to the north, in a field on the other side of the road, the **Pipers** are two tall upright stones supposedly representing the musicians petrified by the same spell. Other than the likelihood that the ring and uprights date from some time between 2400 and 800 BC, nothing is known about their origin or significance though they were probably the focus of some ceremonial function.

Porthcurno and around

Five miles west of Lamorna, **PORTHCURNO** lies in one of the peninsula's loveliest stretches of coast, a succession of picturesque coves and generous sand beaches against a jagged granite backdrop. The scattered hamlet lies around – but mostly out of sight of – the most popular of the beaches, **Porthcurno Beach**, protected by high cliff walls and reachable along a path from the village car park. On the western side of the beach, just along from the date 1812 carved into the granite by an unknown hand, lies a beach-house built by local benefactress Rowena Cade for her nieces and nephews, artfully sandwiched within a fissure in the rock and now sadly cemented up. Cade was the founder of Porthcurno's famous **Minack Theatre**, situated at the top of the cliff, 200ft above the sea, and reached by steep steps from the beach. Originating as a venue for amateur plays put on by Cade's friends and family, the theatre staged its first production (*The Tempest*) in 1932, and subsequently expanded as its fame spread – it now holds 750 seats, though the basic Greek-inspired design remains intact. The spectacular backdrop of Porthcurno Bay makes this one of the country's most inspiring theatres and productions are frequently sold out during the seventeen-week season, lasting from May to September, when an eclectic range of plays, opera and musicals are produced (see box below). The weather can be cold and blowy but cancellations are rare. If you can't make it to a performance, you can at least nose around the site and follow the story of the theatre's creation at the **Exhibition Centre** (daily: April–Sept 9.30am–5.30pm; Oct–March 10am–4pm; closed during matinée performances, currently May–Sept Wed & Fri at 2pm; £2.50).

You can reach more fine beaches along the coast path from here, your steps accompanied to the west by the moaning of the whistling

---

Performances at the Minack

Tickets for shows at the Minack Theatre for afternoon (2pm) or evening (8pm) performances cost £6.50 for the main auditorium or £5.50 for upper-terrace seating. You can book in person at the box office (Mon–Fri 9.30am–8pm, Sat & Sun 9.30am–5.30pm), by phone (same hours; ☎01736/810181) or on the Web site (*www.minack.com*). Cushions can be hired and macs bought on site. Programmes are usually available in local tourist offices or on the Web site, which also gives an informative history of the venue.

---

buoy at the Runnel Stone a mile offshore. The path runs westwards to **Porthchapel**, a wedge of smooth, clean sand, and beyond to a much narrower cleft in the cliffs at **Porthgwarra**, where a tunnel has been bored through a huge boulder to the rocky shore. East of Porthcurno, the coast path skirts the beach of **Pednevounder**, a steep climb down and traditionally popular with nudists, but now equally frequented by the clothed. The Iron Age fort of **Treryn Dinas** once occupied the headland on the eastern prong of Porthcurno Bay, though nothing remains today beyond the earthworks comprising a ditch and bank. The most interesting feature here lies above it and a few steps back on top of a cluster of granite slabs: the rounded square of **Logan's Rock**, a seventy-tonne monster that for centuries rocked – reputedly at the merest touch – until it was knocked off its perch by a nephew of playwright Oliver Goldsmith and a gang of sailors in 1824. In the outcry that followed, they somehow replaced the boulder, but it rocked no more. Beyond Treryn Dinas, the coast path sweeps down to more sandy beaches near the cluster of cottages and a handful of fishing vessels at **Penberth Cove**, where the National Trust has restored the heavy wooden capstan once used to haul boats up the slipway.

Halfway between Porthcurno and Logan's Rock, a white pyramid adjacent to the coast path marks the spot where an undersea telegraph cable was landed in 1870, recalling Porthcurno's important role as a terminus for a network of cables which reached across the world. The history of the telegraphy station, including the serious competition it faced from Marconi's innovations in "wireless" transmissions, is related in the **Museum of Submarine Telegraphy** (April–Oct daily 10am–5pm, last admission 4pm; £3.50), housed in a World War II communications bunker just up from Porthcurno Beach, behind the car park. Brass and mahogany instruments and etchings give a vivid sense of the pioneering work undertaken by the marine engineers and the problems they faced with cables getting broken or snagged – a memorable photo from 1947 shows a fisherman looking in dismay and bewilderment at a tangle of trawl gear entwined with cable. Most cables today are buried under the seabed; a model of one of the submersible vehicles used for putting them in place is also on show.

Practicalities

Buses #1, #1B and #4 stop at Porthcurno on their run between Penzance and Land's End. **Refreshments** can be found nearby on the road climbing above the beach from the car park, either at the *Porthcurno Beach Café* or the *Mariner's Lodge*, which has a formal restaurant and tables outside. The *Cable Station Inn* is more casual, with a veranda, a pool table, table tennis and darts. The *Mariner's Lodge* also provides modern **accommodation** (☎01736/810236; ②); the best rooms have a balcony and ocean views, but they cost more.

The Penwith peninsula

A passport ticket which allows access to Trevithick Trust properties – including Museum of Submarine Telegraphy (see this page), Pendeen Lighthouse (p.233); Levant Beam Engine (p.234); Geevor Tin Mine (see p.233); and Trevithick Cottage (near Camborne) – is available for £10 at any of these attractions.

The Web site of the Museum of Submarine Telegraphy, www.porthcurno.org.uk, gives a guided tour of the museum and also provides useful maps of Porthcurno and the coast around.

Land's End and Whitesand Bay

Four miles west of Porthcurno, **Land's End** can be reached via **buses #1, #1A** and (Sun in summer only) **#10A** from Penzance, or **#15** (Sun in summer only) from St Ives. Unarguably, however, the best way to approach England's extreme western tip is on foot via the coastal path. Although it would be hard to efface the potency of this majestic headland, the amusements complex that dominates the land approach comes close to irreparably violating the spirit of the place. Once past it, however, you can relax: turf-covered cliffs sixty feet high provide a platform to view the Irish Lady, the Armed Knight, Dr Syntax Head and the other wind-eroded outcrops dotted around, beyond which you can spot the Longships lighthouse, a mile and a half out to sea, and sometimes the Wolf Rock lighthouse, nine miles southwest (flashing every fifteen seconds), or even the dim outline of the Isles of Scilly, 28 miles away. From the point or the coast path on either side, look out too for the area's richly diverse **wildlife**, from busy fulmars and herring gulls, to Atlantic grey seals "cottling" out to sea – drifting, as though asleep, with just their heads above the water. In early September, colonies of seals haul themselves out of the water to breed on the rocks below Longships lighthouse. Other regular passengers on the fast currents include dolphins, porpoises and basking sharks, for which a pair of binoculars would be useful.

*One good way
to enjoy the
coast around
Land's End is
on horseback:
contact Land's
End Riding
School at
Trevescan
Farm, 200m
from the
Land's End–
Porthcurno
junction on
the B3315,
opposite the
Glass Gallery.
(April–Sept
only;* ☎*01736/
871989).*

You'll almost always have to share the point with crowds of other visitors, often queuing for the traditional Land's End souvenir: a photo taken next to a signpost showing distances to New York (3147 miles), John O'Groats (874 miles) and the hometown of their choice. It's harmless, unobtrusive fun, unlike the trivializing **Land's End Experience** (daily from 10am; closing times vary – call ☎0870/458 0099; free entry, but parking costs £3), which substitutes a panoply of lasers and unconvincing sound effects for the real open-air experience. If you have kids in tow, you might be swayed to sample the exhibitions and amusements, most of which cost around £2.50; you can also buy an all-inclusive ticket for £9. One exhibition is dedicated to the **"end-to-enders"** – those who have walked, ridden or driven from Land's End to John O'Groats (or vice versa) – showing some of the various means of transport used, for example a motorized bar stool and a powered supermarket trolley. If you opt for one of the sound-and-light shows, the best is probably the Legendary Last Labyrinth, "an exciting multi-sensory experience" which somehow blends the stories of smugglers, wreckers and King Arthur. In August, many come here for the **fireworks displays** that take place on Tuesdays and Thursdays around 9.30pm.

Just behind the point, the *First and Last House* has unremarkable light **refreshments**, but if you want a full meal, the only option is *Longships Restaurant*, part of the *Land's End Hotel*, which has tables outside overlooking the sea and in a conservatory. You might even be tempted to stay in the fancily furnished rooms at the **hotel** itself (☎01736/871844; ⑥); though not all have sea views. The nearest **campsite**, *Sea View* (☎01736/871266), is just a ten-minute walk away, almost opposite the *Wrecker's Inn* on the B3315; there's a shower block and a heated outdoor pool.

A mile and a quarter north of Land's End, the rounded granite cliffs fall away at **Whitesand Bay** to reveal a glistening mile-long shelf of sand, the only substantial beach at this end of the peninsula, and one of the largest in west Cornwall. The rollers here make for good surfing, and boards can be rented and lessons arranged at the more popular southern end of the beach, **Sennen Cove**, where Sennen Surfing Centre, occupying a kiosk in summer, can arrange two–three-hour lessons or longer **surfing** courses, with all equipment provided (☎01736/871458). Alternatively, just hire the wet suit and board from the Surf Hire Shop at the *Beach Café* (each about £5 for a full day, or £4 for the afternoon only, with £10 deposit).

The adjacent esplanade holds some snack bars and a popular **pub**, the *Old Success Inn*, which is also just about the only place around to get anything more than a bag of chips to eat. You can get excellent seafood, meat and veggie dishes in the **restaurant** (moderate) or munch bar snacks. If you want to stay in Sennen, there are a pair of cosy **B&Bs** tucked away on Old Coastguard Row at the southern end of the Strand and right on the coast path: *Myrtle Cottage* (☎01736/871698; no credit cards; ②), which also has a fine café open to nonresidents, and *Polwyn Cottage* (☎01736/871349; no credit cards; ①), offering two rooms with private bathrooms. If only for the stupendous views over the bay, the *Sennen Cove Hotel* (☎01736/871275; ③) makes a good choice, visible on a height from the Strand, and accessible by a path from Coastguard Row or by road from Cove Hill along Maria's Lane. Finally, if you don't mind being a few minutes' walk inland (and uphill), there's a fine backpackers' **hostel** located on the A30 above the cove: *Whitesands Lodge* ☎01736/871776), which offers dormitory accommodation (£10) and single, twin or family rooms (①). You can cook here, and there's a relaxed café/restaurant (also open to nonresidents), as well as a library, studio workspace, and access to bike rental and land and sea tours, making this a viable base for the whole area.

St Just-in-Penwith and Cape Cornwall

Three miles north of Whitesand Bay and half a mile inland from the sea, **ST JUST-IN-PENWITH** is the biggest centre at the peninsula's western end. Formerly a close-knit mining community serving the local tin and copper industry, its rows of trim grey cottages radiate out from the central Market and Bank Squares. It's not a particularly attractive village today, though it gets quite lively in summer with visitors drawn to its limited range of shops, pubs, restaurants and B&Bs. Just off the square, behind the clock tower, **Plain-an-Gwarry**,

You can get a gull's-eye perspective of Land's End and the surrounding area on scenic flights from Land's End airport, midway between Land's End and St Just on the B3306. Ten minutes costs about £20 per adult (minimum two people). Call ☎01736/ 788771 to book.

The Penwith peninsula

or "playing place", is a grassy open-air theatre that was once a venue for old Cornish miracle plays and was later used by Methodist preachers as well as local wrestlers. These days, the occasional concert or play is staged here – the only entertainment you'll find in St Just outside the trio of pubs on Market Square.

There could be no greater contrast to the prosaic tenor of St Just than the dramatic coastline two miles west at **Cape Cornwall**, for which the village is the main access point (from Cape Cornwall Rd, off Bank Square). For years this headland – topped by the stack of the Cape Cornwall Mine (closed in 1870) – was thought to be England's westernmost point, until more accurate means of measurement decided the contest in favour of Land's End. In many ways, though, Cape Cornwall is the more stirring of the two promontories: there are no towering outcrops or lighthouses to look out onto, but neither are there cafés, entertainments or car parks to distract from the vista. Sheltered by the cape, the cove has a few boats hauled up and a foreshore with plenty of rock-pools to explore, though there's no beach to speak of. Southward, the coast path takes in some spectacular cliff scenery on its route to Land's End, while northward towards Pendeen, away from the crowds, it passes close to one of Cornwall's most dramatic engine houses at **Botallack**, just yards from the shore.

Of St Just's rather plain B&B **accommodation**, try the friendly *Swan Cottage* at 29 Cape Cornwall Rd (☎01736/788246; no credit cards; ①), or the *Star Inn* pub on Market Square, offering simple rooms furnished in antique style (☎01736/788767; no credit cards; ②). Alternatively, the *Wellington Hotel* (☎01736/787319; ②), has fully-equipped rooms which can be linked to form a larger suite. There is better choice a short distance outside the village: the *Boscean Country Hotel* (☎01736/788748; ②) on the Cape Cornwall road has a generous garden, oak-panelled public rooms and log fires. There's also a **youth hostel** less than a mile south (☎01736/788437; closed Nov–Feb), with dorm beds for £10; take the left fork past the post office and follow the track at the bottom of the road – it's conveniently close to the coast path. Drivers should take the B3306 Land's End road, turning right at the hamlet of Kelynack a couple of miles south of St Just. Just north of Kelynack, a side road leads to an excellent secluded **campsite**, *Kelynack Caravan and Camping Park* (☎01736/787633), one of the few genuinely sheltered sites on Penwith, which also has bunks in small and clean dorms (£7; bed linen not provided).

You don't need to travel out of St Just for **eating and drinking**. The traditional *Star Inn* is the most congenial of the pubs, describing itself as "stress-free" (children, mobile phones, cameras and dogs off leads are all banned) and serving mead, farm cider and cheap snacks which you can eat in the yard. The *Wellington Hotel* has a separate upstairs restaurant serving simple meals. For lunches and

For bike rental in St Just, ask at the Commercial Hotel *on Market Square or call* ☎01736/788455.

inexpensive dinners, step into *Kegen Teg* at 12 Market Square (closed Sun evening), which offers fish pie, rich chocolate cake and glorious Kelly's ice creams. Alternatively, *St Just Tea Rooms* at 3 Cape Cornwall Rd has filling teas, snacks and full meals (closed Sun evening and Nov–March; no credit cards).

Pendeen and around

A couple of miles north of St Just, two ruined engine houses guard the approach to **PENDEEN**, an unexceptional ex-mining village which has some appealing excursions within an easy radius. The nearest is to see an example of a **fogou**, or prehistoric underground chamber, in nearby farmland; to get there, take the narrow lane to the right of Boscaswell Stores, signposted for the Lighthouse, and then take the signposted right turn for *Pendeen Manor Farm*, where you can ask to view the chamber which is reached across a muddy byre. A torch is useful: the steep entrance leads down to a stone tunnel which bends sharply left after a few yards, and there is a further stretch accessible only on hands and knees. Though the fogou's function is unknown, it suggests the presence of an Iron Age village, possibly on the site of the farm. *Manor Farm* also provides snacks and **cream teas**, and makes a good stopover for B&B **accommodation** (☎01736/788753; no credit cards; ①).

Past the turn-off for *Manor Farm*, the lighthouse road meets the sea at the slate promontory of **Pendeen Watch**. Poised on the edge of this grassy knoll, **Pendeen Lighthouse** – a squat, green-and-cream tower in service since 1900 – affords superb views over the craggy coast and of the derelict engine houses dotted around the surrounding hills. You can **tour** the lighthouse (Easter–Sept daily except Sat 10am–5pm; tours every half-hour 10.15am–4.15pm; £2), which has the last working twelve-inch fog siren in the country – be warned that this can sound without warning, a potentially traumatic experience. The headland also gives access to the lovely rocky **Portheras Cove**, a ten-minute walk east, where you'll find an excellent sandy beach, though there are signs warning of metal fragments from a dynamited shipwreck.

Geevor Mine and the Levant engine

Just south of Pendeen on the St Just road, **Geevor Tin Mine** (April–Oct Mon–Fri & Sun 10am–5pm; Nov–March Mon–Fri 10am–4pm; £5.50) was the area's last working mine, ceasing operations in 1990. Since then, the building has been restored and opened up to visitors to allow a fascinating close-up view of the Cornish mining industry. You can wander at will among the surface machinery and through the vast mill where 98 percent of the valueless rock was separated from the tin ore, but the most thrilling part is the guided tour of an adit, or horizontal passage running into the rock (the main underground area is now flooded to sea level). Here, the hellish working conditions of a tin miner are graphically described by the knowledgeable guides, and you can peer down into the murky depths of vertical shafts, or up them to the sky. A small **museum**, the only part of the site open to visitors in winter (when tickets are £2), shows a model of the mine and explains the complex process of tin production. You might finish up in the on-site café which affords distant views of the coast west, as far as the engine house of the Levant Mine, closed since 1930 when its workings were absorbed within the Geevor mine. Perched on the cliff edge, the brick buildings now hold the **Levant Beam Engine** (Nov–March Fri 11am–5pm; April–May & Oct Tues & Fri 11am–5pm; June Wed–Fri & Sun 11am–5pm; July–Sept Sun–Fri 11am–5pm; £3), Cornwall's oldest beam engine now restored and functioning, as well as a small exhibition. Already locally famous for the number of its "cappens" (captains, or foremen) and for its use of pit ponies – rare in Cornwall – Levant was the scene of a major **disaster** in 1919, when the beam holding the "man-engine", or mechanical lift, broke away from its upper coupling, resulting in the deaths of 31 men and serious injuries to many others. If you don't want to hike it from Geevor, the site can be reached on Levant Road, which branches off the St Just road at the *Trewellard Arms Hotel.*

East of Pendeen: prehistoric remains

East of Pendeen, the landscape of granite and hilly moorland is an apt setting for the cluster of enigmatic relics of Cornwall's prehistory scattered about here. The nearest lies off the B3318 Penzance road, where, after less than a mile from the village, a lay-by on the left marks the start of a track that winds onto the moor and to **Chun Quoit**, one of the most dramatic of Penwith's quoits – granite rocks arranged into what may have been burial chambers, whose outer covering of earth has washed away over the centuries. Chun resembles a giant mushroom from afar, the giant "capstone" poised precariously on four upright slabs, together enclosing a chamber within which bones of ancestors may have been laid.

Equally compelling remains of Penwith's past inhabitants can be reached along a path that threads about a quarter of a mile eastwards from Chun Quoit to the top of a hill, where a rubble of rocks and two upright stones marking a gateway are all that's left of the Iron Age **Chun Castle**. At this ancient hillfort, archeologists have found traces of slag in smelting pits, suggesting that tin mining existed here at least 2000 years ago. From Chun Castle, a track leads southeast and downhill to a farm, from where a lane leads northeast for less than a mile to meet the minor Morvah–Madron road (which drivers can access from the coastal B3306, taking a right turn for Madron and Penzance just past the village of Morvah). Almost opposite the lane from Chun Castle, and a mile from Morvah, a signposted track wanders northeast for just under a mile to where a marked path to the right goes through fields to **Men-an-Tol**, or "stone of the hole". Also called the "Devil's Eye", this rock hoop in open moorland – probably the remains of a neolithic tomb – suggests nothing so much as a giant doughnut. Similar "hole stones" have been found elsewhere as entrances to burial chambers, and in the Middle Ages this one was thought to have great healing powers: people crawled through the hole to rid themselves of rheumatism, spine troubles or ague, while children with scrofula or rickets were passed three times through it before being dragged round it through the grass. Further up the track from the Morvah–Madron road, another five-minutes' walk brings you to **Men Scryfa**, a standing stone with a Latin inscription commemorating "Rialobran, the son of Cunoval" – probably a reference to a sixth-century Celtic chieftain.

Another mile or so down the Morvah–Madron road, and less than two miles northwest of Madron, **Lanyon Quoit** is more easily visited, its roadside location partly accounting for its status as best known of Cornwall's quoits. Its local name of "Giant's Table" is a plain reference to its form – a broad top slab balanced on three upright stones. The quoit has not survived intact over time however: in 1815 a storm caused the structure to collapse, and it was re-erected nine years later with only three of the four original supports. Consequently it is not so high as it once was, though it still makes an arresting sight in the midst of the moor.

Zennor

Back on the coastal B3306, the road snakes eastward from Morvah, bringing you after five or so miles to **ZENNOR**, an ancient village known by *literati* for its associations with **D.H. Lawrence** (see box, overleaf). The village retains no trace of Lawrence's presence today, though you might invoke his memory in the *Tinners Arms* – which lent him the title of a short story which A.L. Rowse grudgingly conceded to be "more true to Cornish life than most other things written about us by foreigners" – or at Higher Tregerthen, where he lived, reachable in about fifteen minutes via the path that runs toward St Ives from behind Zennor's church.

At the bottom of the village, next to the old Methodist chapel, the **Wayside Museum** (mid-April to Sept daily 10am–6pm; Oct Mon–Fri & Sun 11am–5pm; £2.20) is dedicated to Cornish life from prehistoric times. It's a densely packed and eclectic compendium of over 5000 items crammed into fifteen rooms, where you can rummage to your heart's content among the painstakingly labelled exhibits, many of which were found under hedges and in fields. Ancient tools used by carpenters, wheelwrights, plumbers and cobblers are displayed alongside primitive agricultural threshing machinery, ploughs and sheep-shearers, and there are granite pounders and mortars for crushing seed and corn which date from around 3000 BC. You'll also see a reconstruction of a traditional parlour and kitchen, with thick

D.H. Lawrence in Zennor

Seeking escape from the London literary scene as well as inspiration from the "fine thin air which nobody and nothing pollutes", D.H. Lawrence came to live in Cornwall in December 1915, and moved to Zennor the following March. Installed with his wife **Frieda** at Higher Tregerthen, one of a group of cottages about a mile east of the village, he was evidently smitten by the place, describing it in a letter to **John Middleton Murry** and **Katherine Mansfield** in March 1916 as "a tiny granite village nestling under high shaggy moor hills, and a big sweep of lovely sea, lovelier even than the Mediterranean . . . It is all gorse now, flickering with flowers, and then it will be the heather; and then, hundreds of fox gloves. It is the best place I have been in, I think." The following month Murry and Mansfield came to join the Lawrences in what Lawrence envisaged as a writers' community to be called **Rananim**. The experiment was unsuccessful, however; alienated by Lawrence and Frieda's violent quarrels and by Lawrence's evident disapproval of the newcomers' own relationship, Murry and Mansfield left after two months for a more sheltered spot near Falmouth. Lawrence stayed on to write *Women in Love*, spending a year and a half in Zennor in all, though his enthusiasm for the place was gradually eroded by the hostility of the local constabulary and the residents, who took a dim view of the couple's unorthodox lifestyle not to mention Frieda's German associations (her cousin was air ace Baron von Richtofen, the "Red Baron"). In October 1917, after police had ransacked their cottage, the Lawrences were brusquely given notice to quit. His Cornish experiences were later described in *Kangaroo*, while Murry and Mansfield were peeved to find themselves characterized as Gudrun and Gerald in *Women in Love*, with the Lawrences themselves re-created as Birkin and Ursula.

stone walls and a very low doorway to keep out the wind, while, on a very different note, cuttings and photos give the background to Zennor's various literary connections. On your way out, look for the "plague stone" just outside the building – its bowl was filled with vinegar for disinfecting visiting merchants' money during cholera outbreaks in the nineteenth century.

Above the museum, the simple granite **St Senara** has a barrel-vaulted roof typical of many of Penwith's churches, but its most famous feature is the **Mermaid Chair**, made from two sixteenth-century bench-ends carved with an image of a mermaid holding a mirror and a comb. The carving relates to a local legend according to which a mermaid was so entranced by the singing of a chorister in the church choir that she lured him down to the sea, from which he never returned – though his singing can still occasionally be heard. On the left of the church doorway, a plaque commemorates the memory of John Davey of Boswednack, supposed to be the last person to possess any knowledge of the Cornish language when he died in 1891.

Behind the *Tinners Arms*, next to the church, a fairly level path leads less than a mile northwest to the sea at **Zennor Head**, where there is some awe-inspiring cliff scenery above the sandy **Pendour Cove** (the fabled home of Zennor's mermaid). In the other direction, above Higher Tregerthen and just off the St Ives road, a path leads south behind the Eagle's Nest – for many years the home of St Ives painter Patrick Heron – to **Zennor Quoit**, a chambered tomb with one of the widest roof slabs of all Cornwall's quoits. Thought to be some 4500 years old, it's also a rare example of a quoit with two central chambers.

Practicalities

For a **drink**, the homely *Tinners Arms*, though somewhat spoiled by a fake fire in the traditional hearth, serves pub snacks and has a garden. Alternatively, take a **meal** at the *Old Chapel*, a hostel in the former Wesleyan chapel next to the Wayside Museum, where pizzas, baguettes and scrumptious cakes are available from the ground-floor café. If you don't mind sleeping up to six to a room, the hostel makes a fun place to **stay** (☎01736/798307; no credit cards); it's a modern conversion, with bunk-beds at £10; you can also book a room sleeping four for £30. Otherwise, you'll have to venture outside the village to the simple but comfy rooms at friendly *Trewey Farm* (☎01736/798307; no credit cards; ①), on the St Just–St Ives road right by the turn-off to Zennor; on the brow of the hill behind the farm, remote *Tregeraint House* (☎01736/797061; no credit cards; ①) offers clifftop views from two of its rooms, and the owners can provide transport to guests. Smoking is not allowed, nor are young children.

St Ives

East of Zennor, the road runs four hilly miles to the steeply built town of **ST IVES**, which has smoothly undergone the transition to holiday haunt from its previous role as a centre of the fishing industry. So productive were the offshore waters that a record sixteen and a half million fish were caught in one net on a single day in 1868, and the diarist Francis Kilvert was told by the local vicar that the smell was sometimes so great as to stop the church clock. Virginia Woolf, who spent every summer here to the age of twelve, described St Ives as "a windy, noisy, fishy, vociferous, narrow-streeted town; the colour of a mussel or a limpet; like a bunch of rough shell fish clustered on a grey wall together". By the time the pilchard reserves dried up in the early 1900s, St Ives was beginning to attract a vibrant **artists' colony**, precursors of the wave later headed by Ben Nicholson, Barbara Hepworth, Naum Gabo and the potter Bernard Leach, who in the 1960s were followed by a third wave including Terry Frost, Peter Lanyon and Patrick Heron.

St Ives' dual artistic and fishing legacies are continued today in the numerous **galleries** jammed into its narrow alleys, and in the daily landing of **fishing** catches on Smeaton's Pier. The town has little in common with the rest of the Penwith peninsula, its broad sand beaches, higgledy-piggledy flower-bedecked lanes (bearing such

From St Ives, bus #15 runs along Penwith's north coast to Zennor, Geevor and Land's End, providing useful pick-up points for coastal walkers. In summer, some services are open-top.

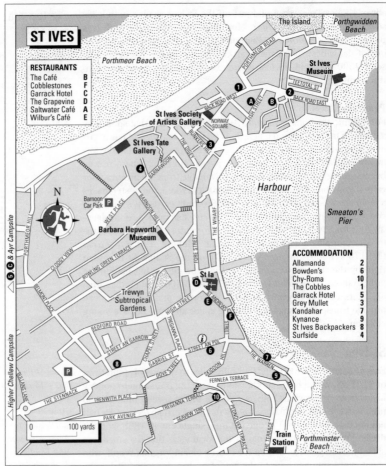

ST IVES

Porthmeor Beach

The Island

Porthgwidden Beach

St Ives Museum

TEETOTAL ST

BACK ROAD EAST

RESTAURANTS

The Café	B
Cobblestones	F
Garrack Hotel	C
The Grapevine	D
Saltwater Café	A
Wilbur's Café	E

St Ives Society of Artists Gallery

NORWAY SQUARE

St Ives Tate Gallery

Harbour

Smeaton's Pier

Barnoon Car Park

WEST PLACE

Barbara Hepworth Museum

THE WHARF

FORE STREET

ACCOMMODATION

Allamanda	2
Bowden's	6
Chy-Roma	10
The Cobbles	1
Garrack Hotel	5
Grey Mullet	3
Kandahar	7
Kynance	9
St Ives Backpackers	8
Surfside	4

St Ia

Trewyn Subtropical Gardens

HIGH STREET

THE WARREN

TRENWITH PLACE

TREGENNA TERRACE

SEAVIEW TERR

PARK AVENUE

Train Station

Porthminster Beach

0   100 yards

© Crown copyright

melodious names as Teetotal Street and Salubrious Place), and the modernistic architecture of the Tate putting it into an altogether different category from the grim granite villages and jagged cliffs that characterize most of west Cornwall. It also receives most of the tourism, but however inundated it gets, St Ives still repays a visit, and its range of accommodation makes it a great base for excursions to the rest of the peninsula.

Arrival, information and accommodation

To reach St Ives by **train**, change at St Erth on the main London–Penzance line, or take a direct service from Penzance. St Ives' train station lies at the eastern end of town, behind Porthminster

Beach, and most **buses** stop just up from here on Station Hill. Buses #16, #17, #17A, #17B and #17C connect St Ives with Penzance, while the town can be reached from Truro by National Express services. The **tourist office** is a few minutes' walk away from Station Hill on the narrow Street an Pol (July & Aug Mon–Sat 9.30am–6pm, Sun 10am–1pm; Sept Mon–Sat 9.30am–5.30pm; Oct to mid-May Mon–Thurs 9.30am–5.30pm, Fri 9.30am–5pm; mid-May to June Mon–Sat 9.30am–5.30pm, Sun 10am–1pm; ☎01736/796297). **Accommodation** is scattered throughout the town, with the most central places generally the most cramped.

The Penwith peninsula

Hotels and B&Bs

Allamanda, 83 Back Rd East ☎01736/793548; *www.allamanda.co.uk*. Classy Georgian conversion in the cobbled heart of St Ives, with two small but elegant en-suite rooms. No smoking, no under-12s and no credit cards. ④.

Bowden's, 4 Trepolpen, Street an Pol ☎01736 796281. Opposite the tourist office, this is a great choice if you're tired of the "fisherman's cottage" style of B&B that rules in these parts, with bold minimalist designs and art on the walls. No credit cards. ②.

Chy-Roma, 2 Seaview Terrace ☎01736/797539; *www.connexions.co.uk/ chyroma*. Convenient for the bus and train stations, harbour views from the three front-facing rooms and a lively Irish proprietor who provides home-made muesli, breads and jams for breakfast. No credit cards. ②.

The Cobbles, 33 Back Rd West ☎01736/798206. Slightly upmarket choice near Porthmeor Beach with lots of art and antique furnishings, gargantuan breakfasts and a relaxed atmosphere. All rooms are en suite. No credit cards. ③.

Garrack Hotel, Burthallan Lane ☎01736/796199; *www.garrack.com*. One of the area's most stylish hotels, outside the town's bustle but within walking distance of Porthmeor Beach. It's family-run with an indoor pool, sauna and top-quality restaurant (see p.243). ⑥.

The Grey Mullet, 2 Bunkers Hill ☎01736/796635. Oak-beamed and drowned in flowers and prints, this eighteenth-century house – claimed to be the oldest in town – is twenty yards from the harbour on a cobbled lane. No credit cards. ②.

Kandahar, 11 The Warren ☎01736/796183; *www.kandahar11.com*. A great choice on the seafront below the bus station, with a range of quite small rooms, some en suite, four with a view. No pets, children under 6 or smoking. Closed late Oct to Easter. ②.

Kynance, 24 The Warren ☎01736/796636; *www.kynance24.co.uk*. From the small patio here you're within 150m of Porthminster Beach and the bus and train stations, where there are some parking spaces. Accommodation is fairly standard, with views of the harbour from the top-floor rooms. No under-7s and no smoking. Closed mid-Nov to early March. ②.

Surfside, Godrevy Terrace ☎01736/793825. Perfect if you want to keep your distance from the hustle of the town's lower lanes, with plain rooms offering great all-round views of St Ives. No credit cards. ②.

Campsites and hostel

Ayr, Higher Ayr ☎01736/795855; *andy@ayrholidaypark.demon.co.uk*. Pleasant campsite half a mile west of the centre, above Porthmeor Beach, affording bird's-eye views over the town. Buses #6B and #15 to Land's End pass close by. Closed Nov–March.

Higher Chellew, Nancledra (☎01736/364532). Good out-of-town alternative to *Ayr*, and much cheaper. Facilities are basic but clean, and include washing machines. Located on the B3311 road, equidistant between St Ives and Penzance.

St Ives Backpackers, Lower Stennack ☎01736/799444; *www.backpackers.co.uk/st-ives*. Usefully located in a Wesleyan chapel school in the centre, this rambling place has lots of dormitories, holding four, six or eight beds for £12 a night. Barbecues and other entertainments are organized in the central courtyard in summer, and there is pool and table football.

The town

You can arrange motor-boat rides from the harbour, starting at £7 for 15min.

Squeezed between no less than four beaches – if you count the sands of the harbour – and steep slopes and headlands, St Ives is a town of picturesque nooks and eye-catching vistas. Threading through its centre, the pedestrianized **Fore Street** is usually a mass of shuffling tourists who spill out onto the wide harbour, where the piercing shrieks of gulls add to the hubbub. Above and at either end of the main drag is a disorienting maze of lanes choc-full with restaurants, bars and galleries.

The galleries

On the north side of town, reached from Back Road West or over Barnoon Hill, Porthmeor Beach is overlooked by the town's greatest cultural asset, the **St Ives Tate Gallery** (Tues–Sun 10.30am–5.30pm, daily in July & Aug; *www.tate.org.uk*; £3.95, combined ticket with Barbara Hepworth Museum £6.50). Anyone expecting something on the same scale as Britain's other Tates may be disappointed by the St Ives collection, which has a much smaller and more local feel, though few would deny the splendour of its beachfront location. The seaside sounds are a constant presence inside the airy white building, creating a lively soundtrack to the paintings, sculptures and ceramics, most of which date from the period 1925 to 1975, and many inspired by St Ives itself. Near the entrance, the tone is set by a massive stained-glass window by **Patrick Heron**, said to be the largest unleaded stained glass in the world, whose great slabs of colour recall the brilliance of the sun, sand and sea outside. Contrastingly, the work of the local naive painter **Alfred Wallis** shows much muter tones, as in his *Houses at St Ives, Cornwall* and *Newlyn Harbour*. Depicting cottages in front of The Island, with the harbour and a glimpse of the open sea with the local fishing fleet, Wallis's *St Ives* was one of the first paintings he sold, bought by Ben Nicholson on his visit to the town in August 1928. The influence of Wallis's diagrammatic designs is apparent in some other work here, for example *Island Sheds* by **Wilhelmina Barns-Graham** and *St Ives from the Cemetery* by **Bryan Pearce**. The interplay between the different generations of artists can also be seen in the painted

Free one-hour tours of the Tate kick off from Patrick Heron's stained-glass window on weekdays at 2.30pm, and on Saturdays and bank holidays at 3pm.

aluminium and wood *Construction* by **Peter Lanyon**, which shows a debt to the constructivist Naum Gabo, who lived in St Ives during World War II. Lanyon's tall, chaotic, partly abstract harbour view, *Porthleven*, in the Lower Gallery is also noteworthy, as is John Wells' *Seabird Forms*, which strikingly depicts the movement and flight patterns of seabirds, in a similar blend of figurative and abstract ideas.

The crescent-shaped **Gallery 2**, which affords views over the beach, has displays of pottery and stoneware by **Bernard Leach** and his school – including Michael Cardew – and **Shoji Hamada**, mostly very simple designs of jugs, cups, plates and bowls. **Barbara Hepworth**'s sculpture *Sea Form (Porthmeor)* is her response to the beach, while her *Menhirs*, carved from a single piece of slate, and *Landscape Sculpture*, a bronze from the late 1950s, take their inspiration from what she called "the pagan landscape" of the Penwith peninsula. As well as this permanent collection, there are constant exhibitions focusing on the St Ives artists and others, usually with a local connection. Finish up your visit at the museum's rooftop **café**, one of the best places in town for tea and cake, with a stupendous panorama.

If your appetite has been whetted by Hepworth's elemental sculpture, the **Barbara Hepworth Museum** (managed by the Tate, and keeping the same hours; £3.75) is an essential stop, a short distance away on Barnoon Hill. One of the foremost nonfigurative sculptors of her time, Hepworth lived in the building from 1949 until her death in a fire here in 1975. Apart from the sculptures, the museum has masses of background on her art, from photos and letters to catalogues and reviews. The clean all-white space is a superb setting for such works as *Infant*, a shiny, alien-looking child sculpted in Burmese wood. In the adjoining garden, a lush area planted with subtropical trees and shrubs, Hepworth herself arranged her stylistically diverse works in striking settings: in one grassy corner, *Conversation with Magic Stones* consists of six irregularly shaped pieces in an intimate huddle, opposite the wildly different *Apollo*, a steel rod fashioned into a geometric shape. At the centre of the garden, the mammoth *Four Square (Walkthrough)* is the most massive work, while *Meridian* is perfectly placed under a tree surrounded by a bush and bracken. Hepworth's famous "wired" pieces, in which the different planes are linked by the threaded string, are also well represented, for example *Spring 1966*. Though the garden attracts plenty of visitors, it remains a tranquil escape from the town's bustling activity. There are a few other Hepworth works dotted around St Ives, including the rather uncharacteristic *Madonna and Child*, a tender work in memory of her son killed during RAF service in 1953, donated to the harbourside church of **St Ia** (open weekdays 10am–4pm and Sun for services), where the High Street meets Fore Street. The steel candlesticks that stand in front of the

The Penwith peninsula

Lasting for about eight days in mid-September, the St Ives Festival features roots music, poetry, theatre and exhibitions. For more information, call ☎01736/ 796888.

For more on
the arts scenes
in Newlyn and
St Ives, see
Contexts,
pp.327-328.

work are also by the sculptress. The church itself is a fifteenth-century building dedicated to a female missionary said to have floated over from Ireland on an ivy leaf.

Most of St Ives' private galleries are small, whose contents can be usually be glimpsed from outside, but most welcome visitors. The **St Ives Society of Artists Gallery** (mid March–Oct daily 10am–4.30pm; 25p) is a much bigger affair, occupying the Old Mariners' Church on Norway Square – as it has done since 1945 when its members included Lamorna Birch, Barbara Hepworth and Ben Nicholson. Following the split with the abstract group in 1947, the gallery has shown chiefly figurative work, much of it of a high quality. In the upstairs Norway Gallery, the members' paintings and sculptures – virtually all on local themes – are constantly replaced by new works, giving a good overview of the group's varying styles, while the Mariners Gallery in the crypt is hired out for private exhibitions (free).

The rest of town

Housed in an old Sailors' Mission at Wheal Dream, between the harbour and Porthgwidden Beach, **St Ives Museum** (Easter–Oct daily 10am–5pm; £1) will appeal to anyone with a magpie curiosity and lots of energy. A wide-ranging trawl through Cornish history, and more particularly of Penwith and St Ives, the densely crowded rooms on two floors throw up such nonessential bric-a-brac as a collection of kettles, a bardic robe, a stuffed turtle that had wandered over to Cornwall from Mexico and a collection of photos including some of the St Ives artists. The sections devoted to the railway in Cornwall, the pilchard industry and of course mining, with a model of the Levant Mine "man-engine" which crashed in 1919 (see p.234), entertainingly fill out the picture. Below the museum, there are views across the bay to Hayle Sands and, directly below, over tiny **Porthgwidden Beach**, a sheltered spot for a quiet paddle on a hot day.

If you need relief from the claustrophobic lanes of St Ives, take a picnic or just a breather in **Trewyn Subtropical Gardens** (open 8am to sunset), a miniature haven furnished with benches, banana trees and wooden sculptures of musicians round the lawns; it's tucked away off Bedford Road, above High Street. For a bit more space, however, you can't do better than a bracing climb up to **The Island**, the undeveloped headland (also known as St Ives Head) which separates the harbour and Porthgwidden Beach from Porthmeor Beach. **St Nicholas Chapel** sits in isolation on this heathy promontory, and there are inspiring views across St Ives Bay. At some point, you'll fetch up on the wide expanse of **Porthmeor Beach**, dominating the northern side of St Ives. Unusually for a town beach, the water quality is excellent, and the rollers make it popular with surfers (boards are available for rent below the Tate); there's also a good open-air café here. South of the train station, **Porthminster Beach**, a long stretch of smooth yellow sand, is another favourite spot for sunbathing and swimming.

Having perused the Tate, devotees of Bernard Leach's Japanese-inspired ceramics can wander to the northern outskirts of town to visit his studio, the **Leach Pottery** (Mon–Sat 10am–5pm; £2.50), in the village of Higher Stennack, three-quarters of a mile outside St Ives on the Zennor road and reachable via buses #16, #17 or #17A. In three exhibition rooms here, Leach's work is showcased alongside that of Shoji Hamada and of former pupils, the various jars and vases almost all made using the high-fired technique introduced by Leach from Japan, and all sharing an emphasis on strong, pure lines. Products of the pottery can also be found in the New Craftsman gallery/shop at 24 Fore St, which has some examples of Leach's work as well as by his wife Janet Leach, Shoji Hamada and Michael Cardew, and other more contemporary artworks are also exhibited here.

Eating and drinking

The huge range of **restaurants** in St Ives takes in Penwith's most sophisticated eateries as well as pizzerias and places serving simple fish and chips and other seaside snacks. Nightlife, however, is limited, and decent **pubs** are few and far between – and often packed: the *Sloop* on the harbourside is usually a good bet for a pint, though, with slate floors and beams, while *Isobar*, listed below, provides a good alternative, with a more up-to-date ambience for its cocktails and lagers.

The Café, Island Square ☎01736/793621. Delicious vegetarian snacks and full evening meals served in a friendly atmosphere. Moderate.

Cobblestones, 5 St Andrews St. Basic English seaside nosh, or just tea and cakes, with few frills and late opening till 10pm in summer (it closes at 5pm in winter). Inexpensive.

Garrack Hotel, Burthallan Lane ☎01736/796199. A bit out of the way, but worth the journey for a slap-up feast. The kitchen excels at fish but meat dishes are also superb, and there are some astounding desserts. Expensive.

The Grapevine, 7 High St ☎01736/794030. This bistro serves breakfasts and lunches and has fresh local fish at night, all in a pleasant woody decor. Highlight dishes might include grey mullet with bacon and cheese or salmon in coconut and coriander. Moderate.

Isobar, Tregenna Place ☎01736/799199; *www.theisobar.com*. Cool bar at the top of Street an Pol serving coffees, chunky ciabattas, salads and seafood. DJs play most evenings downstairs and there's a club upstairs (around £4 entry) open Wed–Sat (but daily except Sun in July and Aug), playing dance music from 1970s onwards. Inexpensive.

Saltwater Café, Fish St ☎01736/794928. Bright, beachy, fishy paintings on the walls and a good choice of seafood, from swordfish to pan-fried scallops wrapped in pancetta. The wild mushroom risotto is also good. Breakfasts, sandwiches and ciabattas are available during the day. Moderate.

Wilbur's Café, St Andrew's St (☎01736/796661). Movie stars on the walls set the tone here, where there's usually a lively atmosphere, with pastas and fish prominent on the menu and a vegetarian option. Moderate.

The Penwith peninsula

The biggest and best pasties in Cornwall are served at Trevaskis Farm, Gwinear Road, *seven miles southeast of St Ives, and a couple of miles south of Hayle in the Connor Downs direction (*☎*01209/713931; closed Mon evening). There's a farm shop attached and inexpensive meals are also served: ring ahead to check for evening opening.*

Listings

Banks The High St holds HSBC, Barclays and Lloyds TSB, while NatWest is nearby on Tregenna Hill; all have cashpoints (ATMs).

Bus information Call ☎01209/719988 for all timetable and route enquiries.

Car hire St Ives Motor Company, Trelyon Ave ☎01736/796695; Parc an Creet, Higher Stennack ☎01736/795442.

Hospital Edward Hain Hospital on Albany Terrace (☎01736/795044) can deal with minor casualties otherwise head for Penzance (see p.221).

Post office The main office is on Tregenna Place, and there's a smaller branch at the end of Fore St, off the seafront near the *Sloop* pub.

Riding Old Mill Stable, Lelant Downs (☎01736/753045); Penhalwyn Trekking Centre, Halsetown (☎01736/796461).

Supermarket The Cooperative on Lower Stennack stays open until 11pm in summer.

Surfing Shore Surf School, 3 Dracaena Ave, Hayle (☎01736/755556), offers half-day "surfaris", or full-day sessions for £30; all equipment is included.

Taxis Ace Cabs ☎01736/797799; DJ's Cabs ☎01736/798103; Cass Cabs ☎01736/799150.

Tours Cambron Tours, 5 Pordenack Close, Carbis Bay (☎01736/796389; *www.cornwall-online.co.uk/cambron-tours*), offers customized full-, half-day and evening tours of the surrounding area for up to five people, as well as weekly town walks around St Ives in season.

Travel details

Trains

Penzance to: Bodmin (1–2 hourly; 1hr 15min); Exeter (1–2 hourly; 3hr); London (9 daily; 5hr 10min–7hr); Plymouth (1–2 hourly; 2hr); St Erth (2 hourly; 12min); St Ives (Mon–Sat 7–8 daily; 20min); Truro (1–2 hourly; 40min).

St Ives to: Penzance (Mon–Sat 6–7 daily; 20min); St Erth (2 hourly; 15min).

Buses

Helston to: Coverack (Mon–Sat hourly, Sun 5 daily; 45min); Falmouth (Mon–Sat 8 daily, Sun 4 daily; 1hr); The Lizard (Mon–Sat hourly, Sun 5 daily; 45min); Mullion (Mon–Sat hourly, Sun 5 daily; 20–30min); Penzance (1–2 hourly; 40–50min).

Penzance to: Helston (1–2 hourly; 40–50min); Land's End (June–Sept hourly, Oct–May Mon–Sat 8 daily; 45–55min); Mousehole (2–5 hourly; 20min); Newquay (1–3 daily; 1hr 30min–2hr 35min); Plymouth (4–5 daily; 3–4hr); St Austell (3 daily; 1hr 30min–2hr 15min); St Ives (2–3 hourly; 40min); Truro (Mon–Sat hourly, Sun 5 daily; 1hr 25min–1hr 45min).

St Ives to: Land's End (June–Sept 1–3 daily; 1hr 30min); Newquay (1–3 daily; 1hr 10min–2hr 15min); Pendeen (Mon–Sat 2–3 daily; 25min); Penzance (2–3 hourly; 35min); Plymouth (3–4 daily; 2hr 30min–3hr); St Austell (1 daily; 1hr 50min); Truro (Mon–Sat 9 daily, Sun 2 daily; 1hr–1hr 45min); Zennor (2–3 daily; 20min).

Chapter 10

The Isles of Scilly

L ying 28 miles southwest of Land's End, the **Isles of Scilly** (the name "Scilly Isles" is strongly disapproved of) are a compact archipelago of 100–150 islands – counts vary according to the definition of an island and the height of the water. None is bigger than three miles across, and only five of them are inhabited. Though they share a largely treeless and low-lying appearance – rarely rising above a hundred feet – the islands nonetheless each have a distinctive character, revealing new perspectives over the extraordinary rocky seascape at every turn.

Free of traffic, theme parks and amusement arcades, The Scillies provide a welcome respite from the mainland tourist trail. The energizing briny air is constantly filled with the cries of seabirds, while the **beaches** are well-nigh irresistible, ranging from minute coves to vast untrammelled strands – though swimmers must steel themselves for the chilly water temperature. Other attractions include Cornwall's greatest concentration of **prehistoric remains**, some fabulous **rock formations**, and masses of **flowers**, nurtured by the equable climate and long hours of sunshine (the archipelago's name means "Sun Isles"). Along with tourism, the main source of income here is flower-growing, and the heaths and pathways of the islands are also dense with a profusion of wild flowers, from marigolds and gorse to sea thrift, trefoil and poppies, not to mention a host of more exotic species introduced by visiting foreign vessels.

ACCOMMODATION PRICE CODES

Throughout this *Guide*, hotel and B&B accommodation is coded on a scale of ① to ⑨, the code indicating the lowest price you can expect to pay per night for a double room in high season. The prices indicated by the codes are as follows:

① under £40	④ £60–70	⑦ £110–150
② £40–50	⑤ £70–90	⑧ £150–200
③ £50–60	⑥ £90–110	⑨ over £200

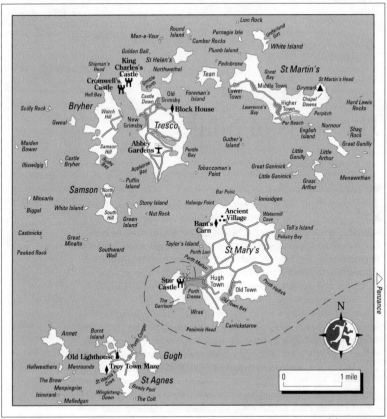

The majority of the resident population of just over 2000 is concentrated on the biggest island, **St Mary's**, which has the lion's share of facilities in its capital, **Hugh Town**. Among the "off islands", as the other inhabited members of the group are known, **Tresco** is the largest, and presents an appealing contrast between the orderly landscape around its abbey – whose subtropical **gardens** are the archipelago's most popular visitor attraction – and the bleak, untended northern half. Three miles northwest of St Mary's, **Bryher** has the smallest population, the slow routines of island life quickening only in the tourist season. The bracing, back-to-nature feel here is nowhere more evident than on the exposed western shore, where **Hell's Bay** sees some formidable Atlantic storms. East of Tresco, **St Martin's** has a reputation as the least striking of the Scillies with the most introverted population, but its beaches are impressively wild and it boasts stunning views from its cliffy northeastern end. On the southwest rim of the main group, the tidy lanes and picturesque cottages of **St Agnes** are nicely complemented by the weathered boulders and craggy headlands of its indented shoreline.

A visit to the isles would be incomplete without a sortie to the **uninhabited islands**, sanctuaries for seals, puffins and a host of other marine birdlife. On the largest of them, **Samson**, you can poke around prehistoric and more recent remains which testify to former settlement. Some of the smaller islets also repay a visit for their delightfully deserted beaches, though the majority amount to no more than bare rocks. This chaotic profusion of rocks of all shapes and sizes, each bearing a name, is densest at the archipelago's extremities – the **Western Rocks**, lashed by ferocious seas and the cause of innumerable wrecks over the years, and the milder **Eastern Isles**.

Although you can get a taste of the islands' highlights on a day-trip from Penzance, the Scillies deserve a much longer sojourn. The chief drawbacks are the high cost of reaching them and the shortage of **accommodation** (advance booking is essential throughout the year). Note that most B&Bs offer – and often insist on – a dinner, bed and breakfast package, and this is anyway usually the most convenient option, considering the tiny choice of places to eat. Many close in winter, but there's usually enough to cater for the trickle of visitors who come in these months. The alternative is a self-catering deal, almost always available by the week, but you'll need to book some time in advance (basic groceries are available on all five inhabited islands, though at higher prices than on the mainland). Apart from Tresco, each island also has one **campsite**, mostly unsheltered with basic facilities; all close during winter, when it would be impractical to pitch a tent in any case – camping elsewhere is not allowed.

A history of the islands

In the annals of folklore, the Scillies are the peaks of the submerged land of Lyonesse, a fertile plain that extended west from Penwith before the ocean broke in, drowning the land and leaving only one survivor to tell the tale. The story may not be complete fantasy, insofar as the isles form part of the same granite mass as Land's End, Bodmin Moor and Dartmoor, and may well have been joined to the mainland in the distant past.

The early human history of the Isles of Scilly is equally obscure. Many have tried to prove that the archipelago was the group of islands referred to in classical sources as the Cassiterides, or "Isles of Tin", where the Phoenicians and Romans obtained their supply of the precious metal – though no trace of tin-mining remains today – while some have also identified the Scillies as the legendary "Isles of the Blest" to which the dead heroes and chieftains of the mainland were conveyed in order to find peace and immortality. This theory is apparently supported by the unusual quantity of **Bronze Age** burial chambers found here, though it is more likely that these were rather

Isles of Scilly

Getting to the islands

Whether you choose to arrive on the islands by sea or air, it's advisable to book in advance – several days ahead if it's high season. **Ferries** to St Mary's are operated by the Isles of Scilly Steamship Company (☎0845/710 5555; *www.islesofscilly-travel.co.uk*) from Penzance's South Pier. Sailings, which can be nauseatingly rough, take place from Monday to Saturday between the second week in April and the end of September, and on Monday, Wednesday, Friday and Saturday between October and mid-November and during the first week of April; there is no service between mid-November and March. Departures are at 9.15am, with returns from St Mary's at 4.30pm or 5pm; journey-time is about two-and-three-quarter hours. Single tickets cost £38, day-returns £32–35, short-break returns (one to three nights) £45–55, and period returns (anything over three nights) £65–74, with discounts for students, families and children. It's worth asking the ticket office about special offers for discounted ferry tickets, sometimes available with vouchers from local newspapers in Cornwall.

Once arrived on the islands, you'll have no difficulty travelling between them, with **inter-island launches** operated by St Mary's Boatmen's Association (☎01720/422541; currently £5.20 return fare) leaving from the quayside for the other islands (the "off islands") soon after the ferry arrives in St Mary's; luggage destined for the off islands should be clearly marked with the name of the island, so that bags can be deposited in the right pile on the dock. Note, however, that there is a much-reduced service in winter and none at all in bad weather – even in summer, the waves can be frighteningly high.

Arriving by **air** is a much more expensive way of reaching the Isles, but quick and memorable, affording a terrific overview of the archipelago and its surrounding litter of rocks (and incidentally revealing how shallow the waters are around here). Fares vary according to whether you opt for a short break (one to three nights) or a period return (over three nights away). The main departure points for Skybus aeroplane flights (also operated by the Isles of Scilly Steamship Company, see above) are Land's End, near St Just (Mon–Sat frequent flights; 15min; £60–98 return), Newquay (Mon–Sat 1–2 daily; 30min; £80–104 return), Plymouth (Mon, Wed & Fri 1 daily; 45min; £110–150 return), Exeter (Mon–Sat 1–3 daily; 50min; £142–196 return) and Bristol (Mon, Tues, Thurs & Fri 1–6 daily; 1hr 10min; £160–220 return). In winter (usually Oct–Easter), there is no service from Bristol, Exeter or Plymouth, and a significantly reduced service from Newquay and Land's End. A free transfer service between the mainline train station and airport is available for all airports except Newquay, which needs a couple of days' advance notification.

Between Monday and Saturday only, British International (☎01736/363871; *www.helicopter-scilly.co.uk*) run **helicopter flights** from the heliport a mile east of Penzance to St Mary's (summer 8–11 daily; winter 1–3 daily) and Tresco (summer 3–5 daily; winter 1–2 daily). Journey time is about twenty minutes, and return fares cost about £95 – though you can buy discounted "Late Saver Returns" the day before departure for a one- to three-night stay (£62), and short-break deals for up to four nights (£69).

the tombs of the first Scillonians, dating from some time between 1900 and 800 BC.

There is evidence of **Roman occupation** from the third and fourth centuries AD, when the isles are thought to have been used as a place of exile for undesirables. Recorded history, however, begins in the twelfth century, when Henry I granted the Scillies to the Benedictine abbey of Tavistock, in Devon, whose monks established a priory in Tresco. Although the **Benedictines** had nominal control for the next 400 years, their rule was always limited by the activities of pirates, and conditions were extremely tough anyway, so that they probably welcomed the opportunity to return to the mainland following the Dissolution in 1539. In 1571, the isles were leased to the **Godolphin family**, a Cornish dynasty which held the archipelago for the crown until 1831, introducing a degree of order and generally improving the lot of the islanders by such measures as dividing the land into manageable plots. They also provided a much-needed protective garrison, though the construction of Star Castle on St Mary's in 1593 was at the behest of Elizabeth I, motivated by the fear of Spanish invasion. The presence of the fort ensured that Hugh Town, rather than Tresco, site of the abbey, should be the islands' capital. It also meant that the islanders were left alone by the pirates, and stability reigned until the eruption of the **Civil War**, when the Scillies upheld the Royalist cause long after the mainland had capitulated to the Parliamentarians. After a brief sojourn by the Prince of Wales (later Charles II) in 1646, the archipelago was occupied by a Roundhead army, whose legacy was Cromwell's Castle in Tresco.

As soon as the Roundheads had departed, the Godolphins resumed their tenure, though their new official responsibilities after the Restoration – a reward for their loyalty to the crown – meant that they were rarely present on the islands. The maladministration and corruption of their local stewards, who demanded high rents while neglecting the plight of the Scillonians, combined with regular crop failure, reduced the local population to a fruitless struggle for subsistence over the next 150 years. Although fishing and piloting continued to be the economic mainstays, the development of agriculture was handicapped by the short leases granted to the tenant farmers, which discouraged any long-term planning. Conditions only improved with the arrival in 1834 of a new proprietor, **Augustus Smith**, a landowner from Hertfordshire who, despite his despotic methods, implemented far-reaching reforms which included the construction of roads, the overhaul of the land-tenure system and the introduction of compulsory education thirty years before it became law on the mainland. Smith's work was continued after his death in 1872 by his nephew Lieutenant Dorrien-Smith, who was mainly responsible for introducing **flower-farming** to the archipelago. This quickly became the economic lifeblood of the community and continues to be of primary importance today, though the advent of

---

Flower-farming in the Scillies

After tourism, **flower-farming** is the most important commercial activity on the isles, introduced towards the end of the nineteenth century by the then-proprietor Augustus Smith and his nephew Lieutenant Dorrien-Smith. The flower farms shape much of the landscape with their narrow fields, or "pieces", intricately divided by tall windbreaks of hardy veronica, pittosporum, euonymus and escallonia, lending a maze-like appearance to some of the inland tracts. Most of the crop consists of various species of narcissi, creating a spectacular effect in March and April when they are in full flower. However, harvesting takes place throughout the winter, just before they flower, when the crop is flown or shipped directly to markets in London and other mainland centres in Britain and abroad.

---

tourism over the last forty years has overtaken it in terms of revenue. The growth of the holiday industry dates chiefly from the 1960s, when the islands were the favourite resort of the then prime minister Harold Wilson. The subsequent demand for second homes and retirement bungalows has transformed the local landscape, most prominently on St Mary's, though development of the off islands has been much less conspicuous, and on most the populations have decreased.

St Mary's

An indented oval with a pair of pincer-like projections from its south-western edge, **ST MARY'S** is the largest of the Isles of Scilly, measuring about three miles across at its widest point. Despite holding the archipelago's highest point, Telegraph Hill, St Mary's is in places as low-lying as its neighbours, with constant fears of flooding in the capital, **Hugh Town**, which straddles the isthmus connecting the island's western limb.

Though pleasant enough, and holding the bulk of the Scillies' accommodation and services, Hugh Town has little to occupy your time once you've exhausted the harbour and museum. The best attractions, which consist of a handful of prehistoric remains and some tempting beaches, are dispersed around the island; all can be reached by easy hikes, and some are accessible by bus.

Arrival, information and getting around

Ferry passengers disembark at the harbour on Hugh Town's sheltered north side, also the departure point for launches to the other islands, while the **airport** lies a mile east of town, connected by regular buses to the centre, whose departures are timed to coincide with plane arrivals. The main drag, Hugh Street, runs between the bus stand at The Parade, at its eastern end, and the harbour.

Hugh Town's **tourist office** is in the Old Wesleyan Chapel on Garrison Lane (Mon–Sat 8.30am–5.30pm; ☎01720/422536,

---

Gig racing in the Scillies

If you're coming to the Isles of Scilly between May and September, try to
time your visit to be here on a Wednesday or Friday evening to witness the
gig races, the most popular sport on the Scillies. Usually performed by
women on Wednesdays, men on Fridays, the races start off from Nut Rock,
to the east of Samson, finishing at St Mary's Quay, and can be followed on
launches. Some of the gigs – six-oared vessels some thirty feet in length –
are over a hundred years old, built originally to carry pilots to passing ships.

---

www.simplyscilly.co.uk), and has information on accommodation, as
well as car rental, walks and other activities in all of the Scillies.

You can easily negotiate the town on foot, and you don't really
need any transport to explore the rest of St Mary's. However, you can
get around the island fast by means of the circular **bus** service leaving from The Parade (mid-March to Oct 7–10 daily; £1), where
there's also a **taxi stand** (contact Scilly Cabs ☎01720/422901). **Car
rental** is another transport option, though an extravagant one (contact Sibley's ☎01720/422431), and in any case, roads do not give
access to the remoter coastal sections, which are only reachable on
foot (off-road biking is not viable).

Hugh Town

Although it can get inundated by ambling tourists in summer,
HUGH TOWN never feels overwhelmed in the way that many mainland towns do, partly on account of the absence of much motor traffic. The twin centres of activity are Hugh Street, lined with shops
and pubs, and the **harbour**, protected by a long pier, where the coming and going of ferries, launches and yachts creates a mood of
quiet industry. As well as the inter-island launches departing from
here, there are daily **boat trips** to view seals and seabirds (excursions to see the puffins run between April and mid-July only): schedules and prices are posted on boards on the quayside and outside
the Isles of Scilly Steamship office, next to Barclays Bank on Hugh
Street.

From The Bank at the western end of Hugh Street, Garrison Hill
climbs up to the high ground west of Hugh Town known as the
Garrison, after the ring of fortifications erected around this headland in the eighteenth century. The promontory was already the site
of the archipelago's major defensive structure, **Star Castle**, which
still dominates the height today just up from Garrison Hill. Built in
the shape of an eight-pointed star in 1593 after the scare of the
Spanish Armada, it sheltered the future Charles II in 1646 when he
was on the run from the Parliamentary forces, and later became the
headquarters of the famous Royalist privateer, Sir John Grenville,
under whom it was the last Cavalier stronghold until stormed by
Admiral Blake in 1651. Now converted into a hotel (see p.254), the

*Between Easter
and October
you can rent
bikes from
Buccabu Bike
Hire at
Porthcressa
Beach, on the
south side of
Hugh Town
(☎01720/
422289).*

Bus tours with commentary leave several times daily according to demand in summer from the end of Hugh Street, providing a good way to see a lot of the island quickly (£4 for about 90min).

Between April and October, Will Wagstaff, a native Scillonian (☎01720/ 422212), offers wildlife tours around St Mary's and other islands, highlighting the local flora and fauna, particularly birdlife. Tours leave from St Mary's Quay or the Town Hall at 9.45am (about £6 per person per full day, plus ferry fares to the other islands).

castle is not visitable today unless you're a guest or you're eating or drinking at the restaurant or bar (see pp.254–255). The interior holds little remaining of the original structure in any case, and the best entertainment is to be had on the circular rampart walk around the headland, which you can complete in less than an hour and which affords spectacular views over all the islands and the myriad rocky fragments around them.

The only other essential stop in town is the engaging **Isles of Scilly Museum** on Church Street, which begins at The Parade (Mon–Sat: summer 10am–noon, 1.30–4.30pm & 7.30–9pm; rest of year 10am–noon & 1.30–4.30pm; £1), well worth an hour or two's wander for background on the archipelago. Most of the exhibits are relics salvaged from the many ships that have foundered on or around the islands, including the rag-bag of finds recovered from the *Cita*, which sank off St Mary's Porth Hellick in March 1997; much of its cargo, ranging from tobacco to trainers, found its way into the islanders' homes.

Adjacent to the harbour on the north side of Hugh Town, the murky waters of the **town beach** do not invite any more than a paddle, and the neighbouring **Porthmellon Beach**, looking out onto a mass of small boats, is not much better, though space can be found for **windsurfing**, with hire and instruction facilities on hand. Both beaches pale in comparison to **Porthcressa Beach**, a lovely sandy hollow in the sheltered bay on the south of the isthmus.

Around the island

East of Hugh Town, St Mary's is a checkerboard of meadows and box-like flower patches, though the most attractive parts are all on the coast, which is best explored on foot. From Hugh Town's Porthcressa Beach, a path wanders south, skirting the jagged teeth of **Peninnis Head**, and passing some impressive sea-sculpted granite rocks on the way, including the formation known as the **Kettle and Pans**, a hundred yards north of Peninnis Lighthouse, where immense basins have been hollowed out by the elements. Past here, the path follows the coast to placid **Old Town Bay**, where the scattered modern houses of **Old Town** give little hint that this was the island's chief port before Hugh Town took over that role in the seventeenth century. These days, Old Town boasts a few decent cafés and a sheltered south-facing **beach**, where a diving school offers equipment for hire and excursions to reefs and wrecks (☎01720/422732).

Three-quarters of a mile east of Old Town, past the airport's perimeter, **Porth Hellick** is the next major inlet on St Mary's southern coast, marked by a rugged quartz monument to the fantastically named admiral Sir Cloudesley Shovell (see box, opposite), sited at the bottom of the bay just back from the beach. On the seaward side of the monument is another rock shape, the aptly named **Loaded Camel**. At the eastern end of the bay, a gate leads to a path

Sir Cloudesley Shovell

Of all the wrecks which litter the seabed around the Isles of Scilly, the most famous are those belonging to the fleet led by Rear-Admiral **Sir Cloudesley Shovell** (1650–1707), a hero of many naval battles including an attack on Tripoli and the capture of Gibraltar and Barcelona. A month after sailing for England from Gibraltar on 19 Sept, 1707, 21 ships of the Mediterranean squadron under Shovell's command were beset by gales and fog which made accurate navigation impossible. The concerned commander convoked a meeting on board his flagship, the HMS *Association*, to establish their position, at which the consensus was that they were off the island of Ushant, 26 miles northwest of Brittany, with the English Channel open and clear before them. Strangely, for such experienced mariners, they were completely wrong: in fact they lay some hundred miles north of that position, so when Shovell issued the command to steer in a northeasterly direction, the fleet converged directly onto the Isles of Scilly. In all, **five ships** and nearly **2000 men** were lost; four ships foundered on the Western Rocks, two – including the *Association* – with all hands lost. One vessel, the *Phoenix*, unintentionally and quite miraculously sailed through Broad Sound, but hit rocks and was beached near New Grimsby on St Agnes, where it was quickly reduced to a total wreck. According to one ghoulish story, Shovell himself escaped the wreckage at first, putting to sea in a small boat accompanied by his treasure chest and pet greyhound, but was wrecked a second time – years later, a St Mary's woman confessed on her deathbed to having found the admiral lying exhausted on the beach and finishing him off for the sake of his gold rings. Other reports, however, claim that his body was found at sea. He was buried on the sands at Porth Hellick where a memorial stone still stands.

Despite his evident responsibility for the tragedy, Shovell's reputation became, if anything, enhanced by it, and he was glorified as a much-decorated war hero who went down with his ship: Queen Anne ordered that his body be exhumed and conveyed to London for an elaborate funeral in Westminster Abbey, where his tomb lies to this day. In 1967, local divers recovered many of the treasures carried in his fleet, which included a hoard of Spanish "**pieces of eight**" and represented one of the greatest troves ever found around the British Isles. A selection of the finds are displayed in Penzance's Maritime Museum (see p.219).

over the hill, from which a signpost points right to a four-thousand-year-old **barrow**, or passage grave, probably used by the Scillies' first colonists. The grave is covered by a circular mound, some forty feet in diameter, with a curving passage leading to the central chamber, composed of large upright stones and four large slabs for a roof.

On the **eastern side** of St Mary's, less than two miles from Hugh Town and a mile north along the coast from Porth Hellick, **Pelistry Bay** is one of the most secluded spots on the island, its sandy beach and crystal-clear waters sheltered by the outlying **Toll's Island**. The latter, joined to St Mary's at low tide by a slender sandbar, holds the remains of an old battery known as Pellow's Redoubt as well as several pits in which kelp was burned to produce a substance used for the manufacture of soap and glass. Grey seals are also a common sight here.

The best remnants of early human settlement on the Scillies are located in the north of the island, reached by path and – part of the way – by road. A mile or so north of Hugh Town, overlooking the sea near the island's cluster of tall TV masts, **Halangy Down**, dating from around 2000 BC, consists of an extensive complex of stone huts, the largest of which gives onto a courtyard with interconnecting buildings. Though evocative enough, the site is not as complete as **Bant's Carn**, above the village at the top of the slope, a long rectangular chamber topped by four large capstones used for cremations. Part of a much earlier site, the Carn is probably contemporaneous with the barrow at Porth Hellick.

Accommodation

Hugh Town is relatively well supplied with **hotels and B&Bs**, all within easy walking distance of the harbour. Near Porthcressa Beach, Porthcressa Road has the small, nonsmoking *Pieces of Eight* (☎01720/422163; no credit cards; ②), while *The Boathouse*, on The Thoroughfare, which gives onto the town beach (☎01720/422688; ③; closed Nov–March), enjoys a good view over the harbour from three of its five rooms; both places have a restaurant. A good alternative is *Veronica Lodge* (☎01720/422585; no credit cards; ②), high up on the Garrison, a large, solid house sheltered by trees, with a spacious garden and great sea vistas from its comfortable bedrooms. Also on the Garrison, the *Star Castle* (☎01720/422317; ⑦; closed Nov–Jan) is the island's most atmospheric hotel, where the steep rates get you access to a pool and tennis court.

There is much to be said for staying **outside Hugh Town**, where you can be assured of peace and quiet. One of the best options is family-run *Atlantic View* (☎01720/422684; no credit cards; ②; closed Dec), in the centre of the island on High Lanes (right off Telegraph Rd heading north), providing comfortable farmhouse accommodation and good facilities; the owners also offer horse-riding excursions and bike rental. The island's only **campsite** is at *Garrison Farm* near the playing field at the top of the Garrison in Hugh Town (☎01720/422670; closed Dec–Feb).

Eating and drinking

Hugh Town has the vast majority of **places to eat** on St Mary's. The *Pilot's Gig* is a cosy basement restaurant below the Garrison Gate at the end of Hugh Street (☎01720/422654; closed Mon), specializing in fish but offering more basic snacks at lunchtime. In the middle of the main street, the popular *Kavorna Bakery* serves simple, hearty snacks as well as coffees and buns. In the Garrison, the *Star Castle Hotel* has three eateries: the high-quality *Castle Dining Room*, with

From Hugh Town's harbour, regular launches connect all the inhabited islands (currently £5.20 return fare), though these are sporadic in winter. Timetables are chalked up at the quayside. For more details, contact the St Mary's Boatmen's Association (☎01720/ 422541)

a magnificent granite fireplace, and good for both meat and vegetarian dishes; the smaller and less formal *Conservatory* restaurant, which gives onto the garden and concentrates on seafood; and the *Dungeon Bar* (lunchtime only), where you can snack on salads, jacket potatoes and sometimes steaks at tables on the ramparts. Out of town, *Juliet's*, located above the seashore between Porthmellon and Porthloo beaches, serves superb cakes and teas, light meals and moderately priced early dinners in its garden (closed Nov–March).

Tresco

Measuring two miles by one mile, **TRESCO** is the second largest of the Isles, and also the most visited of the off islands. Despite its regular boatloads of day-trippers, however, it never feels crowded, and there are ample opportunities to find a solitary beach. There are also more trees and vegetation than on the other Scillies, and the island suffers less wind than the rest of the group. Once the private estate of Devon's Tavistock Abbey, and later the home of the "benevolent despot" Augustus Smith and his family, Tresco retains a privileged air, with short-term accommodation confined to a couple of expensive lodgings.

According to the tide, **boats** pull in at either New Grimsby, midway along the west coast, the smaller quay at Old Grimsby, on the east coast, or Tresco's southernmost point, Carn Near. Wherever you land, it is only a few minutes' walk along signposted paths to the entrance of **Abbey Gardens** (daily 10am–4pm; £6), where the sparse ruins from the Benedictine priory of St Nicholas lie amid extensive subtropical gardens first laid out by Augustus Smith in 1834. Immediately on taking up office as Lord Proprietor of the islands, Smith established his residence in the present Abbey, a tall Victorian mansion to the west of the gardens, and set about clearing the wilderness of undergrowth which then covered most of the island's southern half. Planting belts of cypress and Monterey pines from California as wind-breaks, and erecting a tall wall, he introduced plants and seeds from London's Kew Gardens which formed the core of the botanical garden. His work was continued by his successors – including the present Dorrien-Smith – and was augmented by seedlings brought from Africa, South America and the Antipodes, often by local mariners. Today's dense abundance of palms, aloes, cacti and other tropical shrubs lends an almost jungle-like air, with some strategically sited statuary adding to the exotic ambience. The entry ticket also admits you to **Valhalla**, housed in a building near the entrance, a colourful collection of figureheads and name plates taken from the numerous vessels that have come to grief around here.

Tresco's alluring sandy **beaches** are equally easy to reach: one of the best – **Appletree Bay**, a dazzling strand of white sand and shells – is only a few steps from the ferry landing at Carn Near. Further up the island's western shore, there's another gorgeous sandy bay

General information on Tresco is available at the island's Web site www.tresco .co.uk

You can rent bikes from Tresco's estate office at New Grimsby (☎01720/ 422849).

around the cluster of cottages that make up **New Grimsby**, where there's a store and the island's sole pub, the *New Inn*. You can also rent bikes from the estate office here (see margin note). From the pub, a lane heads across the narrow waist of the island to the village of **Dolphin Town** – named after an early Lord Proprietor of Scilly, Sir Francis Godolphin – where the stout grey church of **St Nicholas** is ringed by fields and trees. The lane then continues across to Tresco's eastern side, where **Old Grimsby** has a pier and another couple of sandy beaches. Close to the *Island Hotel* to the north of the bay, you can hire **sailing dinghies** from a shed on the beach in summer – sailing lessons, windsurf gear and even waterskiing are all also available either here or at New Grimsby. The granite shell on the high ground at the southern end of the harbour is the **Blockhouse**, a gun platform built to protect the harbour at Old Grimsby in the sixteenth century. South of Old Grimsby stretch a succession of wide strands, ending at the glorious curve of **Pentle Bay**, which are probably the island's finest, and good for shell-hunting.

North of the road between the two Grimsbys, tidy fields give way to the heathland of **Castle Down**, an elemental expanse of granite, gorse and heather crossed by narrow paths. Skirting Castle Down from New Grimsby, a path traces the coast to the scanty ruins of **King Charles' Castle**, built in the 1550s. Strategically positioned on high ground to cover the lagoon-like channel separating Tresco and Bryher, this artillery fort was in fact badly designed, its guns unable to depress far enough to be effective. It was superseded in 1651 by the much better-preserved **Cromwell's Castle** nearby, a round granite gun-tower built at sea level next to the pretty sandy cove of **Castle Porth**.

The shore path continues from Castle Porth round the serrated northern edge of Tresco to **Piper's Hole**, a long underground cave accessible from the cliff-edge, which is the source of several legends that variously identify it as the abode of mermaids, ghosts or smugglers. The entrance can be a little difficult to negotiate but it's worth pressing ahead to the freshwater pool some sixty feet within, for which a torch is essential. South of here, the deep indentation of **Gimble Porth** is one of the few sheltered inlets of this northern promontory, its shores crowded by dense ranks of rhododendrons, beyond which extend the orderly fields and flower plantations of Tresco's southern half.

Practicalities

If you're feeling flush, you can join the elite at the *Island Hotel* at Old Grimsby (☎01720/422883; ⑨; closed Nov–Feb), a sumptuous modern retreat with panoramic views and a pool, or head for the less exclusive *New Inn* at New Grimsby (☎01720/422844; ⑦), which charges alarmingly high rates for its rather ordinary rooms. Otherwise the only **accommodation** on the island comprises self-catering homes, usually available only for weekly rent, though it's worth asking if you want a place for less time. Prices run from £220 to £420 per week, according to season and size: contact *Boro Farm* (☎01720/422843) or *Borough Farm* (☎01720/422840) – both closed November–February – or Tresco's Estate Office (☎01720/422849; *www.tresco.co.uk*) for details and bookings. Fresh fish takes pride of place at the *New Inn*'s **restaurant** where a three-course set menu costs around £25, and you can eat pub snacks in its garden.

Bryher

Covered with a thick carpet of bracken, heather and bramble, **BRY-HER** is the smallest of the populated islands, and also the wildest. The prevailing feeling here is of a struggle between man and the environment, with the cultivable parts of the island regularly threatened by the encroaching sea. The seventy-odd inhabitants have introduced some pockets of order in the form of flower plantations, mostly confined to the scattering of houses just up from the main quay that makes up the grandly named **Bryher Town**, facing Tresco on Bryher's eastern side. Just fifty yards from the granite jetty, the church of **All Saints**, dating from 1742, is the archipelago's oldest, its churchyard chock-full of gravestones marked Jenkins, showing the extent to which this Welsh family, that settled here over 300 years ago, once dominated island life.

To the north of Bryher Town, more flower patches creep up **Watch Hill**, one of the island's five Scillonian-scale "hills", whose comparatively steep slopes makes it seem taller than its 138ft. A brief ascent allows you to take in a grand panorama of the whole group of islands. Nearer to hand, the calm corridor of water between Bryher and Tresco, **New Grimsby Channel**, is one of the archipelago's best anchorages, and consequently often crowded with a small flotilla of moored boats. Thrusting out of the water in mid-channel, you'll see the jagged rock pile of **Hangman Island**, which takes its name either from the execution of pirates or of the Cavaliers who were dispatched here during the Civil War.

Barren heathland soon asserts itself to the north, extending as far as the impressive granite promontory of **Shipman Head**, another terrific vantage point offering dizzying views over the foaming Atlantic. Bryher's exposed western seaboard takes the full brunt of the ocean, and nowhere more spectacularly than at the aptly named **Hell Bay**, cupped by a limb of land below Shipman Head, and frequently blasted by ferocious winds and savage waves. It's worth following the island's serrated western coast down its full length to get the full value of the sound and fury, which is the rule even in relatively calm weather. By contrast, peace usually reigns in the south-facing **Rushy Bay**, a small, sheltered and sandy crescent, surrounded by a mass of flowers, that counts among the island's best **beaches**. Its name is

From Bryher's quay, there's a daily year-round boat service to the other islands (from £5.60 return). Frequent tours to seal and bird colonies on the outlying rocks, and fishing expeditions, are also on offer for around £10; contact Bryher Boat Services at ☎01720/ 422886.

derived from the rushes, marram grass and other plants grown here by Augustus Smith in the 1830s in order to stabilize the shore from erosion. Above the bay, **Samson Hill** has a few megalithic barrows submerged beneath a coating of gorse, foxgloves, campion and other wild flowers, and boasts views as good as those from Watch Hill.

Practicalities

Bryher has a tiny range of **accommodation** which, apart from the one hotel, is usually fully booked in August. The cheapest choices are the B&Bs *Soleil D'Or* (☎01720/422003; ③; closed Nov–Feb), north of the main quay and with views over to Tresco, and *Chafford*, a family-run guesthouse near Watch Hill (☎01720/422241; ③; closed Nov–March); both are on the eastern side of the island and offer comfortable rooms and wholesome meals; *Chafford* also offers boat hire. Halfway down the other side of the island, the upmarket *Hell Bay Hotel* (☎01720/422947; ⑦; closed Nov–March) is beautifully situated next to the placid and brackish Bryher Pool, below the Gweal Hill promontory. Each room has its own sitting room, and half- or full-board is obligatory, but discounts are available for short breaks in spring and autumn. *Jenford Farm* on Watch Hill offers basic **camping** facilities (☎01720/422886; closed Nov–March).

For **refreshment**, the *Hell Bay Hotel* has a bar and a good restaurant open to nonresidents. You can eat inexpensively at the friendly *Vine Café*, below Watch Hill, and the *Fraggle Rock Café*, near the post office north of the main quay – the latter is popular with locals and features an upstairs restaurant, which has a fish-and-chips night on Fridays. The island's post office doubles as a general store, selling a limited range of food and good fresh bread; you can also buy fresh veg (and, in season, strawberries) from Hillside Farm, just south of the church, or from the nearby stall it operates in season.

St Martin's

The third largest of the Isles of Scilly, and located a mile east of Tresco, **ST MARTIN'S** is a narrow ridge some two miles in length, its northern side wild and rugged, the southern side sloping gently to the sea and chiefly given over to flower-growing. The main landing stage is on the promontory jutting out from this more sheltered side, at the head of the majestic sweep of **Par Beach**, a bare wedge of pure-white sand. From the quay, a road leads uphill past a public tennis court to **Higher Town**, the island's main concentration of houses and the location of the only shop as well as St Martin's Diving Services (☎01720/422848), which offers **scuba and snorkelling** equipment for rent as well as tuition at all levels. Free of plankton or silt, the waters around St Martin's are said to be among the clearest in Britain, and are much favoured by scuba enthusiasts. Nondivers can go snorkelling among the seals around the nearby Eastern Isles (see p.262).

Beyond Higher Town's church, a road runs westwards along the island's long spine to **Middle Town** – actually little more than a cluster of cottages and a few flower-packing sheds – and from there to the western extremity of the isle. Here, **Lower Town** has a slightly larger collection of houses nestled under Tinkler's Hill, as well as a pub and a second quay, all overlooking the uninhabited isles of Teän and St Helen's (see p.261).

From Lower Town, there's easy access to the long, sandy continuum of **Lawrence's Bay** on St Martin's southern coast, backed by large areas of flowerbeds. However, the best beaches – and among the grandest ones in the Scillies – lie on the desolate northern side, the beautiful half-mile recess of sand at **Great Bay** and the adjacent **Little Bay** reachable from paths branching north off the main east–west track. Utterly secluded, backed by grassy dunes, it's ideal for swimming, and also a nice place to do some exploring. From Little Bay, you can climb across boulders at low tide to the hilly and wild **White Island** (pronounced "Wit Island"), on the northeastern side of which you'll find a vast cave, **Underland Girt**; it's accessible at low tide only, so take care not to be stranded by the returning high waters.

East of Great Bay, paths weave round the rocky coves to the island's northeastern tip, where the heathland of **Chapel Downs** is dominated by a conspicuous red-and-white Daymark, erected in 1683 (not 1637 as inscribed) as a warning to shipping during the day. On the edge of the heathland, the sheer cliffs of **St Martin's Head** confront crashing seas; on a clear day you can make out the foam breaking against the Seven Stones Reef seven miles distant, where the tanker *Torrey Canyon* was wrecked in 1967, causing one of the world's worst oil spills. Working your way round the perimeter of Chapel Downs you can reach another fine beach, **Perpitch**, on the southeastern shore facing the scattered Eastern Isles (see p.262).

Practicalities

St Martin's has just one **B&B**, *Polreath*, in Higher Town (☎01720/422046; ④), where the six comfortable rooms have all-round views. The sole **hotel** is the posh *St Martin's on the Isle* in Lower Town (☎01720/422090; ⑨; closed Nov–March), a cluster of cottages with modern, rather characterless rooms looking onto a sandy beach. However, asking around in the post office in High Town or the store in Lower Town may find you other places offering **rented rooms** in season. In Middle Town, you'll find a **campsite** (☎01720/422888; closed Nov–Feb), just off the road near Lawrence's Bay – the only Scillies site enjoying some degree of shelter, and the best equipped, with clothes-washing, drying and ironing facilities.

For **meals**, *Polreath* has a simple **café** serving teas and snacks and an evening-only bistro. Down the valley south of Higher Town, the wholefood café and restaurant at *Little Arthur Farm* offers a range of delicious home-baked cakes, organic salads and hot meals

(April–Sept daytime only). The only **pub** on the island is the *Sevenstones Inn* in Lower Town, where snacks are available.

St Agnes

The southernmost and most westerly of the inhabited isles, **ST AGNES** – known simply as "Agnes" to locals – is also the craggiest, its rocks weathered to fantastic shapes. Visitors disembark at **Porth Conger** in the north of the island, from where a road leads inland past the most significant landmark on St Agnes, the disused **Old Lighthouse** – dating from 1680, it's one of the oldest in England. From the lighthouse the right-hand fork in the road leads to the western side of the island and **Periglis Cove**, a picturesque spot and a popular mooring for boats, while the left-hand fork heads south to **St Warna's Cove**, where the patron saint of shipwrecks is reputed to have landed from Ireland; the exact spot is marked by a holy well. It's said that in the old days, locals would cast coins into it to persuade the saint to send them a wreck. Between the two coves is a fine coastal path which passes the **Troy Town Maze**, a miniature maze of stones thought to have been created a couple of centuries ago, but possibly much older. Kept in good order over the years, the circular formation appears rather paltry next to the mighty granite boulders close by.

South beyond St Warna's Cove, the path continues past some of the island's most spectacular sections of shoreline, with views over to the Western Rocks (see p.262). St Agnes's southern segment is mostly taken up by the wild heathland of **Wingletang Down**. At its tip, the headland of **Horse Point** has more tortuously wind-eroded rocks. On the eastern side of Wingletang Down the inlet of **Beady Pool** gained its name from the trove of beads washed ashore from the wreck of a seventeenth-century Dutch trader; some of the reddish-brown beads still occasionally turn up. Above the cove, the **Giant's Punchbowl** is one of the island's most remarkable rock sculptures: two immense boulders, one poised above the other, with a wide basin three feet deep in its top.

The eastern side of St Agnes harbours one of the island's best beaches, the small, sheltered **Covean** (accessible from the path opposite *Covean Cottage*, above Porth Conger). Between the cove and Porth Conger a broad sand bar appears at low tide to connect the smaller isle of **Gugh** (pronounced to rhyme with Hugh), creating another lovely sheltered beach. You can cross the bar to Gugh to wander around a scattering of untended Bronze Age remains – including the **Old Man of Gugh**, a tilting standing stone on the eastern side of the island – and to admire the wonderful panorama from the hill at Gugh's northern end.

If you're visiting Gugh, take care not to be marooned on the isle by the incoming tide, which creates an extremely fierce current over the bar. Swimming is not advised at high tide here.

Practicalities

Best of the **B&Bs** on St Agnes is the *Coastguards*, one of a smart row of cottages past the Old Lighthouse and post office on the island's western side (☎01720/422373; ③), where meals are also available. Other good options include the friendly *Covean Cottage* above Porth Conger (☎01720/422620; no credit cards; ③), which has comfortable rooms above its good restaurant, and the *Parsonage* (☎01720/422370; no credit cards; ③), nestled below the lighthouse behind a copse of Cornish elms. There's a good **campsite** at *Troy Town Farm* above Periglis Cove (☎01720/422360; closed Nov–Feb), fairly exposed but enjoying first-rate views over to the Western Rocks and the Bishop Rock Lighthouse. *Covean Cottage* does good snacks and **meals** throughout the summer, while just above the jetty at Porth Conger, the *Turk's Head* serves superb St Agnes pasties to go with its beer.

The uninhabited isles

Many of Scilly's **uninhabited islands** were formerly peopled and reveal fascinating traces of the former habitations and commercial activities. The prevailing impression, though, is of nature holding sway, from the teeming birdlife perched on every ledge to the ocean in full spate beating against their exposed shores. Weather permitting, there are regular boat excursions from Hugh Town's harbour, run by the St Mary's Boatmen's Association (☎01720/422541), and also frequent services from the nearest inhabited islands.

From Bryher's quay, it's just a quick hop to **Samson**, the largest of the uninhabited isles and marked out by its mammary-like twin hills. The island has been abandoned since 1855 when the last impoverished inhabitants were ordered off by Augustus Smith, then the proprietor of all the islands, who decided that their continued existence there was unsustainable. Wildlife reigns supreme, the slopes thickly grown with gorse and sea holly and populated chiefly by divebombing gulls and colonies of black rabbits. Boats usually pull up on a beach on the island's eastern side, from which a path leads up over **North Hill**, the site of several primitive burial chambers dating from the second millennium BC. One of these – without its cover and exposed to the elements on the summit – is thought to be the sepulchre of a tribal chief. Most of the abandoned cottages of the nineteenth-century inhabitants are on **South Hill**, many still with limpet shells piled outside their doors, left over from when these were collected and traded.

There are also regular excursions from Lower Town in St Martin's to the uninhabited isles of Teän and St Helen's, just a quarter of a mile away. **Teän**, a flattish, meandering island with several crescents of sandy beach, was formerly used by families from St Martin's for burning kelp and to graze their cattle; their ruined cottages can still be seen. Behind Teän, **St Helen's** holds the remains of the oldest church on the archipelago, a tenth-century oratory, together with monks' dwellings and a chapel, and you can also see here, at the base

The uninhabited isles

From Porth Conger, there are boat trips to all the islands, and also catamaran trips on the Spirit of St Agnes *(April–Oct 1–2 daily; Nov–March 3 weekly; ☎01720/422704) to St Mary's (£2.80) and the off islands (£5.50), and daily excursions in summer to the Bishop Rock Lighthouse (£9 for two hours), and evening bird-watching trips around the Eastern Isles (£5.50).*

of the island's 144-foot hill, the melancholy ruins of a "pest house" erected in 1756 to house plague-carriers entering British waters.

Out beyond St Agnes, the **Western Rocks** are a horseshoe of islets and jagged rocks which have been the cause of innumerable wrecks, from Cloudesley Shovell's *Association* (see box on p.253) to the American schooner *Thomas W. Lawson*, the largest pure sailing vessel ever built and the only one with seven masts. It came to grief here in 1907, creating what may have been the world's first spillage disaster when its cargo of crude oil washed up on St Agnes. The biggest of these outcrops is **Annet**, probably never inhabited and notable as a nesting-place for a rich variety of **birds**, such as the stormy petrel and Manx shearwater as well as colonies of puffins and shags; however, many species have been chased out or slaughtered in recent years by the predatory Great Black-Beaked Gull, largest of the gull family. The island cannot be visited during the nesting season, which is probably just as well, as the screeching clamour and the stench of the birds' effluvia are said to be unbearable.

The islands forming the western arm of the group are the best place to see **grey seals**, which prefer these remote outposts for breeding. Many visitors come to this farthest edge of Scilly just to view the **Bishop Rock Lighthouse**, however, a lonely column five miles out – at 175ft, it's the tallest in the British Isles and the westernmost one on this side of the Atlantic. The men who built it between 1847 and 1850 lived on the nearby rocky islet of **Rosevear** – hard to believe, given the extremely harsh conditions, especially in light of the fact that they grew their own vegetables here, established a blacksmith's shop and even organized a ball to which guests from St Mary's and other islands were invited. Remains of their constructions can still be seen.

On the other side of the group, scattered between St Martin's and St Mary's, the **Eastern Isles** are mere slivers of rock to which boat-trippers make forays to view puffins and grey seals. Protected from the Atlantic currents by the other islands, these outcrops generally have more soil than the Western Rocks, and several have excellent beaches – notably **Great Arthur** and **Great Ganilly**. Both of these also have prehistoric remains; on **Nornour**, reached at low tide along a rocky bar from Great Ganilly, dwellings have been unearthed which date back to the first century AD – the finds are now on show in the museum on St Mary's (see p.252).

Chapter 11

The North Cornwall coast

Generally cliffier and more ragged than the county's southern seaboard, the **North Cornwall coast** from St Ives Bay to the Devon border is punctuated by a sequence of small resorts which have sprung up around some of the finest beaches in England. Offsetting these, with their attendant caravan parks, the more westerly stretches are littered with the derelict stacks and castle-like ruins of the engine houses that once powered the region's mining industry, and with the grey Methodist chapels that reflect the impact of John Wesley on the local communities. His open-air meetings attracted thousands of listeners in such places as Gwennap Pit outside **Redruth** and **Camborne**, the dual centres of the mining industry. Relics of both mining and Methodism are also evident in the area around **St Agnes**, to the north, though on the nearby coast the accent is on recreation, especially surfing. Surrounded by splendid beaches, **Newquay** has been dubbed surfers' capital, and has an appropriately exuberant air, while, north on the Camel estuary, the fishing port of **Padstow** also attracts young groups and families, and has recently acquired a gastronomic reputation for its fine fish restaurants. Another reason to come here is for the **Camel Trail**, a first-rate cycle and walking route which starts in Padstow and leads inland along the Camel River to the rather nondescript town of **Wadebridge**, and beyond to Bodmin.

North of the Camel, the coast is an almost unbroken line of cliffs as far as the Devon border, the gaunt, exposed terrain sheltering

Useful Web sites covering the north Cornwall coast are www .north-cornwall .co.uk and www .resort-guide .co.uk.

ACCOMMODATION PRICE CODES

Throughout this *Guide*, hotel and B&B accommodation is coded on a scale of ① to ⑨, the code indicating the lowest price you can expect to pay per night for a double room in high season. The prices indicated by the codes are as follows:

① under £40	④ £60–70	⑦ £110–150
② £40–50	⑤ £70–90	⑧ £150–200
③ £50–60	⑥ £90–110	⑨ over £200

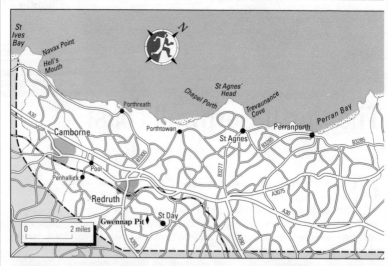

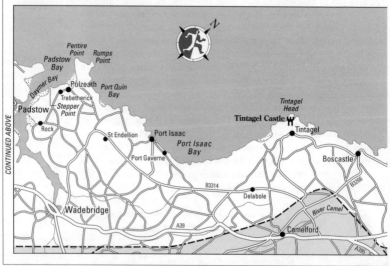

such peaceful havens as **Port Isaac**, and making a melodramatic setting for **Tintagel**, whose atmospheric ruined castle and mythical links with King Arthur have made it the most popular sightseeing destination on this coast. A few miles further on, the exquisite port of **Boscastle** has strong associations with Thomas Hardy, which can be traced on a riverside walk. Summer holiday fun is again the keynote at **Bude**, whose wide strand and nearby beaches draw

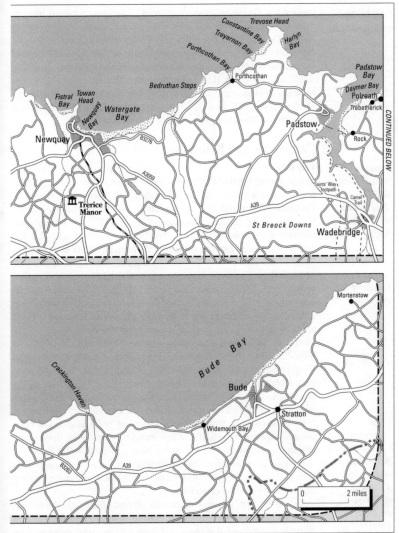

© Crown copyright

legions of surfers in season. Walkers, too, will enjoy the memorable cliff walks around here, particularly those running due north to the Devon border, seven miles away.

North Cornwall's network of **public transport** leaves a lot to be desired. Newquay is the terminus for the cross-peninsula **train** route from Par, while the main line to Penzance stops at Redruth and Camborne, which are connected to St Agnes on the #43 and #57 bus routes. Truronian runs a regular #T1 service (not Sun) from St Agnes to Truro, Helston and The Lizard, while First Western National's #57 from Penzance takes in Perranporth and Newquay. Bus #56 runs between Newquay and Padstow, the latter also served by the regular #55 from Bodmin (not Sun in winter). Services #122, #125 and #X4 link Bude, Boscastle and Tintagel, and #124 runs between Port Isaac, Polzeath and Wadebridge (not Sun in winter). Finally, Bude is linked to Okehampton and Exeter by #X9, and Boscastle to the same places by #X10 (not Sun).

Camborne and Redruth

A passport ticket is available that allows access to all properties, including the Discovery Centre, owned by the Trevithick Trust.

Ten miles west of Truro, the uninspiring towns of REDRUTH and neighbouring CAMBORNE are largely bypassed by tourists speeding down the A30, but merit a stop for anyone interested in Cornwall's industrial history. Nowadays an amalgamated conurbation spreading for six miles along the A3047, the towns once accounted for two-thirds of the world's copper production, the 350 pits in the area employing some fifty thousand workers in the 1850s. Many of the miners were forced to emigrate when cheaper deposits of tin and copper were discovered overseas at the end of the nineteenth century, and the area has never fully recovered, as the numerous ruins of engine houses dotting the area bear eloquent testimony.

You can get an intriguing insight into the world of mining at **Pool**, about a mile west of Redruth's centre on the A3047, site of the **Cornwall Industrial Discovery Centre** (April–July, Sept & Oct Mon–Sat 11am–5pm; Aug daily 11am–5pm; £4.80; NT) on Agar Road (reached through the Safeway car park). Adjacent to the complex's bland visitor centre, Taylor's Shaft is the site of one of the largest (and the last) Cornish pumping engines to be erected, originally built in 1892 to pump water from the nearby Carn Brea mines.

Bissoe Tramways Cycle Hire at Bissoe, signposted off the A393 near Gwennap (☎01872/ 870341), rents out bikes and operates a delivery and collection service to Truro, Falmouth and Portreath.

Now immaculately restored with gleaming brass and wood trimmings, the gigantic cylindrical apparatus is viewable on three levels within the engine house. Across the road you can see the East Pool winding engine or "whim" in clanking action, originally used to haul men and ore up from the mine-shaft when it was worked by steam, and now powered by electricity.

Outside St Day, a couple of miles southeast of Redruth, the grassy, terraced hollow of **Gwennap Pit** (always open; free) was the scene of huge gatherings of miners and their families who came to hear John Wesley preach between 1762 and 1786. The first visits to Cornwall by the co-founder of Methodism were met with derision and violence, but he later won over the tough mining communities who could find little comfort in the gentrified established church. At one time Wesley estimated that the congregation at Gwennap Pit exceeded thirty thousand, noting in his diary, "I shall scarce see a larger congregation till we meet in the air." The present tiered amphitheatre was created in 1805, with seating for twenty thousand, and is today the venue of Methodist meetings for the annual Whit Monday service, drawing adherents from all over Cornwall.

Practicalities

Camborne and Redruth are both **train** stops on the Plymouth–Penzance main line. Camborne's station is south of the centre on South Terrace Road, while Redruth's is just south of the main thoroughfare, Fore Street, on Station Road – frequent **buses** run between the two centres. Buses #57 and #57D pick up from Redruth train station for St Agnes and Portreath. If you need a **bed**, Redruth offers the amiable *Lansdowne House*, five minutes from the bus and train stations at 42 Clinton Rd (☎01209/216002; no credit cards; ①). Best of the bunch in Camborne is the eighteenth-century coaching inn, *Tyacks Hotel*, on Commercial Street, just north of the station (☎01209/612424; ②), with pine-furnished rooms, and offering a moderately priced international menu in its *Trevithick* **restaurant**.

Portreath and around

Redruth's former harbour – once serving the local mining industry and a working harbour until the 1960s – lies two and a half miles northwest at **PORTREATH**. These days the village is better known as a holiday resort, a collection of modern houses surrounding a sea wall which backs onto a sand-and-shingle beach, a draw for surfers from far and wide, despite the local sewage outlets. Though you might be content with the beach here, Portreath is within walking distance of other coastal attractions, notably the awe-inspiring **Hell's Mouth**, a cauldron of waves and black rocks at the base of two-hundred-foot cliffs, five miles south along the coast. Three miles north of the village, **Porthtowan** is another popular surfing beach, which, unlike many of the cliff-bordered beaches around here, still catches the sun from the late afternoon on.

Portreath is connected with Camborne bus station by buses #44B, #44C, #46A and #46B and with Redruth train station by buses #44B, #46A and #46B. **Accommodation** is fairly limited, with the best choices being the light and airy *Cliff House*, just off the harbourside on The Square (☎01209/842008; no credit cards; ①; closed Jan), and the charmingly old-fashioned restored Georgian mansion *Fountain Springs*, Glenfeadon House, Glenfeadon Terrace (☎01209/842650; no credit cards; ①), about a quarter of a mile from the sea – take the second left turning after the school on the B3300.

Rooms are also available at the *Portreath Arms* (☎01209/842259; ①), right next to *Cliff House*, which serves lunch-time and evening bar **food** and reasonably-priced bistro-type meals. **Campers** should head for the *Cambrose Touring Park* (☎01209/890747; closed Nov–Easter), beautifully sited in the Portreath Valley, one and a half miles from Portreath on the Porthtowan turn-off; it has free showers, a heated pool and a store.

Check out the latest walking, cycle and horse-riding routes in the area from the Mineral Tramways Discovery Centre at Penhallick (Mon–Fri & Sun 10.30am–4pm; www.cornwall-online.co.uk/mineral-tramways; free), just south of the Industrial Discovery Centre.

Surfing gear in Portreath can be rented in the summer from Collett's Beach Shop on Beach Road.

St Agnes and around

Five miles north of Redruth and a mile from the coast, and surrounded by ghostly engine houses, the old mining town of **ST AGNES** gives little hint today of the conditions in which its population once lived. Immaculate flower-filled gardens front the straggling streets of grey-slate and granite cottages in Peterville, the lower part of the village, and in Churchtown, the upper, more central part. The two ends are connected by the steep Town Hill, with its picturesque terrace of cottages known as "Stippy-Stappy", a Cornish colloquialism for going uphill.

Before heading for the beaches, there are a couple of sights in and around town that are worth exploring, starting with the unprepossessing **St Agnes Church** in Churchtown, dedicated to a thirteen-year-old Roman girl martyred in 304. Though dating from 1849 in its present incarnation, it merits a glance for its much-older relics, including a quirky Elizabethan alms box.

The local campaigning group Surfers Against Sewage (☎01872/ 553001; www.sas .org.uk) organizes a grand surfers' ball in a tent on the cliffs on the first Friday of September. It's members only (annual membership is £12.50) and tickets, which are usually sold out by September, are £25.

If you're intrigued by the gritty world of tinning in Cornwall, you can find out everything you need to know at **Blue Hills Tin Streams**, a wild spot at Trevellas Coombe, a mile or so northeast of St Agnes (Easter–Oct Mon–Sat 10.30am–5pm; ring ahead in winter ☎01872/ 553341; £3). A member of the resident family will guide you through the processes of vanning, panning and jigging – stages in the process of tin-extraction – and point out examples of tin in its various smeltings in their workshop. Take time out also to sample the home-made biscuits and scones on offer in their small garden café. From St Agnes take the B3285 towards Perranporth, turning left for Wheal Kitty after 250yd and right at the grass triangle.

The real pull around St Agnes, however, is the cliffy, sometimes sandy coast. The best place to take it all in – and one of Cornwall's most famous vantage points – is from **St Agnes Beacon**, 630ft high, from where views extend inland to Bodmin Moor and even across the peninsula to St Michael's Mount. The easiest access is from the free car park on Beacon Drive, a mile west of the village, from where it's a ten-minute walk to the top.

A mile or so north of the Beacon, the knuckle of land that is **St Agnes Head** is edged by cliffs which support the area's largest colony of breeding kittiwakes, fulmars and guillemots, while grey seals are a common sight offshore. There are good beaches on either side: a couple of miles north, **Trevaunance Cove**, the site of several failed attempts to create a harbour for the town, has a fine sandy beach much favoured by surfers and boasts excellent water quality, while south of St Agnes Head, **Chapel Porth** is a wide expanse of white sand at low tide, rocky and stony at other times – swimmers and surfers here should, however, be aware of the strong currents and undertows.

Surfboards and wet suits can be rented from Aggie Surf Shop at 4 Peterville Square.

Practicalities

St Agnes has frequent **bus** connections with Redruth train station and Camborne bus station (#43A, #43B, #43D, #57 and #57D). The local **tourist office** is housed inside a video shop at 20 Churchtown (daily 10am–9pm; ☎01872/554150; *www.stagnes.com*).

There's a good choice of **accommodation** in and around the town, including Peterville's eighteenth-century *Malthouse*, once the village brewing-house, which has a relaxed and bohemian atmosphere (☎01872/553318; no credit cards; ①). Near the museum on Penwinnick Road, *Penkerris* (☎01872/552262; ①) is a spacious creeper-clad house, with log fires in winter, a huge garden, and good home-cooked dinners for £10.

If you want to be near the beach, head down to Trevaunance Cove, where the whitewashed *Driftwood Spars* (☎01872/552428; ②), originally a seventeenth-century tin-miners' warehouse, offers blue-and-white rooms facing the sea, and land-facing rooms with an earthier feel. There's a useful **campsite** a mile south of the centre of St Agnes on Penwinnick Road at *Presingoll Farm* (☎01872/552333; closed Nov–Easter).

Right in the centre of town opposite the church, the large and lively bar at the *St Agnes Hotel* serves triple-decker sandwiches and fuller **meals**, including organic vegetables whenever possible, while the *Taphouse* on Peterville Square attracts a young and lively crowd, thanks to its inexpensive Mexican and Indian food (served until 9pm) and live bands. By the sea, the three bars at the *Driftwood Spars* are always busy, and inexpensive food is available lunchtime and evenings; live bands play throughout the year at weekends. The most interesting **pub** has to be the *Railway Inn* at 10 Vicarage Rd (a continuation of Churchtown), with its idiosyncratic collection of shoes, horsebrasses and naval memorabilia; it has a good selection of ales and snacks and also offers accommodation (☎01872/552310; ①). For a cream tea with a spectacular view overlooking the cove at Trevaunance Point, head for the garden of the *Trevaunance Point Hotel*, formerly the home of actor Claude Rains.

Perranporth

Past the old World War II airfield three miles northeast of St Agnes, the resort of **PERRANPORTH** lies at the southern end of Perran Beach, a three-mile expanse of sand enhanced by caves and natural rock arches, and backed by turf-covered dunes. Once devoted to tin and copper mining, it's now a compact holiday resort that hasn't changed much since the 1930s, when John Betjeman poured scorn on its "bungalows, palm-shaded public conveniences and amenities, and shopping arcades in the cheapest style so that Newquay looks almost smart by comparison". However, the resort's aesthetics have little impact on the thousands of surfers who flock here year-round, drawn by the long ranks of rollers coming in straight off the Atlantic.

Perranporth is well connected to St Agnes by #57, #57D and #T1 **bus**. Thoroughly modernized **accommodation** is provided by the

St Agnes
and
Perranporth

In mid-October Perranporth hosts the Lowender Peran Celtic Festival, which takes place in the Ponsmere Hotel and features Celtic ceilidhs and concerts. A ticket for the full five days, also admitting you into the workshops, displays and concerts, costs £25. For information call ☎01872/ 553413.

huge-beamed and wood-panelled *Seiners' Arms* (☎01872/573118; *www.connexions.co.uk/seiners*; ③), which has a sheltered terrace overlooking the beach. The inn gets a bit busy in summer, however, and you'll find a more peaceful and intimate atmosphere at the small *Tide's Reach Hotel* (☎01872/572188; ②), also close to the beach but tucked away at the end of Ponsmere Road, with big floppy sofas, a pool room and bright bedrooms. The local **youth hostel** (☎01872/573812; closed Oct–March) is dramatically sited in a former clifftop coastguard station less than a mile west of Perranporth. Reached through a locked gate on the coast path (signposted left off Tywarnhale Rd on the B3285 to St Agnes), it has just three small dormitories, where beds are £9.25, and self-catering facilities. The nearest **campsite**, *Perranporth Camping and Touring Park* (☎01872/572174; closed Oct–Easter), lies half a mile northeast of the centre, a five-minute walk from the beach, and is equipped with baths as well as showers.

Between late May and late September, surfing equipment can be rented from Higgin's Outback Surf Shack, next to the beach car park.

Tide's Reach Hotel (see above) is home to *Tidy's Vegetarian Restaurant* (Thurs–Sat evenings only; closed late Dec–Feb), where a three-course **meal**, including such dishes as Oatcake Duvets and "Mule" paella, will cost you under £12. On the beach itself, inexpensive food – and barbecues on Mondays and Thursdays – is available all day at the *Watering Hole*, which is also a great place for a **drink**; it buzzes all year round and puts on live folk and rock at weekends.

Newquay and around

Straddling a series of rocky bluffs seven miles north of Perranporth, **NEWQUAY** has a defiantly youthful air, making it difficult to imagine the town enjoying any history extending more than a few years back. In fact the "new quay" was built as long ago as the fifteenth century in what was already a long-established fishing port, previously more colourfully known as Towan Blystra (Cornish for "boat cove in the sand hills"), concentrated in the sheltered west end of Newquay Bay. For many years the town thrived on the local pilchard industry which reached its peak in the late eighteenth century, when large quantities were exported to the Mediterranean (principally Italy). A century later the town's harbour was expanded for coal imports and a railway was constructed across the peninsula to carry shipments of china clay from the pits around St Austell to Newquay for export. With the trains came a swelling stream of seasonal visitors, drawn to the town's superb position and fine golden sands. These natural advantages, combined with the Atlantic rollers, continue to pull the crowds today, making Newquay north Cornwall's premier resort for surfers, young families and older visitors. The town offers little else, however, and unless you fall into one of the above categories, you'd be better advised to steer clear.

For surfing information on Newquay and the north Cornwall and Devon coasts, check out www.surfnewquay.co.uk

Arrival, information and accommodation

Newquay's **train station** is off Cliff Road, a couple of hundred yards from the bus station on East Street. All **buses** for the beaches stop on Cliff Road and its extension Narrowcliff, and at the bus station, diagonally opposite the town's **tourist office** on Marcus Hill (May–Sept Mon–Sat 9am–5.30pm, Sun 10am–4pm; Oct–April Mon–Fri 10am–4.30pm, Sat 10am–noon; ☎01637/854020; *www.newquay .co.uk*).

Newquay has streetfuls of **accommodation** in all categories, though rooms are at a premium in July and August, when it's strongly advisable to book ahead. The town has the West Country's biggest selection of independent hostels, some fairly scruffy and jam-packed in peak season, but all with TVs, kitchens and places to store your surfboard. Campsites in the area are mostly mega-complexes, many of them geared to families and unwilling to take same-sex groups, or even couples, in order to minimize rowdy behaviour.

Hotels and B&Bs

Bay View House, Fore St ☎01637/871214. Good-value place right in the centre of town, on the cliff between Harbour and Towan beaches, offering superb views, parking and a restaurant (see p.275). Closed Nov–Easter. ③.

The Harbour, North Quay Hill ☎01637/873040; *www.harbourhotel.co.uk*. Poised in a prime position right on the harbour, with five bedrooms furnished in pine and wickerwork, all of which face seaward and have balconies. Bookings for less than one week are not taken July–Sept. ④.

Links Hotel, Headland Rd ☎01637/873211. Handy for Fistral Beach, this place features a pool room and bar and offers use of the sauna and indoor swimming pool at the nearby *Headland Hotel* (£2). Lock-up facilities for wet suits and surfboards are available. No credit cards. ②.

Sea Shells Guest House, 55 Fore St ☎01637/874582; *stokes@shells36 .freeserve.co.uk*. Light and friendly, this low-priced B&B is very central, and offers plain, unfussy rooms. ①.

Seaways Hotel, 20 Pentire Ave ☎01637/874357. Situated close to the western end of Fistral Beach, at the edge of town. With fresh and airy rooms, plus use of heated swimming pool and sauna, staying here represents excellent value, though sea views cost an extra £5. ②.

Hostels

Home Surf Lodge, 18 Tower Rd ☎01637/873387; *www.newquay-online .com/homesurf*. The newest and tidiest of the town's hostels, with pine-furnished rooms all facing seaward; dorm beds cost £9, and there are double rooms (①). There are no self-catering facilities but breakfasts and snacks are served all day, and a chill-out room, Internet facility and computer games are on hand. No credit cards.

Matt's Surf Lodge, 110 Mount Wise Rd ☎01637/874651; *www.matts-surf-lodge.co.uk*. Set slightly further out than the other hostels, but with friendly staff and a licensed bar. Dorm beds are £8, and double rooms ①. There's a car park, and a special rate of £35 per week from September to May. No credit cards.

Pilot gigs (simple six-oared rowing boats), relics of the days when the trading schooners and ketches needed to be guided into harbour – the first to reach the vessel winning its custom – are now raced for pleasure from April to October; for details of fixtures contact Newquay Rowing Club ☎01637/ 876810 or the tourist office.

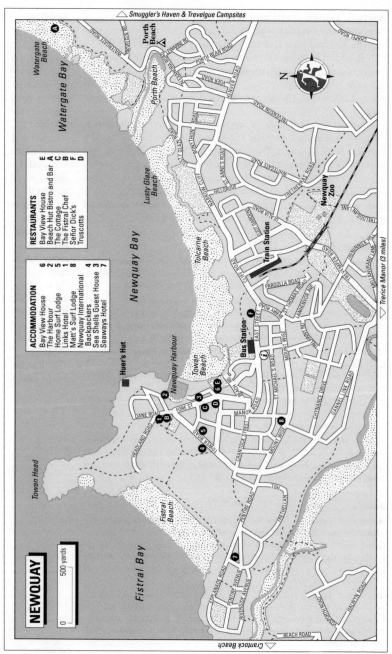

△ Smuggler's Haven & Trevelgue Campsites

NEWQUAY

0   500 yards

Watergate Bay

Fistral Bay

Newquay Bay

Crantock Beach ▷

Towan Head

Watergate Beach

Porth Beach

Lusty Glaze Beach

Tolcarne Beach

Towan Beach

Fistral Beach

Newquay Harbour

Huer's Hut ■

Trerice Manor (3 miles) ▷

Train Station

Bus Station

Newquay Zoo

ACCOMMODATION

Bay View House	6
The Harbour	2
Home Surf Lodge	5
Links Hotel	1
Matt's Surf Lodge	8
Newquay International Backpackers	4
Sea Shells Guest House	3
Seaways Hotel	7

RESTAURANTS

Bay View House	E
Beach Hut Bistro and Bar	A
The Cottage	C
The Fistral Chef	B
Señor Dick's	F
Truscotts	D

Streets: WATERGATE ROAD, TREVELGUE RD, CARNMARTH RD, EWARNE RD, CHAPEL ROAD, PORTH BEAN ROAD, PENTIRE ROAD, VOER ROAD, HENVER ROAD, STEVENSON ROAD, TRETHERRAS ROAD, WHITEGATE ROAD, PENNYTHORN, ST ANNE'S ROAD, HILLGROVE, NARROW CLIFF, ST GEORGE'S ROAD, TRELOGGAN LANE, TREGUNNEL HILL, MELLANVRANE LANE, BENNHICK HILL, BERRY ROAD, PARGOLLA ROAD, CLIFF ROAD, ST THOMAS ROAD, MANOR ROAD, EAST STREET, CRANTOCK STREET, DANE ROAD, HEADLAND ROAD, FORE ST, BEACON ROAD, ST MICHAEL'S ROAD, MOUNT WISE, CHYVERTON AVE, LANHERNE AVE, TRENANCE RD, TOR ROAD, GANNEL LINK ROAD, PENTIRE AVENUE, ESPLANADE ROAD, RIVERSIDE AVENUE, TRETHELLAN, BEACH ROAD, ROSSHILL ROAD, NANKALAN, PRETIRE ROAD

© Crown copyright

Newquay International Backpackers, 69–73 Tower Rd ☎01637/879366; *www.backpackers.co.uk/newquay*. This oldest and largest of Newquay's hostels is always popular with international travellers, so it's essential to book ahead in July and August (when under-18s are not accepted). Dorm beds cost £12, and there are some double rooms (①). Free transport from bus and train stations and airport is on offer, as well as day-trips and discounts on surf rental. No credit cards.

Campsites

Porth Beach, Porth ☎01637/876531; *www.porthbeach.co.uk*. Located behind Porth Beach to the east of town, this site has a villagey feel, and is reached on the B3276, half a mile from the A3058 turn-off. No same-sex groups. Closed Nov to mid-March.

Smugglers Haven, Trevelgue Rd ☎01637/852000; *www.surfshack.co.uk*. This site attracts the 18–30 singles crowd and has bars, a nightclub and a swimming pool.

Trevelgue, Trevelgue Rd ☎01637/851851; *www.cranstar.co.uk*. Next-door to *Smugglers Haven*, this place keeps its caravan, groups and family sites well separate. There's a restaurant, nightly entertainment in summer, and surf rental is available.

The town and beaches

Newquay's partly pedestrianized centre is a somewhat tacky parade of shops and restaurants from which lanes lead to ornamental gardens and sloping lawns on the cliff-tops. The town has plenty of family entertainments, including a steam railway, a water amusements park and aquarium; the best of these, however, is **Newquay Zoo**, in Trenance Gardens off Edgecumbe Avenue (daily: Easter–Oct 9.30am–6pm; Nov–Easter 10am–5pm; £5.50), which has a good programme of talks highlighting its conservation programmes, as well as a maze and play areas for children.

If you feel like escaping the seaside crowds, you'll appreciate the tranquillity of **Trerice Manor** (April to late July & mid-Sept to Oct Mon, Wed–Fri & Sun 11am–5.30pm, closes 5pm Oct; late July to mid-Sept daily 11am–5.30pm; last admission 30min before closing; £4.20), three miles southeast of Newquay. Little changed since it was built by Sir John Arundell in 1571, the house has a Dutch gabled facade and a sequence of period-furnished rooms, most impressive of which is the magnificent Hall, with an ornate plaster ceiling with pendants and a latticed window that preserves much of the original glass in 576 panes. The room's most interesting item is a rare set of fat sixteenth-century wooden skittles, with necks on top and bottom, similar to those used by Francis Drake when playing "bowls" on Plymouth Hoe (see p.123). After the house, the engagingly eccentric Lawnmower Museum in the great barn is worth a once-over, holding over one hundred of the machines in all their diversity, from 1873 onwards.

Trerice Manor is linked to Newquay by the twice-daily #50 bus (week-days only).

Newquay's main attraction, though, is the surrounding coastline. While development has extended unchecked east and north up the

Newquay
and around

All the main beaches are lifeguarded in season, and you should heed all warnings.

coast, the cliffs of **Towan Head** have limited Newquay's growth to the west, and you don't have to walk far to leave the shops behind. You can take in some good views round this headland, up Beacon Road from Fore Street's western end, turning right at King Edward's Crescent, and passing the whitewashed **huer's hut** (not open to the public), a reminder of the town's former fishing role. Stationed here as a lookout for pilchard shoals, the huer would send the fleet docked in the port into action by his cry of *heva!* ("found") bellowed through a three-foot long horn.

Sheltered by the headland and adjacent to the small harbour in the crook of the massive headland, Newquay's most central swimming spot, **Towan Beach**, is a smooth sandy expanse reached from the bottom of Beach Road off Fore Street. It's bound on its eastern side by a tall crag connected to the promenade above by a quaint replica of Bristol's Clifton Suspension Bridge. With the full range of equipment-rental facilities, the beach can get unbearably crowded in full season, and you'll get more elbow room on any of the succession of firm sandy beaches which extend for seven miles to the east. Nearest are **Tolcarne**, accessible from Narrowcliff Promenade, and, past Crigga Rocks, **Lusty Glaze**, reached by steep steps from Lusty Glaze Road, and well protected from the wind by the bordering cliffs. You can reach these spots along the sandy shore at low tide, but for some of the more distant beaches, such as **Porth Beach**, with its grassy headland, or the extensive **Watergate Bay**, two and a half miles north of the centre, it's worth using local buses #53 and #56.

All of the above are popular with surfers, particularly Watergate, but the most challenging is **Fistral Bay**, to the west, which you can reach on foot past Towan Head or across the golf links. Fully exposed to the Atlantic, the fierce breakers make it an ideal venue for surfing championships, but the violent rip currents are hazardous. On the other side of East Pentire Head from Fistral, **Crantock Beach** – reachable over the Gannel River by regular passenger ferry in season or by upstream footbridge – is usually less packed, and has a lovely backdrop of dunes and undulating grassland.

Newquay and around

Because of a stream running into the water, Porth Beach is the only one of Newquay's beaches to have failed the latest EU water-quality tests, while Fistral and Lusty Glaze were graded best.

Eating

Newquay is well equipped with **places to eat**, especially of the fast-food ilk; most are mediocre, but the best are listed below.

Bay View House, Fore St. Set in the hotel of the same name (see p.271), and offering panoramic views, this place serves lobster and wild boar, and a more modest set three-course menu for £8.45. There's a good wine list and a terrace café open during the day for coffee and snacks. Restaurant open evenings only. Closed Nov–Easter. Moderate.

Beach Hut Bistro and Bar, Watergate Bay. Open 9am–midnight all year, this is a trendy hangout for surfers and a good venue for a sundowner. Daily fish specials are available, as well as breakfasts and snacks. Inexpensive –Moderate.

The Cottage, 38 Fore St ☎01637/859200. This funky, lattice-windowed cottage serves all-day breakfasts, cream teas and in the evenings Tex-Mex, steaks and salads in the upstairs restaurant to a jazz accompaniment. Closed Sat lunch and all day Sun. Inexpensive–Moderate.

The Fistral Chef, 2 Beacon Rd. Lively café and takeaway, very close to the *Red Lion* pub (see overleaf), serving breakfasts from 8am (6am Sat) and sandwiches, pizzas and jacket potatoes until 10pm. Inexpensive.

Senor Dick's, East St ☎01637/851601; *res@hotelvictoria.presel.co.uk*. Popular Mexican theme bar and restaurant, with blue, red and yellow decor and up-to-the-minute music. A full range of Mexican dishes is available, plus chargrills and vegetarian options. Upstairs is the only cocktail bar in Newquay to feature fire flaring. Booking essential. Closed Sun–Thurs lunch mid-Sept to Easter. Moderate.

Truscotts, 19 Fore St. Long-established, award-winning fish-and-chip shop, to eat in or take away. Open till 11pm. Inexpensive.

Drinking and nightlife

Newquay's **pubs** overflow in summer, getting rowdy at night when surfers and clubbers take over, though many are still suitable for families during the day. The town has become Cornwall's biggest centre for **nightclubbing**; the magazine *Woz On* (published in summer only) usually has full listings, otherwise ask around for the most happening places, and watch the posters for the current venues. Most places have licences until 2am.

Beach Nightclub, 1 Beach Rd ☎01637/872194; *www.beachclubnqy.co.uk*. One of the most popular places in town, open nightly, with four bars on three floors. The diet is mainstream dance and party, 1970s nostalgia and indie; student night on Thurs has discounted drinks, and there are all-nighters on Fri. Up to £5 entry.

Berties, East St ☎01637/872255; *www.bertiesclub.co.uk*. Newquay's largest nightclub plays commercial, R&B, 1970s and 1980s music. Open nightly in summer; Fri and Sat only in winter. Entry up to £5.

Bowgie Inn, West Pentire, Crantock. Converted pub/disco three miles west of Newquay. The upstairs Surf Bar is open nightly in summer, when entry costs around £5. Aphex Twin began his DJ career here.

Central, Central Square. Very busy pub in the pedestrianized zone, with a large area for sitting out. The Art Deco interior consists of a cocktail bar, sofas, large screen and pool table. Food served all day.

Koola, Beach Rd ☎01637/873415. An up-to-the-minute "style bar" on three levels, attracting music aficionados rather than surfers, with portholes in walls and floor. When live bands aren't playing, hip-hop, UK garage, drum'n'bass and house are usually on the turntables. Open daily in summer, Fri & Sat in winter. Entry free of up to £10.

Red Lion Inn, North Quay Hill. Large pub, popular with surfers, that hums in the evenings and is close to the harbour. Live music on Fridays. Inexpensive pub food, pizzas and skillets served lunchtime and evenings.

Sailors, 11–17 Fore St ☎01637/872838. Lively pub with popular club next door for a young crowd, playing chart sounds, as well as retro, dance and house. Expect long queues in summer. Open May to mid-Sept nightly, Thurs–Sat only in winter. £5–10 entry.

Sandridge Hotel, Headland Rd ☎01637/872089. Newquay's only gay venue, with dance parties on Fri and Sat. Entry from £2.

Skinners Ale House, 58 East St. The relaxed atmosphere, sawdust floor and hops make this the best choice for real ale, and it's an occasional venue for beer tastings and festivals. Beer £1 a pint 6–7pm. Substantial food is served lunchtime and evenings.

Tall Trees, Tolcarne Rd ☎01637/850313. Three rooms play mainstream dance, grunge and indie, and 1970s and R&B – and you can wallow in foam parties on Fridays in summer. Open until 2am Mon–Sat in summer, Fri & Sat in winter (though Fri is pretty dead). Entry £3–6.

Walkabout, The Crescent; *www.walkaboutinns.com*. Rowdy and popular Australian-themed bar featuring crocodiles in hats and authentic tucker, located near Towan Beach. The huge single room is filled with TV screens tuned to different stations, and there is live music every night throughout summer, Fri & Sat in winter, with DJs on Thurs.

The world's longest surfboard can be seen outside Longboard House on Alma Place, just off Fore Street; thirty-six-and-a-half feet long, it was ridden by eleven people in honour of the total eclipse of August 1999.

Listings

Airport St Mawgan ☎01637/860551. British Airways (☎0845/733 3377) operates 4 flights daily to London Gatwick; Skybus (☎0845/710 5555) has daily connections with St Mary's, in the Isles of Scilly, and 3 times weekly (March–Oct) with Bristol and Exeter.

Bike rental From Towan Beach ☎01637/874668, or Newquay Bike Hire at Unit 1, Wesley Yard ☎01637/874040, who will deliver a bike free.

Car rental Europcar, Newquay Airport, St Mawgan ☎01637/860897; *www.europcar.com*; National Car Rental, 8a Quintrell Rd ☎01637/850750.

Fishing trips From May to October, full- (£24) or half-day (£12) trips can be arranged from the harbour (shark-trips £30 for the day). Contact Anchor Fishing ☎01637/877613 or 872605.

Hospital Newquay and District Hospital, St Thomas' Rd ☎01637/893600, has a 24hr minor injuries unit.

Internet café *CyberSurf*, 2 Broad St (daily 10am–10pm; around 10p a minute). Drinks available on the outside deck.

Pharmacy Kayes, 8 East St ☎01637/873353 (nightly until 9.30pm in summer).

Taxis 123, 38D Cliff Rd ☎01637/851234, operate a 24hr service; Yellow Cabs, 2 Beach Rd ☎01637/871000, run 7am–3am.

Tours Western Greyhound Ltd, 14 East St ☎01637/871871; *www.westerngreyhound.co.uk*, run half- and full-day coach tours in and around Cornwall (£4.50–6.50).

Padstow

Twelve miles north of Newquay, **PADSTOW** almost rivals its larger neighbour in popularity, but its compact dimensions and harbour ambience lend it a very different feel. Enclosed within the estuary of the Camel – the only river of any size that comes out on Cornwall's northern seaboard – the town was for a long time the principal fishing port on this coast, and it still shelters a small working fleet, even now that fishing takes second place to tourism. Recently, the town has acquired a reputation for its gourmet **restaurants**, most famously those run by chef superstar Rick Stein. Like Newquay, there are also some first-class beaches within a short distance on the predominantly cliffy coast, and in addition the town hosts one of Cornwall's most famous festivals, the **Obby Oss**, a costumed parade with medieval origins, taking place on May Day (see box on p.279).

Arrival, information and accommodation

Padstow is linked by regular **bus** #55 to Bodmin Parkway train station (see p.298) and Wadebridge (see p.283); the terminus lies south of the harbour on Station Road. The town's **tourist office** is housed in a new red-brick building on the north side of the harbour (April–Sept Mon–Sat 9.30am–5pm, also Sun 11am–4pm in July & Aug; Oct–March Mon–Fri 10am–4pm; ☎01841/533449; *www .padstow.uk.com*). There's no lack of **accommodation**, including

On Sundays throughout summer, at Padstow harbour, promenade brass-band concerts take place at 2.30pm and 7.30pm. There's no seating – listen as you wander around.

the very stylish but expensive options at the three dining establishments run by celebrity chef Rick Stein (see p.282, all ⑤). It's always wise to book ahead in summer, and months ahead if your visit coincides with the Obby Oss festival.

Hotels & B&Bs

Armside, 10 Cross St ☎01841/532271. A few minutes from the harbour, this eighteenth-century town house is elegantly and plainly furnished, with stripped pine and creaky floors. Parking is available – a precious commodity in Padstow. No credit cards. ③.

4 Riverside ☎01841/532383. You'll find this three-storeyed B&B right on the harbour next to the *Old Custom House*. The top bedroom has a prodigiously wide double bed and a French window leading onto a balcony. No credit cards. ②.

Old Ship, Mill Square ☎01841/532357. Family-run eighteenth-century hotel close to the harbour, with antique furnishings and walls stacked with paintings. All rooms are equipped with double showers. Parking is available. ⑤.

Padstow is the start of two of the West Country's most famous long-distance paths: the seventeen-mile Camel Trail (see box on p.283) and the thirty-mile Saints' Way across the peninsula to Fowey (see box on p.281)

Redingtons, 15 Duke St ☎01841/533670. You'll feel pampered in this eighteenth-century cottage on three floors, stuffed with antiques. The attic bedroom has a brass bed and its own sitting area, and in summer breakfast is served in the garden. Booking is essential in summer. No credit cards. ③.

Treverbyn House, Station Rd ☎01841/532855. This spacious and beautifully furnished Edwardian house preserves its original character with contemporary (working) fireplaces in the bedrooms. Ask for the turret room if possible. No credit cards. ③.

Campsites and youth hostel

Dennis Cove ☎01841/532349. Situated in a quiet field along the estuary about a ten-minute walk south of town, this campsite caters mainly for tents, and offers an outdoor heated pool. Closed Oct–Easter.

Trerethern Touring Park ☎01841/532061. A large campsite, with no static caravans, situated one mile southwest of Padstow on the A389, and accessible by footpath. Closed Nov–March.

Treyarnon Bay Youth Hostel, Tregonnan, Treyarnon ☎01841/520322. Four and a half miles west of Padstow, this former farmhouse is sited almost on the beach at Treyarnon Bay, and is the base for the Harlyn Surf School (see p.280), making it a popular surfers' stop. Beds in the 14-bed dorm and smaller rooms cost £10. It's half a mile from Constantine, which is accessible by bus between June and October (#55 or #56, also from Newquay). Closed Nov–March.

The town and around

With its medieval network of largely traffic-free lanes, which are draped for much of the year with window-boxfuls of hydrangeas, fuschias and geraniums, Padstow makes a pleasant place to wander. In summer, the place can be overwhelmed by tourists, but you don't need to walk far to escape the crowds.

The town's focal point is, of course, its harbour, usually crowded with small craft and surrounded by a wide quayside. Above and behind the quays, the parish church of **St Petroc** is worth looking

The Obby Oss festival

Padstow's chief annual festival, the **Obby Oss**, is a May Day – or May 2 if May Day is a Sunday – romp whose origin is obscure but has been variously ascribed as a welcome to summer, a rainmaker, a fertility ritual and even a strategy to ward off the French.

The celebration starts at midnight of the preceding day, when a procession sets off around town to the accompaniment of a special "Night Song", lasting till the early hours. Later in the morning, the "Obby Osses" – circular contraptions draped in shiny black material and hoisted onto fearsomely masked locals – make their appearance in streets bedecked with greenery. Two teams – all dressed in white with red or blue ribbons and bunches of spring flowers pinned to lapels – follow their own obby oss as it prances through the town on set routes, preceded by a club-wielding "teazer" and accompanied by a retinue of musicians, singers, drummers and twirling dancers. The strains of the May Song resound all day:

"Unite and unite and let us all unite,
For Summer is a-come in today.
And whither we are going we all will unite,
In the merry morning of May."

You'll need to book accommodation well ahead if you wish to attend, and it's worth being there the day before to relish the excitement of preparation. For photographs of the oss and renditions of the songs, log onto the Web site *http://home.freenet.bribbonobbyoss*. If you can't make the festival, you can see an authentic oss in the town museum (see below).

into, standing amid the slate tombstones of mariners within a wooded churchyard on Church Lane. A large, mostly slate construction, the church is dedicated to St Petroc, a Welsh or Irish monk who landed here in the sixth century, founded a monastery on this site and eventually became Cornwall's most important saint, bequeathing his name – "Petrock's Stow" – to the town. Inside there's a fine fifteenth- or sixteenth-century font with the twelve apostles, three on each side, carved from Catacleuse stone, and a Tudor-period wine-glass pulpit. Look out too for a lively medieval bench end to the right of the altar depicting a fox preaching to a congregation of geese. The walls are lined with monuments to the local Prideaux family, who still occupy nearby **Prideaux Place**, on Tregirls Lane, the main B3276 into Padstow (Easter to late April & late May to early Oct Mon–Thurs & Sun 1.30–5pm; house & grounds £4.50, grounds only £2), a superbly preserved example of an Elizabethan manor house. Inside, you'll find grand staircases and richly furnished rooms full of portraits and with fantastically ornate ceilings, while outside there are formal gardens, and a deer park affording long views over the Camel estuary.

You can rent bikes from Brinham's on Padstow's South Quay (☎01841/ 532594); see Wadebridge (see p.283) for a greater choice of bike rental.

Unless you're here on May 1, your only chance of seeing an "obby oss" (see box, above) is in the otherwise run-of-the-mill **Padstow Museum** (mid-April to late Oct Mon–Fri 10.30am–4.30pm, Sat

Padstow

Boat Trips and the ferry to Rock

Padstow's **harbour** is jammed with boats offering cruises and fishing trips in Padstow Bay, including excursions to view the razorbills and cormorants, and occasionally puffins, seals and sharks, which can be seen off the shores hereabouts (£5 per hour). The harbour is also the place to board the regular **ferry** (daily 7.50am–7.30pm; not Sun in winter; £1.60 return) across the estuary to **Rock** for the alluring beaches around Daymer Bay and Polzeath (see p.284). Departures are from the harbour's North Pier except at low water when ferries leave from near the war memorial further downstream. In summer, an evening **water taxi** takes over from 8pm till late (☎01208/862815 day or 862217 evenings; £3 single, £4 return).

10.30am–1pm; 50p), hidden upstairs in the Institute on Market Place. The oss dates back to the 1940s and looks a little the worse for wear, but brings to life the photos and descriptions of the revelries on the panels.

For the beaches on the eastern side of the Camel estuary, see p.284.

The coast on the south side of the estuary offers good **beaches**, which you can reach in summer on bus #56 (not Sat), though walking allows you to view some terrific coastline. About a mile out of town, the rivermouth is clogged by **Doom Bar**, a sand bar that was allegedly the curse of a mermaid who had been mortally wounded by a fisherman who mistook her for a seal. Apart from thwarting the growth of Padstow as a busy commercial port, the bar has scuppered some three hundred vessels, with great loss of life.

If you continue north of the Bar, then west round **Stepper Point** you reach after about three miles the sandy and secluded **Harlyn Bay**, good for swimming and surfing. The area's best surfing beach, though, with first-class water quality, is **Constantine Bay**, a mile south of Trevose Head, the promontory located two miles west of Harlyn Bay. The surrounding dunes and rock pools make this one of the most appealing bays on the coast, though the tides can be treacherous and bathing hazardous near the rocks. There are other good surfing beaches in the neighbourhood too, such as adjacent **Treyarnon Bay**, but the surrounding caravan sites can make these claustrophobic in summer. You may find a bit more peace around **Porthcothan**, a long narrow beach with dramatic cliffs and an expanse of sand at low tide, a mile or so south of Treyarnon.

Surfing tuition is offered by the Harlyn Surf School (☎01841/ 533076; www .harlynsurf .co.uk) which runs lessons, as well as residential courses, from the youth hostel (see p.278).

Three or four miles further south lies one of Cornwall's most dramatic beaches, **Bedruthan Steps**, whose jagged slate outcrops were traditionally held to be the stepping-stones of a giant called Bedruthan, a legendary figure conjured into existence in the nineteenth century. You can view the grand panorama from the clifftop path, at a point which drivers can reach on the B3276. From here steep steps lead down the sheer face to the sandy beach, though there is currently no access between November and February. The beach makes a great place to ramble about, but swimming is not

The Saint's Way

Padstow's St Petroc church is the traditional starting point for one of Cornwall's oldest walking routes, the **Saints' Way**, which extends for some thirty miles between Cornwall's north and south coasts. Connecting the principal ports of Padstow and Fowey, the path originates from the Bronze Age when traders preferred the cross-country hike to making the perilous sea journey round Land's End. The route was later travelled by Irish and Welsh missionaries crossing the peninsula between the fifth and eighth centuries, on pilgrimage to the principal shrines of Cornwall's Celtic culture.

The route is well marked and can be walked in stages, the country paths that constitute it stretching for two to six miles each between roads and villages; although it crosses several trunk roads, these do not impinge too much. You should be able to cover the route in a couple of days, allowing time to soak up the rural landscape. It's worth getting hold of the *Saint's Way* information pack (£3.99 from tourist offices), a very useful compendium of route plans, maps and background on what to see along the way, or you can pick up free leaflets giving detailed directions in Padstow, Bodmin and Fowey tourist offices (see pp.277, 299 and 183).

From St Petroc, follow Hill Street, crossing New Street, and continue along Dennis Road and Dennis Lane to the small lake at Dennis Cove, from where the path climbs through fields to a monument to Queen Victoria, the point at which most people stop. From the monument, the route leads along a lane (signposted Trenance) and then a footpath across flattish, open farmland, before climbing **St Breock Downs** seven or eight miles out of Padstow, from where you can enjoy sweeping views stretching from the Camel estuary to the white-clay mountains around St Austell. At this point the path veers southeast to pass through **Lanivet**, the halfway point of the Way, about five- or six-hours' walk out of Padstow, and a couple of miles outside Bodmin. Here you'll find two good places to stay: *Lilac Cottage*, an inexpensive B&B overlooking the village green on Church Road (☎01208/832083; *www.cornwall-online.co.uk/lilac-cottage*; no credit cards; ①; closed Oct–Feb except for advance booking), whose owners like to share their large, beamed sitting room with guests, and *Lower Woon Farm* (☎01208/831756; no credit cards; ①), situated 200yd along the Lanhydrock road from Lanivet, which serves three-course evening meals for £12 in an elegant dining room, has a wood-burning stove for cold evenings, and rents out bikes.

Less than three miles south of here, **Helman Tor** (674ft) holds the trail's most impressive scenery, studded with bare boulders and wind-eroded rocks and flanked by acres of gorse. At Helman Tor Gate, the path divides, giving you the choice of reaching Fowey via **Lanlivery** – home of St Brevita's church with one of Cornwall's landmark towers – or **Luxulyan**, which has a lush gorge crossed by a viaduct and aqueduct built in 1842 and a holy well below the fifteenth-century church. Both ways are around 11.5 miles long and should take around six hours. The eastern route through Lanlivery brings you through the wooded estuary of the River Fowey – legendary meeting place of Tristan and Iseult – to the port, while the western route follows an old cobbled causeway for part of the way, and passes through **Tywardreath**, which once marked the inland extent of the sea before the port of Par was built. Tywardreath means "house on the strand", and was described by Daphne Du Maurier in her novel of that name. Fowey is four miles southeast of here; the end of the route is the church of St Fimbarrus here – see pp.183–184 for accommodation in town.

advised because of the rocks and often violent waves, and you should be careful not to get trapped by the incoming tide.

Eating and drinking

Padstow's quayside is lined with snack bars and pasty shops as well as pubs where you can sit outside, but foodies know the town best for its high-class **restaurants**, particularly those associated with chef Rick Stein, who has reigned in Padstow for 25 years, and whose TV fame has spawned a host of additional restaurants at more reasonable prices. In general, however, you'll have to blow some of your budget to eat in Padstow's famous eating places; all share a fascination for bright Mediterranean colours – uplifting at first, but they soon pall. Always book ahead in summer and at weekends.

If you fancy a picnic, Rick Stein's **delicatessen** is next to his café in Middle Street.

London Inn, Lanadwell St. Adorned with hanging baskets, this pub has an unpretentious atmosphere, with wood panelling and smokey-yellow ceilings. Sandwiches, pasties and more substantial meals are available. No mobiles. Inexpensive.

Margot's Bistro, 11 Duke St ☎01841/533441. An intimate venue with pink and blue decor, offering daily changing menus, from which some items – such as the caramelized walnuts and sticky toffee pudding – can be bought to take away. Vegetarians should call ahead. Closed Mon & Tues and Nov–Jan. Moderate–Expensive.

No. 6, 6 Middle St ☎01841/532359. Mediterranean-style restaurant with black-and-white-tiled floor, white walls and a courtyard, this place uses organic produce whenever possible. Nonsmoking (except in courtyard). Book at weekends. Open evenings only. Closed Nov–Dec. Expensive.

Old Custom House, South Quay ☎01841/532359. Inexpensive food such as chilli and lasagne is served all day in the bar here, while the adjoining spacious *Pescadou* restaurant offers a moderate–expensive menu that includes a selection of steaks alongside the usual fish choices.

Rick Stein's Café, 10 Middle St ☎01841/532700. More casual than the *Seafood Restaurant* (see below), and furnished with stripey banquettes and pine tables, the master chef's café caters for carnivores, with Mediterranean-type snacks at lunch (arrive early) and set-price meals at night, when booking is necessary. Nonsmoking. Closed Sun April–Oct; open Fri & Sat only Nov–April. Moderate.

Rojano's, 9 Mill Square ☎01841/532796. If you're sick of fish, grab a pizza or pasta here, washed down with a Belgian beer. Takeways are available too. Closed Mon and Nov–Feb. Inexpensive.

St Petroc's Bistro, 4 New St ☎01841/532700. This baby-Stein has a cheaper, more French-inspired version of the *Seafood Restaurant*'s menu. You can sit on bentwood chairs at small wooden tables in the main eating area, or you can eat in the bar or garden. Closed Mon. Moderate.

Seafood Restaurant, Riverside ☎01841/532700. One of the country's top fish restaurants, Rick Stein's flagship is classy without being snooty, furnished with green wicker chairs on a parquet floor. Oysters and lobsters feature on the menu and pre-dinner drinks can be taken in the conservatory. A fixed-price dinner will set you back about £40 and lunch about £30. The waiting list often

The Camel Trail

The **Camel Trail** is one of the West Country's best cycle routes, running a total of seventeen miles from Padstow up the River Camel as far as Poley's Bridge, a mile west of Blisland (see p.302) on the edge of Bodmin Moor. The five-and-a-quarter-mile Padstow–Wadebridge section of the trail follows an old railway line and offers glimpses of a variety of birdlife – especially around **Pinkson Creek**, habitat of terns, herons, curlews and egrets. However, this stretch can get very crowded in summer, and you may choose to join at Wadebridge – from the town centre, follow Eddystone Road (from the south side of the bridge) until you reach the trail. From Wadebridge, the route heads five and a half miles southeast towards Bodmin (see p.298), before turning northwards for a further six and a quarter miles to Poley's Bridge, within spitting distance of Wenfordbridge. This, the quieter end of the route, traces the winding river through tranquil woods, always within sight of the moor. The trail is also open to walkers, and to horses between Padstow and Dunmere, a mile west of Bodmin. You can pick up guides, maps and leaflets at the Camel Trail and Wildlife Shop on Eddystone Road or from the tourist offices at Padstow, Wadebridge or Bodmin (see pp.277, below & 299).

Bikes can be rented in Wadebridge from Bridge Cycle Hire on Eddystone Road (open mid-Feb to Nov daily 9am–5pm; ☎01208/ 814545), or across the road at Bridge Bike Hire (open daily all year 9am–5pm; ☎01208/ 813050).

stretches for months ahead, though you could well strike lucky on a weekday out of season. Closed Sun. Very Expensive.

Wadebridge

About eight miles up the Camel river from Padstow, and reachable on frequent buses, **WADEBRIDGE** is nowadays rather a nondescript market town, a far cry from its eighteenth-century heyday as one of Cornwall's main corn-exporting ports. The chief sign of its former stature is the impressive fifteenth-century bridge spanning the River Camel on seventeen arches, and built on a foundation, so it is claimed, of wool packs. You're unlikely to want to spend much time here, though the town makes a useful base for the **Camel Trail** (see box, above).

Practicalities

Wadebridge's **bus station** is located on Southern Way, on the south side of the medieval bridge, from where there are hourly connections to Padstow (#55). The **tourist office** is in the town hall, off the bridge, on The Platt (June–Sept Mon–Fri 10am–5pm, plus Sat 10am–noon late July to early Sept; Oct–May Mon–Fri 10am–4pm; ☎01208/813725). The town has a number of good **accommodation** options, including *Polwhele* (☎01208/814038; no credit cards; ②), south of the centre at Trevanion Road, two minutes from the Camel Trail, which has a couple of light and spacious rooms, and the more characterful *Old Vicarage* in Egloshayle, half a mile south of the centre on the A389, with mullioned windows and antique furniture (☎01208/812210; no credit cards; ①).

You don't need to look far to find a **restaurant** in Wadebridge: in Trevanion Road, the low-beamed *Rowan House* serves up good meat

The Wadebridge Folk Festival is Cornwall's biggest, taking place over three days during the August Bank Holiday, and featuring rootsy European and American artists. Full details can be obtained at the tourist office or ☎01752/ 843510; Wadebridge Folk@ hotmail.com

*Wadebridge
hosts
Cornwall's
biggest agri-
cultural event,
the Royal
Cornwall
Show, over
three days in
mid-June, fea-
turing march-
ing bands,
sheepdog dis-
plays and
sheep racing:
for details call
☎01208/
812183.*

*You can find
out more
information
about Polzeath
at
www.polzeath
.co.uk
Surfing equip-
ment can be
rented from
Ann's Cottage
(open daily all
year;
☎01208/
863317) or
from T.J.'s
Surf Shop,
(April–Dec;
☎01208/
863625).*

and fish main courses for under a tenner; booking is essential (☎01208/813362; closed Sun & Mon). Close to the cycle-rental depots in Eddystone Road, *Simply Food* has a quirky charm, consisting of two small rooms furnished with a 1950s TV, war-time newspapers and board games, and sells baguettes with a vast range of fillings, including clotted cream and chocolate (open 10am–4pm; closed Wed).

Polzeath and Daymer Bay

Situated three miles northwest of Padstow, on the far side of the Camel estuary, **POLZEATH** is renowned for its fine, flat sand beach, where the slow wave is ideal for wannabe surfers – even the babies turn out in wet suits. The large expanse of sand attracts the sand yachters as well, not to mention its fair share of rich kids whose high-spirited shenanigans regularly hit the headlines in the silly season. Surrounded by dunes, and with fine views across the estuary, **Daymer Bay**, a mile or two to the south, is a great place just for sun-bathing, while its shallow waters are a big hit with families. It's also very popular with the windsurfing crowd, and equipment is available to rent from stalls in summer.

Few people are tempted away from the sand and sea to visit the thirteenth-century church of **St Enodoc**, the burial place of the poet **John Betjeman**, whose holiday haunt was here, but it's an appealing spot, the building half buried in the sand dunes and surrounded by a protective hedge of tamarisk. So invasive were the surrounding sands that at one time the vicar and his congregation had to enter through a hole in the roof. It's now incongruously stranded in the middle of a golf course, most easily approached from the Daymer Bay car park, where the footpath is signposted (alternatively, cross the golf course from Rock, following the white stones and keeping a weather eye open for golf balls).

From Padstow, Polzeath can be reached via the Rock passenger **ferry** (see box on p.280) – if you're driving, the journey is five times longer as it involves a detour round the Camel estuary. By **bus** it's accessible on #124 (not Sun) from Wadebridge. Polzeath's **tourist office** is set back from the beach in Coronation Gardens (Easter–Oct Mon–Sat 10am–5pm; ☎01208/862488). Good **accommodation** choices include the well-sited *Pentire View* (☎01208/862484; no cards; ①; no groups), a pleasant B&B a few yards up the hill from the beach, and *Pheasant's Rise*, a modern bungalow a mile inland at Trebetherick with great views, a sunken bath and hash browns for breakfast (☎01208/863190; no credit cards; ①; closed Nov–Feb). The nearest **campsite** lies on the low cliff just above the beach, *Tristram Camping and Caravan Park* (☎01208/862215; closed Nov–Feb; booking advised in July & Aug), and is fully equipped and usually swarming with surfers.

Polzeath has plenty of decent snack stops, including *Finn's* (☎01208/863472; closed Nov–Easter), a brightly painted eaterie with wooden tables and patio just back from the beach, which also offers good and moderately priced à la carte dinners. Further up the road, *Mother's Kitchen* (daytime only) is good for ice cream and *panini*, while the next-door *Hayle Bay Diner* serves decent fish and chips and pizzas till 10pm; both are closed November to Easter. Right on the beach, the cheerful *Galleon Café* (closed Nov–Feb) does a good trade in chips, baguettes, pizzas and treacle tart. The *Oyster Catcher* **pub**, a few steps up the hill, fills up with families during the day and gets fairly merry at night; steaks and pub food are available lunch-times and evenings.

Port Isaac and around

Five miles east of Polzeath and connected by #124 bus, **PORT ISAAC** is wedged in a gap in the precipitous cliff-wall. Only seasonal trippers ruffle the surface of life in this quiet and cramped harbour town which remains largely dedicated to the crab and lobster trade. It makes a lovely secluded spot to hole up for a few days, with granite, slate and whitewashed cottages tumbling down steeply to a largely unspoilt seafront, where a pebble beach and rock pools are exposed by the low tide.

There is some wonderful coastline on either side of the village, best explored on foot, though you face an initial climb out of the port. A couple of miles west, the tiny inlet of **Port Quin** has a few placid cottages but no shops, the place having been abandoned in the nineteenth century when the antimony mine at nearby Doyden failed. The land is now managed by the National Trust who have maintained a tidy appearance. At low tide, you can poke around the patches of sand and the rock pools. Half a mile along the coast road from Port Isaac in the opposite direction brings you to **Port Gaverne** (pronounced Gayverne), a small cove with a pebbly beach and sheltered bathing, where you can grab a bite to eat in the smart *Port Gaverne Inn*.

Practicalities

Parking is limited unless you're staying at the hotel, so drivers to Port Isaac should deposit their vehicles in the car park at the top of the village. The choicest **accommodation** in the village has to be the *Slipway Hotel*, in premier position right on the seafront, some of whose comfortable old rooms have harbour views (☎01208/ 880264; *www.portisaac.com*; ③). It's upbeat and youthfully staffed, and has a good bar and restaurant (see overleaf). Cheaper places lie away from the sea at the top of the village, the best choices overlooking the sea; of these the *Bay Hotel*, 1 The Terrace (☎01208/880380; *jacki.burns@talk21.com*; ②), represents good value, its light and bright rooms decorated in restful colours – there's also a wood-burning stove in winter. A few minutes' further down, but still with sea views on a cliff, the low, white *Old Schoolhouse*

Port Isaac

Surf's Up, at 21 Trenant Close and on the beach in Polzeath (☎01208/ 862003; www .surfsupsurf school.com) runs lessons at 10am and 2pm daily between March and the end of October; booking is advisable in July and August. The surf check number is ☎01208/ 862162.

From Whit Sunday until September Port Isaac's local choir gathers at the harbour from 8pm on Friday nights to regale listeners with shanties.

*Fishing and
sightseeing
trips along the
coast can be
arranged from
Port Isaac's
harbour for £5
per hour.*

*A twice-yearly
classical music
festival is
held at St
Endellion,
two miles
south of Port
Isaac (a week
at Easter and
ten days in
early Aug):
call ☎01208/
850463 for
information.*

(☎01208/880721; ②) has modernized, spacious rooms with exposed beams and slate walls.

Seafood and specifically crab are Port Isaac's specialities, best sampled in the hotel **restaurants**, notably the *Old Schoolhouse*, which mainly serves fresh and reasonably priced fish dishes, and the *Slipway Hotel*, where the oak-beamed restaurant offers crab, lobster and delicious medallions of monkfish with fresh peaches (moderate; book ahead in summer). On Fore Street, *Bones Bistro* in the friendly and atmospheric *Golden Lion* **pub** offers reasonably priced steak and Cornish ale or fish pies, and lunchtime snacks are available in the bar. At Port Gaverne, you can dine cheaply at the *Port Gaverne Inn* on such dishes as Surfer's Lunch – chips topped with cheese and fresh onion rings – or more expensively at the same hotel's *Midge's Restaurant* (☎01208/880151), which specializes in fish and where it's best to book ahead.

Tintagel and around

Seven miles northeast of Port Isaac, reached by inland roads, the village of **TINTAGEL** is a dreary collection of bungalows, guesthouses and souvenir shops milking the area's associations with King Arthur for all they're worth. Thankfully, none of this lessens the impact of the black, forsaken ruins of **Tintagel Castle** (daily: April to mid-July & Sept 10am–6pm; mid-July to Aug 10am–7pm; Oct 10am–5pm; Nov–March 10am–4pm; £2.80; EH), magnificently sited on the rocky littoral a short walk west of the village. Although the castle makes a plausibly resonant candidate for the abode of the Once and Future King, it was in fact a Norman stronghold occupied by the earls of Cornwall, who after sporadic spurts of rebuilding allowed it to decay, most of it having washed into the sea by the sixteenth century. Much older remains are still to be seen, however – notably the remains of a **Celtic monastery** that occupied this promontory in the sixth century, which have become an important source of information on the set-up of the country's earliest monastic houses. Digs begun in 1998 on the eastern side of the island have also revealed glass fragments dating from the sixth or seventh centuries and believed to originate in Malaga, as well as a 1500-year-old section of slate bearing two Latin inscriptions, one of them attributing authorship to one "Artognou, father of Coll's descendant"; some people have taken this as a trace of Arthur's existence, though Artognou was quite a common name at that time. The slate is currently on display in Truro's museum (see p.193).

From the village, the shortest route to the castle is along a well-trodden signposted path; if you can't face the ten-minute walk, a Land Rover service from the end of Fore Street will carry you there and back (Easter–Oct; £1 each way). The most evocative approach to the site, however, is from **Glebe Cliff** to the west (accessed off the B3263), where the Norman parish church of **St Materiana** sits in windswept isolation; the South West Coast Path passes close by, and out of season drivers can park here before descending to the castle. Of the numerous car parks, the private ones closer to the castle are cheapest.

Back in the village, a couple of items among the cafés and B&Bs may excite a degree of interest. On the main Fore Street, **King Arthur's Great Halls** (daily: Easter–Oct 10am–5pm; Nov–Easter 11am–3pm; £2.75), created in the 1930s by Frederick Thomas Glassop, a retired London grocer, is grandiose attempt to re-create the court of King Arthur. A set tour and laser light show picks out the 72 Pre-Raphaelite windows depicting the deeds of the knights, a fake granite throne and round table and much other pseudo-twaddle. On the opposite side of Fore Street, the **Old Post Office** (April–Sept daily 11am–5.30pm; Oct daily 11am–4pm; £2.30; NT) supplies some much-needed authenticity: the rickety-roofed slate-built manor house dating from the fourteenth century has been restored to its appearance in the Victorian era – when it was used as a post office – though the original gallery can still be seen.

South of Tintagel, the coast is wild and unspoiled, making for some steep and strenuous walking, well compensated by some stupendous strands of sandy beaches en route, such as that at **Trebarwith**, two miles down, with its beautiful rock formations, though the beach is only accessible at low tide.

Practicalities

Tintagel is connected by the frequent #124 **bus** from Port Isaac, and #X10, #122 and #124 from Boscastle. Buses stop on the main Fore Street close to the octagonal **tourist office** (daily: March–Oct 10am–5pm; Nov–Feb 11am–3pm; ☎01840/779084), sited in the council car park on the road from Camelford. It has information boards on King Arthur and an audiovisual show on the same theme.

Competition among Tintagel's numerous **accommodation** choices has kept prices – and charm factor – low. However, you'll find both character and good value in the fourteenth-century *Olde Malt House* on Fore Street (☎01840/770461; *www.cornwall-online.co.uk /olde-malthouse*; ①; closed Jan), which also has two restaurants and private parking, and, also on Fore Street, the nonsmoking *Tintagel Arms Hotel* (☎01840/770780; ②; closed Jan), an attractive place with some rooms under the eaves. Further up the same street, the *Wharncliffe Arms* (☎01840/770393; ①), has more basic rooms, including a four-bedded dormitory at £12.50 per person. Alternatively, for a rural treat, you could head for *Trebrea Lodge* (☎01840/770410; ⑨; closed Jan), a mile inland from Tintagel, at Trenale (from the B3263 towards Bosinney, turn right at the Catholic church and right at the crossroads), a Cornish manor house, with an elegant first-floor sitting room, and all bedrooms facing the sea.

At the other end of the scale, but spectacularly sited on Glebe Cliff, the offices of a former slate quarry now house **Tintagel Youth**

King Arthur in Cornwall

The big question about **King Arthur** has always been, "Did he really exist?" If he did, it is likely that he was an amalgam of two people; a sixth-century Celtic warlord who united the local tribes in a series of success-ful battles against the invading Anglo-Saxons, and a local Cornish saint. Whatever his origins, his role was recounted and inflated by poets and troubadours over the ensuing centuries (particularly in Welsh poems, the earliest of which is *Gododdin*, thought to date from the sixth century). Though there is no mention of him in the ninth- to twelfth-century *Anglo-Saxon Chronicle*, tales of Arthur and the knights of Camelot, King Mark of Cornwall, and Tristan and Iseult were prevalent in Celtic folklore by the time Arthur's exploits were elaborated by the unreliable twelfth-century chronicler Geoffrey of Monmouth, who first popularized the notion that Tintagel was Arthur's birthplace. Another chronicler of the period, William of Malmesbury, further embroidered the popular legend that, after being mortally wounded in battle, Arthur sailed to Avalon (Glastonbury, in Somerset), where he was buried alongside Guinevere. The Arthurian legends were crystallized in Thomas Malory's epic, *Morte d'Arthur* (1485), further romanticized in Tennyson's *Idylls of the King* (1859–85) and resurrected in T.H. White's saga, *The Once and Future King* (1937–58).

Although there are places throughout Britain and Europe that claim some association with Arthur, it is England's West Country, and **Cornwall** in particular, that has the greatest concentration of places boasting a link. Relatively untouched by the Saxon invasions, Cornwall has practically appropriated the hero as its own, and, fertilized by fellow Celts from Brittany and Wales, the legends have established deep roots, so that, for example, the spirit of Arthur is said to be embodied in the Cornish chough

Hostel (☎01840/770334; closed Oct–March), where beds cost £10. By foot, it's a mile outside the village, past St Materiana. With only 24 beds and one double room, it's essential to book ahead. Self-catering only is available. At the end of Atlantic Road, the *Headland* site offers scenic but exposed **camping** (☎01840/770239; closed Nov–March).

The **restaurant** attached to the *Tintagel Arms Hotel* is a great place for an evening meal, the accent on Greek and Mediterranean dishes and salads, plus a good choice for vegetarians. The *Wharncliffe Arms* has bar snacks, inexpensive meals and curries on Friday night. Next door to the *Tintagel Arms*, the *Village Tea Rooms* serves tempting snacks and cakes during the day and home-made lemonade in summer.

Boscastle

Three miles east of Tintagel, the port of **BOSCASTLE** is compressed within a narrow ravine carved out by the rivers Jordan and Valency, its tidy riverfront bordered by thatched and lime-washed houses and giv-ing onto a twisty harbour. In its heyday as a port during the nineteenth

– a bird now extinct in Cornwall. The most famous Arthurian site is probably **Tintagel**, while nearby Bodmin Moor is full of places with names like "King Arthur's Bed" and "King Arthur's Downs". Camlann, the battlefield where Arthur was mortally wounded fighting against his nephew Mordred, is thought to lie on the northern reaches of the moor at Slaughterbridge, near **Camelford** (see p.307), which is also sometimes identified as Camelot itself. Nearby, at **Dozmary Pool** (see p.304), the knight Bedivere was dispatched by the dying Arthur to return the sword Excalibur to the mysterious hand emerging from the water – though Loe Pool in Mount's Bay also claims this honour (see p.209). According to some, Arthur's body was transported after the battle to **Boscastle** (see below), from where a funeral barge transported the body to Avalon.

Cornwall is also the presumed home of King Mark, at the centre of a separate cycle of myths which later became interwoven with the Arthurian one. It was Mark who sent the knight Tristan to Ireland to fetch his betrothed, Iseult; his headquarters is supposed to have been at **Castle Dore** near Fowey. Out beyond **Land's End**, the fabled, vanished country of Lyonesse is also said to be the original home of Arthur, as well as being (according to Spenser's *Faerie Queene*) the birthplace of Tristan.

Much of Cornwall's celebration of the Arthurian sagas has the same cynical basis as the more ancient desire to claim Arthur by the various villages and sites throughout England and Wales: the cachet and hence profit to be had from the veneration of a secular saint. Witness the "discovery" of the tomb of Arthur and Guinevere by the Benedictine monks of Glastonbury in the twelfth century, which helped to boost the profile of their powerful abbey. Today in Tintagel you will find Arthurian tack galore, including every kind of Merlinesque hogwash (crystal balls, sugar-coated wands, etc), and even Excaliburgers.

century, sailing vessels had to be "hobbled" (towed) through the entrance by boats manned by eight oarsmen, and centred in the channel by gangs of men pulling on ropes. Horses then hauled the goods, which came from as far afield as Canada, up Boscastle's steep inclines, bringing back in return slate, manganese and china clay for export.

Boscastle grew up around twin settlements around the harbour area and around the site of Bottreaux Castle, built in the twelfth century on a spur above the Jordan valley – below what is now the Methodist chapel on Fore Street – and now disappeared (there's a model of its presumed appearance in the tourist office). The two parts are connected by High Street at the top of the hill, which changes its name to Fore Street, Dunn Street and Old Road, which in turn meets Old Mill Road by the harbour. To take in the village and all its Thomas Hardy connections (see box, overleaf), you can follow a circular walk starting either from Fore Street or the main car park, where there is a local map. The signposted walk traces the valley of the river Valency for three miles or so to the church of **St Juliot** (drivers will find it signposted off the B3263), restored by Hardy when he was plying his trade as a young architect. It's small and nondescript – Hardy later

In rough weather, walk to the end of the harbour an hour either side of low tide to see the Devil's Bellows in action – a blow-hole that shoots water across the harbour entrance.

Boscastle

After eight years working as an architect in London, Thomas Hardy came to Boscastle in 1870 to restore the church of St Juliot. It was in the course of this work that he first met Emma Gifford, the sister-in-law of the rector, and after return visits he eventually married his "West of Wessex girl" in 1874. A year earlier he had published his third novel *A Pair of Blue Eyes*, which opens with an account of an architect arriving in a Cornish village to restore its church, and which is full of descriptions of the country around Boscastle. Although the marriage to Emma was highly strained, her death in 1912 inspired Hardy to return to the village and to write the bitter-sweet love lyrics recalling happier moments in their married life, published in *Poems 1912–1913*, which have been called amongst the most moving love poems in the language. In 1916, he erected a plaque to Emma's memory in St Juliot, still visible on the wall of the north aisle.

regretted his draconian restoration – and pretty much as he left it. The rectory where he stayed lies a quarter of a mile beyond the church, and is now a comfortable B&B (see below).

If you need a break from Hardy, check out the **Museum of Witchcraft**, down by the harbour (Easter to late Oct Mon–Sat 10.30am–5.50pm, Sun noon–5.30pm; £2), an intelligent, comprehensive and nongimmicky account of witchcraft through the ages, displayed in themed galleries. Look out for the "dark mirrors" – supposed to see into the future – and poppets (dolls) used in cursing, with pubic hair and nail clippings sewn onto them.

Practicalities

Boscastle's **tourist office** is situated in the council car park at the bottom of the main road into the village (daily: March–Oct 10am–5pm; Nov–Feb 10.30am–4pm; ☎01840/250010). One of the most appealing **places to stay** is *St Christopher's Hotel* (☎01840/250412; *www.stchristophershotel.co.uk*; ②; closed Dec–Feb), a restored Georgian manor house at the top of the High Street, but for a real Hardy experience, head for *The Old Rectory*, on the road to St Juliot (☎01840/250225; *www.stjuliot.com*; ②; closed Nov–March; nonsmoking), where you can stay in either Hardy's or Emma's bedroom, and roam the extensive grounds. There's fruit from the kitchen garden for breakfast, croquet on the lawn in summer and log fires in winter.

The most congenial area to stay in, however, is by the harbour, where *Sunnyside*, by the flagpole, has three cottagey, comfortable rooms (☎01840/250453; *sunnysidebb@talk21.com*; no credit cards; ①; closed Dec & Jan); you'll need to book ahead. The harbour also has the lovely old **youth hostel** (☎01840/250287; closed Nov to mid-March), housed in former stables; all beds, at £10, are in dormitories in the old hayloft, and parking is in the village. You'll find a couple of peaceful **campsites** at *Trebyla Farm* (☎01840/250308; closed Nov–Easter), one and a half miles from Boscastle on the B3263 towards Bude (on the #122, #124 and #X4 bus routes), and *Lower Pennycrocker* (☎01840/250257; closed Oct–Easter), signposted two miles out of Boscastle on the same road.

For **eating and drinking** the village has some lively pubs that provide food and music nights as well as good ales. Of these, the beamed old *Napoleon* (☎01840/250204; moderate) in the upper part of Boscastle offers such diversions as shove ha'penny, a lawned garden and acoustic folk and rock on Tuesdays; it also houses the popular *Boney's Bistro* (booking advised), excellent for fresh seafood. Down near the harbour, the busy *Cobweb* takes its name from the layers of spider's webs found when it was converted from a warehouse; it serves wholesome fresh bar food (including vegetarian) and has live rock on Saturdays. If you don't like pubs, your best bet for a good feed is the *Harbour* (☎01840/250380; closed mid-Nov to Easter), where you can eat moderately priced organic, Asian-influenced food at wooden kitchen tables; book ahead at weekends.

Bude and around

There is little distinctively Cornish in the seaside town of **BUDE**, just four miles from the Devon border. Built around the mouth of the River Neet and the parallel Bude Canal, the town has become a premier holiday resort in recent times, thanks to the broad sands on either side, but its crop of holiday homes and hotels have not unduly spoiled the place nor the magnificent cliffy coast surrounding it.

The wide seafront is Bude's chief attraction, but there are also a couple of worthy sights if the beaches fail to entice. Right by the canal on Lower Wharf, the **Bude-Stratton Town Museum** (Easter to late Sept daily 11am–5pm; Oct Thurs & Sun 11am–5pm; 50p), housed in an old blacksmith's forge, has some absorbing exhibits to do with the Bude Canal, which was dug in 1825 to transport lime-rich sand and seaweed inland for improving North Cornwall's acid soil, and slate and granite for export. Most interesting is a half-size replica of a canal tub boat, and a model demonstrating how it worked: with six different levels in the canal to negotiate, the tub boats were fitted with wheels at each corner and hauled up each of the inclines by steam engines.

Behind the museum, on the edge of the beach, the battlemented **Bude Castle** was built in 1850 by local inventor and philanthropist Sir Goldsworthy Gurney, who is credited with inventing a steam jet, an oxyhydrogen blowpipe and a bizarre musical instrument consisting of glasses played as a piano. Gurney also improved the lighting

Boscastle and Bude

Look out for the splendidly saggy roof of the Harbour Light, by the youth hostel, a good place to pick up an ice cream.

The Web site www.atlantic -heritage -coast.co.uk has reams of info on Bude and the surrounding coast, including hotels, restaurants, activities, beach reports and surf updates.

Rowing boats on the canal can be rented from Matthew Sampson, close to the tourist office (Easter– Oct).

in the House of Commons by replacing the 280 candles with three "Bude Lights" of his own invention, used for sixty years until the arrival of electricity. He adapted his light – which shone extra brightly by means of oxygen injected into the flame – for use in lighthouses by placing it in a revolving frame, causing a flashing beam as the frame turned. Each lighthouse had its own sequence of flashes – a principle still in use today. Gurney's former home now holds council offices, but his invention is commemorated in front of the castle by the **Bude Light**, the town's newest and oft-derided monument. Resembling a tall, stripey, pointed candle, it comes into its own at night, when the cone itself and the surrounding circle on the ground are lit up by fibre optics in a pattern of constellations.

Around Bude: the beaches

Of the excellent beaches hereabouts, the central **Summerleaze** is sandy and wide, growing to such immense proportions when the tide is out that a seawater swimming pool has been installed near the cliffs – the best place for kids to swim as local sewage discharge makes sea-swimming dubious. Two and a half miles south of Bude, the mile-long **Widemouth Bay** (pronounced "Widmouth") is the main focus of the holiday hordes, backed by a straggle of white bungalows, though bathing can be dangerous near the rocks at low tide. Surfers also congregate five miles south down the coast at **Crackington Haven**, wonderfully situated between 430-foot crags at the mouth of a lush valley. The cliffs on this stretch are characterized by remarkable zigzagging strata of shale, limestone and sandstone, a mixture which erodes into detached formations, vividly contorted.

North of Bude, just beyond Summerleaze Beach, the classic breaks at acres-wide **Crooklets** have made it the scene of **surfing** and lifesaving demonstrations and competitions in summer. A couple of miles further on, beyond the signposted Atlantic Hills Caravan Park, **Sandy Mouth** is a pristine expanse of sand with rock pools beneath encircling cliffs, but it's mainly rocky at high tide. Surfers prefer the tiny sandy cove of **Duckpool**, less than a mile north, flanked by jagged reefs at low tide and dominated by the three-hundred-foot promontory of **Steeple Point**. The beach lies at the mouth of a stream that flows through the **Coombe Valley**, once the estate of the master Elizabethan mariner Sir Richard Grenville, and now managed by the National Trust.

Practicalities

Bude's helpful **tourist office** is in the centre of town at the Crescent car park (April & May Mon–Sat 10am–5pm, Sun 10am–1pm; June–Sept Mon–Sat 10am–5pm, Sun 10am–4pm; Oct–March Mon–Fri 10am–4pm, Sat 10am–2pm; ☎01288/354240; *www.bude.co.uk*).

Most of Bude's **hotels** are along Downs View, north of the golf course, but there are much better alternatives in the town and around. *Clovelly House*, 4 Burn View (☎01288/352761; no credit cards; ②), is the best of a tidy row of terraced B&Bs near the centre and south of the golf course, with simple but comfortable rooms and a coffee shop open all day for "Celtic" organic food, fresh fish dishes and cream teas. Within sight of the tourist office on Breakwater Road, the turreted, white *Falcon Hotel* (☎01288/352005; ⑤), which claims to be the oldest coaching house in north Cornwall, is a much fancier affair, with great views, a lovely secluded garden and a bar serving a variety of generously portioned meals. A mile inland from Bude, hidden away on Cot Hill, Stratton, in a small, whitewashed, sixteenth-century building, the *Stratton Gardens Hotel* (☎01288/352500; *www.cornwallonline.co.uk/accommodation*; ②; closed Jan–March; nonsmoking) also provides superb value and has a great restaurant (see below); book ahead in June and September.

In Widemouth Bay, the *Bay View Inn* (☎01288/361273; *www.bayviewinn.co.uk*; ①) occupies a premier position right on the beach but has fairly basic accommodation – you'd be better off heading down the coast to Crackington Haven, where *Nancemellan*, St Gennys (☎01840/230283; *lorraine.ruff@ondigital.com*; no credit cards; ②; closed Oct–Easter; nonsmoking), a lovely Arts and Crafts house set in nine acres of gardens, makes an excellent spot for a stay. Rooms (including the bathroom) are light and spacious, and the Aga-cooked breakfast is eaten in the family kitchen.

There are numerous **campsites** around Bude, the nearest of them *Upper Lynstone Caravan and Camping Park* (☎01288/352017; closed Nov–March), three quarters of a mile from the centre on the coastal road to Widemouth Bay, while *Wooda Park* (☎01288/352069; closed Nov–March), away from the sea at Poughill (pronounced "Poffil"), is two miles north of Bude.

Unless you eat in the central hotels, there are few good **restaurants** in the centre of town, one exception being the elegant *Villa Restaurant* at 16 The Strand (☎01288/354799; closed Sun, Mon & Nov–Easter; evenings only; moderate), which serves superior fish dishes, and has a long wine list. For fast food, head for the upbeat, cactus-painted *Buffalo Bill's*, a few minutes' north of the centre on Crooklets Beach, which sells inexpensive to moderate Tex-Mex snacks and full meals from noon till 10pm. Otherwise, you could try one of two notable choices in the village of Stratton, a mile and a half west of the centre: the small, smokey-green wainscotted restaurant in the *Stratton Gardens Hotel* (open to nonresidents Easter–Oct Wed–Sat; Nov–Easter Sat & Sun), which offers an international *table d'hôte* menu for £15 between 7.15 and 8.30pm, including old-fashioned puddings (booking advised, see above for number), or the historic thirteenth-century *Tree Inn*, where you can pick up inexpensive-to-moderate bar meals including good vegetarian dishes.

In Crackington Haven, *Coombe Barton Inn* (closed Nov–Easter) serves charcoal-grilled steaks, fresh fish and a Sunday carvery, and a wide range of Cornish ales, while the more casual *Cabin* (open school

Bude and around

Close to Crooklets Beach, Maer Stables (☎01288/ 354141) is open all year for one-hour pony treks along the coast; Efford Down Riding Stables (☎01288/ 354244), provides the same service from Easter to October, two hundred yards past the Falcon Hotel *off Vicarage Road.*

Bikes are available for rental from North Coast Cycles at 2 Summerleaze Ave, off Downs View (☎01288/ 352974).

A weekly general market is held at Crooklets Beach on Fridays.

holidays and half terms Nov–March; check for weekend openings) offers snacks, lunches, pizzas and suppers in the cosy dining area.

Morwenstow

Tucked into Cornwall's northwest tip, seven miles due north of Bude and just two miles south of the Devon border, **MORWENSTOW** has an appealing end-of-the-road feel to it. Surrounded by windswept cliffs and fields, this isolated hamlet is best known for its colourful opium-smoking poet-vicar **Robert Hawker**, credited with introducing to England the custom of the Harvest Festival in 1843. You'll find his church of **St John the Baptist** nestling in a wooded coombe to the right of where the road through the village peters out. In the graveyard, look out for the white figurehead of the *Caledonia* which serves as a gravestone for its wrecked captain. Numbering a good proportion of smugglers, wreckers and dissenters among his parishioners, Hawker insisted on giving shipwrecked sailors a churchyard rather than a traditional beachside burial, with the result that forty mariners now repose here. If the state of decomposition of the corpse was far advanced, he would encourage his gravediggers with liberal doses of gin. Inside the church are some impressive Norman arches carved with bearded men, menacing bird-like creatures and what is reckoned to be a hippopotamus, and a wonky tub font that's the oldest of its type in the country. Below the church, Hawker's vicarage sports a diversity of chimneys in imitation of various church towers known and loved by him.

For a hack in the area, ex-racehorses are available at Gooseham Barton Stables (☎01288/ 331204), two miles east of Morwenstow, signposted from the A39.

Hawker's tiny driftwood **hut** (always accessible; free; NT) complete with stable door, lies embedded in the cliffs, down steep steps, four hundred yards along a footpath from the end of the road. Opposite the church, the *Rectory Tea Rooms* (Easter–Oct 11am–5.30pm) is a handy spot for **lunch** or tea, on stone flags and high-backed settles inside, or in the garden when it's hot.

The rugged coast on either side of Morwenstow makes for strenuous but exhilarating walking. Immediately to the north of the village, **Henna Cliff** is at 450ft the highest sheer drop of any sea-cliff in England after Beachy Head, and affords magnificent views along the coast and beyond Lundy to Wales.

Travel details

Trains

Newquay to: Par (Mon–Fri 8 daily, Sat 4 daily, Sun 5 daily; 50min).

Buses

Boscastle to: Bude (Mon–Fri hourly, Sat 4 daily, also late May to late Sept Sun 8 daily; 35min); Camelford (Mon–Fri hourly, Sat 4 daily, also late May to late Sept Sun 8 daily; 35min); Port Isaac (Mon–Sat 3 daily, also late May to late

Sept Sun 4 daily ; 35min); Tintagel (Mon–Fri hourly, Sat 7 daily, also late May to late Sept Sun 5 daily; 10min).

Bude to: Boscastle (Mon–Fri hourly, Sat 4 daily, also late May to late Sept Sun 8 daily; 35min); Clovelly (Mon–Sat 4 daily, Sun 2 daily; 45min); Morwenstow (Mon, Tues, Thurs 3 daily, Wed & Fri 1 daily; 30min).

Morwenstow to: Bude (Mon, Tues, Thurs 3 daily, Wed & Fri 1 daily; 30min).

Newquay to: Bodmin (3 daily; 1hr); Padstow (3 daily, also late May to late Sept Sun 4 daily; 1hr 10min); Perranporth (hourly; 25–35min); St Austell (Mon–Sat hourly, also late May to late Sept Sun 5 daily; 45min–1hr); Truro (Mon–Sat hourly, also late May to late Sept Sun 6 daily; 1hr–1hr 30min).

Padstow to: Bodmin (Mon–Sat 10 daily, Sun 4 daily; 45–55min); Newquay (3 daily, also late May to late Sept Sun 4 daily; 1hr 10min); Wadebridge (Mon–Sat 10 daily, Sun 5 daily; 30min).

Perranporth to: Newquay (hourly; 25–35min).

Polzeath to: Port Isaac (Mon–Sat 5 daily, also late May to late Sept Sun 5 daily; 20min); Wadebridge (5 daily, also late May to late Sept Sun 5 daily; 35min).

Port Isaac to: Boscastle (Mon–Sat 3 daily, also late May to late Sept Sun 4 daily; 35min); Polzeath (Mon–Sat 5 daily, also late May to late Sept Sun 5 daily; 20min); Tintagel (Mon–Fri 2 daily, also late May to late Sept Sun 4 daily; 20–35min).

Portreath to: Redruth (Mon–Sat 9 daily, Sun 5 daily; 15–25min).

Redruth to: Portreath (Mon–Sat 9 daily, Sun 5 daily; 15–25min); St Agnes (Mon–Sat 4 daily, also late May to late Sept Sun 2 daily; 25min); Truro (Mon–Sat 2 hourly, Sun 5 daily; 30min).

St Agnes to: Helston (Mon–Sat hourly, Sun 5 daily; 1hr 35min); Perranporth (6 daily, Sun 5 daily; 12min); Redruth (Mon–Sat 4 daily, also late May to late Sept Sun 2 daily; 40min); Truro (9 daily; 35min).

Tintagel to: Boscastle (Mon–Fri hourly, Sat 7 daily, also late May to late Sept Sun 5 daily; 10min); Camelford (Mon–Sat hourly, also late May to late Sept Sun 4 daily; 15–25min); Port Isaac (Mon–Fri 2 daily, also late May to late Sept Sun 4 daily; 20–35min).

Wadebridge to: Bodmin (Mon–Sat hourly, also late May to late Sept Sun 4 daily; 25min); Padstow (Mon–Sat 10 daily, Sun 5 daily; 25–30min); Port Isaac (Mon–Sat 5 daily, also late May to late Sept Sun 5 daily; 45min); Tintagel (Mon–Fri hourly, Sat 2 daily, also late May to late Sept Sun 4 daily; 55min–1hr 5min).

Chapter 12

Bodmin and Bodmin Moor

Just ten miles in diameter and effectively bound in by a quartet of **rivers** – the Fowey, Lynher, Camel and De Lank – **Bodmin Moor** is the smallest, mildest and most accessible of the West Country's great moors, its highest tor rising to just 1375ft from a platform of 1000ft. Though bisected by the main A30, the moor's bare, desolate appearance conveys a sense of loneliness quite out of proportion to its size, its emptiness only accentuated by the scattered relics left behind by its Bronze Age population. Like Exmoor and Dartmoor, the moor also has a small population of wild ponies, though its most celebrated animal occupant – if it exists at all – is the **Beast of Bodmin** (see box on p.298), whose phantom presence might add some frisson to your ramblings.

The information Web site for Bodmin Moor is www.bodmin-moor.co.uk

This miniature wilderness is best experienced away from the roads. Having parked your vehicle at one of the numerous parking places scattered around, you can sally forth – armed with a good map (Ordnance Survey Explorer 109 takes in the whole moor at a scale of 1:25,000) – on tracks across the moorland. The highest tors lie to the west of the A30 and can easily be reached from **Bolventor** at the centre of the moor, an area steeped in both literary and Arthurian associations, not least in nearby **Dozmary Pool**. The southeastern moor holds some of Cornwall's most important prehistoric sites, including **The Hurlers** and **Trethevy Quoit**, while some of the region's finest exam-

---

Accommodation price codes

Throughout this *Guide*, hotel and B&B accommodation is coded on a scale of ① to ⑨, the code indicating the lowest price you can expect to pay per night for a double room in high season. The prices indicated by the codes are as follows:

① under £40	④ £60–70	⑦ £110–150
② £40–50	⑤ £70–90	⑧ £150–200
③ £50–60	⑥ £90–110	⑨ over £200

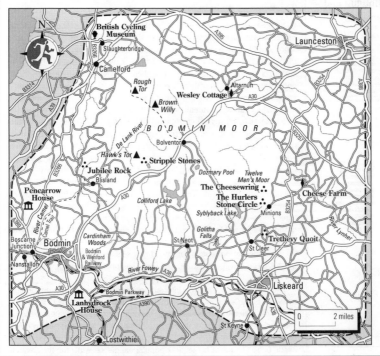

ples of fifteenth-century church art can be seen nearby in the attractive village of **St Neot**, which makes the best base for the southern reaches of the moor. Other good bases on the perimeter of the moor include **Blisland**, on its western fringe, and **Altarnun** on the northeastern edge, while up near the Devon border, **Launceston** is an unsung off-moor town with a better choice of food and accommodation.

The town of **Bodmin** itself lies to the west of the moor, and, with the widest range of accommodation in the area, makes the most viable base for excursions. In addition it has some impressive local sights, including the notorious Bodmin Jail, and, just outside town, a pair of impressive country piles, including **Lanhydrock**, one of the West Country's grandest mansions. Along with the unexceptional town of **Liskeard**, thirteen miles to the northeast, Bodmin is the main **public transport** junction for the moor – both are stops on the main train route to Penzance. The moorland villages are on the whole poorly served by buses, the only useful services being the sporadic #X3 from Bodmin to Launceston via Bolventor (Tues & Thurs, plus Sat in summer); Tilley's Coaches #225, running four times daily on weekdays between Launceston and Altarnun, and the hourly #77 and #X77 from Liskeard to St Neot (Mon–Sat). Liskeard is also connect-

The Beast of Bodmin Moor

Of all the many myths and strange stories spawned on the Moor, one of the most enduring in recent years has been that of the **Beast of Bodmin Moor**. Moorland farmers were the first to raise the issue of this phantom mauler of their livestock in the 1980s, and there have been around 60 big-cat sightings recorded in the area since then, as well as six-inch paw prints and cat droppings. An official investigation in 1995, during which wildlife experts examined photos, footprints and livestock thought to have been attacked by the wild animal, concluded there was no evidence of the so-called beast or of any other big cats on the moor. However, some of the best evidence put forward for the existence of the creature emerged after the investigation in 1997, when a photograph taken in the St Austell area apparently showed two creatures, one an adult female puma, possibly pregnant – or anyway looking "very fat, fit and contented" in the words of the curator of Newquay Zoo – and measuring about two and a half feet tall, the other possibly a cub. This was followed up in August 1998 by a twenty-second video which seemed to show a sleek, black animal about three-and-a-half foot long. These two findings prompted a systematic trawl of the moor by RAF reserve volunteers in 1999, using state-of-the-art night vision and seismic equipment, but again they failed to unearth anything. All the same, farmers have continued to lose sheep to what they maintain to be a large, savage creature, and there has been continuing pressure to persuade the Government to reopen the inquiry.

The farmers do not entirely lack support within the scientific community, however. Some scientists believe the moor could well be home to a species of wild cat which was thought to have become extinct in Britain more than a century ago, though other sightings of mysterious large animals in other parts of the country suggest rather that these are all escaped or abandoned exotic pets. The puma is the most popular candidate, while the lynx, which would be well suited to the often cold British weather, also has a strong claim, and it is even possible that jaguars could live in the wild in the British Isles (black-coloured varieties exist). Most likely of all, however, is that any big cat on the moor would be a hybrid – the result of different species cross-breeding. Such an animal could easily survive on a diet of rabbits and other mammals – plentiful food on the moor – though would only attack sheep or other stock in extreme desperation. Its normal routine would consist in hunting in the early morning or at dusk and sleeping during the day. To date nobody has ever been attacked by a large cat on Bodmin Moor, but if you chance to encounter one, your best bet is to walk nonchalantly by – but not before taking a precious photograph of the fabulous beast.

ed by bus #73 from Plymouth via St Cleer and Darite, and by #73A and by branch-line trains with Looe (see p.177), while #268 runs four times daily (Mon–Sat) between Liskeard and Launceston, with some services stopping at Minions.

Bodmin and around

The no-nonsense town of **BODMIN,** the largest of those at the edge of the moor, lies two or three miles west of Bodmin Moor proper, equidistant from the north and south Cornish coasts and the Fowey and Camel rivers. This central position encouraged Bodmin's growth as a trading town, and it also became an important ecclesiastical centre with the establishment of a priory by Saint Petroc after he moved here from Padstow in the sixth century. Bodmin became Cornwall's county town in 1835, but sacrificed much of its administrative role by refusing land for the Great Western Railway in the 1870s, resulting in many local businesses transferring down the road to Truro.

Bodmin and around

Arrival, information and accommodation

Bodmin Parkway **train station** lies three and a half miles southeast of town, with a regular bus connection (#55) to the centre. The same **bus** provides access to the town from Padstow (Mon–Sat only) and from Wadebridge (daily); you can also get here from St Austell on #29A, #29B or #29C (Mon–Sat), and the #55 (Sun only). The main **bus stop** is located in Nicholas Street, close to the town's pedestrianized central area, Mount Folly. From Penzance, Plymouth or Newquay it is easiest to take National Express coaches, which go to Bodmin three times a day, stopping at Priory Road, just off Mount Folly. Bodmin's on-the-ball **tourist office** (Mon–Sat 10am–5pm; ☎01208/76616), located in Shire Hall, Mount Folly, can supply **information** on all parts of the moor, including walks, rides, transport and accommodation.

Pedal Power, 15 Honey St (☎01208/ 72557), rents bikes daily between Easter and September.

Two of the best **accommodation** options in town are the comfortable and centrally located *Higher Windsor Cottage*, 18 Castle St (☎01208/76474; no credit cards; ①), and, further up at 68 Castle St, *Agan Chy* (☎01208/75339, *agan.chy@btinternet.com*; no credit cards; ①), a modern house with large windows overlooking pleasant gardens. Dating from the seventeenth century, the lattice-windowed *Priory Cottage*, 34 Rhind St (☎01208/73064; *www.priorycottage1 .co.uk*; no credit cards; ①), is conveniently sited near St Petroc's church. **Outside town**, close to the Lanhydrock estate near Lanivet, *Bokiddick Farm* (☎01208/831481; no credit cards; ②) feels more like a guesthouse than a farm, and boasts fantastic views from the conservatory; call ahead for directions. There's a decent **campsite**, the *Camping and Caravanning Club Site*, on Old Callywith Road, a fifteen-minute walk north of the centre from Castle Street, which starts behind St Petroc's church (☎01208/73834; closed Nov–Feb).

The town

Bodmin's most prominent landmark is the **Gilbert Memorial**, a 144ft obelisk occupying a commanding location on Bodmin Beacon, a high area of moorland south of the town centre. The monument honours Sir Walter Raleigh Gilbert (1785–1853), a descendant of Walter Raleigh (the Elizabethan knight), who distinguished himself as a general in the Bengal army. The all-round views from here are stupendous.

On Mount Folly, at the junction of the main Fore Street, Priory Road (A389) and St Nicholas Street, the Gilberts and other local worthies in the town's history are recalled in **Bodmin Museum**, next to the tourist office (Easter–Sept Mon–Sat 10.30am–4.30pm; Oct 11am–3pm; free); amongst the small and unsensational collection of local oddments, look out for a sixteenth-century granite font later used as a corn measure. More absorbing, though, is the next-door **Courtroom Experience** (Mon–Sat 11am–3pm; £2), housed in the Georgian Shire Hall – formerly the assize court and now part-occupied by the tourist office. The exhibition features an hourly re-enactment, using film and moving waxworks, of the trial of Matthew Weeks, controversially indicted for the murder of Charlotte Dymond on Bodmin Moor in 1844, a verdict which was widely questioned at the time – visitors are invited to cast their own vote at the end of the show. You can also visit the holding cells below the courtroom, its ambience enhanced by such refinements as the rancid smell of urine.

Across Fore Street, the granite hulk of **St Petroc** (April–Sept Mon–Fri 11am–3pm; at other times, ask at the rectory next door or call ☎01208/73867) represents Cornwall's largest church, mainly fifteenth-century but with its Perpendicular windows restored in the nineteenth century. Its interior reveals a typical Cornish wagon roof embellished with fine bosses and, in a glass case embedded in the south wall, an ivory casket that once held the bones of Petroc (now lost). Between the chancel and the north chapel is the **Vyvian tomb**, a powerful recumbent effigy of one of the last priors of the abbey carved from black Catacleuse stone. The most striking item here, though, is the formidable **Norman font** near the entrance, its base resting on one column and its bowl, encrusted with fearsome beasts and deeply carved with interlacing trees of life, supported by four others and topped by impassive angels.

West of the church on Berrycombe Road, **Bodmin Jail** (daily 11am–6pm; £3) is menacingly redolent of the executions that were once guaranteed to pull the crowds, for which special trains were hired. After 1862 the hangings continued behind closed doors until the jail's closure in 1909. You can explore parts of the original eighteenth-century structure, including the condemned cell, all now considerably run down and gloomily eerie. Pinned up on the cell walls, the stories of the inmates incarcerated for such crimes as stealing milk from a cow recount a far more telling story than the bedraggled dummies which re-enact their foul deeds.

Around Bodmin

There are several easy excursions you can make from Bodmin for which you don't need a car. Further up from Bodmin Jail, Berrycombe Road holds a section of the **Camel Trail**, linking the town by a one-and-a-half mile cycleway and footpath to the main route along the Camel river a mile northwest (see box on p.283). In summer, you can also approach the Camel Trail on steam locomotives of the **Bodmin & Wenford Railway** (April–Sept 2–4 daily; ☎01208/73666), which run to Boscarne Junction, about two miles from the trail, in fifteen minutes from Bodmin General station. The renovated Bodmin General, situated a few minutes' walk south of the centre on the Lostwithiel road, formerly served trains of the Great Western Railway and now offers train buffs the chance to watch the locomotives being restored in the Engine Shed.

The same line from Bodmin General station goes in the opposite direction to Bodmin Parkway (20min), for connections with main-line trains and for the footpath to Lanhydrock (see below). Halfway along this line, there's a stop at Colesloggett Halt, from where a half-mile path takes you to the nature trails and cycle tracks of **Cardinham Woods**, a mixed-forest plantation where Douglas fir is grown for the timber industry. It's a lovely spot for a ramble, with waymarked trails and other paths winding through ravines and alongside small streams which run down to the main river, Cardinham Water, where there's a small clapper bridge. Deer roam the woods, buzzard wheel overhead and if you're lucky you might catch sight of an otter.

From Parkway train station, it's less than two-miles' walk westwards along a signposted path to one of Cornwall's most absorbing country houses, **Lanhydrock** (April–Sept Tues–Sun 11am–5.30pm; Oct Tues–Sun 11am–5pm; house & grounds £6.80; grounds only £3.70; NT). The frequent #55 bus from Bodmin also stops at the car park, from where, if you wish to arrive in style, you can transfer to a vintage Humber to take you the 600 yards to the house (£1 each way). Entered through an imposing pinnacled gatehouse, Lanhydrock was originally constructed in the seventeenth century, but was totally rebuilt after a disastrous fire in 1881. The granite exterior remains true to its original form, however, but apart from the north wing, containing the long **picture gallery** with its remarkable barrel-vaulted plaster ceiling depicting 24 Old Testament scenes, it's all High Victorian in tone. You're free to wander around the fifty rooms at will (guidebooks cost £2.95), where the grand style in which the local Robartes family lived is best illustrated by the quantities of equipment in the nurseries, luggage room, linen lobby and livery room. Most illuminating of all is the **kitchen**, built in the style of a college hall with clerestory windows, and supplemented by an unending series of dairies, sculleries, larders and pantries, with a spit large enough to roast an entire cow. The small **museum** in the north wing shows sundry photographs and letters relating to the family, and the thousand acres of wooded parkland bordering onto the River Fowey are worth a prolonged wander, especially in spring for the spectacular beds of magnolias, azaleas and rhododendrons. A leaflet available at the ticket desk details the choice of walks you can take.

In the opposite direction to Lanhydrock, four and a half miles northwest of Bodmin, the mile-long drive at **Pencarrow** (April–May & late Aug to mid-Oct 1.30–4.30pm, June to late Aug 11am–4.30pm; £5, gardens only £2.50; *www.chycor.co.uk/pencarrow*) might suggest something on the same scale, but this country house has a very different, more intimate feel. The Georgian building was begun

Bodmin and around

You can rent bikes from Glynn Valley Cycle Hire (daily June–Sept 10am–5pm; Oct–May Sun 10am–5pm; ☎01208/ 74244), by the main car park in Cardinham Woods. Touring bikes and off-roaders are both available for the cycle route through the woods.

Denby Stables (☎01208/ 72013) at Nanstallon, two miles west of Bodmin and signposted off the A389 Wadebridge road, arranges rides along the Camel Trail (see box, p.283) and through the Camel Valley.

by Sir John Molesworth, co-founder in 1771 of the banking house that was the forerunner of Lloyds Bank. A portrait of him by Joshua Reynolds is one of the many paintings on display here. The present scions of the family have stamped their personality by saucily placing hats on the busts of the various worthies, though the exquisite carpets and furnishings are what make the deepest impression. A guide will give you the lowdown on the family's history and encourage you to tinkle the piano on which Sir Arthur Sullivan, a guest here in 1882, composed much of the music for *Iolanthe*. Again, leave time to explore the beautiful wooded grounds.

Eating, drinking and nightlife

Most of Bodmin's best places to **eat and drink** are clustered close together in the centre of town. In Crockwell Street, off Fore Street, the *Hole in the Wall* **pub** has a pleasant back room bar in what used to be the debtors' prison, with exposed fourteenth-century walls enclosing a collection of antiquities and bric-a-brac. In summer you can drink or eat bar lunches in the courtyard, or go for fuller, moderately priced meals in the upstairs *Lion's Den* **restaurant**. Good wholesome snacks are served during the day at the *Maple Leaf*, just across from St Petroc's at 14 Honey St (closed Sun). Opposite the tourist office at 3 Folly Square, *The Fountain of Food* (closed Sun & evenings Mon–Thurs) has comfy sofas for lounging on with a coffee or speciality tea, and offers Mediterranean-type evening meals.

For **nightlife**, head for *Club 15s* in the *Cornish Arms*, at Crockwell Street (Thurs–Sat), as long as you fancy old school techno, hard house and trance tunes.

Blisland

Three miles northeast of Bodmin, **BLISLAND**, tucked into the Camel valley on the western slopes of Bodmin Moor, is mostly interesting for its Norman **church** in amongst the Georgian and Victorian houses scattered around the village green. It has the distinction of being the only one in England dedicated to **St Protus and St Hyacinth**, brothers who were martyred in the third century. Sensitively restored at the end of the nineteenth century, the church has a seventeenth-century carved pulpit and a startlingly colourful Victorian Gothic rood screen, while overhead, the beams of the wagon roof are as wildly wonky as the columns in the nave.

You can make an easy and rewarding ramble less than half a mile north of the village to the gigantic **Jubilee Rock** on Pendrift Common, reached along a signposted and well-trodden path across the moor. The rock is inscribed with various patriotic insignia commemorating the jubilee of George III's coronation in 1809, but the view is the main attraction from this seven-hundred-foot vantage point, looking eastward over the De Lank gorge and the boulder-crowned knoll of **Hawk's Tor**, three miles away. On the shoulder of the tor stand the neolithic **Stripple Stones**, a circular platform once holding 28 standing stones, of which just four are still upright. Blisland also lies a couple of miles east of the **Merry Meeting** crossroads, a point near the end of the Camel Trail (see box, p.283).

If you want to **stay** in Blisland, head for *Lavethan* (☎01208/850487; *www.cornwall-online.co.uk/lavethan*; no credit cards; ②), a beautiful sixteenth-century manor house set in thirty acres of park-like fields and gardens sloping to a small river and with a guests' piano in the drawing room; it's ten-minutes' walk from the village towards St Mabyn. The best option for campers is the small *South Penquite*, one and a half miles north of Blisland on the St Breward road (☎01208/850296; *www.bodminmoor.co.uk/the-farm*; closed Oct–April), which has mountain bikes available for hire.

Back on the village green, the *Blisland Inn* is a popular place for an inexpensive pub lunch or evening **meal**, or just a fruit wine; it sells newspapers too.

Jamaica Inn and around

Lying at the centre of the moor, on the A30 midway between Bodmin and Launceston, **Jamaica Inn** is one of the area's chief focuses for walkers, sightseers and coach parties alike. The inn, located just outside the unprepossessing village of Bolventor, was a staging-post even before the precursor of the A30 road was laid in 1769, and was described by **Daphne Du Maurier** in her book of the same name as being "alone in glory, four square to the winds". The combination of its literary association and its convenient position has led to its development as a hotel and restaurant complex, and to the establishment in an annexed building of **Mr Potter's Museum of Curiosities** (daily: Easter–Oct 10am–5pm, and 10am–8pm during school holidays; winter 11am–4pm; closed Jan; £2.50; combined ticket with Smuggler's Museum £4); even if you're not staying or drinking at the inn, this entertaining fairground assortment of mummified and stuffed animals jammed together with such wildly diverse items as hookahs, fossils and nineteenth-century Chinese dolls, is well worth a stop. The animals include both freaks (for example a two-headed lamb and a six-legged piglet) and tableaux such as *The Death of Cock Robin* featuring 96 birds, a guinea pigs' cricket match and a wedding of kittens decked out in full bridal kit.

Across the road, the **Smuggler's Museum** (same hours as Mr Potter's; £2.50), while not in the same league as its neighbour, still provides some amusement, showing the diverse ruses used for concealing contraband, such as secret pouches in corsets and hollowed-out turtles. A downstairs section documents the history of smuggling up to the present day. In the same building, the story of *Jamaica Inn* can be resurrected at the touch of a button by means of waxworks and sound-and-light gimmickry. In the inn itself, a room devoted to Daphne Du Maurier displays her Sheraton writing desk and a dish of her favourite sweets.

The inn's car park is a useful place to leave your vehicle and venture forth **on foot**, although you should notify staff if you plan to leave your vehicle there. A free leaflet is available at the *Inn* detailing the three-mile walk to Brown Willy, and the well-travelled route to **Dozmary Pool**, a mile south. According to Arthurian mythology, after King Arthur's death, Sir Bedivere is supposed to have hurled the king's sword, Excalibur, into this desolate pool, where it was seized by an arm raised from the depths (Loe Pool, on the Lizard, also claims the honour: see p.209). Despite its proximity to the A30, the diamond-shaped lake usually preserves an ethereal air, though it's been known to run dry in summer, dealing a bit of a blow to the legend that the pool is bottomless.

The lake is also the source of another, more obviously Cornish myth, that of John Tregeagle, a steward at Lanhydrock in the seventeenth century (see p.301), whose unjust dealings with the local tenant farmers are supposed to have resulted in a curse condemning his spirit to endlessly baling out the pool with a perforated limpet shell. As if this were not enough, his ghost is said to be further tormented by a swarm of devils that pursue him as he flies across the moor in search of sanctuary; their infernal howling is claimed to be audible on windy nights.

Though it's the obvious **place to stay** hereabouts, with splendid views on all sides, the completely revamped and modernized *Jamaica Inn* (☎01566/86250; *www.jamaicainn.co.uk*; ③) lacks much character, even if the bedrooms have retained their old doors and low ceilings. Otherwise your best bet is to press on to Altarnun (see below).

For details of the walk from Jamaica Inn to Brown Willy, see box on p.308.

Altarnun and around

Three miles northeast of Bolventor, just off the A30 at Five Lanes, **ALTARNUN** is a pretty, granite-grey village snugly sheltered beneath the eastern heights of the moor, the front doors of its cottages approached by slate slabs crossing the trickle of a stream. By the picturesque packhorse bridge here, its fifteenth-century church, dedicated to **St Nonna**, mother of David, the patron saint of Wales, has been dubbed the "cathedral of the moors" on account of its lofty west tower and spacious interior. The fine solid Norman font here was the prototype of the dozen or so "Altarnun fonts" in the area, characterized by their square shape, with geometric flowers surrounded by snakes on the four sides and fierce faces at the corners. Look out too for the set of 79 superb bench-ends, carved at the beginning of the sixteenth century, boldly depicting secular and sacred subjects – such as saints, musicians, clowns, moorland sheep and even a bagpipe player. Some of the slate memorials in the churchyard were carved by local sculptor Nevil Northey Burnard, also responsible for the effigy of John Wesley, the co-founder of Methodism, over the door of the Methodist chapel on the village's main street. A regular visitor to the neighbourhood, Wesley used to stay at **Wesley Cottage** (daily 9am–dusk; free), half a mile to the southwest at Trewint and now within earshot of the A30's roar. You can visit his two small rooms in the "Prophet's Chamber" area of the house, and view a few of his letters, but there's not a lot to fire the imagination.

Accessed by a private gate from St Nonna's (and also from the road), *Penhallow Manor* (☎01566/86206; *www.penhallow-manor .co.uk*; ③), originally the vicarage, now offers **accommodation** in a variety of well-furnished rooms. There are huge creamy sofas, a library, a conservatory for breakfast and a set three-course dinner at £23 (book ahead if you're not staying); morning coffees and afternoon teas are also available. Five hundred yards towards the A30, the unspoilt *King's Head* (☎01566/86241; no credit cards; ①) has beams, saggy ceilings, patchwork quilts on the beds and **meals** for under a fiver.

Launceston

Unpromoted as a tourist town, **LAUNCESTON** (pronounced Lanceson) was Cornwall's capital until 1835, and still retains much of its original architecture, overlaid with a sedate, well-to-do charm. Situated less than a mile from the Devon border, it was, until the construction of its bypass twenty years ago, literally the "Gateway to Cornwall", since all traffic entering the county passed through the narrow twelfth-century **Southgate Arch** – the last remaining of the three original gateways to the county's only walled town.

Launceston developed around its **castle** (April–Sept daily 10am–6pm; Oct daily 10am–5pm; Nov–March Fri–Sun 10am–1pm & 2–4pm; £1.90; EH), which still dominates the skyline from the top of a grassy mound just west of the centre, though all that now remains is the rough-hewn cylindrical keep and round curtain walls. In the thirteenth century this was the chief fortress of Richard, Earl of Cornwall and brother of Henry III, but later fell into decay until repaired by the Black Prince. In a sturdy cell near the castle's north gate, George Fox, founder of the Society of Friends, or Quakers, was imprisoned in 1656 for "disturbing the peace" in St Ives. Launceston had earlier taken a stand against religious dissenters when St Cuthbert Mayne was hung, drawn and quartered in its main square in 1577 – the first Roman Catholic seminary priest to be executed in England.

North of the castle, Castle Street was described by John Betjeman as the finest Georgian street in Cornwall. Its red-brick buildings include **Lawrence House Museum** (April–Sept Mon–Fri 10am–4.30pm; free), a graceful setting for some well-displayed local exhibits, which include a reconstructed Victorian kitchen and, on the upper floor, mourning clothes and other costumes, a Victorian bier, and a collection of nineteenth-century Christmas decorations. The museum also has items relating to John Couch Adams (1819–92), co-discoverer of the planet Neptune, who was born in nearby Lidcot.

Launceston

East off Castle Street on Church Street, the church of **St Mary Magdalene** is unique in England for its prolifically carved exterior walls – no mean feat, considering the unyielding qualities of granite. Completed in 1524, the church was commissioned by one Henry Trecarrel, whose coat of arms and that of his wife can be seen on the upper storey of the south porch, among a profusion of leaves, quatrefoils, pomegranates and heraldic shields. In the east wall, a recumbent figure of Mary Magdalene was the subject of a poem by Cornwall's most celebrated living poet and local resident, Charles Causley. According to local lore, if you throw a stone over your shoulder and it lands on the effigy's back, you will receive good luck. Highlights inside the church include the fine Perpendicular pulpit painted red, black and white, and contrasting Art Nouveau carved bench ends.

From St Thomas Road, just west of the castle, **Launceston Steam Railway** runs frequent five-mile round-trips to New Mills through the Kensey Valley on the original Waterloo to Padstow line (Easter to late May & Oct Tues & Sun 11am–4.30pm; late May to Sept Mon–Fri & Sun 11am–4.30pm; £5.20; ☎01566/77665). The narrow-gauge steam locomotives, built in the 1880s and 1890s, formerly worked in the slate quarries of North Wales. There are also veteran cars and motorcycles on show in the small transport museum here (free).

Practicalities

A few yards south of St Mary Magdalene, Launceston's **tourist office** (April–Oct Mon–Thurs 8.45am–1pm & 1.45–5pm, Fri 1.45–4.30pm, Sat 9am–1pm & 1.30–5pm; ☎01566/772333) is located in the Market House Arcade in Market Street. For the pick of the town's **accommodation**, head next door to Lawrence House museum at 11 Castle St (☎01566/773873; nonsmoking; no credit cards; ①/②; closed Nov–Feb), with stylish rooms – including a great attic room – and a Savoy-trained chef to supply Finnan haddock or grilled kipper for breakfast. To the other side of the museum, another Georgian house, the *Eagle House Hotel* (☎01566/772036; ③), has a more upmarket feel, with elaborate plaster moulding and cool, spacious rooms, while close to the car park, through the Southgate Arch, *Glencoe Villa*, 13 Race Hill (☎01566/775819; nonsmoking; no credit cards; ①) has a sunny breakfast room and comfortable, colour-co-ordinated bedrooms. The nearest **campsite** is *Chapmanswell Caravan Site* (☎01409/211382; closed early Nov to mid-March) at St Giles on the Heath, six miles north of town along the A388.

For **food**, *Three Steps to Heaven*, 1 Southgate Place, next to Southgate Arch (closed Sun & Mon), offers good-value breakfasts, snacks and full meals, including fish and steaks. During the day, the *Mad Hatter's Tea Shop* at 28 Church St is a great spot for tea and imaginative sandwiches, baguettes and *panini*. For a cocktail or bistro meal, *Cloisters Wine Bar and Cellar Bistro* at 13 Church St fits the bill (closed Sun & Mon; ☎01566/772558).

Camelford and around

The northern half of Bodmin Moor is dominated by its two highest tors, both of them easily accessible from **CAMELFORD**, a small town once thought to be the site of King Arthur's Camelot. Though the town itself hardly lives up to the expectations raised by its associations or its exotic name – the latter is probably derived from a contraction of Cam meaning "crooked", and Hayle meaning "estuary" – it makes a useful touring base and is easily negotiated, its one main street starting as Victoria Road at its northwestern end and changing its name to Market Place, Fore Street and High Street. In addition, a trio of museums provide some diversion, the most conventional of which is the **North Cornwall Museum** on The Clease (April–Sept Mon–Sat 10am–5pm; £1.50), at the junction of Fore Street and High Street, which displays a low-key collection of domestic items, tools and farming implements from the last hundred years, alongside background information on the local slate industry. In complete contrast, the **British Cycling Museum**, housed in the old train station a mile north of town on the B3266 Boscastle road (Mon–Thurs & Sun 10am–5pm; ring ahead for Fri & Sat; ☎01840/212811; £2.50) is a cyclophile's dream, with some four hundred examples of bikes through the ages filling every inch of floor, ceiling and wall space. Among the oddities are a reverse penny farthing, a four-wheeled quadracycle and a pentacycle (one large wheel, four small), and there's a library on site as well.

The third museum lies on the River Camel a mile or so north of town at **SLAUGHTERBRIDGE**, possibly the site of King Arthur's last battle of Camlann – at which the king was mortally wounded by Mordred – though the identification of this site probably has more to do with the fact that a decisive battle between the Saxon King Egbert and the Celts was fought near here in the ninth century. Despite the tenuous connection, you'll now find the **Arthurian Centre** here (mid-Feb to Dec daily 9am–6pm; *www.kingarthur.co.uk*; £1.75), which includes the Land of Arthur exhibition, covering Arthur-related art and poetry by means of a video and photographs, and an interpretation centre, which highlights the background to the site, focusing particularly on Lord Tennyson's visit here in 1848, when he was inspired to write his Arthurian elegy *Idylls of the King*. There are also gardens with riverside walks, and a tearoom overlooking a children's play castle. The main basis of the centre, however, is the sixth-century inscribed **King Arthur's Stone**, below the tearoom, which supposedly marks the site of the final battle. Inscribed in Latin and an ancient Celtic script which is thought to indicate the former presence of southern Irish people in North Cornwall, the funerary stone was first recorded in 1602 but had lain on the banks of the Camel for a thousand years before that.

Otherwise, the area's attractions are all to do with the wilderness of moorland all around, easily accessible to the southeast of

Camelford and around

The walk to Rough Tor and Brown Willy

One of the best hikes on Bodmin Moor, and one which can be accomplished without too much difficulty, is to its two highest peaks of **Rough Tor** (1311ft) and **Brown Willy** (1375ft), accessible either from Camelford (see previous page) or *Jamaica Inn* (see p.303). Though the ascents don't present particular hazards, you'll need suitable clothing and footwear, and a good map, such as OS Explorer 109, which covers the moor at a scale of 1:25,000. Do not attempt the walks in poor visibility.

Rough Tor (locally pronounced Row – as in argument – Tor) lies about a mile south of the car park at Rough Tor Ford, which is three miles southeast of Camelford and reachable on foot or by car from Rough Tor Road, a right turn off Victoria Road at Camelford's northern end. From the bridge over the stream below the car park, walk about a mile over springy turf and a well-worn trail, past a stone monument to Charlotte Dymond (see p.300) and the three boulders of **Showery Tor**, before bearing left along the ridge to the slight elevation of **Little Rough Tor**. From here, continue in a southeasterly direction to the summit, a gentle but steady uphill trudge over the heath, as often as not accompanied by a biting wind. The sides of Rough Tor are very rocky and the last stretch is not well defined, so care is needed. The piles of flat precariously balanced rocks crowning the summit present a different aspect from every angle – an ungainly mass from the south, and a nobly proportioned mountain from the west – and were described by Daphne Du Maurier as "shaped like giant furniture with monstrous chairs and twisted tables". Nearby are the ruins of a medieval chapel, and the whole area is scattered with Bronze Age remains.

Originally named Bronewhella, or "highest hill", Bodmin's loftiest peak, **Brown Willy**, is easily visible less than a mile and a half to the southeast of Rough Tor. Like the latter, Brown Willy shows various faces, its sugarloaf appearance from the north sharpening into a long, multipeaked crest as you approach. To reach it, continue from the summit of Rough Tor in a southeasterly direction, towards a ruined building near which is a bridge over the upper reaches of the De Lank river. From here the ascent is clearly marked, with the final stretch along a steep but well-defined track. Both Rough Tor and Brown Willy can be climbed in a couple of hours from the car park.

Brown Willy can also be accessed **from Jamaica Inn** (see p.303), a three-and-a-quarter-mile walk from the car park there. Turning left out of the car park, follow the old road down the hill, and take the second turning on the left under the A30. From here, take the first turning on the right, then first left, walking along this road for 150yd until you see a signed footpath on the right. Follow this path for the length of three fields until it becomes a broader track, and continue up this, bearing to the right of the buildings in front, from where a lane leads to a gate after 750yd. Pass through the gate and onto the moorland, bearing right for 250yd to Tolborough Tor, the highest point of the surrounding downs and a mile from *Jamaica Inn* as the crow flies (but more like 1.5 miles walking). From here, Brown Willy is clearly visible less than two miles to the northwest across bare moor: walk towards it for another 250yd to a gate, beyond which you should continue for another mile and a half with a wire fence on your left, crossing this over a stile and climbing the steep slopes of the tor. From the summit, the highest point in Cornwall, you get a grand panorama of the rock-strewn green-and-brown patchwork of high moorland on all sides.

Camelford. For a good walk up to Rough Tor and Brown Willy, in the heart of the moor, see the box opposite.

Practicalities

Camelford's **tourist office** is housed in the North Cornwall Museum (April–Sept Mon–Sat 10am–5pm; ☎01840/212954). Among the town's central **accommodation** is the thirteenth-century, slate-hung *Darlington Inn* on Fore Street (☎01840/213314; ①), which has spacious rooms, and the *Countryman Hotel* at 7 Victoria Rd (☎01840/212250; *www.cornwall-online.co.uk/countryman*; ①), where walkers can pick up plenty of advice and information. There are two **campsites** in the area, both a mile or so north of Camelford on the B3266: the very quiet and small *King's Acre* (☎01840/213561; closed Nov–Easter) and *Lakefield Caravan Park*, Lower Pendavey Farm (☎01840/213279; closed Nov–March), a much larger site with more facilities and providing **horse riding**.

The lively *Mason's Arms* on Market Place serves generous portions of pub **food**, both evening and lunch-times, and has a beer garden, while the *Darlington Inn* makes another good pub-stop. *Tiffins*, at 5 Market Place, serves all-day breakfasts and other inexpensive meals (closed Sun & evenings).

The southeastern moor: St Neot and around

Seven miles east of Bodmin, **ST NEOT** is one of Bodmin Moor's prettiest villages and is a good access point for the southern part of the moor, reachable from the A38, two miles to the south, or by bus #77 or #X77 from Liskeard, six miles southeast. It also merits a visit for its fifteenth-century **church**, overlooking the village, which contains some of the most impressive medieval stained-glass windows of any parish church in the country. The set begins with the oldest glass, at the east end of the south aisle, where the fifteenth-century **Creation Window** shows God with mathematical instruments and Seth planting in Adam's mouth the seeds from which the wood of the cross will grow. The first window in the south aisle, **Noah's Window**, continues the sequence with lively scenes of the ark as a sixteenth-century sailing ship. However, the narration soon dissolves into windows portraying saints and – due to the need of sponsorship when the money ran out – patrons and local bigwigs, as well as the ordinary men and women of the village.

St Neot is the most pleasant **place to stay** in this southern part of the moor, with options including the seventeenth-century *Dye Cottage* (☎01579/321394; *www.cornwall-info.co.uk/dye-cottage*; no credit cards; ①), which offers attractively furnished rooms and a large sitting room that looks onto a summer-house and a garden sloping down to a stream; breakfasts are luscious, with home-grown produce and home-made bread. Opposite, and next door to the church,

The south-eastern moor

the *London Inn* (☎01579/320263; ②) also has comfortable accommodation, and provides a cosy setting for lunch-time and evening **meals**.

The southern edge of Bodmin Moor is far greener and more thickly wooded than the north due to the confluence of a web of **rivers** into the Fowey, which tumbles through the **Golitha Falls**, a couple of miles east of St Neot, below Draynes Bridge. One of the moor's best-known beauty spots, this is actually more a series of rapids than a waterfall, enlivened by the dippers and wagtails that flit through the surrounding beech trees. There's also an attractive woodland walk to the dam at the Siblyback Lake reservoir just over a mile to the northeast: follow the river up to Draynes Bridge, then walk north up a minor road until a path branches off on the right after a half-mile, leading down to the water's edge.

North of Siblyback Lake, and reachable from the B3254 Launceston road, **Twelve Men's Moor** holds some of Bodmin Moor's grandest landscapes. The quite modest elevations of **Hawk's Tor** (1079ft) and the lower **Trewartha Tor** appear enormous from the north, though they are topped by **Kilmar**, highest of the hills on the moor's eastern flank at 1280ft. Three miles east of Siblyback Lake, and reachable on the twice-daily Launceston–Liskeard bus #268 (Mon, Wed & Fri only), Cornwall's highest village, **MINIONS**, makes a good base for exploring these bleak areas, and also lies within easy distance of a cluster of prehistoric remains which are worth visiting en route. The closest of these can be reached by following the signposted path a few steps west of the centre of Minions, which brings you after a quarter-mile to **The Hurlers**, a wide complex of three stone circles dating from about 1500 BC. The purpose of these stark upright stones is not known, though local lore declares them to be men turned to stone for playing the Celtic game of hurling on the Sabbath. Following the path a further half-mile or so north, **Stowe's Hill** is the site of the moor's most famous stone pile, **The Cheesewring**, a precarious pillar of balancing flat granite slabs that have been marvellously eroded by the wind to resemble a hamburger in a peaked cap. Gouged out of the hillside nearby, the disused **Cheesewring Quarry** is a centre of rock climbing. Three miles south of Minions and less than half a mile south of the village of Darite (off the Tremar road), **Trethevy Quoit** is another Stone Age survivor, a chamber tomb nearly nine feet high and surmounted by a massive capstone. Originally enclosed in earth, the slabs have been stripped by centuries of weathering to create Cornwall's most impressive megalithic monument. Bus #73 from Liskeard calls at Darite and St Cleer, both of which are close to Trethevy Quoit; alternatively, it's a three-mile walk from Liskeard.

Off the southern limits of the moor, where the B3254 meets the A390 and the A38, **LISKEARD** is a useful bus and rail junction at the head of the East Looe Valley, connected by a summer branch line with

At the Cheese Farm, *two miles north-east of Minions, sign-posted a mile east of Upton Cross on the B3254, (April–Oct Mon–Fri 10am–4pm, Sat 10am–2pm; £2.50), guides in cowskin-patterned trousers reveal how Cornwall's distinctive Yarg cheese, with its coating of nettle leaves, is made; tastings are on offer and there's a shop and café attached.*

Looe, on the coast (see p.177). The only distraction hereabouts lies out of town at the exhibition of **Magnificent Music Machines** (Easter–Oct daily 11am–5pm; £4), three miles south in St Keyne (a request stop on the line to Looe, and signposted off the B3254), where an hour's enthusiastic tour brings you face-to-face with a delicate 1895 polyphon, a Wurlitzer cinema organ from 1929 and various fairground and café organs (watch out for the Turkish cymbals in action). Back in Liskeard, just below St Martin's Church at 27 Church St, the *Bay Leaf* is a great place for something to **eat** (closed Wed & Sat lunch); the Bosnian chef likes to include Eastern European dishes on the menu as well as early-evening specials for under a fiver (6–7pm), and there's a cellar bar downstairs for smokers.

Travel details

Travel details

Trains

Bodmin Parkway to: Liskeard (twice hourly; 13min); Penzance (hourly; 1hr 20min); Plymouth (every 30min; 45min).

Liskeard to: Bodmin Parkway (hourly; 12min); Looe (June–Sept 8–11 daily; 30min); Penzance (hourly; 1hr 30min); Plymouth (hourly; 30min).

Buses

Altarnun to: Launceston (Mon–Fri 3 daily; 25min).

Blisland to: Bodmin (Mon–Sat 5 daily; 20min); Camelford (Mon–Sat 3 daily; 20min).

Bodmin to: Blisland (Mon–Sat 5 daily; 20min); Bolventor (Tues & Thurs 2 daily, Sat 1 daily; 15min); Camelford (Mon–Sat 4 daily; 45min); Launceston (Tues & Thurs 2 daily, Sat 1 daily; 35min); St Austell (Mon–Sat hourly; 1hr 10min; Sun 4 daily; 50min); Truro (3 daily; 45min); Wadebridge (Mon–Sat hourly, plus late May to late Sept Sun 4 daily; 25min).

Bolventor to: Bodmin (Tues & Thurs 2 daily, Sat 1 daily; 15min); Launceston (Tues & Thurs 2 daily, Sat 1 daily; 25min).

Camelford to: Blisland (Mon–Sat 3 daily; 20min); Bodmin (Mon–Sat 4 daily; 45min); Tintagel (Mon–Sat hourly, plus late May to late Sept Sun 4 daily; 15–25min).

Launceston to: Altarnun (Mon–Fri 3 daily; 25min); Bodmin (Tues & Thurs 2 daily; 35min); Bolventor (Tues & Thurs 2 daily, Sat 1 daily; 25min); Liskeard (Mon–Sat 4 daily; 1hr).

Liskeard to: Launceston (Mon–Sat 4 daily; 1hr); Plymouth (Mon–Sat hourly, Sun 2 daily; 50min); St Austell (Mon–Fri 5 daily; 45min); St Neot (Mon–Sat 8 daily; 25min).

St Neot to: Liskeard (Mon–Sat 8 daily; 25min).

The Contexts

A brief history of Devon and Cornwall

Remote from England's main centres of political and industrial activity, the counties of Devon and Cornwall have played a largely peripheral role in the country's history. The region has been most pre-eminent in matters related to the sea, namely fishing, smuggling and buccaneering, while inland, Devon's cloth industry and Cornwall's mines for centuries provided a solid economic base.

Prehistory

The **first evidence of human settlement** in the region is from around 30,000 BC – a teenager's jawbone found in Kent's Cavern, Torquay – but the subsequent prehistory of the region is a succession of long blanks of which next to nothing is known. In general, however, it seems likely that England's westernmost counties shared much the same experiences as other parts of the land, the scattered tribes relying on hunting and gathering with a rudimentary social organization. In common with the rest of England, the region was settled by **Neolithic** tribes from mainland Europe during the fourth millennium BC, who introduced relatively advanced domestic and industrial skills. Strangely, despite the unearthing of large quantities of flints and arrowheads from Neolithic sites, relics of habitation are paltry, though Cornwall

has numerous examples of quoits, or chambered tombs set in open country with a giant slab, or capstone, for a roof. The beginnings of cereal cultivation and livestock farming are also traced to these times.

More prolific are finds associated with the **Bronze Age** peoples who began to arrive on the scene during the second millennium BC. These tribes left a contrastingly rich legacy of granite menhirs, kistvaens, stone rows, stone circles and hut circles throughout the region – more than 1200 barrows (burial mounds) have been discovered in Devon alone, of which a significant number lie on Dartmoor. In Cornwall, remains are concentrated particularly on the Isles of Scilly, the Penwith peninsula and Bodmin Moor, where The Hurlers, a complex of three circles dating from about 1500 BC, represent a fine example. Most of these sites were rifled centuries ago, and the surviving relics have yielded frustratingly little information about the life and structure of the society which occupied them.

In around 500 BC, another wave of immigrants, the **Celts**, established themselves in the region, bringing with them weapons and tools made of iron. Much given to tribal wars, the Celts established sturdy hillforts throughout the peninsula, though the best-preserved relic from these times is the village of Chysauster in Penwith, established in around the first century BC and occupied until long after. Good examples of the form and layout of the fields farmed in these times still exist hereabouts, notably the small, stone-hedged field systems around Zennor.

The Romans and the Dark Ages

Recorded history begins with the coming of the **Romans**, who occupied Exeter (known by them as Isca Dumnoniorum) in the first century AD but did not venture much further. Little interested in this extremity of their empire, the Romans left few traces in the West Country, content to establish a strong military presence at Exeter to keep an eye on the Celtic tribes which were left to their own devices further west. Although the region as a whole benefited from the *Pax Romana*, Roman ways were never greatly assimilated, as far as historians can tell, and the Roman interlude left less impression here than on most other areas of the country.

The accelerating disintegration of the Roman Empire towards the end of the fourth century led to the withdrawal of the legions and a rapid reversion to pre-Roman practices in the West Country. Almost immediately, there began incursions by the **Saxons**, a Germanic people, who settled in much of the region during the sixth and seventh centuries. The invaders were at first unable – or unwilling – to subdue the Britons in the far west, however, making an enclave of Cornwall. As the last stronghold of Celtic resistance in England and the torch-bearer of Christianity, the "Dark Ages" here were actually a golden age during which much of the county's rich folklore originated. In this scantily recorded era, saints and mystics were said to wander the pilgrimage routes between Wales, Ireland and Brittany, and the various strands of the Arthurian saga were first woven together, probably based on the exploits of a Celtic chieftain resisting the Saxons. The county's isolation aided the survival of the Celtic tongue, and while Cornish has not been spoken as a living language since the eighteenth century, Celtic place-names are still much in evidence today.

Cornwall was not fully conquered by the Saxons until the time of Athelstan in around 926. In Devon, the local Dumnonii more readily absorbed the Saxon newcomers, who by the **eighth century** were at least nominally Christians. Much of the work of conversion was undertaken by such individuals as Saint Boniface (c. 680–754), born Wynfrith in Crediton, who went on to spread the faith in Devon and later among the Frisians in Germany and the Lowlands. The integration of Saxons and Celts was further strengthened by the need to confront the threat of **Danish raids** which afflicted the region, in common with the rest of the country, during the **ninth and tenth centuries**. Unlike in other parts, however, there was little Viking settlement in the West, but a constant skirmishing between invading armies and the forces of the West Saxons under Alfred the Great and his descendants. The Danes occupied Exeter for the last time in 1003, but the Anglo-Saxon state was not to last much longer, for the entire region was shortly to be absorbed into the

new Norman kingdom following William the Conqueror's capture of Exeter in 1068.

The Middle Ages

The **Normans** built castles at Exeter, Totnes, Okehampton, Restormel and Launceston, which acted as nuclei for the growth of towns. This urban development was also spurred on by the **cloth trade**, Devon's principal industry at this time, as it continued to be throughout the medieval and early modern periods. Wool from the county's fertile inland pastures was processed locally or in the towns, and exported to mainland Europe from the great estuary ports of the south coast, establishing both a robust rural economy and a strong mercantile class in such towns as Topsham, Totnes and Dartmouth. Exeter's primacy in Devon was assured when the diocese was transferred here from Crediton in 1050, and the great cathedral constructed soon afterwards.

In Cornwall, the indigenous Saxon manors were taken over by the Normans to form the basis of an earldom, which was granted to Edward III's son, the Black Prince, in 1337, since when the earldom has belonged traditionally to the eldest son of the English sovereign, who acts as duke of Cornwall. On the whole, the Norman yoke was accepted here, the greater links with France and centralized economy promoting the growth of commerce and of such inland ports as Truro and Fowey.

Although Cornwall played a comparatively minor part in the region's cloth trade, it had a much greater role in the region's **mining** industry. Tin had been extracted here since prehistoric times, when it was alloyed with copper – also found in the region – to make bronze. Though the Romans do not appear to have utilized the resource, the greater level of protection and organization that existed under the Normans made Cornwall Europe's biggest supplier of tin in the twelfth century. Over the next hundred years Helston, Lostwithiel, Truro and Liskeard in Cornwall, and Ashburton and Tavistock in Devon were made stannary towns, according to which they were granted special privileges and placed by the crown under the separate legal jurisdiction of the stannary (tin mine) courts. Stannary towns were visited twice a year by officials from London who came to test the smelted tin, chipping a corner if it was approved – "coigning" it, from the French for "corner", hence the English word, *coin*.

After farming and mining, the third most important activity in Devon and Cornwall was **fishing**, and many of the ports of the southern coast in particular – such as Beer, Brixham, Polperro and Mevagissey – have retained their medieval layout and miniature scale. In 1272, however, the imposition of custom duties for the first time gave birth to another lucrative spin-off which existed side-by-side with fishing – **smuggling**, for which the inlets and estuaries proved ideal terrain. The activity was to carry on until well into the nineteenth century, and there are even echoes of it in the present era with shipments of drugs regularly apprehended off the peninsula's indented coasts.

The fifteenth and sixteenth centuries

While the region had consolidated its wealth in comparative peace during the later part of the Middle Ages, the **fifteenth and sixteenth centuries** saw Devon and Cornwall increasingly drawn into the turmoil of national events. Stirrings of **revolt** against the new centralizing Tudor state surfaced in 1497 when Thomas Flamank, a Bodmin lawyer, and Michael Joseph, a blacksmith from the Lizard area, led 15,000 Cornishmen to London to protest at high taxation. By the time the force arrived in Blackheath, they were much depleted and easily crushed by Henry VII's army. Feelings still ran high, though, inflamed by the execution of the rebellion's leaders, so that there was widespread support for **Perkin Warbeck**, who just three months later landed at St Ives claiming to be Richard, Duke of York – one of the disappeared "Princes in the Tower" who had in fact probably been dispatched by Richard III in 1483. Warbeck received a rapturous welcome in Bodmin and attracted some support from local gentry who proclaimed the pretender Richard IV. Crossing the Tamar in September 1497, however, the rebels failed to take Exeter and Warbeck's army melted away when confronted by the king's forces at Taunton.

A further revolt took place in 1549 against the Act of Uniformity and its insistence on the Book of Common Prayer and the simplified service in English rather than the old Latin Mass – a particular aggravation to the non-English-speaking Cornish. The **Prayer Book Rebellion** began in the village of Sampford Courtenay, near Okehampton, and drew support in both Devon and Cornwall,

but the rebels were defeated in battle at Clyst St Mary, outside Topsham, by Lord Russell, who happened to be the principal beneficiary of dissolved monastery lands in the West Country.

As England's defence came to rely more heavily on its maritime prowess, and trade began to focus increasingly on the Atlantic, so Devon assumed an increasingly important naval role, both for its geographical position and for its colourful crop of highly qualified mariners – Drake, Grenville and Raleigh, among others. All of these men were to take a leading role in the defence of the realm and the expansion of trade to the Americas, and all were also involved in piracy and slavery. **Francis Drake** (c. 1540–96), born near Tavistock, was plundering the coast of Guinea and the Spanish Main when he was only in his twenties and was a popular hero on his return to Plymouth, of which he later became mayor. **Walter Raleigh** (1552–1618), born in Hayes Barton, east Devon, also indulged in piratical activities in addition to his attempts to colonize America, and represented the county in parliament. His cousin **Richard Grenville** (1542–91) commanded the fleet that carried English colonists to Roanoke Island in present-day North Carolina in 1585, and died heroically against overwhelming odds in a celebrated tussle with a Spanish treasure fleet in the Azores – his ship, the *Revenge*, was crewed by "men of Bideford in Devon". Grenville's preparations for a voyage of discovery to the South Pacific were adopted by Drake when the latter circumnavigated the world in 1577–80, the first Englishman to do so. As the home port of these and other maritime adventurers, Plymouth became the western centre of Britain's maritime power and remains the home of the Royal Navy today. Devonport Dockyard here is still one of the area's biggest employers, while Appledore on the northern coast also continues its centuries-old shipbuilding activities.

Elsewhere on the south coast, defences were strengthened against French and Spanish raids, with fortifications erected or expanded in Dartmouth, Fowey, St Mawes, Falmouth and St Mary's, on the Isles of Scilly. The ever-present fear of Spanish invasion during the second half of the **sixteenth century** culminated in 1588 with the sailing of the **Spanish Armada**, whose approach was first announced from the Cornish coast at the Lizard, and which was eventually scuppered by Elizabeth I's fleet docked in Plymouth – the occasion of Drake's famous sang-froid when he insisted on finishing his game of bowls on Plymouth Hoe before putting to sea to fight the enemy. Far more dangerous than the Armada for Cornwall was the Spanish invasion of Brittany in 1590, allowing a convenient base for raids on Cornwall, including the devastating attack on Mousehole, Newlyn and Penzance in 1595, when two separate Spanish assault parties joined forces to sack and burn these three ports.

The Civil War

Fifty years later, the **Civil War**, when it erupted, engulfed and divided the West Country no less than other parts of England. Although most places preferred to keep their options open and observe the course of events before rallying to either side, sentiment here was pretty squarely behind the Royalist cause – with the notable exceptions of Exeter and Plymouth, which declared both ways. Where it was necessary to come out in favour of one side over another, most people followed their religious and political beliefs. Thus, in Cornwall for example, Bevil Grenville – celebrated warrior and hero of Robert Hawker's ballad, *Song of the Western Men* – together with many others sided with the king in defence of the Anglican church, while Lord Robartes, a Presbyterian merchant, and others who rejected absolutism, sided with parliament. The royalist mint was established in Truro in 1642–3 and Cornwall became a major theatre of war. Battles were fought and won by the Royalists at Braddock Down and Stratton in Cornwall and at Lansdown near Bristol, where Bevil Grenville fell. There were two campaigns in 1643, and the following year Charles I defeated the Earl of Essex's army at Lostwithiel. However, Royalist fortunes were reversed when the New Model Army under the command of Thomas Fairfax appeared in the West in 1645. This final brutal campaign culminated in the Royalist surrender at Tressillian, near Truro, 12 March, 1645, although St Michael's Mount, Pendennis Castle and Exeter held out until the following year.

The main legacies of this sequence of sieges and small battles – there was none on the scale of Naseby or Marston Moor – were harvest failure, starvation and the destruction of many great houses and forts, though some of the latter were simply decommissioned and converted to domestic use. The wool trade in Devon, however, was largely unscathed, and entered a hugely prosperous phase in the second half of the seventeenth century.

The eighteenth and nineteenth centuries

Tin and copper mining brought a degree of prosperity to Cornwall in the **eighteenth century**, with the introduction of beam engines in 1716 allowing ever-deeper shafts to be excavated, pumped and mined. The more extensive underground networks were largely made possible by the innovations of such engineers as Thomas Newcomen of Dartmouth (1663–1729), who constructed a steam engine for pumping water out of pits, and the Cornish scientists Humphry Davy (1778–1829), famous for his "Davy lamp", and Richard Trevithick (1771–1833), who invented a steam carriage for use in the mines. The beam engines were fuelled by coal from South Wales which helped to keep the peninsula's northern ports busy. For the miners themselves, however, the working conditions were both squalid and dangerous, and the conditions in which their families lived were equally appalling. These impoverished communities provided a fertile ground for the preaching of **John Wesley**, the co-founder of Methodism who travelled extensively in Devon and Cornwall between 1743 and 1786. His first visits met with a hostile response, but he later found a receptive audience for his pared-down version of the Christian message, and it is from this period that many of the Methodist chapels dotted around the region date.

The copper industry peaked during the 1840s, focused on the area around Redruth and Camborne, but shortly afterwards the mining industry collapsed when deposits of both copper and tin were found cheaper elsewhere in the world market. Pit closures during the nineteenth and twentieth centuries were followed by large-scale emigration from Cornwall, chiefly to Australia and South America.

On a much smaller scale, the region's extensive deposits of slate and granite continued to be quarried as they had been for centuries, while the eighteenth century also saw the beginning of the **china clay** industry in Cornwall. The deposits were first discovered by William Cookworthy (1705–80) of Kingsbridge in the area around Helston, and more significantly north of St Austell, where the conical white mountains of debris are still a feature of the landscape, and where extraction remains an important industry today. First used in the making of ceramics, the kaolin is now used in a wide range of products.

On the coasts, Devon's seaside towns were finding a new source of income in the tourist industry that expanded throughout the **nineteenth century**. Since the Napoleonic Wars in 1803–15 had prevented "society" from taking the fashionable Grand Tour of continental Europe, there was an increasing trend to sojourn in the comparatively mild climate of such towns as Exmouth, Torquay and Sidmouth, on the south coast, and, on the north, the villages of Lynton and Lynmouth, which were said to recall an Alpine landscape. The extension of Brunel's railway to Exeter in 1840 had the immediate result of accelerating this phenomenon, and the railway's extension over the Tamar into Cornwall in 1859, and to North Devon in 1872 brought these regions for the first time into the ambit of mass tourism. Ilfracombe became an archetypal Victorian seaside resort, while Falmouth, Newquay and St Ives in Cornwall found their full flowering in the twentieth century. Along with the tourists, the railways also brought down other groups from metropolitan England: artists, who congregated first in Newlyn, at the end of the nineteenth century, and later in neighbouring St Ives (see pp. 327-328).

The twentieth century

Along with the steady stream of artists who were drawn to Devon and Cornwall, the **twentieth century** also saw the region associated with various writers, though again these were mainly outsiders who settled in or had links with the West – D.H. Lawrence, Virginia Woolf, Henry Williamson (of *Tarka the Otter*), Daphne Du Maurier and Agatha Christie, among others.

However, here, as elsewhere in the country, all else was overshadowed during this period by the two world wars. Although **World War I** had little direct effect on the region beyond cutting a swath through its adult male population, the south coast of Devon and Cornwall in particular suffered from both military requisition and enemy bombing during **World War II**. While most of the West Country was designated safe from German aerial attack – and accordingly received many evacuees from London and the Midlands – Plymouth suffered the highest bombardment of any British seaport, and Exeter too was targeted

in the so-called "Baedeker raids" (directed at centres of cultural interest). The subsequent reconstruction in these two cities followed very different paths, more conservative in Exeter, bolder in Plymouth, but arguably less successful. Neither city has escaped the brutalizing of large tracts, and the imposition of unsympathetic shopping centres and unsightly car parks.

In the 1950s, the designation of Dartmoor and Exmoor as **national parks** was a significant indication of both the new importance of tourism to the area and the urgency of conservation for the future well-being of the region. However, the decade was also marred by tragedy when heavy rain on Exmoor in 1952 caused the River Lyn to burst its banks, resulting in the catastrophic flooding of Lynmouth and the loss of 31 lives.

The closure of most local rail lines in the 1960s had no significant effect on the region's economy as it was well compensated by the huge expansion of motor traffic, encouraged by the extension of the M5 motorway to Exeter and the building of the link road to North Devon. However, the volume of traffic, which intensifies during the peak summer months, has brought its own massive environmental problems and today remains one of the most pressing concerns for the well-being of the region.

The last thirty years have seen major shifts in Devon and Cornwall related to Britain's membership of the **European Union**, with both the farming and fishing communities losing out as a result of agricultural and fisheries policies. Fishermen have also been hard hit by declining fish stocks and the imposition of quotas which have met stiff resistance. Many in both groups have turned to tourism as a source of a secondary income, though only a small fraction can benefit from this sector, and many businesses have folded for good. The choice of Devon and Cornwall as places of retirement or for second homes has also played a significant effect in pricing locals out of the area, while farming and fishing have been superseded by the shorter-term benefits of service industries. Cornwall has qualified for European aid, and has recently adopted a higher national profile by opening a branch of the Tate Gallery in St Ives and creating the Eden Project, an ambitious exhibition of the planet's ecosystems, near St Austell. Considerable investment has accompanied these large-scale schemes, though, again, this can only have a marginal effect on the local economy.

The wildlife of Devon and Cornwall

Devon and Cornwall are rightly famous for the beauty of their landscapes and the richness of their coastline, which is proportionately the longest shared by any two counties in Britain. The peninsula on which these counties lie drives a wedge deep into the Atlantic and ensures a strong maritime influence, with the benevolent effects of the Gulf Stream giving the region's fauna and flora an almost subtropical diversity that's unmatched in the British Isles. Given this range, the following description treats each of the main habitats separately, summarizing their main features and the kind of wildlife you can expect to find there.

The sea itself is at the junction of the warm southern and cool northern water bodies, and is amongst the richest marine habitats in the world, though most people's experience of the **marine environment** is confined to the occasional glimpse of a dolphin or seal. More accessible is Devon and Cornwall's **coastline**, which as a rule is exposed and heavily weathered on the peninsula's northern littoral and much more sheltered and indented on the southern seaboard. The long walls of **sea cliffs** are interspersed by bays and **estuaries**, whose **rivers** shelter colourful birdlife as well as the occasional otter, while their mouths are fringed by extensive areas of **sand dunes**. Elsewhere, on or just behind the shoreline, **reedbeds** survive in isolated patches and are an important habitat for a range of rare insects, plants and birds.

Inland, too, the geological peculiarities of the region have contributed to the peninsula's range of habitats. The upland granite outcrops which characterize the high moorland were created long ago by violent volcanic intrusion, which also strongly contorted the overlying strata of mudstones and limestones. These bare expanses of moorland, composed of **lowland and upland heaths** and **blanket bog**, fringed by **upland oakwoods**, cover Exmoor, Dartmoor and Bodmin Moor. In complete contrast, Devon and Cornwall's agricultural heartland has been heavily influenced by the historic patterns of human settlement and land use. Although modern farming methods have squandered vast quantities of species-rich **hedges**, **meadows** and banks, enough have survived to preserve large numbers of thriving plants and birds – all linked in a rich mosaic of rolling countryside.

Most of the other habitats, too, have been severely degraded by human activity, particularly changes in agricultural practice, though this process is only an intensification of an influence which has moulded and influenced British wildlife throughout the human settlement of these islands. Nowadays, some of the best examples are entirely limited to nature reserves, precious but beleaguered resources about which you may gather more information from the specialist organizations detailed in the box, opposite.

The marine environment

The **marine environment** of Devon and Cornwall constitutes one of the finest to be found around British shores. In spring and early summer especially, the coasts are bright with an abundance of **sea campion**, **kidney vetch**, **sea lavender**, orange **lichen** and green **algae**. Rarer flora to look out for include **golden samphire**, a nationally scarce plant quite common along the Cornish coastline where it grows on bare rock just above the high-water mark.

Most ubiquitous of the fauna around the coasts of Devon and Cornwall, from rugged cliff to fishing village, are the various populations of **seabirds** which, according to the season, may be nesting or wintering here, or passing through on migration. Among the many species, **fulmars** and **kittiwakes** are numerous around **St Agnes Head** in Cornwall, while **razorbills** and **guillemots** are plentiful on almost all Cornish coasts. One of the most rewarding birds to look out for is the **gannet**, with long, black-tipped white wings, known or its vertical plunges into the sea as it fishes. Of the many species of gulls, most common is the **herring gull**, distinguished by its grey mantle, flesh-coloured feet and black-and-white-spotted wing tips. Chiefly a scavenger, its numbers have greatly increased in recent years as a result of expanding food supplies, which include refuse and sewage, though the birds are also known for their trick of dropping shellfish on rocks to crack them open. The richest variety of marine birds are found on the **Isles of Scilly**, including large flocks of **puffins**, which also breed on the island of Lundy, off north Devon's coast, in April and May.

As for the waterborne marine life, **grey seals** may occasionally be seen by observant coastal walkers, though they're most commonly spotted from a boat at such sites as Godrevy Island, Mousehole Rock, Falmouth Bay or, in greater numbers, the Isles of Scilly. Here, you'll encounter them hauled out onto rocks to bask in the sun or on remote beaches where females ("cows") – lighter and smaller than the males ("bulls") – often return each year to give birth. West Country seal pups are smaller than those of other UK populations, and they learn to swim earlier due to the milder conditions. You'll sometimes see seals wearing a necklace of the fishing nets with which they sometimes become entangled – one of the main hazards they face.

Dolphins and **porpoises** can also be seen off the Devon and Cornwall coasts, though they live in family groups with territories covering hundreds of miles, so there are no specific places where sightings can be guaranteed – your best bet for land-based viewing would be at the far west of the peninsula, at Land's End, Sennen Cove, Cape Cornwall or Mount's Bay. The last century has seen a dramatic decline in porpoise and dolphin populations in the English Channel and southern Celtic Sea, partly due to their being a by-catch of fishing boats, but also due to the fact that fish stocks – their prey – have drastically fallen. It's now recognized that almost all the dolphins stranded on our beaches have been caught accidentally in fishing nets. **Whales** have also fallen prey to fishing methods and sightings are quite rare: the best chances of seeing minke, pilot, humpbacked or even orca (or killer) whales is from **Sennen Cove**, or else from the ferry en route to the Isles of Scilly.

In summer **basking sharks** follow the warm Gulf Stream currents up Britain's west coast, allowing numerous sightings from spots on the Cornish coast (over 500 may be sighted in a typical year in the southwest). A large cartilaginous fish – the world's second largest, at 35 feet – they are harmless to humans, as their huge jaws are designed to scoop up plankton, tiny plants and animals that form the basis of the ocean food chain. Less common are **leatherback turtles**, which grow to over two yards in length and also follow a migration route from their tropical breeding grounds in late summer and early autumn. They're occasionally washed up on Cornish beaches, but you're more likely to see them stuffed in local museums.

In 2001, the EU banned the notorious "wall of death" drift nets which have been responsible for countless dolphin, whale, shark and turtle deaths – to date the only statutory protection for these creatures, which are also regularly maimed if not maimed by jet skis and private pleasure craft. Make sure if you book up with one of the many operators of wildlife cruises that a respectful distance is kept at all times from these creatures, which, unless they join you, is around 100yd. Any instances of harassment can be reported to the police or the Whale and Dolphin Conservation Society (see box overleaf).

Sea cliffs

Many of the long and highly scenic stretches of **cliffs** which dominate Devon and Cornwall's coastline enjoy the protection of the National Trust (see box, overleaf), and can be explored along the South West Coast Path. Robust granite makes up most of the cliffs, though east Devon's striated and undulating red cliffs are softer sandstone, where landslips have led to the creation of thickly vegetated undercliffs. The dense scrub of **privet**, **dogwood**, **maple** and **spindle** here has encouraged the **nightingale** and the rare **dormouse**, while the close-cropped grassland at the cliff tops is usually home to a rare community of flowers such as **wild thyme** and several species of **orchid**.

One of the best wildlife sites on the south coast is **Berry Head National Nature Reserve**

near Brixham, which is home to a substantial **guillemot** colony nesting on cliff ledges, while more unusual **skuas** and **shearwaters** can be seen offshore. The area is also rich in rare plants, with over 500 species recorded on the cliffs and surrounding scrub and limestone grassland. Many, such as **autumn squill** and the delightfully named **autumn ladies tresses** orchid, are national rarities.

The sea cliffs on the peninsula's northern coast are almost unbroken, though the fine stretch of hogback cliffs on north Devon's Exmoor coast is cut by deep wooded coombes which merge into upland moor. Here and further west, small ledges on the sheer faces provide protected habitats for many species of rare plants and nesting sites for birds such as **ravens** and the anchor-shaped **peregrine falcon**. On north Cornwall's cliffs, attempts are being made to reintroduce the **chough**, a rare, red-billed member of the crow family and the emblem of Cornwall – though extinct here since 1973.

In west Cornwall, the **Land's End's Wildlife Discovery Centre** has nesting **razorbills**, while the **National Nature Reserve** at the Lizard headland holds a fantastic variety of wild flowers. The serpentine which makes up much of the Lizard peninsula is rich in magnesium, which allows rare species of plant to flourish, notably the colourful **Cornish heath** (*Erica vagans*) heather, unique to the Lizard. The magnesium also contributes to the floristically rich grasslands running up to the cliffs, harbouring plants normally found around the Mediterranean. These grassland slopes may include thirteen species of **clover**, as well as **vetch**, **ox-eye daisy**, **wild chive** and **orchid**, and are grazed by robust rare breeds such as **Soay sheep** and wild **ponies**.

Estuaries

Devon and Cornwall's **estuaries** hold some nationally rare species of waders and wildfowl, including the beautiful, pure-white **little egrets**. Among the most important areas for wintering wildlife are the **Tamar** complex around Plymouth, the **Hayle estuary** in Cornwall, and, most significantly, the **Exe estuary**, whose broad and shallow waters shelter around 20,000 **waders** as well as **brent geese** and **wigeon** in winter. These last two feed on **zostera**, an unusual flowering marine grass which thrives in the soft, muddy sediments adjacent to the saltmarsh and also helps to stabilize the mud. The best site to watch these wintering flocks is **Dawlish Warren** at the mouth of the estuary, where, just before high tide, you can usually see around twenty species. Other winter species that frequent the Exe estuary include **shelduck, dunlin, curlew, redshank**, the **black-** and **bar-tailed godwit**, as well as large flocks of **oystercatcher**, while one of the country's largest winter flocks of the rare and elegant **avocet** (symbol of the Royal Society for the Protection of Birds) is commonly seen higher up the estuary at **Topsham**.

The coast around Exmouth and Dawlish Warren is also a good spot for picking out a range of **sea** and **sawbilled ducks, grebes** and **divers**, though you'll need patience, expertise and a good telescope to identify these.

Many of the estuaries of Devon and Cornwall's southern seaboard are **rias**, or river valleys drowned long ago by a rise in sea level, with narrow, deep and well-defined channels and high levels of salinity. The **Helford** in the south of Cornwall is a delightful example of one, its winding creeks and wooded shorelines a haven for **eelgrass**. The salty water is also ideal for **cuttlefish** and **oysters**, while the rich rockpools at the estuary mouth shelter numerous **sea anemones** and **crabs**. The other important ria on the south coast is the **Kingsbridge estuary** in Devon, around which the rare **cirl bunting** has its stronghold.

Rivers

The **rivers** of Devon and Cornwall, fast-flowing and varied in character, tend to run south from the high ground of the region's three moors, for example the Teign, Dart and the Fowey. Along their banks, it's not difficult to spot **kingfisher, heron, dipper, sand martin** and **grey wagtail**, among other birds, while in the evening you may glimpse a **Daubenton's bat** skimming low over the water. These rivers are also home to the migratory **Atlantic salmon** and the resident **brown trout**, as well as many species of dragonfly and damselfly. The most important of the rivers that empty from the region's northern coast are the **De Lank** and **Camel** in Cornwall, and the **Taw** and **Torridge** in Devon, all of which are habitats of the highly secretive **otter**. The best chance of spotting these elusive mammals is on one of the guided excursions organized by the Devon or Cornwall Wildlife Trusts (see box on p.321).

Reedbeds

Reedbeds constitute a highly scarce habitat nationally, much depleted after the drainage and reclamation of wetlands that occurred in previous centuries. However, the National Nature Reserve at **Slapton Ley**, between Dartmouth and Kingsbridge in south Devon, is one of the nation's finest freshwater reed and aquatic areas. Its main feature is the Ley itself, the largest natural lake in southwest England and only separated from the sea by a narrow shingle bar. The extensive areas of reedbed surrounding the lake shelter an abundant aquatic flora, including the rare **convergent stonewort** and the only British occurrence of the **strapwort**, while the monotonous call of **sedge** and **reed warblers** can be heard through much of the summer.

You'll also find reedbeds on the **River Exe** just upstream from Topsham on RSPB and Devon Wildlife Trust reserves, where it is possible to see **bearded tits**. Further west, **Marazion**, near Penzance in Cornwall, harbours a discreet and picturesque little RSPB reserve where the reedbeds are becoming famous for rare migrant **dragonflies** and such **butterflies** as the migrant **clouded yellow** and **painted lady**.

Sand dunes

Extending northwards from the tip of the Taw/Torridge estuary in north Devon, **Braunton Burrows** is one of the largest **sand dune** systems in Britain, nearly four miles in length and over a mile wide. Rated of such international importance to be designated by UNESCO as an International Biosphere Reserve, the dunes, which reach up to thirty yards high, are composed of wind-blown marine sand and crushed shells held loosely together by **marram** grass. These dynamic natural systems are continually – if imperceptibly – on the move, and the site's rich community of highly specialized plant and animal species has excited botanical interest since the seventeenth century. Among the 400-plus species of plants recorded here, the myriad wild flowers include **evening-scented sea-stock**, vivid patches of **biting stone crop**, deep-blue **vipers-bugloss**, and the tall, lemon-coloured **evening primrose**, while throughout the summer months, the ground is carpeted with an abundance of **bird's foot trefoil** and **wild thyme**. In damper areas **yellow flag iris** and **marsh marigolds** are replaced later in summer by **marsh orchids** and **marsh helleborines**.

Other notable dune sites are at **Dawlish Warren**, in south Devon, and on the edges of the **Hayle estuary**, near St Ives in Cornwall, where **kestrels** may sometimes be seen hovering overhead.

Meadows and hedges

Unimproved neutral grassland – or **meadow** – constitutes one of Britain's most picturesque habitats, sheltering a wealth of colourful flowers and insects. This is particularly true of rush pasture, which occurs on poor soils. Flower-rich meadows are relatively plentiful in north Devon where they are known as **Culm grassland**, which features a range of highly attractive and increasingly rare plants such as **devil's bit scabious**, the sublime **meadow thistle** and various **orchids** and **sedges**. Meadows are also very important for the rapidly declining **marsh fritillary butterfly**, whose remaining stronghold is in Devon, notably in Exmoor and Dartmoor National Parks; for more on these, information is best acquired from the relevant Wildlife Trusts (see box on p.321).

Small fields, woodland and thick, banked species-rich **hedgerows** are characteristic elements of the southwest's meadows, harbouring a rich variety of wildlife such as the **blackbird, bullfinch** and **song thrush**, which nest here. The hedges – which might include **hawthorn, honeysuckle** and other woody plants – are also an important refuge for the predatory **aphids** that control agricultural pests. Over these fields and copses, the **buzzard** is a common sight wheeling above, one of the region's most common birds of prey.

Upland oakwood

Devon and Cornwall hold some remarkable relics of **upland oakwood**, the majority of which are to be found on Dartmoor, Exmoor and Bodmin Moor. The woods were traditionally managed for charcoal and tanbark through **coppicing** – stimulating woodland plant growth through regular cropping – but the post-World War II era has seen a dramatic decline in this form of management and some change of character in these woods as the coppice stools grow out and gradually revert to forest. On Dartmoor, **Yarner Wood** has probably existed as woodland since prehistoric times, a mixture of sessile oak, holly, rowan, beech, ash and wych elm with an undercarpet of bilberry. It's rich in woodland **butterflies, moths** and **wood-ants**. Breeding birds include **sparrow-**

hawk and all three British **woodpeckers,** while **red, roe** and **fallow deer** may occasionally be seen. Adjoining Yarner Wood, **Trendlebere Down** is a mixture of typical upland oakwood and heath where over 400 species of plants have been recorded. Many stands of trees on the higher ground show the multiple stems and stunted growth typical of abandoned coppice, with a dense cover of **bilberry** on the ground. On Bodmin Moor, **Golitha** is a stunning, steep-sided, tree-lined gorge formed by the River Fowey which tumbles down a waterfall and rapids, creating the humid conditions that allow **lichens** and **mosses** to thrive.

Heathland and blanket bog

The southwest peninsula's wide swaths of **lowland heath** typically comprise open ground poor in nutrients and dominated by **heathers** and **gorse**, with a scattering of scrub and trees (often Scots pine). There are excellent examples of this habitat near Exmouth in east Devon, where the pebblebed heaths of **Aylesbeare** and **Harpford Common** are managed as reserves by the RSPB and are a refuge for the nocturnal moth-eating **nightjar**, the **Dartford warbler** and the agile falcon, the **hobby**. To the west of the Exe estuary, **Haldon Forest** is a heavily wooded ridge interspersed with heath, where the woodland rides reveal glimpses of **high brown fritillary** and other rare species of butterfly – you can sometimes also spot the insect-eating **honey buzzard** along with the rare **goshawk** overhead.

The warm and wet nature of the climate in Cornwall's Lizard peninsula harbours outstanding examples of **maritime heath** of a type not found elsewhere in Britain. The unusual mix of maritime species creates a glorious spectacle in summer, when the ground is a blue carpet of **autumn** and **spring quill, rock sea lavender** and **golden samphire**, and later in the year, when the flowering purple **heathers** and golden **gorse** add a regal blaze. Maritime heathlands also range along the coasts of Penwith and north Cornwall, and on the Isles of Scilly. On the Cornish mainland, **adders** may be found basking on rocks in hot sunny weather, identifiable by their brownish colour with a lozenge pattern down the back.

In global terms, Britain holds a high proportion of **upland heath**, characterized by poor-quality soil and vegetation consisting of **heather, bil-**

berry, **crossleaved heath** and **western gorse**. The largest area of this type of terrain is to be found on **Exmoor**, where such unusual plants as **lesser twayblade** grow, while **crowberry** and **cranberry** occur at the very southern edge of their geographical range. Exmoor is the most important stronghold of the endangered **heath fritillary** in the UK, but its most famous long-term residents are its **red deer** and ponies. **Exmoor ponies**, descended from wild ponies, have a total population lower than many more recognized rare species, but they are hardy and well adapted to the tough conditions of winter on the exposed hills, and their numbers seem to be holding up. A significant cause of casualties to the pony population is accidents with cars and visitors are requested to drive carefully on the moor. This is also particularly appropriate at lambing time, when many lambs are killed by careless visitors driving too fast.

Ponies are also a feature of the upland heaths of **Dartmoor**, which is characterized by granite tors which came about as a result of erosion of granite outcrops. Tors are regionally important for their **lichen** communities. You'll see the best examples at the edges of the Dartmoor plateau, rising above a patchwork of heath, bracken and valley mire, where scattered trees and shrubs may provide important nesting sites for birds such as **raven** and the agile and rare hawk, the **merlin**.

Blanket bog is restricted to plateau areas where the wet conditions have allowed a mantle of **peat** to develop, with a high proportion of **heathers**, **cottongrasses** and **bogmosses** and very small populations of breeding **golden plover** and **dunlin**. Other typical birdlife of these moors includes the summer visitors **wheatear** and **ring ouzel**, while **peregrine falcons** occasionally nest on the sheer rock faces.

Peter Hack

The arts scene in Devon and Cornwall

Stuck on the margins of British cultural life, Devon and Cornwall have produced few artists of great renown, though the last century or so has seen the establishment of two of Britain's rare "art schools" linked to a particular place – namely, the Newlyn and St Ives schools, both in west Cornwall. The same factors which drew those art colonies – the combination of picturesque charm, rugged grandeur and the clear light – have continued to work on successive generations of artists, so that the region now has one of the highest concentrations of the arts and crafts community in the country.

The eighteenth and early nineteenth centuries

Before the advent of the Newlyn and St Ives schools, Devon and Cornwall saw a relatively low level of artistic activity, though in the **eighteenth century**, each of the counties produced one nationally acclaimed figure. Of these, **Joshua Reynolds** (1723–92), born in Plympton, near Plymouth, achieved more lasting fame. After a sojourn in Italy, he found rich patrons who adored his Grand Manner and heroic style. Closely identified with formal "Academy art" (he was the first president of the Royal Academy in

1768), Reynolds advocated above all history painting, though he excelled at what he considered the inferior (but better-paid) field of portraiture.

John Opie (1761–1807), the first Cornish artist of any significance, was also highly esteemed for his portraits, though these were of a very different ilk. Something of a child prodigy, the untutored Opie was discovered by the Devon-born political satirist John Wolcot, then practising as a doctor in Truro, who in 1780 accompanied Opie to London to launch his artistic career (and simultaneously Wolcot's own as "Peter Pindar", author of a series of caustic poetical pamphlets). An instant success, the "Cornish wonder", as he came to be known, was most comfortable with his portraits of simple country folk – old people and children in particular – for which he used plenty of chiaroscuro in a style reminiscent of Caravaggio and Rembrandt. Opie was commissioned to paint seven illustrations for John Boydell's Shakespeare Gallery in 1786, the same year he exhibited his first historical work, *The Assassination of James I of Scotland*. This was followed a year later by *The Murder of Rizzio*, which secured his election as a member of the Royal Academy. Although his later work is now deemed undistinguished and repetitive, he was made a professor of painting at the Academy in 1805, and his death two years later was met with universal grief. Buried with great pomp in St Paul's, next to Joshua Reynolds, Opie attracted the largest gathering of artists since Reynolds' own funeral, including Benjamin West, Henry Fuseli, John Flaxman and Joseph Turner.

Reynolds' and Opie's West Country successors included such figures as the marine artist, **Thomas Luny** (1757–1837), associated with Teignmouth, and the Irish-born Romantic painter **Francis Danby** (1793–1861), who settled in Exmouth in 1847 and was famous for his bombastic, apocalyptic biblical scenes but better liked for his sunsets and landscapes.

ART GALLERIES AND MUSEUMS IN DEVON AND CORNWALL

The prolific output of Joshua Reynolds is well represented in stately homes throughout the country, a good number of them in Devon, such as **Hartland Abbey** and **Saltram House**. Most of the region's major public collections also hold examples of his oils, notably Exeter's **Royal Albert Memorial Museum**, which, along with Truro's **Royal Cornwall Museum**, is also the place to see works by John Opie. You'll find a few paintings by Thomas Luny among other local nineteenth-century artists exhibited in Torquay's **Abbey Mansion**.

The central role of St Ives in the region's art was confirmed by the siting there of the **Tate St Ives**, which opened in a beachside location in 1993 to show the works of the local school. Under the same management, the town's **Hepworth Museum** showcases Barbara Hepworth's sculptures, while the **Leach Pottery** is the place to see work by Bernard Leach, Shoji Hamada and their various pupils and disciples. Contemporary work by local artists is on view at the **St Ives Society of Arts Gallery**. Some of the other current art on display in town is arresting, but much of it is ignorable.

Most of the important works of the Newlyn School are in major collections, but a good representation is on view in Penzance's **Penlee House**. The **Newlyn Art Gallery**, on the other hand, features contemporary art by local and other artists. In recent years a thriving arts scene has also emerged in Falmouth, which you can sample at **Falmouth Arts Centre** and **Falmouth Art Gallery**.

Apart from these places, you'll find tiny galleries in scores of smaller towns and villages throughout Devon and Cornwall, which are often worth a glance or more. Local tourist offices can sometimes provide a list if you're seriously interested; alternatively pick up a copy of one of the local **arts magazines**, such as *Cornwall Arts*, published four times yearly (free from tourist offices).

The Newlyn School

The arrival of the railway in Devon and Cornwall in the late nineteenth century generated a huge growth of interest in the region. Artists were particularly drawn to the far west of the peninsula, encouraged by the mild climate and exceptional light, which together with the strong fishing culture, recalled a corner of continental Europe. Two Birmingham artists, **Walter Langley** (1852–1922) and **Edwin Harris** (1855–1906), had already settled in Newlyn in 1882, but it was the arrival of **Stanhope Forbes** (1857–1947) two years later which really set the ball rolling for the "**Newlyn School**". Inspired by the fishing port's resemblance to villages in Brittany where he had studied, Forbes showed his fascination with the effects of the luminous light and with the life of the local fishing community in such works as *Fish Sale on Newlyn Beach* (1884). When displayed at the Royal Academy, this lively depiction of men and women trading fish on the wet sand established Forbes and the Newlyn School as the most prominent exponents of the new French-influenced styles, which contrasted with the predominantly insular and backward-looking tone of most British painting of the time. The Newlyn painters tried to immerse themselves in the life of the fishing community in order to represent it

more faithfully, and their work shows great sympathy with the people of the locality, even if it is occasionally prone to sentimentality. Other prominent members of the school included **Norman Garstin** (1847–1926), an Irishman who came to Newlyn in 1886, who was supposedly the most "intellectual" member of the group. His most famous work, *The Rain it Raineth Everyday* (1889), was accepted by the Royal Academy but never shown there – it's currently viewable in Penlee House, Penzance. **Henry Scott Tuke** (1858–1929), born in York but brought up in Falmouth and London, had already spent some time painting in Newlyn before he settled in Falmouth in 1885, with the stated intention to "paint the nude in open air". Unable to find suitable models locally he imported one from London, Walter Shilling, and, though his numerous depictions of nude boys aroused controversy, his work did gain some respectability and was actively encouraged by Stanhope Forbes. Truro's museum has some of his homoerotic nudes together with maritime subjects and a self-portrait.

Although most Newlyn artists shared Forbes' devotion to open-air painting, another member of the school, **Frank Bramley** (1857–1915), made his reputation with *A Hopeless Dawn* (1888), an interior scene suffused with light from different sources. Elizabeth Armstrong, later to become Stanhope Forbes' wife and better known as **Elizabeth Forbes** (1859–1912), also painted domestic scenes and portraits characterized by a directness and warmth sometimes missing in her husband's works. Her output was at one time valued more highly by the critics than that of her husband, but her career was cut short by her early death.

There was another wave of artists to Newlyn some twenty years after Forbes first arrived in the town – including **Dod Proctor** (1892–1972), then known as Doris Shaw, and **Laura Knight** (1877–1970), who became better known for her later paintings of ballet and the circus – but Newlyn's golden period had ended by the beginning of the twentieth century and interest subsequently focused on St Ives.

The St Ives School

Across the neck of the Penwith peninsula, St Ives had also previously attracted the attention of the art world, starting with a visit by Turner in 1811. With the new age of rail travel, other artists followed in his footsteps, including Whistler and Sickert in 1883–4, who left a few tiny oil studies as evidence. A trickle of foreign and English artists set up studios during the ensuing years, so that by the 1920s there were scores of artists working locally, including many amateurs alongside more established names. Among the latter were **Ben Nicholson** (1894–1982) and **Christopher Wood** (1901–30), who, on a day-trip to St Ives in 1928, were jointly responsible for discovering and later promoting the work of **Alfred Wallis** (1855–1942), a retired sailor born in Devonport. Having previously worked on fishing boats both inshore and out to sea for over twenty years, Wallis later took up a variety of jobs such as dealing in marine scrap and selling ice cream, and following the death of his wife in 1925, he turned increasingly to painting, often on scraps of driftwood, depicting primitive scenes of ships and seascapes around St Ives and the adjacent coasts. Despite his rapid rise to fame as Britain's best-known naive artist, he nonetheless ended his days in a St Ives workhouse.

Wood produced some of his best work during his short residence in Cornwall (1929–30), while Nicholson went on to be the guiding spirit of the **St Ives School** which flourished between the late 1940s and the early 1960s. He shared with the other artists of the group a preference for non-figurative work, his delicate reliefs and semi-abstract still-lifes acknowledged to have had a greater influence on abstract art than any other British artist. He had settled in the town in 1939, together with his second wife **Barbara Hepworth** (1903–75), a sculptor who had abandoned figure-based art in favour of abstract geometric forms, and whose work was increasingly inspired by the rock and sea landscape of the Penwith peninsula. Nicholson left St Ives in 1958, but Hepworth spent the rest of her life in the town, eventually dying in a fire in her studio there, after which her house and garden became a museum dedicated to her work.

Probably the most influential of the group during the war years was the Russian constructivist **Naum Gabo** (1890–1977) whose spatial geometric sculptures had a profound effect on Nicholson and Hepworth as well as other members of the community. Though Gabo left for the USA in 1946, many of his ideas are reflected in the work of younger St Ives artists such as **Wilhelmina Barnes-Graham** (b. 1912), whose work is alternately abstract and figurative, and **Peter Lanyon** (1918–64), who was born in the town and lived there most of his life; such works of his as *Porthleven* (1951) mix abstract themes with allusions to the local landscape.

On the periphery of the group, **Bernard Leach** (1887–1979) arrived in St Ives from Japan in 1920, accompanied by Shoji Hamada (1894–1978). Together they set up the St Ives Pottery which over the next six decades remained at the centre of the studio pottery movement in Britain. Among the foremost potters who studied under Leach in St Ives were Michael Cardew and Katherine Pleydell-Bouverie.

In the late 1950s and 1960s, a third wave of artists rose to prominence in St Ives, including **Brian Wynter** (1915–75), **Roger Hilton** (1911–75), **Terry Frost** (b. 1915) and **Patrick Heron** (1920–99). Contemporary artists working out of St Ives include **Bryan Pearce**, whose vibrant colours and simple lines in his still-lifes, church interiors and scenes of St Ives, recalling those of Alfred Wallis, have made him one of the country's foremost living naive artists.

Books

We've highlighted a selection of books below which will give you a flavour of Devon and Cornwall, past and present.

Publishers are detailed with the UK publisher first, separated by an oblique slash from the US publisher, in cases where both exist. Where books are published in only one of these countries, UK or US follows the publisher's name; where the book is published by the same company in both countries, the publisher's name appears just once. Titles which are out of print are shown as "o/p".

Apart from local libraries, the best places to track down these and other books on the region are the numerous secondhand bookshops scattered about. These always stock a sizeable section of books relating to the locality, though the same books are always cheaper – if harder to find – in secondhand bookshops outside the West Country.

History and travel

Evelyn Atkins *We Bought an Island* (Fowey Rare Books, UK). Humorous account of the purchase of Looe Island off the coast of Cornwall and the various characters encountered. *Tales from Our Cornish Island* was the sequel.

John Betjeman *Betjeman's Cornwall* (John Murray; o/p). Collection of prose and poetry relating to Cornwall, with illustrations by John Piper and photos.

John Betjeman *Cornwall* and *Devon* (Shell Guides, UK). First published in 1933 and 1936 respectively, and revised in 1964 and 1953, these are now collector's items, imbued with Betjeman's forthright views on churches and architecture in general, and still pertinent – a welcome antidote to glossy brochures.

Anthony Burton *Richard Trevithick: The Man and his Machine* (Aurum). The extraordinary story of Cornwall's greatest engineer and inventor (1771–1833), who built his first locomotive in 1801, the first of many innovations for which the world was not ready. He spent ten years wandering South America in pursuit of ever-more speculative ventures, but died penniless in England.

S.H. Burton *The West Country* (Robert Hale, UK; o/p). Often impassioned survey of the region by local historian who has written extensively on Devon and Cornwall.

Daphne Du Maurier *Vanishing Cornwall* (Penguin; o/p). The book chronicles all aspects of the place where Du Maurier lived for most of her life, fusing history, anecdote and travelogue in a plea for Cornwall's preservation.

Arthur Mee *Cornwall* and *Devon* (Hodder & Stoughton, UK; o/p). Chunky volumes from the 1930s in the King's England series, precious troves of anecdotes and historical snippets among the dense text interspersed with sepia photos.

Nikolaus Pevsner and Enid Radcliffe *The Buildings of England: Cornwall* (Penguin). Pevsner's monumental series was researched on long car journeys with his wife. Now updated and in parts rewritten to reflect recent changes and new knowledge, this volume tells you everything you wanted to know about every building of note in the county, and plenty that you probably have no wish to know.

Nikolaus Pevsner and Bridget Cherry *The Buildings of England: Devon* (Penguin). First published as two volumes in 1952 (*North Devon* and *South Devon*), this single fat volume has been updated and enlarged. It's comprehensive but cumbersome and expensive, best consulted in libraries.

C.J. Stevens *The Cornish Nightmare (D.H. Lawrence During the War Years)* (John Wade, US). The story of Lawrence and Frieda's Cornish sojourn during World War I, as told to the author by Stanley Hocking, "the boy" in *Kangaroo* (see overleaf). This is a day-to-day Lawrence seen fondly, sometimes critically and with some amusement, by the Cornish locals.

A. L. Rowse *A Cornish Childhood* (Truran/Potter; o/p). Autobiography by the distinguished historian and scholar covering his early years in Cornwall at the beginning of the twentieth century.

Fiction

Daphne Du Maurier *Frenchman's Creek* (Arrow/John Curley). Named after the creek off Cornwall's Helford River, this love story with piracy is set in Cornwall during the Restoration and concerns Dona St Columb, who escapes from London to her house in Cornwall where she gets embroiled in nefarious activities, mainly to do with contraband.

Daphne Du Maurier *Jamaica Inn* (Arrow/Avon). A young girl goes to live with her aunt and her husband who own the stark and forbidding inn of the title (which stands today on Bodmin Moor) – a gripping yarn of smugglers.

Daphne Du Maurier *Rebecca* (Arrow/Avon). From the first line, "Last night I went to Manderley again. . . ", this tale of deception and paranoia gallops along at an unput-downable pace – "Manderley" was Menabilly, near Fowey, where Du Maurier lived.

Winston Graham *Poldark* series (Pan and Macmillan/Ballantine and Libsa). *Ross Poldark*, *Demelza* and *The Angry Tide* are among the ten novels set around Perranporth and St Agnes through the late 1700s and early 1800s, featuring Ross Poldark, his wife Demelza, his arch-rival George Warleggan, and a colourful supporting cast of characters – filmed for TV and extremely popular.

Thomas Hardy *A Pair of Blue Eyes* (Penguin/Oxford World's Classics). Partly based on Hardy's own experiences as an architect in Cornwall, this tragic story of Elfride Swancourt, caught between the love of handsome, gentle Stephen Smith and the intellectually superior Henry Knight, sheds light on the struggle between the classes and sexes in the England of that time.

D.H. Lawrence *Kangaroo* (Penguin). The semi-autobiographical tale follows Richard and Harriet

Somers arriving in Australia from the decay of postwar Europe and incorporates a nightmare sequence recounting the Lawrences' trauma of being chased out of Cornwall.

Arthur Quiller-Couch *The Delectable Duchy* (J.M. Dent/Scribner; o/p). Fowey was "Troy Town" in the works of this formidable critic, best known for his literary studies. This collection of short stories highlights different facets of social history and the Cornish psyche as it was in the late nineteenth century. See also the author's *From a Cornish Window* (o/p), if you can find it.

Derek Tangye *The Minack Chronicles* (Warner, UK; o/p). A local hero in west Cornwall, Tangye was a former deb's delight who came to Cornwall to find the "good life", revealing all in his "shocking" tales. Minack is the Cornish flower farm where he and his wife Jeannie lived. Other titles include *The Time was Mine*, *The Gull on the Roof* and *The Cat on the Window*.

Henry Williamson *Tarka the Otter* (Puffin/Beacon). The natural history of north Devon is a minutely detailed backcloth to this animal tale which has spawned an industry.

Virginia Woolf, *To the Lighthouse* (Flamingo/ Harcourt Brace). Though set on a Hebridean island, the lighthouse of the title is Godrevy, near Hayle, where Woolf spent her summers, and the story recalls strands of her Cornish sojourns.

Guidebooks

The Beach and Cove Guide (Westcountry Books, UK). Gives a description of 150 beaches, facilities offered and small area maps. Surfing beaches are listed.

Alf Alderson *Surfing – A Beginner's Manual* (Fernhurst Books, UK). The best guide to the ins and outs of surfing by the editor of *Surf* magazine.

Anthony Burton *Dartmoor* and *Exmoor* (Aurum, UK). The fourteen circular walks in each volume range between 10 and 15 miles and have Ordnance Survey mapping and colour photos. Routes are described in detail and take in sites of archeological, historical or literary interest.

Nick Cotton *Ordnance Survey Cycle Tours: Cornwall and Devon* (Philip's OS Publications, UK). Fourteen on-road and ten off-road routes in Devon and Cornwall, including rides across Dartmoor and Exmoor. 1:50,000 Landranger mapping is used, and there are introductions to each route, with gradient diagrams, information on length and difficulty and notes to places of interest en route.

Nick Cotton and John Grimshaw *Guide to National Cycle Network* (Sustrans, UK). The official guide to all the routes of the National Cycle Network so far opened in the UK. Well presented with good maps and pictures, the guide also provides info on surfaces, traffic hazards and refreshment stops, and has useful advice for families.

John Macadam *The Two Moors Way* (Aurum). Detailed 90-mile walking itinerary between Ivybridge in southern Dartmoor and Lynmouth on Devon's northern coast, crossing the length of Dartmoor and Exmoor. Uses 1:25,000 OS maps and has colour photos.

David Norman and Vic Tucker *Where to Watch Birds in Devon and Cornwall* (Helm/Routledge Kegan & Paul). An excellent introduction to birdlife and other aspects of the region, including bird-watching sites, information on access for the car-bound or disabled, and an update of recent occurrences at each site.

Mark Norton *Classic Walks: Cornwall* (Norton, UK). Two guides to the whole of Cornwall, each covering 60 circular walks, with directions, background information and maps. Contact Norton Publishing Limited, PO Box 12, Camborne, Cornwall TR14 0YG, ☎07000/782688 to obtain a copy.

Richard Sale *The Rambler's Guide: Dartmoor* (HarperCollins, UK). Thirty walks on Dartmoor of varying lengths with maps, pictures and information about the topography, geology, wildlife and history of the area.

Ben Searle *Ride Your Bike: West Country* (Haynes, UK). Routes, tips and maps in this spiral-bound book, part of a series covering the whole of Britain.

Index

L

M

N

O

P

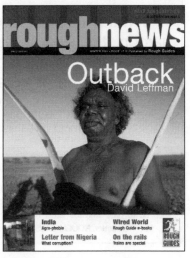

around the world

Alaska ★ Algarve ★ Amsterdam ★ Andalucía ★ Antigua & Barbuda ★
Argentina ★ Auckland Restaurants ★ Australia ★ Austria ★ Bahamas ★
Bali & Lombok ★ Bangkok ★ Barbados ★ Barcelona ★ Beijing ★ Belgium &
Luxembourg ★ Belize ★ Berlin ★ Big Island of Hawaii ★ Bolivia ★ Boston
★ Brazil ★ Britain ★ Brittany & Normandy ★ Bruges & Ghent ★ Brussels ★
Budapest ★ Bulgaria ★ California ★ Cambodia ★ Canada ★ Cape Town ★
The Caribbean ★ Central America ★ Chile ★ China ★ Copenhagen ★
Corsica ★ Costa Brava ★ Costa Rica ★ Crete ★ Croatia ★ Cuba ★ Cyprus ★
Czech & Slovak Republics ★ Devon & Cornwall ★ Dodecanese & East
Aegean ★ Dominican Republic ★ The Dordogne & the Lot ★ Dublin ★
Ecuador ★ Edinburgh ★ Egypt ★ England ★ Europe ★ First-time Asia ★
First-time Europe ★ Florence ★ Florida ★ France ★ French Hotels &
Restaurants ★ Gay & Lesbian Australia ★ Germany ★ Goa ★ Greece ★
Greek Islands ★ Guatemala ★ Hawaii ★ Holland ★ Hong Kong & Macau ★
Honolulu ★ Hungary ★ Ibiza & Formentera ★ Iceland ★ India ★ Indonesia
★ Ionian Islands ★ Ireland ★ Israel & the Palestinian Territories ★ Italy ★
Jamaica ★ Japan ★ Jerusalem ★ Jordan ★ Kenya ★ The Lake District ★
Languedoc & Roussillon ★ Laos ★ Las Vegas ★ Lisbon ★ London ★

in twenty years

London Mini Guide ★ London Restaurants ★ Los Angeles ★ Madeira ★
Madrid ★ Malaysia, Singapore & Brunei ★ Mallorca ★ Malta & Gozo ★ Maui
★ Maya World ★ Melbourne ★ Menorca ★ Mexico ★ Miami & the Florida
Keys ★ Montréal ★ Morocco ★ Moscow ★ Nepal ★ New England ★ New
Orleans ★ New York City ★ New York Mini Guide ★ New York Restaurants
★ New Zealand ★ Norway ★ Pacific Northwest ★ Paris ★ Paris Mini Guide
★ Peru ★ Poland ★ Portugal ★ Prague ★ Provence & the Côte d'Azur ★
Pyrenees ★ The Rocky Mountains ★ Romania ★ Rome ★ San Francisco ★
San Francisco Restaurants ★ Sardinia ★ Scandinavia ★ Scotland ★
Scottish Highlands & Islands ★ Seattle ★ Sicily ★ Singapore ★ South Africa,
Lesotho & Swaziland ★ South India ★ Southeast Asia ★ Southwest USA ★
Spain ★ St Lucia ★ St Petersburg ★ Sweden ★ Switzerland ★ Sydney ★
Syria ★ Tanzania ★ Tenerife and La Gomera ★ Thailand ★ Thailand's
Beaches & Islands ★ Tokyo ★ Toronto ★ Travel Health ★ Trinidad &
Tobago ★ Tunisia ★ Turkey ★ Tuscany & Umbria ★ USA ★ Vancouver ★
Venice & the Veneto ★ Vienna ★ Vietnam ★ Wales ★ Washington DC ★
West Africa ★ Women Travel ★ Yosemite ★ Zanzibar ★ Zimbabwe

also look out for our maps, phrasebooks, music guides and reference books

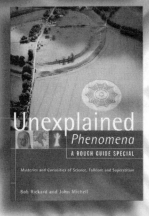

Will you have enough stories to tell your grandchildren?

Yahoo! Travel

Do You YAHOO!?

©2000 Yahoo! Inc.